THE BATTLE
FOR PAKISTAN

PRAISE FOR THE BOOK

'In *The Battle for Pakistan* Shuja Nawaz delivers a forensic and illuminating investigation of the troubled relationship between the United States and Pakistan. His work is informed by valuable original interviews and delivers new details and evidence—including about the hunt for Osama Bin Laden—that will be of great interest to scholars, analysts and the general public in both countries'.

—STEVE COLL, Pulitzer Prize–winning author of *Ghost Wars* and most recently *Directorate S: The CIA and America's Secret Wars in Afghanistan and Pakistan*

'An intriguing, comprehensive and compassionate analysis of the dysfunctional relationship between the United States and Pakistan by the premier expert on the Pakistan Army. Shuja Nawaz exposes the misconceptions and contradictions on both sides of one of the most crucial bilateral relations in the world'.

—BRUCE RIEDEL, senior fellow and director of the Brookings Intelligence Project, and author of *Deadly Embrace: Pakistan, America and the Future of the Global Jihad*

'A superb, thoroughly researched account of the complex dynamics that have defined the internal and external realities of Pakistan over the past dozen years. *The Battle for Pakistan* is a compelling read that provides enormous insights on the forces at work within Pakistan as the country's civilian and military leaders determine Pakistan's way forward at a critical juncture in time'.

—GENERAL DAVID PETRAEUS, former commander of the US Central Command and Coalition Forces in Iraq and Afghanistan, and former director of the CIA

'With well-researched and meticulously collected information, in-depth analyses and scholarly insights, Shuja Nawaz has produced an impressive and invaluable study of the twists and turns of US–Pakistan relations. Only a person with his understanding of the political dynamics in the two countries could provide such an authoritative and cogent account of how the dissonant but important respective interests of the two countries brought about periods of consequential cooperation. And yet these interests failed to create a basis for a stable relationship which continues to have critical relevance to the complex circumstances of the region. This book will be essential reading on the subject and for examining the past six decades of developments in the region'.

—RIAZ MOHAMMED KHAN, former Foreign Secretary of Pakistan, and author of *Afghanistan and Pakistan: Conflict, Extremism, and Resistance to Modernity*

'Packed with inside information from the ruling circles in both Pakistan and the United States, this book is essential reading for everyone trying to understand the international community's most tortuous bilateral relationship'.

—OWEN BENNETT-JONES, journalist and author of *The Bhutto Dynasty*

'Shuja Nawaz has followed up his earlier tour de force on the Pakistan Army— *Crossed Swords: Pakistan, Its Army and the Wars Within*—with a superbly researched study of the US–Pakistan relationship in all its dimensions. *The Battle for Pakistan* is essential reading for anyone attempting to fathom the fundamentals of the relationship between the two countries now and in the future. Shuja's view is truly panoramic and he has masterfully pieced together the many facets of a complex and evolving relationship. His insights and deep analyses are invaluable for understanding the forces of change that are shaping the relationship and Pakistan's future'.

—GENERAL JEHANGIR KARAMAT, former Chief of Army Staff
and Pakistan ambassador to the United States

'An engaging and insightful exploration of the realities and dynamics that have shaped present-day Pakistan and the US–Pakistan relationship. Nawaz captures the essence of Pakistan's seventy-year difficult and rocky journey. A relevant and important book'.

—CHUCK HAGEL, former US Secretary of Defense and US senator

'A must read for anyone who seeks to understand the complexities of forming and executing foreign policy any place, but especially in South Asia. Written with insight, detailed knowledge, keen analysis, and true conviction'.

—AMITAI ETZTONI, The George Washington University;
author of *Reclaiming Patriotism*

'Shuja Nawaz has written with deep knowledge and arresting eloquence about what he calls the "misalliance" between two nations that often misunderstand each other, but must ultimately reach an understanding as two vital partners in a necessary alliance. And he writes as a citizen and insider of both countries, with matchless personal knowledge of the personalities who have both made history and will make the future. There is no better or more compelling volume to read about this often troubled, but imperative relationship between two nations on other sides of the world that have been brought into the same orbit by geopolitics, and an increasing diaspora of human talent'.

—SCOTT SIMON, Peabody Award–winning host of
National Public Radio's Weekend Edition Saturday

'Shuja Nawaz's new book, *The Battle for Pakistan*, makes a critical contribution to our understanding of the turbulence of the last decade in US–Pakistan ties and Pakistan's fight for its democracy and security. US–Pakistan relations have long suffered because of mutual mistrust, suspicion and misunderstanding. Shuja's unique access in Washington and Islamabad has allowed him to tell both sides of the story. In doing so, hopefully this book can contribute to improved relations between our two countries in the coming decade and beyond'.

—GENERAL JAMES JONES, former Supreme Allied Commander in Europe, and
National Security Advisor to President Barack Obama

'Shuja Nawaz's important book is as timely as tomorrow's headlines. He's delivering vital guidance to US policy makers—surprisingly misinformed about ties with Pakistan—while, for general readers, he's telling a suspenseful story of diplomacy and intrigue in the toughest of neighborhoods. No one is more authoritative than Mr. Nawaz on the US–Pakistani political-military relationship, and that makes the choices he lays out vital for all of us to understand'.

—DEREK LEEBAERT, author of *Grand Improvisation:
America Confronts the British Superpower, 1945–1957*

'His unique access to centres of power in Washington, Islamabad and Rawalpindi enable Shuja Nawaz to offer rare and fascinating insights into the roller-coaster US–Pakistan relationship. As the Afghanistan–Pakistan drama heads for denouement, *The Battle for Pakistan* promises to be an invaluable guidebook for politicians, diplomats and soldiers attempting to navigate this South Asian quagmire'.

—ADM. ARUN PRAKASH, former chief of the
Indian Navy and chairman, Chiefs of Staff

'Writing about Pakistan is often like travelling through the looking glass, given the vast difference in perception of the nation from the outside and the perception that those within have of the world outside. Just as he did with his last book, in *The Battle for Pakistan*, Shuja Nawaz deftly manages the journey between what he calls "both homelands", US and Pakistan: balancing a critical look of Pakistan's actions on terror and foreign policy in the past decade and a half, with an insider's account of who said what to whom, unravelling events like the killing of Osama Bin Laden to civil–military tensions, and all that led up to the Imran Khan election. The suggestions Mr Nawaz proffers at the end of the book bear some careful study as well'.

—SUHASINI HAIDAR, diplomatic editor, *The Hindu*

'Nawaz has produced a book essential to anyone's South Asia library. . . . [In] writing with serious intent, Nawaz has created, perhaps, inadvertently, another dark, tragic comedy of duplicity, chaos, misunderstanding, miscommunication, backstabbing, and betrayal. . . . [As] his book illustrates, Pakistan has yet to make [the right] choices and is today as was once described of late 19th century Prussia—not a country with an army but an army with a country'.

—ARNOLD ZEITLIN, *South Asia Journal*

'In this seminal work . . . Shuja Nawaz explores what Pakistan's war against itself means for the new version of the Great Game now being played in Central Asia, for Pakistan, the US, and the alliance between them. . . . It is a remarkable work by an acclaimed writer on the Pakistani military. . . . It also sheds light on the deep involvement of the US and UK in Pakistan's internal political battles. The horizontal and vertical fragmentation of the society along political, religious and ethnic lines, which has intensified since 9/11, poses the most serious problem for Pakistan. . . . What makes *The Battle for Pakistan* substantive and authoritative is that it is based on interviews with senior Pakistani and US military officials directly involved in policymaking during that period. The author has unique access to the centres of power in the US and Pakistan, both of which he considers home. That makes the book extremely objective, covering all sides and dimensions of a roller-coaster relationship'.

—ZAHID HUSSAIN, *Dawn*

'This book should stimulate a much-needed debate among policy circles in Washington and Islamabad. It is a must-read for policy makers, top military officers, diplomats, academics and scholars, not just in the two countries that are its focus, but throughout the globe'.

—AHMAD FARUQI, *Naya Daur*

THE
BATTLE FOR
PAKISTAN

The Bitter US Friendship and a Tough Neighbourhood

SHUJA NAWAZ

ROWMAN & LITTLEFIELD
Lanham • Boulder • New York • London

Published by Rowman & Littlefield
An imprint of The Rowman & Littlefield Publishing Group, Inc.
4501 Forbes Boulevard, Suite 200, Lanham, Maryland 20706
www.rowman.com

6 Tinworth Street, London SE11 5AL, United Kingdom

First published in English by Penguin Random House India in 2019; subsequently published in English by Liberty Publishing, Pakistan in 2019.

British Library Cataloguing in Publication Information Available

Library of Congress Control Number: 2020932756

ISBN 9781538142035 (cloth) | ISBN 9781538142042 (paperback) | ISBN 9781538142059 (epub)

*This book is for the future generations of leaders in Pakistan and
the United States.
More specifically, our beloved and fearless granddaughters
Karam, Lina and Norah . . .*

Contents

Important Milestones 2007–19

2007

9 March	Chief Justice of the Supreme Court Iftikhar Muhammad Chaudhry removed by President Musharraf.
3–11 July	Assault on Red Mosque in Islamabad under Operation Silence.
20 July	Chief Justice Chaudhry reinstated.
23 August	Supreme Court rules exiled former PM Nawaz Sharif can return to Pakistan.
10 September	Nawaz Sharif returns, only to be deported again from Islamabad airport.
14 September	Benazir Bhutto announces she will return from exile on 18 October.
5 October	National Reconciliation Ordinance promulgated to allow indemnified politicians to return from exile.
6 October	Pervez Musharraf re-elected as president. Pakistan Peoples Party (PPP) boycotts presidential election.
18–19 October	Benazir Bhutto returns from Dubai to Karachi. Double bomb blasts greet her caravan from the airport to Bilawal House. Over 160 killed.
3 November	State of Emergency declared. Chief Justice removed, lawyers and political workers arrested; private TV channels shut down; Abdul Hameed Dogar installed as new Chief Justice.
12 November	Pakistan Army sends 12,000 troops to begin Operation Rah-e-Haq against local Taliban in Swat.
18 November	Caretaker Prime Minister Mohammad Mian Soomro installed.
24 November	Suicide bomber near army headquarters in Rawalpindi kills at least thirty-five persons.

25 November	Nawaz Sharif and his brother Shehbaz return to Pakistan.
4 December	Twenty-four high court judges retired. Chief Justice Chaudhry and Justices Rana Bhagwandas and Khalilur Rehman Ramday also dismissed.
14 December	International Republican Institute of United States poll shows Musharraf and army popularity dramatically decreased; orders to amend Constitution issued to allow waiver of two-year ban on government officials to run for president; National Command Authority established under president to control nuclear policy and assets.
27 December	Benazir Bhutto assassinated after speech at Liaquat Bagh in Rawalpindi. Additional twenty-one persons killed in associated bomb blast.
30 December	Bilawal Zardari named chairperson of the PPP. Both PPP and Pakistan Muslim League-Nawaz (PML-N) announce that they will participate in elections.

2008

2 January	Election Commission announces elections to be held on 18 February; Asif Ali Zardari repeats his demand for UN investigation of his wife Benazir Bhutto's assassination.
18 January	Director CIA Gen. Michael Hayden blames Al-Qaeda and Baitullah Mehsud of Tehrik-i-Taliban Pakistan (TTP) for Bhutto murder. Mehsud denies any link.
19 January	Pakistan claims fifteen-year-old boy captured who claims to be part of five-person team headed by Baitullah Mehsud that was involved in Bhutto killing. Mehsud says he has no link to the boy.
8 February	Scotland Yard investigation states Bhutto was killed by the impact of the explosion and not by bullets fired at her.
19 February	Election results indicate big win for PPP. PML-N keeps Punjab.
21 February	PPP and PML-N agree to coalition at the Centre.
25 February	A suicide bomber kills an army three-star general and seven others on a street in Rawalpindi. Six injured.
7 March	Army Chief Gen. Ashfaq Parvez Kayani denies differences between him and President Musharraf.
24 March	Yousaf Raza Gilani of PPP elected prime minister.
26 March	Senior American officials John Negroponte and Richard Boucher land in Islamabad to meet politicians.
24 May	Zardari unveils sixty-two-point plan to change Constitution and reduce the powers of the president.

26 May	Nawaz Sharif says Musharraf should be tried for 'high treason' under Article 6 of the Constitution for overthrowing Sharif's government.
7 June	Musharraf tells press conference he will not resign.
10 June	US air strike on Frontier Corps post on Afghan border leaves eleven FC soldiers and twelve alleged militants dead.
15 June	Gen. Stanley McChrystal takes over as twelfth coalition commander and third US commander in Afghanistan since 2002. (He was to resign on 23 June 2010, following publication of remarks critical of President Obama and Vice-President Biden in *Rolling Stone* magazine.) Succeeded by David Petraeus, then commander United States Central Command (CENTCOM).
17 June	For the first time in Pakistan's history, the senate discusses the defence budget.
30 June	Assistant Secretary of State for South Asia Richard Boucher returns to Pakistan to meet government and military officials.
2 July	The US will strike inside Pakistan if Bin Laden is found to be there, according to a *Washington Post* report.
16 July	The US did not know about the location of the FC post that the US attacked in June, according to a *New York Times* report.
26 July	Government notification places Inter-Services Intelligence (ISI) and Intelligence Bureau under Minister of Interior. Decision reversed within hours following pushback from military.
7 August	Zardari and Sharif announce they are ready to impeach Musharraf and restore judges removed by him, after his impeachment.
8 August	Pakistan Army reportedly asks Musharraf to step down within a week, according to the *Daily Telegraph*.
18 August	Musharraf resigns. Chairman of the senate Muhammad Mian Soomro takes over as president, according to the Constitution.
21 August	TTP-owned suicide bomb blast kills seventy and injures over sixty outside Pakistan Ordnance Factory in Wah Cantonment.
22 August	Election Commission announces presidential election on 6 September.
23 August	Zardari will be a candidate for the presidency, according to the PPP.
3 September	North Atlantic Treaty Organization (NATO) and International Security Assistance Force (ISAF) forces

	land via helicopters and attack suspected militant targets at Angoor Adda in South Waziristan border region.
6 September	Asif Ali Zardari elected president of Pakistan.
11 September	President George W. Bush authorizes US troops to carry out ground attacks inside Pakistan without seeking Pakistani permission, according to the *New York Times*.
20 September	The JW Marriott Hotel in Islamabad attacked by truck bomb. fifty dead, over 200 injured. Next day, hitherto unknown Fadayan-e Islam takes credit.
25 September	Inter-Service Public Relations (ISPR) directorate states Pakistan fired on two intruding US helicopters.
27 September	President Zardari denies exchange of fire with NATO forces. US Admiral Mike Mullen says Pakistani forces did fire and American forces returned small arms fire.
29 September	Major shuffle announced in army high command by Gen. Kayani. Lt. Gen. Ahmed Shuja Pasha appointed director general (DG) ISI.
16 November	International Monetary Fund (IMF) announces $7.6 billion programme to assist Pakistan.
26–29 November	Militants attack sites in Mumbai, India. As many as 195 persons killed over three-day period. India accuses Pakistani-based militants of attack.
7 December	US Secretary of State Condoleezza Rice says Pakistani soil was used in planning Mumbai attacks.
28 December	Islamabad Marriot reopens after massive and rapid renovation.

2009

1 January	US drone strike kills four in South Waziristan, presaging increased drone attacks.
7 January	Pakistan National Security Adviser Maj. Gen. (retd) Mahmud Ali Durrani admits Ajmal Kasab, captured in Mumbai attacks, is a Pakistani. Minister for Information and Broadcasting Sherry Rehman also reportedly confirms the same. PM Gilani sacks Durrani.
20 January	President Barack Obama takes oath of office.
27 January	US Defense Secretary Gates, holdover from the Bush administration, says drone strikes will continue inside Pakistan.
4 February	UN Secretary-General Ban Ki-moon announces formation of a UN Commission under the Chilean

	ambassador to the United Nations to investigate the death of Benazir Bhutto.
9 February	Islamabad High Court frees nuclear engineer Dr A.Q. Khan. The US is concerned about this measure.
13 February	US Senate Chair of the Intelligence Committee, Senator Dianne Feinstein, says US drones are also being flown from bases inside Pakistan.
3 March	Terrorists strike Sri Lankan cricket team in Lahore. Six policemen and one civilian killed. Two Sri Lankan cricketers injured.
15 March	Nawaz Sharif starts the Long March from Lahore to Islamabad.
	PM Gilani concedes to demand for the reinstatement of the Chief Justice after intervention by army chief with the PM and President Zardari.
27 March	President Obama announces new US strategies on Afghanistan and Pakistan, after review led by Bruce Riedel. 'The future of Afghanistan is inextricably linked to the future of its neighbor Pakistan. In the nearly eight years since 9/11, Al Qaida and its extremist allies have moved across the border to remote areas of the Pakistani frontier . . . or the American people, this border region has become the most dangerous place in the world.'
30 March	TTP attacks police academy in Lahore. 8 killed, 100 injured.
3 April	Video emerges of young girl being flogged by the Taliban in Swat.
6 April	Admiral Mullen says top Taliban leaders hiding in Quetta, Balochistan.
16 April	PML-N says it will not rejoin the government of Zardari.
21 April	Taliban reported to be entering Buner in Swat.
22 April	Secretary of State Hillary Clinton says the Pakistan government is abdicating to Taliban.
23 April	Taliban enter Shangla, threatening Karakoram Highway.
26 April	Pakistan Army launches operations in Buner. Locals asked to vacate area.
6 May	Presidents Obama, Karzai and Zardari meet at the White House to determine future trilateral strategy.
7 May	PM Gilani announces full-scale military operations in Malakand division.
29–30 May	ISPR states both Mingora and Peochar Valley in Swat cleared of the Taliban.

5 August	Baitullah Mehsud, head of the TTP, killed by two Hellfire missiles from a US drone in South Waziristan.
14 September	President Zardari announces that former President Musharraf has left Pakistan under a deal.
24 September	US Senate passes Kerry–Lugar Bill.
7 October	Pakistan Army issues public reservations against Kerry–Lugar–Berman (KLB) bill to aid Pakistan over five-year period.
10 October	Terrorists attack Pakistan Army General Headquarters in Rawalpindi. Five attackers killed. Four militants manage to enter GHQ and take hostages. Initial reports indicate at least four army men killed. One militant captured.
11 October	Pakistan Army launches attack to regain GHQ and free hostages. Final tally: nineteen killed, including eight militants.
15 October	Terrorists attack Federal Investigation Agency, Manawan Police Academy and Elite Force Headquarters in Lahore. twenty killed. Over forty injured.
	President Obama signs KLB law to give Pakistan $7.5 billion over five years.
17 October	Pakistan Army launches offensive Operation Rah-e-Nijaat (Path to Salvation) to retake territory from militants in South Waziristan.
1 December	After another review of his Afghanistan and Pakistan policy, President Obama declares at West Point:

'I have determined that it is in our vital national interest to send an additional 30,000 US troops to Afghanistan . . . After eighteen months, our troops will begin to come home . . . First . . . a military strategy that will break the Taliban's momentum and increase Afghanistan's capacity over the next eighteen months . . . Second, we will work with our partners, the UN, and the Afghan people to pursue a more effective civilian strategy . . . Third . . . our success in Afghanistan is inextricably linked to our partnership with Pakistan . . . [T]he absence of a timeframe for transition would deny us any sense of urgency in working with the Afghan government . . .'

Taliban emboldened by withdrawal timetable. Pakistan's hedging policy on Afghan Taliban bolstered.

30 December	All provinces agree on 7th National Finance Commission Award on revenue-sharing among the provinces of the federation and between them and the federal government.

2010

6 February	US jury trial of Dr Afia Siddiqui finds her guilty on seven counts, sentences her to eighty-six years in jail.
2 March	FC says it has taken back control of all of Bajaur Agency of FATA.
9 March	DG-ISI Lt. Gen. Pasha given one-year extension.
8 April	18th Amendment of the Constitution passed in the National Assembly. Massive devolution of powers of the president and other changes.
16 April	Pakistan Senate passes 18th Amendment.
19 April	President Zardari signs the 18th Amendment into law.
4 May	Pakistani American Faisal Shahzad is caught in a failed attempt to blow up a car in Times Square, New York.
22 July	PM Gilani announces three-year extension for Army Chief Gen. Kayani.
29 July	Massive floods and heavy rains in Pakistan. Death toll reaches 108 in Khyber Pakhtunkhwa.
11 August	Marine Gen. James Mattis takes over as Commander CENTCOM from acting commander Lt. Gen. John Allen. (Mattis was later prematurely removed by President Obama on 22 March 2013 due to differences on a number of issues, including the number of troops needed to remain in Afghanistan and how to deal with Iran.)
26 September	NATO helicopters intrude into Pakistan and kill thirty suspected terrorists. Two Pakistani soldiers killed. Ground Lines of Communication (GLOC) shut down.
9 October	Pakistan reopens GLOC for NATO supplies to Afghanistan.
20 October	During strategic dialogue at White House, Gen. Kayani hands President Obama thirteen-page White Paper outlining Pakistan's concerns and suggesting the way forward in Afghanistan and the region.
27 October	New US Ambassador Cameron Munter presents his credentials to President Zardari.
28 October	Afghanistan and Pakistan sign historic Transit Trade Agreement (TTA), supported by Secretary of State Hillary Clinton.

2011

3 January	Muttahida Qaumi Movement (MQM) resigns from coalition with PPP.

4 January

Punjab Governor Salmaan Taseer killed by his own police guard Malik Mumtaz Qadri because he asked for a review of the blasphemy law and justice for accused Christian woman Aasia Bibi.

27 January

US CIA contractor Raymond Davis kills two persons on the streets of Lahore and is taken into custody.

1 March

Minister for Minority Affairs Shahbaz Bhatti, a Christian, killed for pleading on behalf of Aasia Bibi in her blasphemy case.

16 March

Raymond Davis released under blood money deal with the families of the two persons he killed in Lahore, flies out of Pakistan with US Ambassador Munter.

2 May

US Navy Seals invade Pakistan on helicopters from Jalalabad, Afghanistan, and kill Osama bin Laden in Abbottabad—take his body, documents and computer drives back to Afghanistan. Pakistan shuts down GLOC.

22 May

Militants attack and occupy Mehran Naval Station in Karachi. Nine killed. Two P3-Orion aircraft destroyed.

31 May

Journalist Saleem Shahzad who wrote an exposé about the Mehran attack found dead in a canal near Jhelum, some 70 miles away from Islamabad, after being abducted from Islamabad.

8 July

Admiral Mullen blames Pakistan government for Shahzad's death. According to BBC: 'I have not seen anything that would disabuse that report that the government knew about this,' Adm. Mullen told journalists in Washington on Thursday. 'It was sanctioned by the government, yeah,' he said. Adm. Mullen added that he did not have a 'string of evidence' linking the death to the ISI. ISI denied any link. Crime remained unsolved.

11 September

Gen. Kayani presents Pakistan's regional perspective on the tenth anniversary of 9/11 at NATO defence chiefs' meeting in Seville, Spain, as a follow-up to a paper given to President Obama and the US reply of February 2011.

23–24 September

US General Jim Mattis arrives to deliver tough message to the Pakistani military after attack on the US embassy in Kabul, reportedly linked to Pakistan-based terrorists. Kayani shares the paper delivered at NATO meeting in Seville with Mattis.

10 October

Pakistani American Mansoor Ijaz publishes an article in the *Financial Times*, hinting at Pakistani civilian government's conspiracy to seek US help in cutting Pakistan Army down to size. He later suggested that

Pakistan ambassador to the US, Husain Haqqani, had worked with him on drafting a secret memorandum in May, after the bin Laden raid, from the civilian authorities in Pakistan asking for US help against the Pakistan Army. Thus began the so-called 'Memogate' issue leading to Amb. Haqqani's resignation.

26 November   US forces attack two Pakistani posts on the Afghan border near Salala and kill twenty-four Pakistani soldiers and officers. Pakistan closes the GLOC again and asks US to evacuate the airbase at Shamsi, used for drone launches, among other things. ISAF commander Gen. John Allen, Maj. Gen. John W. "Mick" Nicholson Jr and Maj. Gen. James Laster arrive in Rawalpindi to discuss past and future operations, among other things, with Pakistani counterparts, but do not mention operation near Salala. Pakistan stops GLOC to Afghanistan. ALOC kept open.

2012

5 January   TTP murders fifteen Frontier Constabulary soldiers in Orakzai Agency after kidnapping and keeping them for over a year. Each body had forty bullet wounds and showed signs of torture.

9 January   Ten Pakistani soldiers missing since December 2011 found dead in upper Orakzai.

12 January   Baloch Liberation Front insurgents ambush and kill fourteen soldiers.

15 May   After Pakistan's foreign minister says it would consider reopening the GLOC to Afghanistan, NATO says it will invite Zardari to NATO Summit in Chicago, where Zardari fails to reach agreement on the opening of GLOC.

18 May   While debating the National Defence Authorisation Act, US lawmakers in the House of Representatives vote 412-1 for an amendment to block up to $650 million in proposed payments to Pakistan unless Islamabad reopens the GLOC.

23 May   A senate panel approves a foreign aid budget for the following year that slashes US assistance to Islamabad by more than half, and threatens further reductions if it fails to reopen supply routes for NATO in Afghanistan.

25 May   The Senate Appropriations Committee votes to cut aid to Pakistan by a symbolic $33 million—$1 million for

	each year of jail time handed by Pakistan to Shakil Afridi, a Pakistani doctor who allegedly assisted the Central Intelligence Agency (CIA) in locating Osama bin Laden.
3 July	After talks by Peter Lavoy in Islamabad, followed by discussions in Washington involving Amb. Sherry Rehman, and negotiations by Foreign Minister Hina Rabbani Khar, Pakistan agrees to reopen supply routes into Afghanistan. US Secretary of State Hillary Clinton says she is sorry for the loss of life in a 'horrendous' air raid on Salala in November 2011.
17 July	Amb. Richard Olson named for Pakistan post, replacing Amb. Cameron Munter.
9 October	Taliban shoot Malala Yousafzai in her face and two of her friends are wounded on a bus in Swat. She is evacuated to Birmingham, England, for treatment.
31 October	US Ambassador Rick Olson starts in Islamabad.

2013

10 January	Terrorist attacks in Quetta kill some 100 persons.
25 March	Mir Hazar Khan Khoso appointed caretaker prime minister to conduct fresh elections.
11 May	General elections held in Pakistan.
5 June	Nawaz Sharif elected prime minister for the third time.
30 July	Manmoon Hussain of PML-N elected twelfth president of Pakistan.
1 November	Hakimullah Mehsud, leader of TTP, killed by a US drone attack in North Waziristan.
29 November	Pakistan Chief of Army Staff (COAS) Gen. Ashfaq Parvez Kayani retires. Gen. Raheel Sharif becomes the next COAS.
11 December	Chief Justice Iftikhar Muhammad Chaudhry retires. Succeeded by Justice Tassaduq Hussain Jillani.

2014

9 February	Gunmen attack an Islamic religious gathering in Karachi, eight persons killed.
17 February	Former president Pervez Musharraf appears in a civil court for the first time.
31 March	A Pakistani court charges former president Musharraf with high treason under Article 6 of the Pakistan Constitution for imposing Emergency rule in 2007, but

avoiding the same issue of high treason for his 1999 usurpation of elected PM Nawaz Sharif.[1]

21 May

Pakistan Air Force jets bomb suspected militant hideouts in North Waziristan, killing approximately sixty militants and injuring another thirty.

13 August

Another Long March and dharna or sit-in organized by the Pakistan Tehreek-e Insaf (PTI) of Imran Khan and Pakistan Awami Tehreek of cleric Tahir-ul-Qadri in Islamabad.

10 October

Malala Yousafzai becomes the second Pakistani to win a Nobel Prize, sharing the Nobel Peace Prize for her efforts on behalf of girls' right to education.

16 December

Taliban gunmen storm a military-run Army Public School in Peshawar, killing at least 141, including 132 children and nine school employees. All seven gunmen killed by the military.

24 December

Prime Minister Sharif announces twenty-point National Action Plan (NAP) to fight terrorism and militancy and that envisages the establishment of special courts for speedy trial of terror suspects and a crackdown on jihadi and sectarian outfits.

2015

25 January

A massive blackout strikes Pakistan, leaving as much as 80 per cent of the country without electricity.

13 February

Pakistan announces the arrest of twelve TTP members in connection with the attack on the Army Public School in Peshawar in December 2014.

11 March

Sindh Rangers, under direction of the military, though reporting to the interior ministry, move into MQM headquarters in Karachi and arrest dozens of party workers and uncover arms and ammunition.

15 March

A church bombing in Lahore kills at least eleven people, with forty-eight more injured.

19 May

Russia closes down a key military transport corridor that allowed the US and its NATO allies to supply forces serving in neighbouring Afghanistan via the Russian transhipment hub at Ulyanovsk.

---

[1]   Constitution of Pakistan, Article 6, high treason: 1. Any person who abrogates or subverts or suspends or holds in abeyance, or attempts or conspires to abrogate or subvert or suspend or hold in abeyance, the Constitution by use of force or show of force or by any other unconstitutional means shall be guilty of high treason; www.infopakistan.pk/constitution-of-pakistan/article/6-High-treason

	The transit route was used by NATO for non-lethal cargo since 2008 and for military shipments since 2010. The official reason cited by Russia is the end, in December 2014, of the UN mandate authorizing the US-led military mission into Afghanistan.
16 June	PPP co-chairman and former president Asif Ali Zardari lashes out publicly at the Pakistani military establishment for overstepping its domain. He was reportedly disturbed over the corruption cases lodged against some of his key colleagues.
23 July	A three-member judicial commission headed by the Chief Justice of Pakistan rejects all three allegations of the PTI on rigging in the 2013 general elections.
18 September	Terrorists attack a Pakistan Air Force camp near Badaber area of Peshawar, killing twenty-nine personnel, including an officer.
17 November	US Ambassador Rick Olson leaves his post to become US SRAP for one year. He is succeeded by Amb. David Hale.
25 December	Indian Prime Minister Narendra Modi pays a surprise visit to Lahore and Raiwind on his way back from a visit to Kabul, kindling hopes of an entente cordiale. He attends Nawaz Sharif's granddaughter's wedding.

2016

18 January	Former president Pervez Musharraf acquitted in the murder trial of Akbar Bugti, the Baloch tribal leader who died in a military operation in 2006.
3 April	The International Consortium of Investigative Journalists and a German newspaper *Süddeutsche Zeitung* publish millions of confidential documents from the Panamanian legal firm Mossack Fonseca, which provide detailed information on more than 214,000 offshore companies, the identities of shareholders and directors, including noted personalities and heads of state. PM Nawaz Sharif's family is named in the papers, as are other leading Pakistanis. 'Panamagate' comes into being.
29 April	US Department of State, under instructions from the senate, refuses to subsidize sale of F-16 planes to Pakistan.
23 May	Afghan Taliban leader Mullah Akhtar Mohammad Mansour reportedly killed by US drone strike inside Pakistan en route from a visit to Iran.

2017

20 January	Donald J. Trump is sworn in as the forty-fifth president of the United States of America. Names former CENTCOM Commander Gen. James Mattis as Secretary of Defense.
21 January	A bombing at a vegetable market in Parachinar kills twenty-five people.
16 February	A suicide bombing at the shrine of Lal Shahbaz Qalandar in Sehwan, Sindh Province, kills over ninety people.
14 March	Pakistan's sixth census launched. Slated to be decennial, this one was held nineteen years after the previous census in 1998.
28 July	The Supreme Court of Pakistan unanimously disqualifies Prime Minister Nawaz Sharif from office for life, over the controversy emerging from the Panama Papers, regarding withheld information of business interests abroad and potential earnings from those interests.
1 August	Shahid Khaqan Abbasi sworn in as prime minister, succeeding Nawaz Sharif.
21 August	President Trump announces a new strategy on Afghanistan and criticizes Pakistan's lack of cooperation.
13 October	Trump tweets: 'Starting to develop a much better relationship with Pakistan and its leaders. I want to thank them for their cooperation on many fronts.'
23 October	President Ashraf Ghani of Afghanistan states the Afghanistan–Pakistan Transit Trade Agreement of 2010 is to end since Pakistan did not allow Afghan trucks to go into Pakistan, while Pakistani trucks could enter Afghanistan fully loaded.
24 October	US Secretary of State Rex Tillerson gets frosty welcome in Pakistan. Tillerson later said he told Pakistani leadership that Washington would implement its new strategy with or without their support.
4 December	US Secretary of Defense James Mattis visits Islamabad for the first time in his new position. He meets with Prime Minister Shahid Khaqan Abbasi and Minister of Defence Khurram Dastigir Khan, and with COAS Gen. Qamar Javed Bajwa and the DG-ISI Lt. Gen. Naveed Mukhtar. While acknowledging Pakistan's earlier efforts, Mattis reiterates that Pakistan must redouble its efforts to confront militants and terrorists operating within the country.

2018

2 January	In his first tweet of the year, President Trump threatens to cut aid to Pakistan for allegedly lying to the US and offering 'little help' in hunting 'terrorists' in Afghanistan. 'The United States has foolishly given Pakistan more than $33 billion in aid over the last 15 years, and they have given us nothing but lies and deceit, thinking of our leaders as fools,' Trump said. 'They give safe haven to the terrorists we hunt in Afghanistan, with little help. No more!'
3 January	US suspends about $900 million of assistance for Pakistan. Calls suspension temporary, depending on Pakistan's change of behaviour regarding war in Afghanistan.
25 July	General elections held in Pakistan. Imran Khan's PTI wins big at the Centre and in Khyber Pakhtunkhwa, forms government in Punjab and in coalition in Balochistan. PPP wins big in Sindh. MQM loses support.
17 August	Imran Khan elected prime minister—pledges to fight corruption and bring corrupt politicians to justice. Faces huge economic issues, including repayment of loans. Foreign exchange reserves falling.
4 September	In advance of Secretary of State Mike Pompeo's 5 September visit to Islamabad with Gen. Joseph Dunford, chairman, US Joint Chiefs of Staff, Pentagon spokesman Lt. Col. Kone Faulkner states: 'Due to a lack of Pakistani decisive actions in support of the South Asia Strategy the remaining $300 million was reprogrammed.' The cancelled aid was to come from the Coalition Support Funds (CSF).
19 September	Imran Khan visits Saudi Arabia to seek economic assistance. Returns with $6 billion aid package.
3 November	Imran Khan in China seeking financial concessions and aid. China also pledges to support IMF programme for Pakistan.
10 November	IMF team arrives to begin discussions with Pakistan on a potential financial programme. (US Secretary of State Mike Pompeo had earlier opposed the idea of US taxpayers' funds going via IMF to repay Pakistan's Chinese loans.)

2019

14 February	A local Kashmiri suicide bomber Adil Ahmad Dar attacks an Indian security convoy on the Srinagar National

Highway at Pulwama killing forty personnel of the Central Reserve Police Force. The attack is linked to the Jaish-e-Mohammed. India blames Pakistan for the attack. Pakistan condemns it.

25 February   Afghanistan peace talks begin in Doha, Qatar, between the United States and the Taliban. Amb. Zalmay Khalilzad, the US special envoy and the Taliban founder Abdul Ghani Baradar lead the discussions. Baradar was earlier released from custody by Pakistan.

26 February   In response to the Pulwama attack, Indian Air Force aircraft attack a site in Balakot across the Kashmir Line of Control and claim to have killed 300-350 'terrorists' at a religious seminary.

27 February   Pakistan claims no damage or human losses and takes foreign journalists subsequently to the site of the attack. It retaliates with an air attack across the LOC in Jammu and Kashmir without claiming any Indian casualties. IAF sends aircraft to meet the PAF attack and loses one aircraft, with its pilot being captured by Pakistan. He is subsequently released as a gesture of goodwill by the Pakistan prime minister, Imran Khan.

5 March   Pakistan takes into custody members of the JeM, including relative of the Jaish leader Masood Azhar. It seeks Indian evidence for support of these individuals for the Pulwama attack.

29 April-May 3   Afghanistan convenes a Loya Jirga to pursue peace but the Taliban refuses to attend. Meanwhile, direct US–Taliban talks continue, focused on four key issues: a Taliban guarantee that it will not allow fighters to use Afghanistan as a base to launch attacks outside the country, the withdrawal of US and Coalition Forces, an intra-Afghan dialogue and a permanent ceasefire.

3 July, 2019   IMF approves $6 billion programme to help Pakistan.

10-11 July   Pakistan joins trilateral US, Russia, China talks on the Afghanistan peace process in Beijing. The trio says, 'They believe that Pakistan can play an important role in facilitating peace in Afghanistan.' Earlier the Taliban sent a team to Beijing. Khalilzad says he is aiming for a September deadline on an agreement.

20-23 July   Prime Minister Imran Khan visits Washington DC, principally to meet President Donald J. Trump and congressional leaders, and brings his army chief and

DG-ISI to connect with US military counterparts. Trump appreciates Pakistan's help in Afghanistan and promises renewal of ties and financial flows, provided Pakistan takes further positive actions. He also says he had offered to mediate or arbitrate between India and Pakistan on Kashmir at the request of Indian PM Narendra Modi. India's Ministry of External Affairs denies that. US State Department later walks back third-party intervention in Pakistan–India bilateral issues. US–Pakistan apparent reset raises Pakistani hopes for the future.

5 August

India announces the end of Articles 370 and 35A that accorded special constitutional status for Kashmir. Deems it an internal matter for India. Pakistan objects and tries to involve the United Nations on the basis of historical bilateral discussions between India and Pakistan. Tensions rise on the Line of Control with exchanges of fire.

13 August

The US and Afghan Taliban are near a deal to end fighting in Afghanistan and allow US troops to withdraw, as well as intra-Afghan talks to proceed.

19 August

Prime Minister Imran Khan announces a full-term three-year extension for Army Chief General Bajwa in light of 'the regional security environment'.

November 26

Pakistan's Supreme Court suspended the government's extension of the term of office of army chief General Qamar Javed Bajwa, followed up on December 16 by asking for Act of Parliament within next six months to specify and regularize length of term and possibility of extension.

December 17

A special court sentenced former military ruler General Pervez Musharraf to death in absentia for treason over his 2007 imposition of emergency rule. The case had been pending since 2013. Musharraf was in Dubai when the verdict was announced. The army, via its Inter Services Public Relations Directorate, expressed its anguish and said that the former general cannot be called a traitor. The government also opposed the verdict and said it would appeal it.

Abbreviations and Acronyms

Agency for International Development	USAID
Border Coordination Centres	BCCs
Central Intelligence Agency	CIA
Chief of General Staff	CGS
China–Pakistan Economic Cooperation Corridor	CPEC
Coalition Support Funds	CSF
Counter-insurgency	COIN
Counterterrorism	CT
Defence Housing Authority	DHA
Department of Defense (US)	DoD
Director General Inter-Services Intelligence	DG-ISI
Director General Military Operations	DGMO
Director General	DG
Economic Affairs Division	EAD
Foreign Military Financing	FMF
Foreign Military Sales	FMS
Forward Operating Base	FOB
Frontier Corps	FC
Frontier Force	FF
General Officer Commanding	GOC
Improvised Explosive Device	IED
Inspector General Training and Evaluation	IGT&E
Inspector General	IG
International Military Education and Training	IMET

International Security Assistance Force	ISAF
Inter-Services Public Relations	ISPR
Inter-Services Intelligence	ISI
Joint Chiefs of Staff	JCS
Joint Special Operations Command	JSOC
Junior Commissioned Officer	JCO
Low-intensity Conflict	LIC
Memorandum of Understanding	MoU
Ministry of Defence (Pakistan)	MoD
National Action Plan	NAP
National Counter Terrorism Authority	NACTA
National Counterterrorism Center	NCTC
National Defence University	NDU
National Directorate of Security	NDS
National Disaster Management Authority	NDMA
National Security Adviser	NSA
National Security Council	NSC
National Training Mission, Afghanistan	NTMA
Non-commissioned officer	NCO
North Atlantic Treaty Organization	NATO
Office of Defense Representative in Pakistan	ODRP
Pakistan Military Academy	PMA
Pakistan Muslim League-Nawaz	PML-N
Pakistan Tehreek-e-Insaf	PTI
Navy Sea, Air and Land Team	SEAL
Special Operations Command	SOCOM
Special Representative for Afghanistan and Pakistan	SRAP
Strategic Plans Division	SPD
Supreme Allied Commander, Europe	SACEUR
Tactical Exercises Without Troops	TEWTs
United States Central Command	CENTCOM

Author's Note

The Pakistan edition of this book was produced by Liberty Publishing in the third week of November 2019, roughly two-and-a-half months after the South Asian edition was released in India by Penguin Random House. Pakistan's trade ban with India to protest the Indian actions in Kashmir had prevented copies from India to be imported into Pakistan, hence the need for a separate Pakistan edition. Advance copies of the book were hand delivered on my behalf to both the Pakistan prime minister and the army chief in early October. Soon after that the extension of the army chief's position became a contentious legal issue. An unintended victim of that situation was this book.

It provoked a reaction from the Pakistan army high command to the public launch of the book's Pakistan edition, although the book had already been released in the market. After I arrived in Pakistan in early December, the military high command asked me to delay the launch events to a later, undetermined date. The concern was that the public events might give rise to controversial discussions.

I refused to voluntarily scrub the events. So the military high command directly interacted with the key participants and organizers of the public book events and canceled them in all three cities, Lahore, Islamabad, and Karachi, though the book continued to sell inside Pakistan. The civilian government remained noticeably silent. I did not wish to fuel the controversy or become the story, so I returned to the United States to begin preparing for this US and world edition.

Preface

Salvaging a Misalliance

The US–Pakistan relationship has often been compared to a bad marriage. Some have also described the relationship using the Chinese and Japanese sayings about an estranged couple that share the same bed but dream different dreams. It has been a true misalliance that is hurtling towards a bad break-up, but one that needs to be rescued for the sake of both parties and for the region in which Pakistan is located and where it can play a crucial role.

The French word '*mesalliance*' was borrowed by George Bernard Shaw's brilliant satirical play on the class battle in British society. It was based on an unequal partnership between the daughter of a businessman who made his money selling underwear, and the son of an upper-crust British proconsul in an Indian province. Indeed, the Shavian commentary from the father of the boy may also apply to the case of Pakistan and even Trumpian America today: 'Democracy reads well; but it doesn't act well.'[1]

In many ways, the seventy-year-old US–Pakistan relationship, with its many ups and downs, alternately filled with both tantrums and fulsome praise for each other, has become a tragicomedy on a regional political stage, with numerous bad actors and confused heroes and heroines. Meanwhile, the sorry chorus of their hoi polloi tries to make sense of the 'tangled web' that the often-cynical leadership of both countries has woven. Pakistan

---

[1]   If memory serves me well, I first came to know this play and *Arms and the Man* by Shaw as a young man and occasional member of the Rawalpindi Amateur Theatrical Society (RATS), which was formed by members of the diplomatic corps and locals in Rawalpindi and Islamabad in the late 1960s.

continues to struggle to craft a democracy, as its successive governments continue to battle for supremacy with the military, even while they pretend to be 'on the same page'. It also faces a hostile, much larger India to the east that continues to inform its security policy and its regional relationships. The US fails to fully appreciate this aspect of Pakistan's existential struggle. The internal Battle for Pakistan forms one side of a triangle of turmoil that reflects the country's roller-coaster relationship with the US. The other two sides are the US relationships with the civil and the military in Pakistan.

Today, as at critical junctures in the past seventy years, the US is trying to shape a new global strategy that involves preparing for economic and even military conflict with potential enemies in distant parts of the world. China is one major target of the administration of President Donald J. Trump, reflected in the Indo-Pacific alliance with India and preceded by the pivot to the Pacific of President Barack H. Obama. The US brushed off all Pakistani concerns about its tilt towards India. Russia may be another US target, though Trump, whatever his reasons, remains silent on that very real and growing conflict. The US persists in stumbling into the darkness of an ill-defined 'war on terror', as it struggles to place the Band-Aid of military intervention on numerous wars across the world against irregular forces of extremist Islamic warriors. It is trying to fight ideologies with military weapons. And failing. At the same time, it is preparing to confront poor Central American civilians attempting to breach its southern frontier in search of economic and political freedom. For eighteen years, the US struggled to find a direction in the seemingly endless and losing war inside Afghanistan. How it manages its military exit out of that battlefield will determine its relationship with Pakistan, Afghanistan's larger neighbour to the east, and the US's role in greater South Asia.

The US appears to have chosen the path of regional partnerships with powerful surrogates in pursuit of its global aims and to help stabilize or police regions. A closer relationship with India in the context of the US antipathy towards China on the global stage, and India's tremendous potential as a rising economic power, a market for American goods and services and the world's major arms importer, all give great impetus to the US courtship. This de-hyphenation of the India–Pakistan relationship and the US focus on economics and military cooperation with India colour Pakistan's view of its American 'friends'. Fear of India and its hegemonic potential in South Asia informs Pakistan's paranoia about the growing US–India relationship.

Against this background, Pakistan has tried unsuccessfully to maintain a relationship with the US. But, its own regional dynamics and the unending conflict with India has made it a sometime ally of the US, often at odds with emerging US policy aims in the neighbourhood. Both the US and Pakistan depend heavily on each other, but periodically have lapses of memory and judgement that allow the relationship to become transitional and mercenary rather than truly strategic and long-lasting. As Peter Lavoy, an experienced regional hand, explained to me, 'The problem in Pakistan . . . is that the expediency often trumps the more considerate long-term benefits.'[2] This could well apply to the US too. In spades.

The US, a superpower, has yet to exhibit the full gravitas and sense of history that is demanded by its position as a modern-day Global Gulliver. Its goals often appear to the world to be fixed on the near horizon of the next domestic election, rather than distant, demanding and persistent global needs. It calls the shots on the world stage, yet it keeps changing the goal posts to its own detriment and thus confounds friends and enemies alike. Over the past two decades or so, for example, it professed deep friendship for Pakistan, elevating it to a non-NATO ally status, but then proceeded to bomb its territory from drones in an undeclared war, oddly enough with the connivance of Pakistan's own governments. In the process, it lost the trust of the Pakistani population. And its troops invaded Pakistani territory at will since 2001, notably in the border region with Afghanistan at Angoor Ada and Salala. In May 2011, its forces went into the heart of Pakistan to kill Osama bin Laden in Abbottabad.

Pakistan, meanwhile, struggles to define itself. Harking back to its founder's vision of a modern and tolerant polity and paying lip service to Mohammed Ali Jinnah's Pakistan, its people and leaders have yet to clearly define what country Jinnah wanted to place on the map of the world in 1947—an Islamic state or a more liberal entity where Muslims could pursue their lives alongside other religious groups. Its people are now increasingly besieged by highly contentious and divisive arguments of dogmatic Islamic sects trying to expand their influence beyond the mosque. Recent governments have chosen not to challenge the extremist Islamists who use religion to gain a political foothold and are eroding the writ of the state. Even the powerful Pakistani military has been seen by many as abetting this behaviour in two successive governments, becoming

---

[2]   Interview with Peter Lavoy, February 2017, Washington DC.

party to written agreements that conceded to a new Islamist group known as the Tehreek Labaik Pakistan, a group that celebrated the killing of the governor of the Punjab for having committed blasphemy by seeking justice for a Christian woman accused of having insulted Prophet Muhammad. Leadership of the Tehreek Labaik Pakistan publicly preached the murder of the Chief Justice of Pakistan, and mutiny in the armed services against the army chief, whom it was accusing of being a non-Muslim. And it remained at large till late 2018, when the new government of Imran Khan attempted to rein it in. But the final chapter of that story has yet to be written.

Pakistani society is riven by linguistic, provincial, caste (yes, caste or 'zaat', often inherited from its Indian societal origins) and class distinctions. The military remains the strongest political force and source of continuity and security in the country. However, the state has been losing its monopoly on weaponry as an instrument of power, allowing the formation of armed militant groups, some even with the blessing of the state. And, the military's leadership, even when it means well, does not have the ability to effect massive societal change without the change emerging from the heart of the general population itself. Pakistan's major political parties often are family businesses or autocratically run enterprises, largely intent on making money and often using that wealth to purchase elections and overseas real estate. Their interests and those of the military clash frequently. The better-organized and disciplined military tends to win those battles. Indeed, in the words of a sympathetic US observer, 'It is like a huge tree that does not allow other plants to grow under its shade!' Pakistan also tends to treat the US as a gullible partner that can be fooled to part with its money in return for vague promises that may or not be fulfilled.

Located at a strategically important point on the map, Pakistan inhabits a tough neighbourhood. It abuts Afghanistan, Central Asia, Russia, China, Iran, India and the Arabian Peninsula. It trumpets its location as an asset, but its myopic leadership has, as yet, refused to take advantage of its position as a potential trade hub and source of economic and political stability for the neighbourhood, especially for its benighted cousins in war-torn and landlocked Afghanistan.

The Pakistani people are resilient, hardworking and adventurous. They have spread throughout the world and have done extremely well, whether it is in building up the economies of the Gulf States, or in business and politics in Britain, Europe or the US. Contemporary Pakistan has given the world some of the best poetry, plays and fiction in the recent past. There is much to celebrate Pakistan; beyond the seemingly ubiquitous images of bearded terrorists or angry mobs burning the American flag. The majority of Pakistanis are honest and enterprising. But their leadership has often not served them well.

There is much that can bring the US and Pakistan together. The frontier spirit that is embodied in the striving expatriate Pakistani men and women. The rebellious youth, brilliant women, path-breaking scientists and intellectuals operating on a global level. Their spirit cannot be bottled up. Indeed, the dreams of the people of America and Pakistan do intersect despite the hurdles their governments keep throwing in their paths. The challenge is to make their respective dreams and realities converge, inside both countries, and between them, improving the possibilities for greater trade, travel, educational and cultural exchanges. For the longer run, the US will be looking for stable partners in the Near East and Central Asian region, as sectarian conflicts create conflagrations in the Arab world and between Shia and Sunni Islam. Pakistan could become one such partner, provided the US works with the Pakistani people more than with corrupt and self-serving politicians to help ordinary Pakistanis achieve their aspirations. Here, the US can revisit its early relationship with Pakistan when it connected the people of the two countries together with exchange of expertise, technology and knowledge, while helping build for the long term much-needed infrastructure and educational institutions.

What Do Pakistanis Need?

In order to create a prosperous and stable Pakistan, its people need an enabling environment that gives them room to breathe and the tools to build their lives, unfettered by the heavy and dead hand of government and regulations and laws that are rooted in the stifling and dusty history of colonial rule or increasingly buried under religious obscurantism. No wonder they do well outside Pakistan and no wonder that the huge informal sector of the economy operates so effortlessly and well outside the reach of the taxman in Pakistan today. Its biggest asset and most critical part of security is its people. Then why has it invested less in them than it has in acquiring unproductive debt or in physical or military security? The symbiotic relationship between human development and security needs to be better understood for both sectors to be properly developed, so Pakistan can become the great state that its founders envisaged. An uneducated and growing population cannot help sustain a growing military, nor contribute to economic development in general.

Pakistan also needs to learn to live with its neighbours and to trade with them more than it does with distant friends. This will need much more than the ritualistic lip service that this goal has garnered. The opportunity cost of lost time in pursuing this goal is very high in terms of forgone benefits to the economies of the region. A connected South Asia remains Pakistan's best hope for growth and development. It cannot continue to rely on the kindness of friends around the world, nor the conditionality-based largesse of international financial institutions. Neither can Pakistan be seen as the petri dish for the growth of militancy and terrorism across borders and, worse, within its own society.

It has the wherewithal to become a stronger and more vibrant society. A politically awakened population, a large and enterprising middle class, a strong business community, a powerful and disciplined military, a critical mass of urban and educated men and women, and more than 60 per cent of its population that is still classified as youth. More than 150 million persons in the total population of 210 million now have a cell phone.[3] The Pakistani middle class is now around 50 million, largely urban, and generally invests in greater education for its male and female children.[4] If Pakistan makes the right policy choices and investments, it could become an important part of a developed South and Central Asia, the potential centre of gravity of global stability and development. This is the Peace Dividend that it must seek from itself and its leaders. If Pakistan gets its own house in order, its friends abroad will come knocking to help further. The counterfactual is unimaginable and unacceptable.

The US needs to weave a fresh strategy for the region, with a better and more active policy framework for bringing the countries of Greater South Asia together. Apart from introducing stability and growth for the countries of the region and reducing the possibility of intra-regional conflicts, it could help create a larger market than China for American

---

[3]   'Mobile Phone Users in Pakistan 150 Million in May 2011', Telecoalert, 27 June 2018, https://www.telecoalert.com/mobile-phone-users-in-pakistan-150-million-in-may-2018/

[4]   Umair Javed, 'Pakistan's Middle Class', *Dawn*, 20 November 2017, https://www.dawn.com/news/1371675

and European goods and services and open up its market for Pakistani exports at more reasonable tariff rates. In the process, it could provide in an integrated South Asian market, a global counterweight to the rapid rise of China as the dominant power in Asia. After all, for the first time in modern history, it has close relations with Afghanistan, Pakistan and India. It can and should be able to maintain a balance between them and assist actively in bringing them together rather than sit passively on the sidelines of their wasteful regional conflicts. It also needs to reopen ties to Iran and Central Asia and knit them back into the fabric of traditional South Asia, a natural and historically connected region of the world, home to great empires. The absence of conflict in the region would also create conditions for domestic and foreign investments in social and scientific sectors.

The US must avoid dividing the Muslim World into Arabs and non-Arabs or Shia and Sunni. And increasingly, it must speak to and for the people of the countries that it befriends, so it is not seen as beholden to or linked with despots and ruling bigots. Washington must come back to being that Shining City on the Hill that most Americans aspire to create and most non-Americans see when they conjure up the American Dream. Not the profit-seeking fickle 'friend' of dictators that the poor and dispossessed people of the Third World often see in action in their countries.

It is against this background that I undertook to write this new book, as a follow-up to *Crossed Swords: Pakistan, Its Army, and the Wars Within*, when I stepped aside in 2014 as the founding director of the South Asia Center of the Atlantic Council in Washington DC. My aim was to help focus attention on key events and personalities over 2008–19 and to use them to illustrate the challenges facing both the US and Pakistan, as well as the opportunities that await their people. I have used first-hand interviews, archival research and contemporaneous notes from conversations with key players in the region and in the US over this period to recount recent history as well as shed light on background events that influenced it.

In some ways, this book is a follow-up to my earlier *Crossed Swords*, since continuing wars in the region and the powerful role of the military remain key parts of the narrative. Without understanding these key ingredients, we cannot understand the potential solutions. With the removal of Benazir Bhutto and Pervez Musharraf from the political scene, the focus shifted not just on their political successors but also on the military chief, Gen. Ashfaq Parvez Kayani, and his director general of the Inter-Services

Intelligence (DG-ISI), Lt. Gen. Ahmed Shuja Pasha, and their successors. The extraordinary effect of these military leaders on the Pakistan Army as well as on the US–Pakistan relationship helps us understand the deeper issues in this misalliance as well as the persistent civil–military divide inside Pakistan.

This book starts by tracing the sorry end of the military rule of Gen. Pervez Musharraf and his controlled democracy that had been supported by the US, since it needed Musharraf's help in invading Afghanistan. Simultaneously, it sheds light on some of the background machinations inside Pakistan and the involvement of the US and the UK in the rehabilitation of Pakistani political leaders, such as Benazir Bhutto and Mian Muhammad Nawaz Sharif, in order to bring them back to Pakistan. It then delves into the internal battles raging inside Pakistan and the gradual deterioration of the US–Pakistan relationship during the two terms of President Barack Obama, while focusing on the massive changes that have occurred in the Pakistani Army, a key institution of Pakistan today. I chose to spend more time looking at the watershed year of 2011 when the US–Pakistan relationship began careening out of control. That single, most horrible year captures the essence of the disconnect between these so-called 'allies'.

During the period 2008–18, the US chose to continue to deal with the powerful Pakistani military as its preferred and main interlocutor, despite the emergence of a fledgling democracy in Pakistan. Meanwhile, both Pakistan and the Pakistani military were undergoing rapid and deep-seated changes, in response to the conflicts raging on its eastern and western borders, along with the rise of Islamist and ethnic militancy and terrorism inside the Pakistani heartland. Today the Pakistan military is better equipped for irregular warfare than at any time in its history, even while it retains its advanced nuclear weaponry.

America failed Pakistan by relying too much on its military partners in Pakistan and mollycoddling the corrupt civilian leadership. It also failed the Pakistani people by ignoring them in the main—as much as Pakistani leaders, civil and military, failed to recognize the centrality of their own youthful and highly urbanized population to the future strength and stability of their country. The arrival of President Donald Trump in 2017 brought with it a new muscular US foreign policy and a short-sighted view of regional relationships. Hence, the US risks losing not just the war in Afghanistan and peace in South Asia, but also losing Pakistan as a potential friend in stabilizing the Middle East. All the more reason to understand how things reached this pass.

The election of a political maverick, Imran Khan, as prime minister, with a broad national base for his Pakistan Tehreek-e-Insaf Party (PTI), offers an opportunity to recast the system of government inside Pakistan as an Islamic welfare state. But, his strength in the national assembly will be countered by the composition of the senate that is still dominated by recalcitrant opposition parties. And the shadow and suspicions of the military looms large over the civilian government despite their apparent entente. This mistrust can only be removed by active and frank discussions amongst the two, and good governance by the civilians, which will inoculate them against the military's interference. How the new government handles relations with militant Islamists will shape domestic and external views of Pakistan and its ability to operate effectively on the regional and global stage. Prime Minister Khan has been viewed with suspicion by the West for his own Islamist tendencies and rhetoric, as well as his ties to the military establishment. He brought to government a reputation for probity, and, unlike other politicians, appeared to be free of the taint of corruption. How he conducts his government will shape his ability to create a Big Tent coalition of political forces in Pakistan that can lay the foundation for a viable and flourishing polity and economy, and eventually as a counter-weight to the military.

Since the invasion of Afghanistan in 2001, a number of important books have tried to explain decision making in Washington DC (including insider accounts by Bob Woodward and former officials of the Bush and Obama administrations), and the role of the US military and intelligence services. Among others, Steve Coll's penetrating *Directorate S,*[5] a follow-up to his seminal *Ghost Wars,*[6] focused on the Pakistani ISI, but also showed how the war was badly conducted on the ground, and included other micro-level examinations of the losing war inside Afghanistan. Bob Woodward's books on the Obama and Trump presidencies provide an insight into decision making in the White House.

---

[5]   Steve Coll, *Directorate S: The CIA and America's Secret Wars in Afghanistan and Pakistan,* Penguin Random House, 2019.

[6]   Steve Coll, *Ghost Wars: The Secret History of the CIA, Afghanistan, and Bin Laden, from the Soviet Invasion to September 10, 2001.* Penguin Press, 2004.

But, the US–Pakistan relationship and especially the massive changes that occurred inside the Pakistani military and civil society during this period have not been adequately explained or understood from the perspective of those who were involved in making key decisions on both sides of this sensitive bilateral relationship. I had an opportunity to observe all this from my perch at the Atlantic Council's South Asia Center, and interacted with US, NATO, UK, Afghan and Pakistani civil and military officials, politicians and civil society groups, as an observer, adviser and commentator. Hence this book.

For those who know me, this will not be news: I belong to an old military family and a warrior clan, the Janjua Rajputs, and take pride in my heritage. I respect all those who wear the uniform for their desire and willingness to serve and protect their homeland against all enemies. But I do not support the military as a substitute for civil government. Nor do I favour the politicization of the military, in Pakistan and the US, both. At the same time, I take seriously my responsibility, as an observer and commentator, to cast light on the strengths and weaknesses of the militaries in both countries, and the political systems that they serve, so that they can be improved. It is important that informed observers continue to tell truth to power in Pakistan and not be seen as traitors. Constructive criticism will help Pakistan improve itself, so its narrative can be based on verifiable reality.

In 2008, I began working on the events that led to *The Battle for Pakistan* as a Pakistani citizen and ended it as an American. I wrote this as much as an American as a Pakistani. Dedicated to the well-being of both countries. My hope is that that this book will help spark a fresh debate in Washington and Islamabad about what is possible to make the dream of Pakistan a reality and make this relationship a long-lasting one so that they are not condemned to re-live their mistakes. America must not abandon the region again, nor write off Pakistan. For its part, Pakistan needs to build trust and more open economic relationships with its neighbours. Mark Twain is said to have famously quipped: 'History does not repeat itself but it sometimes rhymes.' I pray that this recent history of the US–Pakistan relationship can help bring both my homelands together.

Shuja Nawaz
Alexandria, VA

1

The Revenge of Democracy?

'Democracy substitutes election by the incompetent many for appointment by the corrupt few.'

—George Bernard Shaw, *Maxims for Revolutionists*

Ambitious Pakistani politicians have made frequent pilgrimages to Washington DC thinking that the path to government in Islamabad goes through this 'City of Magnificent Intentions'.[1] In recent decades, ancillary pilgrimages meandered through Saudi Arabia, China and the UK too. As President Pervez Musharraf's political orbit turned to its perigee, Nawaz Sharif headed from his exile in Saudi Arabia to London under an elaborate scheme for national reconciliation, a fig leaf for the transfer of power that was becoming inevitable. The aim was to absolve his major political opponents, former prime ministers Nawaz Sharif and Benazir Bhutto, of all legal cases against them or previous convictions under his rule, to allow them to return to Pakistani politics. Musharraf had begun digging a political hole for himself by taking on civil society and the legal community. He refused to recognize the political realities of the opposition to his long stay in power. Meanwhile, the Opposition had begun coalescing. In London, a coalition of sorts was cobbled together by Sharif and other political leaders, including Benazir Bhutto, under the rubric of a Charter of Democracy, an impressively long document that encompassed all the

---

[1] Charles Dickens described it thus in his nineteenth-century book *American Notes* (Penguin Classics, reprint 2001), though he referred more to the architectural plans of Pierre L'Enfant than the machinations of American politicians in Washington DC.

1

issues that they could collectively agree upon and that they hoped would prevent a recrudescence of military dictatorship in Pakistan and preserve their own fiefdoms.[2] The Charter made many promises to the people of Pakistan for improving governance, providing, in effect, benchmarks for a report card on the performance of whichever political party inherited power after Musharraf's departure.

But, Pakistan, like many other struggling former states once governed by colonial Britain, suffers from the same disease of empty rhetoric and unfilled promises, arising out of the degradation of public institutions and absence of good governance. The talk by the political class was of democracy. Its actions veered towards autocracy, kleptocracy and dictatorship, both civil and military. Governments tended to accumulate whatever power they could, and if they were military governments, they had little faith in the speed and efficacy of the democratic process. Almost as a rule, civilian governments that succeeded military ones tended to acquire all the coercive powers of the state of the regimes they upended, and resorted to non-democratic means to retain and consolidate their control. All the instruments of power that they decried in military rule, such as misuse of intelligence agencies and coercion, were employed to pressure and constrain opponents. Over time, civilian successor governments began to resemble their autocratic predecessors. But their rhetoric relied heavily on the lexicon of democracy.

Benazir Bhutto arrived in Washington DC in September 2007, connecting with her 'Washington family' of retired officials and Pakistanis in exile who provided her financial, political and logistical support. Among the many former officials who flocked to her support were Judge William Webster, a former attorney general, and director of the CIA. She also had a small but effective group of expatriate Pakistanis and Pakistani Americans who provided her continuous information and support within the Beltway. Her friend and former official lobbyist for the government of Pakistan, Mark Siegel, used his knowledge of the Hill to link her with key members of the Congress. The media loved her, seeing her as a modern Muslim woman who lived comfortably in her two worlds and spoke the language of the West with ease. She was also well regarded on Capitol Hill, especially as a counterpoint to President Musharraf who was losing his lustre as a

---

2   *Dawn*, 'Text of the Charter of Democracy', 16 May 2006, http://www.dawn.com/news/192460

teammate of President George W. Bush in the Global War on Terror. There, she had a very crowded and sympathetic audience on 26 September 2007, as she declared her intention to return to Pakistan in October. Terming Pakistan a 'petri dish of the international extremist movement', she suggested that fighting the Taliban and Al-Qaeda 'requires a national effort that can only flow from legitimate elections'.[3] The malleable nature of Pakistan's legal system was evident a few days later as the Supreme Court allowed President Musharraf to run for re-election despite holding the dual offices of army chief and president of the country.

Behind the scenes, efforts had been under way for some time on clearing the way for a return to a new formula for political 'co-habitation' between Musharraf and the political leaders whom he had summarily turfed out of Pakistan.

Prompted by Musharraf, jointly and separately, the UK and the US pushed for a return to some semblance of representative democracy in Pakistan. On Musharraf's team, the main interlocutor was Tariq Aziz, a civilian bureaucrat and ex-college mate of Musharraf at the Forman Christian College in Lahore. Aziz had earned his trust as a key adviser and as secretary to the National Security Council (NSC), and had even supplanted some of Musharraf's military confidantes in political decision making on behalf of the president. Others included his Chief of Staff Lt. Gen. Hamid Javed,[4] DG-ISI Lt. Gen. Ashfaq Parvez Kayani, a Musharraf favourite who had successfully investigated an assassination attempt against Musharraf, and Maj. Gen. Syed Ehtisham Zamir,[5] a Kayani deputy at the ISI who kept tabs on domestic political issues and reportedly even helped

---

[3]   Agence France-Presse report posted by AAJ TV: AAJ News Archive, 'Benazir to Put Up Amin against Musharraf', 26 September 2007, http://aaj. tv/2007/09/benazir-to-put-up-amin-against-musharraf/

[4]   Hamid Javed was a classmate of mine in the lower school at St. Mary's Cambridge School on Murree Road, Rawalpindi, and we reconnected briefly when he was named Defence Attaché at the Pakistan embassy in Washington in the early 1990s.

[5]   He passed away in 2015 after having retired from the army and starting a not-for-profit foundation in the name of his late father, the brilliant, humorous Urdu poet, Syed Zamir Jafri. Zamir Jafri, who also came from Jhelum, our home district, was a classmate of my father at Zamindara College, Gujrat. General Zamir worked closely with CIA Station Chief Robert Grenier also. Grenier refers to him under the name Imran in his book *88 Days to Kandahar*.

in rigging elections. Kayani had earlier served as a deputy military secretary to Prime Minister Benazir Bhutto, and this was considered a plus in using him as a conduit for the exchange of views. Once Kayani took over as army chief, the new DG-ISI, Lt. Gen. Nadeem Taj, a relative of Musharraf's wife, took over his function as an interlocutor on the deal Musharraf was negotiating with Bhutto for a National Reconciliation Ordinance.

On the American side, Richard Boucher, the assistant secretary of state for South and Central Asian Affairs since February 2006, was the point man for the Pakistani transition, with Secretary of State Condoleezza Rice entering the discussions, as needed and, in the words of then Amb. Anne W. Patterson, 'to close the deal'.[6] In the UK, Mark Lyall Grant, a former UK High Commissioner to Islamabad with a family history linked to the area that is now Pakistan, played a key role in his new position as DG for Political Affairs at the Foreign and Commonwealth Office.[7] He received help from fellow Trinity College graduate, Adam Thomson, later High Commissioner to Islamabad.[8] Boucher and Grant sometimes shared ideas, as needed, to coordinate their efforts in persuading Musharraf as well as the exiled Pakistani political leaders to reach a negotiated settlement on the political future of Pakistan.

---

[6] Interview with Amb. Richard Boucher, Washington DC, 14 June 2016, and with Ambassador Anne Patterson, Washington DC, 8 January 2016.

[7] Faisalabad, a city in the Punjab, formerly known as Lyallpur, was founded in 1890 and named after Mr Lyall Grant's great-great uncle, Sir James Lyall, the lieutenant governor of the Punjab, who built the world's largest canal system that transformed the formerly desiccated Punjab into India's breadbasket. The original town was laid out, like Khartoum, along the lines of the Union flag. See: Isambard Wilkinson, Notebook: 'The Sun Hasn't Yet Set on the British Raj', 5 October 2006, http://www.telegraph.co.uk/comment/personal-view/3632887/Notebook.html

[8] Amb. Thomson, later Sir Adam Thomson, was educated at Trinity College, University of Cambridge, and the Kennedy School of Government at Harvard. His father Sir John Thomson was a former High Commissioner to India, and even in his retirement years played a vigorous role in trying to build relations between India and Pakistan from his perch at the Massachusetts Institute of Technology. Both were a great help to me in my work at the Atlantic Council on 'waging peace' in South Asia.

Boucher met with Bhutto in different locations around the world. He recalled that her spouse, Asif Ali Zardari, was spending most of his time in New York City and therefore did not participate in the meetings held in Dubai and London. Boucher used to meet Bhutto roughly every month, and in between would travel to Islamabad to meet Tariq Aziz, often at the home of the Deputy Chief of Mission of the US embassy, Gerald Feierstein, the same DCM who later called Tariq Aziz to protest the 'thuggish implementation' of the emergency laws by Musharraf.[9]

Aziz had conveyed to Boucher that Musharraf and Bhutto were in touch with each other, but wanted the US to 'guarantee the outcome'. Secretary Rice did not approve of this formulation. She thought 'guarantee' was too strong a word. She suggested replacing 'guarantee' with 'witnessed' as a substitute. Boucher spent most of 2007 talking to Musharraf and Bhutto in search of the outcome that the US could comfortably sign on to as a witness. His sense from those exchanges and visits to Pakistan was that the military was getting tired of running things. He discerned that Bhutto seemed to favour an arrangement that would allow her to govern, even if Musharraf was titular president. But neither of them trusted the other. Musharraf also evinced an obligation to his 'King's Party', the Pakistan Muslim League (Quaid-e-Azam Group) or PML-Q, that had given him political support and legitimacy during his reign. As a result, no clear or explicit understanding emerged between Musharraf and Bhutto.

Boucher saw a number of reasons for the mistrust. Musharraf knew that Bhutto was coming back, but in Boucher's reading, 'hoped she would not'. A particular bone of contention was the re-election of Musharraf before Bhutto's return. Musharraf also felt that his PML-Q would do better than others expected it to do. Bhutto saw a downside to being seen as too closely associated with Musharraf. She had to weigh this against the upside of her party's potential election victory.

Against this backdrop, Bhutto decided to return to Pakistan and to run for elections. The Washington lap was to be her final move to consolidate her foreign support. She was eager to soak up whatever intelligence she could on the state of affairs in Pakistan as well as the level of US support

---

9   WikiLeaks SECRET/NO FORN cable of 11/4/2007 from Amb. Anne Paterson to the Secretary of State. *Dawn*, '2007: US Protested "Thuggish Implementation" of Musharraf Emergency', 31 May 2011, http://www.dawn.com/news/633237/2007-us-protested-thuggish-implementation-of-musharraf-emergency

for her efforts. After the speech on Capitol Hill, she invited me through her party loyalist, Senator Akbar Khawaja, to join her for coffee at the Ritz Carlton Hotel on 22nd Street NW, where she had two tables set up for meetings in the café at the ground level. She moved to the central table and with her came her husband and a few other local supporters, including Khawaja, an ex-World Bank staffer who had gone back to represent the PPP in the Pakistani Senate.

As usual, she was all business, shooting questions about the thinking inside the Pakistan military and their likely reactions as well as thinking inside the Beltway in Washington DC. Mr Zardari did not play an active role in the conversation, as he continued to take his phone calls. (At one point late in our conversation, she stopped our conversation and peremptorily suggested that Mr Zardari take his cell phone calls into another room, since she wished to 'hold a serious conversation'.) Among other things, we spoke about her personal safety in Pakistan.[10] This was the subject of American warnings to Bhutto about her planned return to Pakistan.

While in Washington DC, Bhutto met a second time within the year with Musharraf's ambassador to the US, Maj. Gen. (retd) Mahmud Ali Durrani, courtesy of a Pakistani American couple, Rafat 'Ray' and Shaista Mahmood, who had cultivated political connections on both sides of the aisle over the previous few years. Durrani had earlier been Defence Attaché at the embassy in Washington DC, then military secretary to Gen. Zia-ul-Haq, and, as commander of the armoured division in Multan, had invited Zia to the fateful tank trials near Tamewali, close to Bahalwalpur, in

---

[10] Earlier in our exchange, I raised with her a question about her personal safety and asked if she had body armour. Mr Zardari responded that they had a bulletproof vest at Bilawal House, the party citadel, in Karachi. I said that this was probably outdated by now and the danger would be imminent upon arrival at the airport. I suggested they look into using a product similar to Dragonskin that was custom designed for women too and provided protection with a lightweight material up to the neck. Later, I connected both Bhutto and Zardari with the company producing Dragonskin via e-mail. The company was prepared to fly to Dubai to outfit her with the protective gear. However, it needed a licence from the US government to export the protective clothing, and that could only be obtained via the Pakistan government's application. Bhutto later sent me a message that she had decided against that since she did not wish to ask Musharraf for any favours. After her caravan was attacked in Karachi, Mr Zardari suggested he would try to get body armour via the UAE.

August 1988, soon after which Zia's plane crashed after take-off. Durrani retired a few years later and devoted himself to an effort to bring India and Pakistan together through a Track II peace process named BALUSA. Musharraf had called on him to represent Pakistan when Gen. Jehangir Karamat left his post in Washington. Bhutto appeared to take a liking to him and saw him as a useful conduit to Musharraf, with whom she had begun a secret dialogue.

Durrani had had his first meeting with Bhutto at the Mahmood home in Mount Vernon, Virginia, eight months earlier, after clearing the visit with Musharraf. He also recalls that over lunch for about twenty persons in September 2007, arranged by the Mahmoods, at the Willard Inter-Continental Hotel in Washington DC, Bhutto said to him that he was her 'favourite ambassador', probably because he was the only one of Musharraf's envoys who met her. The host, 'Ray' Mahmood, suggested to Bhutto: 'When you become the PM you can make Ambassador Durrani the NSA.'[11]

'We all laughed and this issue did not come up during the lunch or even later at the dinner we had together,' said Durrani. He recalled that 'on both occasions I informed Musharraf personally that I was meeting *Bibi*.[12] I also asked him if he wanted me to pass on any message to her. He told me that he was already in communication with her and there was no need for me to get involved.' Bhutto's wish eventually came to be fulfilled by Zardari in May 2008, who recalled the Willard conversation as a 'promise' by his then late wife, and invited Durrani to become his government's national security adviser (NSA).[13] Durrani recalls that Bhutto came to sit across from him at the dessert stage of the lunch at the Willard and, among other things, asked him to tell Musharraf that 'he should administratively remove all these false cases' against her. Durrani demurred by repeating that Musharraf had asked him to stay out of the exchanges with Bhutto: 'He doesn't really want me to get involved.' But Bhutto insisted: 'No. No. No! He is like a brother to you! . . . Please communicate with him and tell him this is what I am

---

[11] In fact, Mahmood, an American citizen, was also rewarded later by Zardari with the honorary title of Ambassador at Large.

[12] Bibi is the polite way many friends and colleagues referred to Bhutto, that doubled as the Urdu equivalent of 'lady' as well as her initials BB. She often signed her emails as Bibi.

[13] Email from Maj. Gen. Mahmud Ali Durrani.

saying.' Durrani states she kept this up for nearly forty-five minutes. At one point, Zardari also joined in by saying, 'You know there are false cases against me [too]. I need a break. I've been in difficulty.'[14]

Bhutto arrived in Karachi to a tumultuous welcome and took many hours traversing down the main Shahrah-e-Faisal from the airport to Bilawal House. But security was poorly organized by her party and even poorly provided by the authorities. Musharraf was signalling his displeasure with her breaching of what he thought was an implicit contract that she would not come before the elections. The promised scanners for use by her vehicles against remote-controlled bombs did not work. Streetlights were switched off en route. A major bomb attack on her convoy took place that resulted in the death of 115 persons and wounding of 200 on Friday, 19 October. Bhutto escaped by chance as she had gone into the depths of the armoured truck for a breather at the time of the explosion.

President Pervez Musharraf said the attack represented 'a conspiracy against democracy'. The White House also condemned the attack. Meanwhile, in Dubai, Bhutto's husband Asif Ali Zardari, told ARYONE World Television: 'I blame government for these blasts. It is the work of the intelligence agencies.'[15]

Soon after, Musharraf suggested that Bhutto should confine her campaigning to the use of broadcast media. Bhutto would not have any of that. She wanted to re-energize her supporters across the country and was determined to continue on her march across Pakistan. The regime imposed all the bureaucratic hurdles it could to prevent her from connecting with supporters, including restricting public gatherings of four or more persons under the draconian Section 144, a vestige of colonial rule, and barricading her behind rolls of barbed wire—all in the name of protecting her. But as later events and investigations were to indicate, it did little to prevent her from being attacked and may even have condoned or assisted her attackers, if Bhutto's supporters are to be believed. Musharraf was alleged to have threatened Bhutto when he spoke with her on the telephone during her Washington visit in 2007.[16]

---

[14]   Interview with Gen. Durrani on telephone, 30 November 2016.

[15]   Asim Tanveer, 'Pakistan Blasts Kill 115 as Bhutto Returns', 18 October 2007, http://www.reuters.com/article/us-pakistan-idUSISL24512920071018.

[16]   Mark Siegel, 'Face the Truth, Musharraf', *New York Daily News*, 21 March 2012.

Her quest took her to the north, to Rawalpindi, where she planned a huge gathering on 27 December 2007 at the famous Liaquat Bagh, a historic site just across the River Leh and at shouting distance from the General Headquarters of the army in Rawalpindi cantonment. Pakistan's first prime minister had been assassinated there in October 1951. Her father Zulfikar Ali Bhutto had delivered many memorable speeches there too, including on 3 December 1971, when full-scale war began with India.

Bhutto referred to Rawalpindi as her 'second home' in her speech before a massive gathering that was waving a sea of the PPP's signature red, black and green tricolours. She presented herself as the legatee of Zulfikar Ali Bhutto and a 'sister' of the people of Rawalpindi as she went through a litany of the charges against Musharraf's regime in the preceding year: among others, the removal twice of the Chief Justice of Pakistan, the attack on the Lal Masjid (Red Mosque) in Islamabad and the attack on her own convoy in Karachi. She recognized the successful return to Pakistan of former prime minister Sharif and herself, as she whipped up her frenzied supporters with the battle cry that would prove to be sadly ironic in a matter of minutes after her speech was over: 'This land is calling out for me!' she yelled out hoarsely a number of times, as the crowd roared its approval of her father's party's promised goals of providing food, clothing and shelter (*roti, kapda aur makaan*) for the masses.[17]

The sun set in Rawalpindi that day at 5.07 p.m., leaving behind a hazy twilight when Bhutto got into her bulletproof vehicle with a foldable escape hatch or sunroof to leave the site of her speech. She then stood up in the vehicle, poking out of the escape hatch to acknowledge her cheering followers. At 5.16 p.m., three shots rang out, followed by an explosion. She fell inside the vehicle, wounded and bleeding from the side of her head. Her staff quickly moved her to the nearest public hospital. According to a report prepared by the staff who attended her at the emergency department of the Rawalpindi General Hospital, where she was received by Dr Aurangzeb Khan and Dr Saeeda of Surgical Unit II: 'A wound was present on the right temporoparietal region through which blood was trickling down and whitish materials which looked like brain matter was visible in

---

[17] 'Last Speech of Shahid Benazir Bhutto: Hope Is Lost', Video, *Daily Motion*, http://www.dailymotion.com/video/xyvkk2_last-speech-of-shaheed-benazir-bhutto-hope-is-lost_news

the wound. Her clothes were soaked in blood.'[18] The cause of death was determined to be 'open head injury with depressed skull fracture, leading to cardiopulmonary arrest'. Various conflicting reports emerged after this attack regarding the nature of the attack and the cause of death. No autopsy was requested by Bhutto's husband and none was performed by the authorities. The site of the attack was quickly hosed down and much of the evidence washed away.

The major agency involved in the handling of the assassination and its aftermath was Musharraf's Interior Ministry. Its spokesman, Brig. Javed Cheema, came on television the following day to present evidence that, he believed, linked the assassination to Baitullah Mehsud, the leader of the Tehrik-i-Taliban Pakistan (TTP), playing a recording of an 'intercepted' conversation that purported to indicate that the TTP had contracted out the killing. Cheema informed the media that Bhutto had died from a fractured skull resulting from her fall against a lever of the sunroof of her vehicle. The government of the day wanted to solve the murder in short order and move on. The US embassy also believed that the government's explanation was the right one. The jihadis were out to get her. But Zardari did not believe that. Sherry Rehman said that when they washed her body there were bullet wounds.[19]

Much later, President Zardari wanted to send the case of Bhutto's death to the United Nations for investigation, since he clearly did not trust the local authorities, even when his own party was running the government. He was cautioned against bringing the UN into the inquiry since Pakistan would lose control of the matter once it landed in the UN's lap. Foreign Secretary Riaz Mohammed Khan, who counselled against the move, was quickly sidelined and retired. According to the detailed reporting of Heraldo Munoz, the head of the UN team that investigated the death at the request of President Zardari, many questions remained unanswered about the government's handling of the crime scene, the speed with which they produced the evidence against the TTP, and the behaviour of Bhutto's

---

[18] Medical report of Mohtarma Benazir Bhutto, hand-dated 28 December 2007 and signed by seven doctors. See: 'Documents: Medical Examiners' Report on Benazir Bhutto', *Washington Post*, http://www.washingtonpost.com/wp-srv/world/articles/bhutto_medicalreport_010108.html

[19] *Newswire*, 'Bhutto Aide Says Bathed Body, Saw Bullet Wound', *Outlook*, 29 December 2007, https://www.outlookindia.com/newswire/story/bhutto-aide-says-bathed-body-saw-bullet-wound/530981?utm_source=bottom_floater

own party staff before, during and after the attack. He cites reports of suspicious behaviour of Khalid Shahenshah, one of the security guards, while she was speaking at Liaquat Bagh, including making a signal with his fingers across the neck. Shahenshah himself was killed later in Karachi under suspicious circumstances.

The person in charge of the security for Bhutto was Rehman Malik, a former official of the Federal Investigation Agency and interior minister in Bhutto's government. He was in a back-up car that immediately after the attack reportedly headed to Islamabad instead of following his wounded leader to the hospital. Later, as Minister of Interior (for the second time) in the Zardari government, he presented a bound report to Munoz dated 20 June 2009 and entitled 'Summary of Investigation and Trial Conducted So Far for UN Fact-Finding Commission'.

'I think your work will be made easy when you read this document,' said Malik, adding, 'This is very complete. This is your own report ready to be issued, of course, with the changes and additions that you may see fit.'[20] Munoz concluded that Malik 'never satisfactorily answered our questions about his role and actions during the moments surrounding Bhutto's assassination'. Yet Malik was President Zardari's confidant and the main interlocutor with the Commission. He had been convicted of corruption in 2004. Zardari used his 'discretionary powers' to pardon him after taking over as president and then made him Minister of Interior again. Why? Among other things, a senior US official dealing with Pakistan told me confidentially, 'because he knew too much'.

Faced with incomplete evidence and changing stories by police officers, neither the UN nor Scotland Yard, which had been called in by the Pakistan government, produced any definitive results. Rumours ran rife. Some people pointed the finger at Zardari as the most likely beneficiary of Bhutto's death. Others pointed to Musharraf. US Ambassador Anne W. Patterson thought, 'Zardari believed in conspiracies. He honestly believed that Musharraf could have killed her [Benazir].'[21] The US had the technological capability to track and isolate electronic communications, for instance, and would have been able to either corroborate or rebut the

---

[20] Heraldo Munoz, *Getting Away with Murder: Benazir Bhutto's Assassination and the Politics of Pakistan* (New York and London: W.W. Norton & Co., 2014), p. 77.

[21] Op. cit., Patterson.

Musharraf claim that the TTP had ordered the hit. It did neither. As Patterson told Zardari, the US believed the story that Baitullah Mehsud was behind the Bhutto murder.[22] A later and very detailed examination of the Bhutto murder by veteran BBC journalist Owen Bennet-Jones was presented in his podcast, 'The Assassination', and generally supported the theory that the TTP may have been involved, although it is not clear if wittingly or unwittingly. Yet another dead end emerged in the history of major Pakistani political murders.

Bhutto's untimely death forced Musharraf to delay the elections beyond 8 January 2008 to 18 February. The leaderless party of Bhutto faced a crisis in the middle of the campaign. Zardari, who had remained in Dubai when his wife had travelled back to Pakistan for the campaign, suddenly produced a handwritten document reportedly prepared by his wife naming him as the heir of the party command and control. A compliant PPP leadership team quickly accepted this evidence and his new role as the head of the party of Zulfikar Ali Bhutto. To add to the popular appeal of the Bhutto name, Zardari announced on 30 December 2007 that his nineteen-year-old son Bilawal would become party chairman and take over the party on completion of his studies at the University of Oxford in England. He added that the three children would add the middle name Bhutto to their given names. Hence, Bilawal Zardari became Bilawal Bhutto Zardari, only to be referred to as a norm as Bilawal Bhutto, so his name could be used for electioneering with the emotional slogan, '*Kitne Bhutto maarogey? Har ghar sey Bhutto niklega!*' (How many Bhuttos will you slay? Every home will produce a Bhutto!) Bilawal said, 'My mother always said democracy is the best revenge,' as he took on the titular role while his father ran the party.[23]

Zardari took to the hustings and used the death of his wife as a prominent feature of his campaign. He would often place a photo of Bhutto on the table or podium whenever he spoke publicly or to the media. Unwittingly, Musharraf had given the PPP a huge advantage in the

---

[22] This cable from Patterson to Washington reported on the condolence call by Patterson on Zardari. It mentioned that Zardari shared with her a copy of the one-page so-called will of Benazir Bhutto handing over the party to him. Zardari also sought 'U.S. blessing for his leadership'. *See:* https://wikileaks.org/plusd/pdf/?df=96891

[23] *BBC News*, 'Bhutto's Son Named as Successor', 30 December 2007, http://news.bbc.co.uk/2/hi/south_asia/7164968.stm

electoral campaign, allowing it to garner the sympathy vote of the public on top of the PPP's well-established vote bank as the party of the Bhuttos. At the same time, Zardari began establishing his own control over Bhutto's party, appointing his relatives and friends to key positions and making the party's central committee, populated by aging party faithfuls, into a rubber stamp for his views. In the process, he managed to alienate some diehard PPP followers, especially in the heartland of the Punjab where the elder Bhutto had established his stronghold.

Musharraf was quickly beginning to understand his own diminished position, even as president, now that he had somewhat reluctantly relinquished the command of the powerful army to his protégé, Gen. Kayani. The latter began introducing changes into the military system while attempting to turn the army from being a political instrument of the president to a professional body. Kayani ordered that all serving officers who had accepted civil positions should either resign from the military or return to their posts in the army. He also forbade any direct contact between military officers and politicians. And, when some officers sneaked meetings with Musharraf, he reminded the army that he considered Musharraf a politician too.

On 13 February 2008, US Ambassador Patterson reported in detail back to Washington and US outposts at United States Central Command (CENTCOM) as well as to allies in the UK on the moves that allowed Kayani to take charge of the army and leave Musharraf on his own, while raising the popularity of the army among the masses. He focused on improving the lot of the lower ranks, declaring his first year as chief as the Year of the Soldier, and following up with the Year of Training.[24] Kayani also dealt Musharraf and his PML-Q Party supporters a death blow by taking a public position of neutrality in the upcoming elections. He guaranteed the security of the elections, a code word for ensuring that no one would be allowed to tamper with the voting process at the polling stations.

The US ambassador summarized the changes succinctly. She had earlier been ambassador to Colombia and was familiar with the cut and

---

[24] In a conversation with me in his office, he referred to my book *Crossed Swords* that he had read and indicated that he wanted to follow the lead of my late brother and Army Chief Gen. Asif Nawaz, who had attempted to professionalize the army after years of martial law.

thrust of civil–military relations in a nation beset by an insurgency. An understated but steely diplomat, who had even challenged Musharraf by trying to visit the former Chief Justice when he was under virtual house arrest, she had travelled widely in Pakistan cultivating her sources and was in regular contact with both the civil and military, often acting as Mother Confessor to disgruntled local officials. She wrote to Washington:

> 1. (SBU) Summary: Following through on his public pledges to reduce military involvement in civilian politics, Chief of Army Staff General Kayani decided February 7 to withdraw military personnel who are currently serving in civil departments and return them to military positions. On February 11, he ordered the immediate return of approximately 150 Army officers working in various GOP offices. In a move to improve soldier morale, Kayani also approved a robust welfare package for soldiers and young officers. End summary.
>
> [. . .]
>
> 5. (C) Comment: The most recent IRI [International Republican Institute] poll shows the Army's popularity has been rebounding under Kayani's leadership, and Kayani's statements and the ensuing press coverage almost certainly will continue the trend. As the last army pay raise benefited high-ranking officers, the new welfare package [aimed at lower ranks] will increase morale among the junior commissioned officers (JCO) and the lower officer ranks who have suffered the most casualties in recent actions against militants. These operations, along with the young retirement age of JCOs, suggest that Kayani is looking to ensure the Army's ability to recruit new troops. Kayani's father was a junior commissioned office [*sic.*] which helps explain his sympathy for the lower ranks. PATTERSON[25]

Kayani had impressed his American colleagues with his dedication to the common soldier and JCOs. A senior US military officer recalled flying

---

[25] WikiLeaks, 'Kayani Withdraws Officers from Civil Departments', Public Library of US Diplomacy, 13 February 2008, https://wikileaks.org/plusd/cables/08ISLAMABAD651_a.html

with Kayani over various housing schemes that Kayani proudly pointed as new quarters for soldiers and Junior Commissioned Officers. He also took great pride in his indigenous efforts to set up counter-insurgency training sites replicating villages and towns of FATA so that his troops were prepared for action when they were deployed in the border fight.[26] Once Kayani distanced himself from Musharraf, the president was isolated politically. Sharif and Zardari then formed an alliance with a view to impeach Musharraf and force him to be tried for treason for upending the Sharif government in 1999. 'I gave concessions to Sharif brothers to get rid of Musharraf,' Zardari explained later, while interacting with newspaper editors and workers of his Pakistan Peoples Party (PPP) at the Governor's House . . . He further said, 'The Sharifs have stiff necks and I know how to humble them.'[27]

The marriage of convenience between the PPP and the PML-N resulted from their respective strong showing in the elections and common hatred of Musharraf. The PPP had garnered eighty-six out of the 342 seats in the parliament to the PML-N's sixty-six, and the forty seats of the PML-Q, Musharraf's supporting party. By promising to bring other parties into the fold of the new 'national consensus' and producing a two-thirds majority, Zardari threatened Musharraf with impeachment.[28] This unlikely partnership was doomed from the outset, but its immediate target, Musharraf, kept it hanging together for six months.

August, the month when Pakistan was born in 1947, remained among the cruellest months in Pakistan's calendar. On 18 August 2008, Musharraf succumbed to pressures from home and abroad and negotiated a departure to avoid impeachment, citing his devotion to Pakistan in his farewell television address. 'If I was doing this just for myself, I might have chosen a different course,' he said, wearing a Western suit and tie but speaking in Urdu. 'But I put Pakistan first, as always . . . Whether I win

---

[26] Background interview with senior US military commander with long experience in the region.

[27] *Indian Express*, 'PPP Formed Alliance with PML-N to End Musharraf's rule: Zardari', 7 April 2012, http://archive.indianexpress.com/news/ppp-formed-alliance-with-pmln-to-end-musharrafs-rule-zardari/933798/

[28] *CNN*, 'Pakistan Leaders Agree on Coalition', http://edition.cnn.com/2008/WORLD/asiapcf/02/21/pakistan/index.html?iref=nextin

or lose the impeachment, the dignity of the nation would be damaged, the office of the president harmed.'[29]

Many in Pakistan must have noticed the irony in that date—twenty years to the day that the previous military ruler Gen. Zia-ul-Haq was killed in a plane crash. Not only had the Pakistan Army distanced itself from Musharraf, even his American friends recognized the futility of trying to keep him in power. Surreptitious visits of emissaries from the White House, including some claiming to be from the vice-president's office, accompanied by their Pakistani fixers,[30] traipsed through the luxury hotels and corridors of power in Islamabad, cobbling together the deal that allowed Musharraf to escape without being held accountable for his extraconstitutional actions.

A very senior member of Musharraf's government told me that he had been informed by senior staff of the Crown Prince of Abu Dhabi that during a visit of Crown Prince Mohammed of Abu Dhabi to President George W. Bush at Camp David, the idea was bruited that Musharraf could be encouraged to depart Pakistan with a promise of 'protocol' and property. Bush was reported to have referred to Musharraf as a 'protocol President', that is, someone who enjoyed the perks of his position. As a result of that exchange, the Saudi King Abdullah bin Abdul Aziz Al Saud was approached and provided a reported $2 million, and the ruler of Abu Dhabi approved another $2 million, according to this Musharraf confidant. The amounts were reportedly deposited in Musharraf accounts in Dubai and London and used by him to make cash purchases of apartments in both cities. Musharraf later acknowledged the gift by the Saudi king. He did not name the second Arab nation that had provided help to purchase property in Dubai. A senior British officer recalls some discussion about the possibility of London being a destination for Musharraf once he left Pakistan. But he said he was not aware of the financial background to the move. Richard Boucher, the American emissary, would often brief senior Abu Dhabi and Saudi officials between visits with Bhutto and Musharraf.[31]

---

[29] Saeed Shah, 'Pervez Musharraf Resigns as President of Pakistan', *Guardian*, 18 August 2008.

[30] I ran across one of these Pakistani facilitators in the Serena Hotel and he told me of his mission for the Americans.

[31] In an interview with Nadeem Malik on Samaa TV, Musharraf claimed that he had received 'financial assistance' from King Abdul Aziz back in 2009.

Once the glue of hatred for Musharraf that was holding the tenuous coalition together gave way, the PML-N and PPP had little reason to stay together. Sharif announced the break-up within a week of Musharraf's departure from his office. Sharif's excuse: 'Zardari's party had failed to restore judges ousted by former President Pervez Musharraf according to a timetable they had agreed on.' Sharif said the two coalition partners also had failed to agree on a neutral successor to Musharraf.[32] Zardari offered himself as the replacement for Musharraf. Sharif found a retired judge to run for president against him. Zardari outplayed Sharif in creating a coalition across the political spectrum, except with the Islamist parties.

However, Musharraf avoided disclosing the details, saying that it was a 'private affair' so he would not go into details.

'Shah Abdullah was like a brother to me,' Musharraf said, adding that they had family relations and he even had access to the residence of King Abdullah bin Abdul Aziz. 'I was the only one with whom he used to smoke,' said Musharraf while trying to cement his claim.

Musharraf claimed that no one could prove that he had purchased any property abroad while enjoying power in Pakistan. 'I would be held accountable, if I had make property while being in power. But I went abroad in 2009 and then established the property in my individual capacity, so it is my private matter,' he said.

Musharraf offered a different explanation about the receipt of money from the Saudi King:

He said he stayed in London in the house of a friend Brigadier Niaz for six months which is located in a posh area of the city because he had no money to pay for the rent.

The former president disclosed that after a few months of leaving Pakistan he went to Saudi Arabia to perform Umra and King Abdullah then asked him where he was staying. Musharraf said King Abdullah considered him as a younger brother and gave him a big amount of money by opening a bank account in his name in London. He said a team of Saudi officials came to him at midnight and got his signatures on papers to open the bank account.

The former military ruler said that he used to deliver lectures abroad and receive payments ranging between $100,000 and $150,000 per lecture.
See: Ansar Abbasi, 'Musharraf Admits to Untaxed Rs 1 Bn in Foreign Accounts', *News International*, 9 November 2016, https://www.thenews.com. pk/print/163506-Musharraf-admits-to-untaxed-Rs1-bn-in-foreing-accounts

32   'Former Premier Sharif Quits Pakistan's Ruling Coalition', Radio Free Europe/ Radio Liberty, 25 August 2008, http://www.rferl.org/a/Former_ Premier_Sharif_Quits_Pakistans_Ruling_Coalition/1193720.html

The army kept a low profile as the presidential campaign unfolded. The US, however, continued to have an active interest in aiding the departure of Musharraf and in some ways clearing the way for Zardari to ascend to the presidency. Deputy Secretary of State John Negroponte, Assistant Secretary for South and Central Asia Richard Boucher, and Ambassador Patterson were the point persons for Pakistan. Unbeknownst to them, US ambassador to the United Nations Zalmay Khalilzad had developed a relationship with Zardari when the latter was living in New York, and he continued to provide information and advice to Zardari until Boucher found out and had to rein him in. 'Can I ask what sort of "advice and help" you are providing?' Mr Boucher wrote in an angry e-mail to Mr Khalilzad. 'What sort of channel is this? Governmental, private, personnel [*sic*]?' Copies of the message were sent to others at the highest levels of the State Department. 'Why do I have to learn about this from Asif after it's all set up?' Mr Boucher wrote in the 18 August message, referring to the planned Dubai meeting with Mr Zardari.

> We have maintained a public line that we are not involved in the politics or the details. We are merely keeping in touch with the parties. Can I say that honestly if you're providing 'advice and help'? Please advise and help me so that I understand what's going on here.[33]

Even Special Representative Richard Holbrooke complained about this 'freelancing'. Khalilzad does not mention this episode in his book but does mention an older relationship with Pakistan that was marked by a palpable disdain for Pakistani politicians. During a visit to Pakistan when Zia-ul-Haq was in power, suggested by Pakistan ambassador to Washington Lt. Gen. (retd) Ejaz Azim, he noted that 'there is always a gap between declaratory policy and actual policy, but never had I seen officials tell flat-out lies to their American counterparts so frequently and with such impunity'.[34] Khalilzad's own ambitions, beyond his meteoric rise in US officialdom, apparently extended to his native Afghanistan where he had

---

[33] Helene Cooper and Mark Mazzetti, 'UN Envoy's Ties to Pakistani Are Questioned', *New York Times*, 25 August 2008.

[34] Zalmay Khalilzad, *The Envoy* (New York: St. Martin's Press, 2016), p. 54. Interestingly, Khalilzad ended up being appointed as a special representative of President Trump to handle Afghan reconciliation, and effectively returned to the region to try to coerce or cajole the Pakistanis to cooperate in that effort.

been a powerful US ambassador and virtual kingmaker in local politics. Reports on his telephone conversations, captured by the British agency GCHQ (General Communications Headquarters) reportedly had him speaking from his New York perch with Afghan 'warlords and politicians' with a view to assessing his chances of running for the Afghan presidency himself.[35] (Khalilzad later become instrumental in President Trump's efforts to end the Afghanistan war on the basis of peace talks amongst Afghans, with help from Pakistan.)

This contretemps among US colleagues did not obscure the fact that the US, in the midst of its Afghan adventure, was actively seeking a new ally in Pakistan, having had to jettison its relationship with Musharraf. It worried about Pakistan's nuclear activities; after all, the architect of nuclear proliferation Dr A.Q. Khan was still at large. And the US needed a counterterrorism (CT) partner in the region that could buttress its efforts inside Afghanistan by reducing the footprint and ability of Al-Qaeda operatives to function inside Pakistani territory. Terrorism was on the rise inside Pakistan. The number of fatalities from terrorist violence rose from 1,471 in 2006 to 3,598 in 2007. (In 2008 they nearly doubled to 6,715 and then further to 11,704 in 2009.)[36] The total number of terrorist attacks inside Pakistan more than doubled from 260 in 2007 to 567 in 2008.[37] This deterioration could not be ignored by the US or by Pakistan.

But the US saw Sharif as an unsure partner, and he had never cultivated the Americans as much as he had cultivated the British and the Saudis. In Zardari, the Americans saw the potential for a more vulnerable and hence pliable ally. He took advantage of their attitude and, as WikiLeaks later revealed, was prepared to play the game of shadow puppetry, criticizing US policies in public to gain support at home, while privately applauding US actions in the region, especially their drone attacks inside Pakistan. In truth, he was not alone in playing this game. His prime minister, Yousaf

---

[35] Steve Coll, *Directorate S* (Penguin Random House, New York, 2018), pp. 376–77.

[36] South Asia Terrorism Portal, 'Fatalities in Terrorist Violence in Pakistan 2000–2019', http://www.satp.org/satporgtp/countries/pakistan/database/casualties.htm

[37] Umer Mahasin, 'Analyzing & Visualizing Terrorist Attacks in Pakistan & India (2002–2015)', Towards Data Science, 18 July 2017, https://towardsdatascience.com/analyzing-visualizing-terrorist-attacks-in-pakistan-india-2002-2015-24a03424f5e3

Raza Gilani, and army chief confided similar thoughts in their interactions with US officials.

> Against this background, Zardari entered the presidential race. The presidential election in Pakistan is indirect, with voting only by lawmakers in the National Assembly, the Senate and in the four provincial assemblies around the country. Under Pakistan's constitution, the president is elected by a majority vote.
>
> According to the chief election commissioner of Pakistan, Qazi Muhammad Farooq, Zardari received 481 votes. Retired Chief Justice Muhammad Saeed Uzaman Saddiqi (sic) [of the PML-N] received 153 votes and Senator Mushahid Hussain [of the PML-Q] received 44 votes . . .
>
> 'The (sic.) democracy talks, and everybody hears,' Zardari said in a televised address Saturday evening. 'And to those who would say the People's Party or the presidency would be controversial under our guardianship and under our stewardship, I would say, listen to democracy.' The president-elect said he would hand over many responsibilities to the parliament. 'Parliament is sovereign, this president shall be subservient to the parliament . . .'[38]

The PPP had come into power without a great deal of preparation. There was no blueprint for the transition in hand when its leadership returned from exile overseas. When I had asked Bhutto in Washington about her plans, whether she had set up a shadow cabinet and if she intended to reform the Federally Administered Tribal Areas (FATA) in particular, her reply was, 'We'll deal with all that once we are back in government.' Some of her party colleagues in Pakistan had been preparing plans, including one for the reform of FATA. But they were sidelined by Zardari as events unfolded.

Bhutto's death changed the internal dynamics of the party. Zardari, who prided himself on his loyalty to friends and sought the same from his friends and colleagues, brought in his own team of friends and relatives into key positions. The Bhutto loyalists of the ancient regime fell into line.

---

[38] CNN, 'Bhutto Widower Zardari Elected Pakistan's New President', 7 September 2008, http://www.cnn.com/2008/WORLD/asiapcf/09/06/pakistan.presidential.election/

He inherited an economy on the downswing and headed a coalition that was beset by continuous blackmail by his various partners. Soon, he had to turn to the International Monetary Fund (IMF) to get assistance to stabilize the economy. But lack of institutional mechanisms and whimsical decision making produced less than ideal results. Zardari was also wont to reverse rules and regulations to please business groups from Karachi. He did favour improvement of relations with India and Afghanistan. Inviting Afghan president Hamid Karzai to his inauguration as president was a smart PR move. But he could not follow up since the Afghan policy was largely made in army headquarters in Rawalpindi with controlling input from the ISI Directorate. The civilian government did not devote the manpower or resources needed to formulate sound or sustainable policy on security or foreign relations.

Capturing the ISI

From behind the scenes, Zardari began exerting his power through his compliant prime minister, Yousaf Raza Gilani, and his own hand-picked group of ministers, including Rehman Malik. Similar to Benazir Bhutto's attempted internal coup against the military during her first term, when she appointed a retired general to head the ISI, Prime Minister Gilani attempted an administrative coup against the ISI on 26 July 2008. He did this by issuing a notification that placed both the civilian IB and the military's ISI under the Minister of Interior. Technically, the ISI head was supposed to be picked by the prime minister and reported to him. In practice, he worked closely with and under instructions of the army chief.

The news that appeared in Pakistani media the next morning came as a surprise:

> In an unprecedented move on Saturday evening, the government placed Inter-Services Intelligence (ISI) and Intelligence Bureau (IB) under Interior Ministry, which according to defence analysts could undermine the role of the supreme spy agencies.
>
> Prime Minister Syed Yousuf Raza Gilani has approved the placement of IB and ISI under the administrative, financial and operational control of the interior division with immediate effect, according to a cabinet division notification . . .

Adviser to the prime minister on Interior Rehman Malik talking to
The Nation from London hailed the decision, which according to him
would boost coordination between different security institutions. He said
even before the move the security agencies had been working against
terrorism in a well-coordinated manner and helped a lot to curb the
menace of terrorism in the country.[39]

The notification was issued in the name of the prime minister while he was
en route to London. NSA Gen. Durrani recalls Malik informing a small
group of officials on the prime minister's London flight of the notification
with some glee. With the prime minister out of the country, it was expected
that the action would be a fait accompli.

According to later explanations, the decision was made after a
seemingly innocuous exchange between the PM and the Army Chief Gen.
Kayani at the end of a meeting on security matters when the PM suggested
en passant, according to Kayani, that there needed to be better coordination
between intelligence agencies. Kayani recalls that he agreed to that general
principle. A similar exchange had reportedly occurred with President
Musharraf. Malik then proceeded to act upon the transfer of power to the
Interior Ministry but gave no prior warning to the military leadership.

Almost the entire senior brass of the army was gathering that evening
in Rawalpindi at an officers' mess to mark the wedding of the daughter of
a senior colleague at army headquarters. Word of the notification spread
rapidly among the gathering. When Kayani arrived, a knot of senior
officers surrounded him to ask about the change that had been made by the
prime minister. Kayani confessed to have been unaware of the notification,
though one report states Musharraf had called him to ask about it. His first
reaction was cautious. He suggested to his senior colleagues that he would
speak to the PM on the latter's return from his foreign trip. He was told in
no uncertain terms that delay would allow the decision to take root. So, he
agreed to speak to the prime minister in London.

On the plane carrying the prime minister, Durrani recalls raising a
warning about the reaction of the military to this attempted coup by Malik.
He was asked to call Kayani to placate him. By the time the army chief

---

[39] Maqsood Termizi, 'Interior Ministry Gets ISI, IB Control', *Nation*, 27 July
      2008.

spoke with Gilani at 11 p.m. Pakistan time, a clear decision had been made by the military.

Gilani was informed that the army, and especially the ISI, was trying its best to stay away from politics for the past many months but his decision to place the ISI under the control of Rehman Malik would be seen as an attempt to again politicize the ISI for achieving certain political objectives.[40]

The notification had to be rolled back and put into abeyance. This was done in a matter of hours. The army had won back control.

According to Hamid Mir, who spoke with Zardari about these events:

> Prime Minister Gilani immediately contacted PPP co-chairperson Asif Ali Zardari in Dubai and informed him about the 'feedback'. Asif Ali Zardari suggested to the prime minister that the country could not afford any misunderstandings between the armed forces and the civilian government, so it will be better to reverse the decision immediately . . .
>
> Asif Ali Zardari said that there was no bad intention in placing the ISI under the control of the Interior Ministry and stressed: 'We don't want any confrontation between different state organs and that was why the prime minister tried to remove some misunderstandings through a clarification released by the Press Information Department.'
>
> Asif Ali Zardari accepted that some more homework and detailed consultations were needed before such a sensitive decision was announced but claimed: 'It's a new government with a lot of challenges and problems. Anybody can make mistakes in such a situation but nobody should doubt our intentions.'[41]

Looking back on this misstep, I wrote at that time:

> The incident illustrated the civilian government's lack of understanding of the nature and role of security organizations, especially those under the military's jurisdiction. Only one of the ISI's six wings actually deals with domestic political issues. Most of the rest of its operations deal with military matters at home and abroad. In addition to the three-star general

[40] Hamid Mir, 'Pakistan Politics: How Decision Regarding ISIS Was Reversed So Soon', Overseas Pakistani Friend blog, http://www.opfblog.com/3389/pakistan-politics-how-decision-regarding-isi-was-reversed-so-soon/
[41] Ibid.

head of the ISI, there are six two-star major generals responsible for each of the wings of the agency, more than even in a corps headquarters of the regular army. The overwhelming majority of the staff at senior levels is from the army. The idea that such an organization would report to a civilian entity with a narrow remit of law and order inside Pakistan was never examined or tested in debate or discussion, even if it had merit in the context of strengthening the civilian role in an emerging democracy. But for that to happen, the civilian establishment would need to prepare itself with knowledge and experience to handle high-level decision making related to the military and especially to intelligence—as in India and the United States, among others, and as intended in Pakistan's 1973 constitution.[42]

In India, both, the IB and the ISI-equivalent Research and Analysis Wing (R&AW) are under civilian leadership. Military Intelligence resides in the Indian military's domain.

But in Pakistan, the ISI had carved out a special territory for itself. Ostensibly reporting to the prime minister, it acted fairly autonomously and often in concert with the army chief, who effectively controlled its budget and provided its staff, especially at the top levels. Generally, it operated within the broad remit of the official policy, determined by whichever branch of government, the civil or the military, had the greater power at any point. However, it also took advantage of operational secrecy to act independently at the tactical level, guided by the ambivalent loyalties of local field operatives, particularly locals in the tribal areas, who guided senior officers in Islamabad. The senior officers were often temporary, rotating in and out of the regular military. They did not have complete knowledge or control over many aspects of the detailed operations below them, as a result.

The fledgling government clearly had much to learn about managing the country and especially the armed forces. Yet, as later events indicated, they continued to miscalculate the power of the military, creating a jungle of misunderstandings that led to backtracking during the next few years. One of Zardari's few victories was largely due to his deft handling of the army chief on the matter of the latter's extension of service beyond his first

---

[42] Shuja Nawaz, 'Who Controls Pakistan's Security Forces', Special Report 297, United States Institute of Peace, December 2011, p. 4.

three-year term. Zardari had a clear notion that he wished the PPP to complete its five-year term. But he faced serious odds that weakened his ability to govern effectively.

Ungovernable

The heartland province of Punjab was in the hands of the Sharif brothers and they did little to assist Zardari in managing what could truly be called an 'ungovernable' country.[43] In Sindh, he had a coalition with the MQM, and in Balochistan, the provincial assembly was marked by cronyism and corruption to the extent that nearly every member of the provincial assembly also had an official position so they could double-dip for salaries and privileges. 'At one time 61 out of 65 members of the assembly were ministers, advisors or parliamentary secretaries.'[44] In the North West Frontier Province (NWFP), later to become Khyber Pakhtunkhwa, the Awami National Party resisted attempts by the federal government to actively govern the fractious region. Zardari took to deal-making across the board to keep his head above the turbulent politics of Pakistan, even signing into law a bill approved by parliament that allowed Islamic Sharia to be applied in the Malakand division of NWFP (comprising one-third of the NWFP) to assuage the rising Islamist nationalism of the Tehreek-e-Nifaaz-e-Shariat-e-Mohammedi (TNSM) of Sufi Mohammed and his son-in-law Mullah Fazlullah (the future head of the TNSM and then the TTP).[45] The bill gave cover to the ANP's signed deal with the Islamist insurgents who had effectively taken over Malakand, including Swat, Buner and Shangla, and threatened the Karakoram Highway.

Zardari also continued to be dogged by accusations of corruption and cronyism and was given little respite by the newly invigorated media, especially the large numbers of broadcast news organizations, which produced a steady drum beat of criticisms and abuse. Meanwhile, the Islamist groups captured the airwaves and built up their base using threat and skilful application of radical Islamic thought to create divisions inside

---

[43] Shuja Nawaz, 'Ungovernable', *American Interest* 7, no. 1, 1 September 2011.

[44] Adnan Aamir, 'Corrupt Balochistan Assembly Members Are a Major Part of the Province's Problems', *Nation*, 21 August 2015.

[45] Bill Roggio, 'Pakistan Signs Sharia Bill into Law', *FDD's Long War Journal*, 13 April 2009.

Pakistan while fostering hatred for 'Hindu India'. The army also continued to keep up the pressure on him, as he tried to build relations with India and even with the US. He took to a whirlwind of foreign tours to China, Saudi Arabia and Iran, among others. But none of these trips yielded the aid that he was seeking.

China promised few investments in Zardari's Pakistan, even though Zardari presided over the signing of many MoUs between Chinese and Pakistani businesses. The Saudis were wary of him and favoured Sharif, whom they had harboured in exile. 'According to a January 2009 cable, Saudi King Abdullah described Zardari as "the 'rotten head' that was infecting the whole body"; other cables suggest the Saudis would prefer Pakistan to lose its weak civilian leadership in favour of strong military rule.'[46] According to a senior Pakistani diplomat, Zardari was briefed prior to his visit to Saudi Arabia not to directly discuss aid with Saudi King Abdullah, since that was normally left to officials to work out once they had discerned the wishes of the Saudi monarch from his conversation with his visitor. Zardari, according to the Pakistani diplomat, was very confident of his own persuasive powers and launched into a request for financial help soon after the Saudi monarch had welcomed him. A chill descended on the meeting, according to the diplomat.[47] Needless to say, no aid was forthcoming as a direct result of that visit.

The Empire Strikes Back: Mumbai 2008

The new and still weak government was faced with a huge challenge before the year was out. An attack on civilian targets in the heart of the Indian city of Mumbai (erstwhile Bombay) on 26 November by a well-armed and well-trained group of terrorists with links to Pakistani-based jihadi outfits nearly brought India and Pakistan to war, while putting Pakistan in the dock of international public opinion. As many as 163 persons were killed by the attackers. One of them, Ajmal Kasab, was wounded and captured, tried and eventually executed by Indian authorities. The ensuing case reverberated across the globe, as evidence mounted that the terrorists

---

[46] Ishaan Tharoor, 'WikiLeaks: The Saudis' Close but Strained Ties with Pakistan', *TIME*, 6 December 2010, http://content.time.com/time/world/article/0,8599,2035347,00.html

[47] Private communication from Pakistani diplomat.

were linked to the Lashkar-e-Taiba, a group that once was supported by the ISI for operations in Kashmir. A Pakistani-born informant of the US intelligence services, David Coleman Headley (original Pakistani name Daood Gilani), who apparently was involved in planning the attack, reportedly gave damaging testimony implicating Pakistan and its ISI in the attack. But India managed to botch the handling of the evidence as well as obscure the role of local and Bangladeshi groups in the planning and execution of the attack on Mumbai, producing a legal impasse with Pakistan in proving the case against official Pakistan.[48]

Despite the lengthy chargesheet offered by Headley against the ISI and Pakistan, Headley was not a credible witness, with dubious loyalties. He had been working as an informant for the US Drug Enforcement Administration to track heroin shipments from Pakistan and been turned by the Pakistanis. He ended up training with the Lashkar.[49] His multiple employments, often simultaneous, seemed to indicate an innate ability to turn each adverse event to his own advantage. Though he linked the Lashkar to the ISI directly, the ISI challenged that assumption and maintained that it had cut ties to the Lashkar. When Musharraf was attempting to thaw relations with India with a view to seeing a resolution of the Kashmir dispute, the ISI reportedly cut the jihadi groups off. But it did not follow up in disbanding or disarming the group. It is not clear if this was done purposefully or not. It allowed LeT to remain active, especially in Kashmir and later in Afghanistan. The LeT and others had built up a financial base of their own inside Pakistan and with patrons in the Arabian Peninsula, public and private. It appears many ISI handlers of the Lashkar continued to retain their links with the newly banned organizations and some may have even joined their ranks.

Regarding the ISI's links with the LeT, the ISI chief Lt. Gen. Ahmed Pasha explained to the Pakistan ambassador to the US Husain Haqqani that 'these were our guys but not our operation'. At the end of his meetings with his CIA counterpart Gen. Michael Hayden, 24–25 December 2008, Pasha had reportedly visited Haqqani at the latter's residence on S Street

---

48　HT Correspondent, '10 Things David Headley Told NIA about Mumbai Terror Attacks', *Hindustan Times*, 8 February 2016.

49　Ellen Barry and Hari Kumar, '2008 Mumbai Attacks Plotter Says Pakistan's Spy Agency Played a Role', *New York Times*, New Delhi, 8 February 2016.

NW in Washington DC. 'Pasha said to me *"Log hamaray thay, operation hamara nahin tha"*,' Haqqani writes in the book *India Vs Pakistan: Why Can't We Just Be Friends?* [50]

'General Pasha had also told General Hayden that "retired military officers and retired intelligence officers" had been involved in the planning of the attacks.'[51]

Haqqani took that to mean they were ISI agents, though the Urdu formulation, '*Log hamaray thay, operation hamara nahin tha*', could also mean the terrorists were 'of Pakistani origin' though the 'operation was not ours'.

The Pakistani government made some initial attempts to seal the offices of the jihadi outfits. None of the ex-ISI officers named in the charges by India were charged. Indian investigations into the attacks made little immediate progress. Pakistan blamed India for not sharing enough information to make a legally sustainable case in Pakistani courts. There was also internal friction between the civilian government and the military inside Pakistan on how to handle the investigation.

According to the *New York Times*, Prime Minister Gilani was reported to have offered to send ISI chief Gen. Pasha to India to discuss the investigation:

> Pakistani officials said the decision to send Gen. Pasha to India was reached during a conversation between the prime ministers of both countries . . .
>
> 'Prime Minister Syed Yousaf Raza Gilani called the Indian prime minister, Manmohan Singh, Friday morning at 11 a.m. to condemn the attacks,' Zahid Bashir, Mr Gilani's spokesperson said by telephone.
>
> 'The Indian prime minister stressed the need of intelligence sharing and evolving a joint strategy to counter terrorism,' Mr Bashir said. 'Dr Singh requested the prime minister to send the DG ISI to India to help in the investigations.'
>
> 'Once the modalities are worked out, the ISI chief will leave for India,' Mr Bashir said.

---

[50] Husain Haqqani, *India Vs Pakistan: Why Can't We Just Be Friends?*, Juggernaut Books, India, 2016.

[51] Suhasini Haidar, '26/11 Planners "Our People" Says Former ISI Chief', *Hindu*, 10 May 2016.

Officials here said President Asif Ali Zardari also called Mr Singh
to promise cooperation 'in exposing and apprehending the culprits and
the master minds [*sic*] behind the attack,' according to a presidential
spokesperson.

Mr Zardari said both countries should avoid being manipulated by
militants.[52]

The military thought the offer to send Pasha to India was inappropriate,
and the government had to withdraw that offer. NSA Durrani said the
offer had been made without consulting the DG-ISI. The military's
response was, 'He doesn't go. This is an intelligence service', and 'his going
would be counterproductive. You are putting yourself in a spot.' Little did
Durrani realize that he himself would become a major senior casualty on
the Pakistani side.

The NSA was publicly fired by the Pakistani prime minister for
having confirmed that the captured terrorist Ajmal Kasab was a
Pakistani. Kasab's family and village had been identified by journalists
in the Punjab before the relatives were removed by security officials from
public sight. Durrani had called his Indian counterpart M.K. Narayanan
immediately after hearing about the Mumbai attack. 'I called my
counterpart in India whom I knew . . . I told him that we need to
cooperate, see what happened, but we would love to send a couple of
investigators to talk with your people in Bombay.' But 'he didn't get
back to me'. Durrani recalled that 'there was this great threat of the
Indians attacking us. There were rumors about them [the Indians]
hitting Muridke [the headquarters of the LeT] . . . we carried out an
assessment, our [ISI] agency and others and the air force . . . were of the
view that there were about 50 per cent chances, 50–60 per cent, that they
might do something by the movement of their forces, their helicopters,
their aircrafts.' So Durrani called Steve Hadley, the US NSA. 'I told
him, "Listen, if they do something as a reprisal . . . I can guarantee
you one thing . . . Pakistan will be forced to respond. If they have any
illusion that we will not. Please respect us." Hadley called him back the
next day: 'I want to assure you that they will not do this.' Durrani told

52 Salman Masood, 'Pakistan's Spy Chief to Visit India', *New York Times*,
28 December 2008.

him about the Pakistani assessment of a possible attack by India. Hadley assured him, 'No. No. That is incorrect.'[53]

Durrani had been freelancing on his contacts with his India and American counterparts. He did not have a clear remit from the president or the prime minister. He recalls preparing a three-page document on the role and operations of the NSA's office soon after he was appointed. The president asked him to remove the role of the finance ministry from the NSA's orbit since the president wished to handle finance himself. On Mumbai, he stated that the PM 'did not ask for an assessment. I was on my own . . . I was even calling the Indian embassy et cetera et cetera.' Even the call to Hadley and the threat that Pakistan would react to an Indian provocation was Durrani's own initiative. He explained that no regular briefings were expected or sought by the civilian leadership. Out of that lack of clear communications and regular relationships emerged the conflict that led to Durrani's firing. Durrani states that everyone who had been tracking Kasab's origins, including the journalists, knew he was from Pakistan. 'The whole world knew about it', but 'we were keeping quiet. The day I made the announcement I had a chat with the DG ISI. I said, "Don't you think we need to announce? We are looking like fools." He said, "Sir, I have spoken with the president, and he supports that . . . we should announce."' Durrani recalls the PM was in Lahore that day. Durrani tried unsuccessfully to reach him. After that, 'I made the determination myself, rightly or wrongly.' He told the world that Kasab was a Pakistani on 7 January 2008.

Later that evening he saw on the local television that the PM had fired him!

Durrani said that Zardari told him that he was unaware of the Gilani decision to fire him. But he suspects now that the president was dissembling, and perhaps, the army chief, who came to see him the next day and spent an hour with Durrani, may also have been glad to see the back of Durrani. The plot may have been more complex. Apparently, the military was chary of the civilians autonomously bringing in a senior retired military officer to be NSA. The so-called Deep State jealously guarded its territory.[54]

---

[53] Interview with Maj. Gen. (retd) Mahmud Ali Durrani, on telephone from Alexandria, VA, 30 November 2016. He was in Islamabad.

[54] Interestingly, it was willing to sacrifice its own in that quest. Apart from Durrani, a second NSA general found himself on the skids, and even the role of the NSA was removed in 2018 when Lt. Gen. Nasser Khan Janjua resigned as NSA. The new government of Imran Khan eliminated the office of the

As usual, US Ambassador Patterson was quick to get to the source of the firing, and her cable to the Department of State offers multiple views on what transpired, while exposing the confusion inside the Pakistan government about what to do and when:

His dismissal has more to do with internal GOP [Government of Pakistan] dynamics than about Pakistani views on India or the Mumbai investigation. As is increasingly the case, PM Gilani was out of the loop and reacted angrily that he had not been consulted before the media announcement. Durrani told Ambassador that President Zardari had called him to apologize; both Interior Minister Malik and Ambassador to the US Haqqani confirmed to Ambassador that Zardari did not know Gilani was going to take this action. Durrani told Ambassador that Zardari promised that he would place Durrani in another position, but that he (Durrani) would decline if a new position were to be proffered. Zardari told Ambassador that he would try to find another high-level position for Durrani, but he had some sympathy for Gilani, who had heard about Durrani's statements on the news and was blindsided . . .

Ambassador called Durrani January 8 to confirm the story. Durrani said he had consulted with ISI Director General Pasha and gotten his concurrence about announcing that Kasab was Pakistani. Pasha had been very specific that the government wanted to disseminate that information. Durrani said he was one of four people authorized, in writing, to make such statements on behalf of the government. (This is contradicted by others in government.)

Her report than went on to outline the chaotic handling of information by the government of Pakistan:

Despite Durrani's assertion, the GOP did not coordinate release of the information. Foreign Secretary Salman Bashir first denied the report, then confirmed it. Separately, Information Minister Sherry Rehman confirmed it. When Gilani heard about these statements, said Durrani, he was in Lahore and out of the loop, and decided to fire Durrani for not consulting with him. (According to visiting Ambassador Haqqani, a

---

NSA without much public debate or publicity most likely because the military thought the role was redundant.

Durrani ally, Gilani was a recipient of the memo authorizing Durrani to confirm Kasab's nationality, but Gilani may not have seen it.) . . .

5. (C) In a meeting January 8 with Ambassador, Interior Minister Rehman Malik confirmed Zardari did not know that Gilani had fired Durrani. He said Durrani had never managed to develop good chemistry with the PM. As you know, he said 'the PM is not very smart.' The PM had been smarting [sic] for weeks that he was out of the loop and not kept informed by his ministers on a range of issues. Speaking about his own relations with Gilani, Malik said that he had an air-clearing session with Gilani a few days ago and arranged to have better cell phone connections with him. Malik said he reminded the PM that he had tried to get in touch with him for a full day in the PM's home town of Multan recently about one of his operations but could not find him.[55]

This episode reflected the lack of trust and poor communication between the civil and military on the one hand and among government officials in general on the other. It also showed a lack of confidence of the politicians and how civilians were loath to confront the military. They chose to offer human sacrifices on the altar of political expediency—people who had little political value in their minds when the military pushed the government. Zardari was not alone in this behaviour. Nawaz Sharif also suffered from the same timidity, even when he had a strong political base. The military continued to be the key dealmaker.

The Long March

As Zardari's government lurched from one issue to the next, he could not escape the active participation and interest of the army in each imbroglio. The following year, Zardari faced a new challenge from Nawaz Sharif's party that had signed on to the lawyers' movement demand for the reinstatement of the yet again deposed Chief Justice Iftikhar Muhammad Chaudhry. Ironically, a PPP stalwart lawyer, Aitzaz Ahsan, continued to be one of the key players in the movement and was in the procession, in the car with Nawaz Sharif, that took off from Lahore towards Islamabad. Their objective: force the government to put Chaudhry back in his position as head of the Supreme Court.

---

[55] WikiLeaks document, https://wikileaks.org/plusd/pdf/?df=61598

The army realized that it was caught in the battle between two powerful political forces—the government and the Opposition—and that it would be invited to protect the capital against the invading hordes accompanying the lawyers' caravan. According to the US ambassador in Islamabad, Army Chief Gen. Kayani had sent ISI officers to persuade Nawaz Sharif to call off his 'Long March'.

Aitzaz Ahsan recalls a more direct approach: receiving a call from Gen. Kayani near Gujranwala on the night of 15 March 2009.[56] Sharif was sitting in the car with him when Ahsan took the call from Brig. Zubair Mahmood Hayat, the private secretary to the army chief, around 11.30 p.m., who then connected him with Kayani.[57] It was a short conversation, recalls Ahsan. 'He wanted to inform me that the Prime Minister Yousaf Raza Gilani would address the nation at 3 or 4 a.m. It might be useful to break the journey and hear him,' Kayani said to Ahsan.

'Why should I do that?' responded Ahsan.

'Your concerns might be addressed by the PM,' said Kayani, listing the concerns:

1. No 'Minus 1 Formula' and the Chief Justice to be reinstated. [Minus 1 referred to the idea being floated around that the senior judges would be restored minus the Chief Justice].

2. Reinstatement should take place without requirement of taking a fresh oath.

This was crucial, Ahsan thought, to 'our position since some judges had been taken back by Zardari on a fresh oath. This restored the *status quo ante*. I said, "You are right." He [Kayani] said again, "If it is expedient,

---

56   Interview with Aitzaz Ahsan at his home in Islamabad, 29 February 2016.

57   Brig. Hayat, a tall bespectacled US- and UK-trained artillery officer with a commanding presence, was essentially *chef de cabinet* for Kayani. He ran the office with great efficiency and a serious demeanour, though privately he had a wry sense of humour. Kayani later created a new post for a major general to be DG-SD or Director General Staff Duties to manage office systems and processes for the army chief. Hayat was promoted and then sent to command 8 Division in Sialkot, and later promoted to three stars to command a corps in Bahawalpur. That positioned him as the senior-most general when Kayani's successor, Raheel Sharif, completed his three-year tenure. After Bahawalpur, he was sent by Sharif to head the SPD that was responsible for Pakistan's nuclear assets, before being promoted to four stars as chairman of the JCS Committee.

please stop and listen [to the PM's speech]." Kayani said, "I know where you are and how many are with you.'"

Ahsan said that he had managed to build up a massive army of supporters across the country with his call for protests in every city centre. Supporters of the judiciary had even blocked the Karakoram Highway for fourteen hours, he claimed. He said he had 50,000 persons with him on the march to Islamabad. Another 150,000 were waiting to join the procession in Gujranwala, and his plan called for a drive through Rawalpindi down the busy Murree Road to Islamabad, instead of taking the Islamabad Highway directly from Rewat to Islamabad, which was the preferred route of the army if the march had continued. He would have picked up a huge crowd inside Rawalpindi on the final leg of the march on Islamabad. (It is difficult to verify the crowd sizes. All politicians tend to magnify such numbers.)

Interestingly, Ahsan's party leader Zardari never called him during the march. Nor did the prime minister. Zardari called only a week after the Chief Justice was reinstated. Ahsan regretted that Zardari had not called, and believes that the president had been fed 'stories' by Rehman Malik of smaller crowds than was the case. Ahsan represented the Old Guard of the PPP, the committed workers who had joined the party of Zulfikar Ali Bhutto and remained loyal to the Bhutto family and the original progressive message of the party. Malik was a relative newcomer and more loyal to Zardari than the PPP of old.

Ahsan thought the army could have taken over, but he did not fear an army takeover since the lawyers' movement had been bolstered by its success in forcing Musharraf from the presidency. 'We could have changed "Go, Musharraf, Go!" to "Go, Kayani, Go!"' said Ahsan. (Kayani on the other hand later confided to me that if he wanted to he could have taken over during this crisis since the public had lost faith in the government and disruption caused by the lawyers' movement had created a backlash in the public mind. But he stayed his hand.)

With these calculations racing through his mind, Ahsan found a large farmhouse near Gujranwala and pulled in. A puzzled Sharif asked Ahsan, 'Whose phone call was that?' He was surprised when Ahsan told him it was Kayani because Sharif said Ahsan had not used the respectful term 'General Sahib' when speaking to the army chief. The break allowed them to hear the prime minister's announcement.

'I announce today that Iftikhar Chaudhry and all other deposed judges will be reinstated from March 21,' Gilani said in a televised address to the nation.

'The current Supreme Court Chief Justice will retire on that date, allowing Chaudhry to take over,' the premier said.

He directed provincial governments to release all those arrested during a stringent government clampdown aimed at foiling a so-called long march organized by lawyers and political activists, due to reach Islamabad on Monday.

He also immediately lifted Section 144, a nineteenth-century British law, put into effect in the capital and the provinces of Punjab, Sindh and North West Frontier Province, outlawing public gatherings and demonstrations.

'I order all the provincial governments to release political workers, lawyers and all those arrested during the long march,' he said.

'I want to congratulate the nation. Let us celebrate this with dignity . . . This was the promise made by our late leader Benazir Bhutto that the chief justice will be restored and I had also made the promise after I took over as prime minister,' said Gilani.[58]

Civil society had won a major victory over both the government and the military, using mass media and a committed and cohesive movement to achieve its objective. The PPP government had to make the best of a bad thing, as the prime minister's speech indicated. But they were not entirely out of the woods. And the military–civil divide had been merely papered over again.

The US ambassador reported back to Washington DC on the outcome on 16 March 2009 as divulged via WikiLeaks:

16. (C) None of the Pakistan Army units alerted to support civil authorities during the march were deployed, and all other Pakistani Army units were restricted to their cantonments throughout the protests. Pakistani military officials highlighted the fact that Army units, not placed on alert, were deliberately ordered to remain in their cantonments in an effort to telegraph the military's neutrality during the crisis.

17. (C) There is a growing consensus among mid-grade Pakistani military officers that the Chief of Army Staff (COAS), General Kayani, was the primary interlocutor responsible for convincing President Zardari to restore the Supreme Court judges, including the Chief Justice, and end

---

[58] 'Gilani Announces Restoration of Deposed Chief Judge', *Dawn*, 16 March 2009.

governor's rule in Punjab Province, thus averting the potential chaos that would have resulted if the marchers had reached Islamabad. USDAO [US Defence Attaché Office] reporting also indicates that the COAS dispatched ISI officers to meet with Nawaz Sharif to explain the Army's role in mediating between the government and the PML-N and to advise him to call off the march if the President acquiesced to the PML-N's and lawyers' demands.

18. (C) ODRP [Office of Defence Representative in Pakistan] discussed situation with Director General of ISI (Pasha) and DGMO (Javed Iqbal) and found that both were relieved at the outcome. Pasha remarked that there is still much to be done. When ask [*sic*] for his comment regarding winners and losers, he commented diplomatically that everyone won. When ODRP commented that it appeared Zardari had lost popularity, Pasha merely chuckled. PATTERSON[59]

Pasha the Soldier would have responded sharply and verbally. Pasha the Spymaster was learning to be guarded and circumspect. He had mastered the act of the Cheshire Cat by hiding behind his enigmatic and polite smile to shield his thoughts!

More Governance Challenges

Natural events beyond his control further showed up the weakness of the Central government of Zardari. Floods ravaged Pakistan while he was visiting France and the UK with his young son Bilawal, a student at Oxford, in July and August 2010. The juxtaposition of photographs of his helicopter landing near his French chateau and more than 20 million Pakistanis flooded out of their homes was damning. He chose not to return to Pakistan. From France he proceeded to the UK and a reported visit with the British Prime Minister David Cameron at the PM's country residence at Chequers.[60] Facing severe criticism at home and from others around the world, the best he could do was to return and accompany the UN Secretary General on an aerial survey of the damage. In the aftermath

---

[59] '2009: Army's Role in Long March Conclusion', *Dawn*, 5 June 2011, http://www.dawn.com/news/print/634414.

[60] Isobel Villiers, 'What Is Zardari Doing at Chequers', *Spectator*, 7 August 2010.

of the 2010 floods, the Saudis offered no help till the Army Chief Gen. Kayani called them. He was told they would only give money since the army chief had called, and that too via the United Nations, not to the Zardari government.[61]

The US did its best to help Pakistan cope with the floods that inundated an area roughly equivalent to the Eastern Seaboard of the continental US. The damage was estimated at 5.9 per cent of GDP. The US rushed aircraft and supplies, and its intrepid new Ambassador Cameron Munter was seen everywhere trying to help out, even to the extent of offloading bags of grain from an airplane. The National Disaster Management Authority (NDMA) had been set up after the earthquake of 2005. In 2010 it was being run by an army general, Nadeem Ahmad. The NDMA had produced a report in 2009 that promised a proactive approach. The 2010 report, among other things, predicted the possibility of a massive flood, but the new devolved governmental structure meant that the provinces were unprepared. The full report was not published till April 2011, delaying implementation. Hence, aid was slow in reaching the people.

Civil society groups leapt up to help, including the social services arm of the jihadi groups. The army was the principal actor in flood relief, rushing equipment and manpower into the most seriously affected areas and deploying in aid of civil power up and down the country. Its performance tended to put the civil authorities in a bad light relative to the speed and efficiency of its relief efforts.

US Special Representative for Afghanistan and Pakistan (SRAP) Richard Holbrooke immediately flew to Pakistan and wanted to visit the affected areas and refugee camps. This forced the prime minister also to act and visit the displaced persons' camps. International aid also began arriving. UN Special Envoy and famous actress Angelina Jolie flew to Pakistan, and she and her partner Brad Pitt together donated $1 million.[62] The US also helped set up a group to provide multilateral and multinational aid to Pakistan under the rubric of Friends of Democratic

---

[61] Private conversation with a senior Pakistani military official.

[62] I met Jolie at an event in September at the Newseum, Washington DC, before she left to meet the UN Secretary General on Pakistan, and suggested she ask him to appoint a special representative to seek and coordinate assistance. She took to the idea and did so, resulting in faster action by the Secretary General. A few days later, he appointed Rauf Angin Soysal of Turkey as his special envoy for assistance to Pakistan.

Pakistan. Surprisingly, participation and contributions were spotty. China only sent its UN envoy to the meeting in New York. The Saudis, as mentioned earlier, failed to contribute until the army chief intervened. As usual, pledges were hard to fulfil.

Ambassador Holbrooke was struck by the need to act quickly and saw an opportunity to show the Pakistani public how much the US cared for them. He fought hard to get $500 million released from the US bureaucracy from the $7.5 billion programmed for the Kerry–Lugar–Berman (KLB) funds for Pakistan over five years. That cash infusion allowed the US to assist Pakistan in meeting the immediate needs of the flood-affected population.

Throughout this period, the civilian government was generally seen as missing in action. At the provincial level, Punjab Chief Minister Shahbaz Sharif was operating at full throttle. Sindh was a battleground for publicity between the PPP and the MQM, as the latter even hijacked general public donations and labelled train shipments with the MQM banner. The more successful flood relief efforts were organized privately by groups of individuals and local foundations, such as the Jehangir Siddiqui Foundation that rushed supplies to the interior of the country. Other relief workers belonging to the social service units of the Islamic militant organizations, such as the Lashkar-e-Taiba, and other Islamic charities from overseas also quickly established their presence in the flood-affected areas, much to the discomfort of the government.

Again, the military was doing its own thing, autonomously, while the civilians were trying to play to the public gallery with photo ops for ministers seemingly parachuting into the flood-affected areas, distributing supplies and leaving. In some cases, groups of locals were posed as victims of the floods and tents set up to show that they were being housed and well looked after. As a detailed series of reports from *Scientific American* showed in a camp near Nowshera:

> Salma Begum, 32, fumes when asked what the government and international community have done for her family in the weeks since the disastrous flooding here. The only support she has seen comes from the local branch of the Ummah Welfare Trust, a UK-based Islamic charity.
>
> Many in Pakistan are in the same position, but the people in the Ummah camp are especially furious, as their tents sit right next to a much-better-provisioned camp that has received extensive

UN and government help. Other camp residents speak of a federal government relief operation just 15 minutes down the road that has been set up as something of a Potemkin village, used for tours to show celebrities and top-ranking non-governmental organization (NGO) officials.[63]

US flood aid was welcomed, but not for long. Neither the civil nor the military wished to allow the US to be seen as a major benefactor. As often happens, the incumbent Central government failed to fully liaise with provincial authorities or the military. Aid was thus delayed or diverted for political purposes. This left a lasting negative impression of the Zardari government on the country's mind and he suffered its consequences in the following elections in 2013.

Internal Situation Deteriorates

The internal security situation continued to deteriorate, as the Taliban and their allies established a strong foothold outside FATA. Incidents of suicide bombings continued to rise in the heartland. As the Department of State's annual report on terrorism stated:

> In 2010, Pakistan continued to experience high levels of terrorism and Pakistan-based terrorist organizations continued to threaten internal, regional, and global security. Violence resulted from both political and sectarian conflicts throughout the country, with terrorist incidents occurring in every province. While government authorities arrested many alleged perpetrators of terrorist violence, few convictions resulted. The Pakistani military continued to conduct operations in areas with known terrorist activity but was unable to expand its operations to all areas of concern. Increased sectarian violence between the Sunni and Shia communities and against religious minority communities also resulted in numerous attacks with high casualties. These attacks continued the trend of employing suicide bombers and remotely detonated explosives to

---

[63] Nathaniel Gronewold, 'After the Pakistan Floods, Why Relief Help Was Slow to Arrive', *Scientific American*, 16 October 2010, https://www.scientificamerican.com/article/in-pakistan-floods-scale/

perpetrate violence. Attacks using similar methods were also carried out against government and police facilities.[64]

The 2010 report from the National Counterterrorism Center (NCTC) of the US showed that Pakistan had suffered 2,150 deaths from terrorist attacks.[65]

Meanwhile, Karachi too fell into a renewed and downward spiral of sectarian and ethnic conflict, as did FATA. The new US administration upped its use of drone attacks. Each public complaint by the Pakistani government (despite its private support for such attacks) raised public anger against the US and its Pakistani allies. Terror struck the heart of Islamabad soon after Zardari became president on 10 September 2008. An explosive-laden truck rammed the gate of the Marriott in Islamabad on 20 September, reducing much of the famed hotel to a heap of rubble and ashes. Zardari claimed the attack was aimed at him because he was supposed to attend a celebration at the hotel after his inauguration. The owner of the Marriott, Sadruddin Hashwani, with whom Zardari had allegedly had some run-ins over business deals, claims Zardari was behind the attack and that Hashwani was the likely target since he was supposed to attend a family celebration at the hotel. Hashwani also says there was no official booking for any event at the hotel that evening, so Zardari could not have been the target. He also writes about earlier attacks on his office and the Pearl Continental in Peshawar.[66] None of these claims was proven.

Zardari struggled to reshape the political system of Pakistan, to alter the constitutional balance between the president and the prime minister on the one hand and between the Centre and the Provinces on the other. He had a vision of change that he felt would be true to the original plan of the elder Bhutto as spelled out in the 1973 constitution.[67] This involved

[64] US Department of State, *Country Reports on Terrorism 2010*, https://www.state.gov/j/ct/rls/crt/2010/170258.htm

[65] National Counterterrorism Center, *2010 Report on Terrorism* (Washington DC: Office of the Director of National Intelligence, NCTC, 30 April 2011), https://www.dni.gov/files/documents/2010_report_on_terrorism.pdf

[66] Sadruddin Hashwani, *Truth Always Prevails: A Memoir* (India: Penguin Portfolio; UK: Penguin Books, 2014), pp. 204–16.

[67] He conveyed this vision to me in a brief conversation on the telephone from London on 24 September 2016, when I spoke with him about recording an interview for this book. He ended that brief exchange by asking to see the

reducing the powers of the president in favour of the prime minister and returning Pakistan to the original federation that was envisaged, with greater devolution of portfolios to the provinces. For a man who had inherited an all-powerful presidency, this appeared to be politically suicidal. But he recognized his pre-eminence in the power structure of the PPP, and the fact that he would retain total control of the party even if the prime minister had titular power under the changed constitution. Zardari played his cards well. Many of these objectives were consonant with the Charter of Democracy that Sharif had signed. Sharif publicly vowed to work towards the implementation of the charter even though he was sitting on the Opposition benches. In quick order, Zardari succeeded in the passage of the 18th Amendment that reduced his own powers and strengthened the prime minister's hand, in effect removing the possibility of summary dismissal of a prime minister by the president.

Continuous infighting within the government and competition between the government and the military created separate centres of gravity for action against terrorism and militancy. Pakistan tried to assist the US's CT efforts, especially drone strikes in FATA from bases in Afghanistan, within boundaries established by both sides. Map grids defined where the drones could attack. But the collaboration was spotty and not whole-hearted. The civilian government was desperately trying to keep its head above the choppy political waters, even as it faced economic challenges.

The next few years were marked by tumult and challenges to the security of the country and to its economy. Pakistan had become truly 'ungovernable'. The need to constantly satisfy the needs of hungry coalition partners made it impossible for the PPP to pass economic reforms. It had some extensive ones in mind aimed at reordering Centre–Periphery relationships and restoring fiscal stability and growth to the economy, but these ambitions far outstripped the PPP's fragile capacities. So try as it might, the PPP government failed to reduce the fiscal deficit, to reform tax policy, or to streamline tax administration in line with its own promises to, and the demands of, the IMF. That, in turn, meant that Pakistan was unable to draw the last two tranches (totalling $3.5 billion) of its $13 billion IMF loan.

---

topics or questions I wished to cover in the interview and then promised to set a date for the actual interview. I immediately shared the list of topics and questions. Despite efforts to follow up, the interview never took place.

The PPP government lacked a clear vision of what it wanted to achieve. It could have supported the new technocratic economic team it put in place in 2010 without much new legislation, if it had a clearer set of goals. As a result, by year's end, it sought and received a nine-month waiver from the IMF with a promise to meet the Fund's stringent conditions in 2011 that included full implementation of a reformed GST involving a broader base, reduced exemptions and input crediting, both at the federal and provincial level; parliamentary passage of the amendments to the State Bank Act and the Banking Companies' Ordinance; agreement on measures to achieve the revised fiscal deficit target, including a realistic envelope for energy subsidies in 2010–11 based on a plan that was yet to be endorsed by the Asian Development Bank and World Bank staffs; and third-quarter fiscal performance that would be consistent with achieving the full-year target.

None of this has happened, effectively killing the IMF Programme.

Meanwhile, the Pakistani state's *Titanic* steamed toward the economic iceberg. President Zardari appeared to be relying on the relatively large cushion of Pakistan's foreign exchange reserves of $16.7 billion, disregarding the fact that most of these reserves were themselves borrowed. His government was also dependent on Western aid donors, primarily the US, to come to Pakistan's rescue if its economy tanked. The false premise was that if defence spending had to rise to meet US demands to fight the Taliban, the US would pay for the increase. False, because if the Americans became convinced that Pakistan was playing a double game they would back out of aid to Pakistan. Pakistan believed it had to play that double game of condoning or abetting some Afghan Taliban to protect itself against the day when the Americans would leave Afghanistan.[68]

Insurgency

Meanwhile, Pakistan did little to prepare for the wars within the country, letting the military take the lead in a conflict that demanded a whole of government and whole of society approach. The government made ritualistic efforts to show that it was concerned about the insurgency raging in its borderlands with Afghanistan. But the reality of the continuing power struggle between the civil and the military negated the rhetoric.

---

[68] Nawaz, 'Ungovernable'.

In my own assessment at that time I was less than sanguine about the ability of the government to craft a practicable policy:

In October 2008, during the early days of the current government, there was an attempt to get a joint resolution in parliament to fight terrorism within Pakistan. After much arm twisting and cajoling, members of parliament across the political spectrum consented to create the resolution, even if they disagreed politically with the government. The joint resolution they produced essentially ceded all powers to the army chief, even though martial law had not been declared in the Northwest Province or the Federally Administered Tribal Areas (FATA) . . . The military also reserves the right to detain persons until it finds civil authority capable of taking detainees over. In effect, a quasi-martial law exists.

Thus the civilian government has ceded control to the military. It retains some semblance of involvement with administration in the insurgency-prone areas: Recently the Apex Group [in each province] brought together civilians and military personnel at the highest levels in the province of KP. However, the military has more or less determined and approved the group's agenda.

The military has a wider national stance than during earlier civilian regimes. Beyond the traditional areas of India and Kashmir, the military has exerted control over national policy concerning Afghanistan, nuclear weapons, and US relations.[69]

The civilians had effectively lost control of the security forces of Pakistan. But even the military was not fully prepared to act decisively without clear support from the government and civil society.

When the insurgents tied up with the local Taliban in Malakand Division and threatened the Karakoram Highway, the military did not act immediately, apart from preparing the X Corps headquartered in Rawalpindi to protect that lifeline to China. Looking for public support and the government's direction, then Army Chief Gen. Kayani went to Islamabad and briefed the political leadership as a group, including Opposition leaders, on the security situation, and purposely stopped short

---

[69] Shuja Nawaz, *Who Controls Pakistan's Security Forces*, Special Report 299, US Institute of Peace, December 2011, p. 5.

of suggesting specific actions, asking them to think about the issues and then instruct the army to take specific actions. He recalled to me in a conversation in his office that he did not hear back from the leadership for a few weeks and then had to call again to ask for direction. The message he got was that the army should proceed with its plans; the government would catch up. It never did.

Public outcry against the depredations of the Tehreek-e-Nifaaz-e-Shariat-e-Mohammedi Taliban in Malakand gave Kayani the popular support he needed. The proximate cause was the video of the Taliban whipping a young girl who was accused of adultery. Civil society wanted the army to move. It did, and rapidly, though it risked legal issues in handling the thousands of Taliban whom it captured and whom it suspected of perpetrating violence and cruelty on unarmed civilians less than 100 miles from the nation's capital. The regular army was not well-trained in handling the sort of violence perpetrated on civilians and captured soldiers by the local Taliban and their supporters. It also was angry that captured militants often ended up being released by overburdened courts. They ended up keeping many militants in their own custody, as a result. There were reports of summary executions by the military, and a video surfaced at one point showing a Pakistani military unit firing squad killing blindfolded 'insurgents'. The army denied this action. But the US embassy in Islamabad managed to identify the regiment involved in this action 'within six hours', according to a senior US embassy official,[70] and subsequently specific sanctions were placed on the unit involved. The US did not make a public issue of this matter to avoid problems with Congress at home at a time when Pakistan was needed for the egress from Afghanistan. I recall discussing with Gen. Kayani at that time that he and other senior officers could be in legal jeopardy for extrajudicial actions of their subordinate officers and soldiers. Sadly, the celebrated 12 Punjab Regiment was one of the formations accused by Human Rights Watch of having taken in to custody persons whose bullet-riddled bodies were later found in fields in Swat.[71]

---

[70] Background briefing to the author.

[71] Human Rights Watch, 'Pakistan: Extrajudicial Killings by Army in Swat', 16 July 2010, https://www.hrw.org/news/2010/07/16/pakistan-extrajudicial-executions-army-swat

12 Punjab was a storied regiment to which my grandfather belonged. He had fought in the North West Frontier in 1902 and 1908 and then in

The army then sought legal cover for its counter-insurgency (COIN) operations. Zardari was happy to oblige.

In June 2011, President Zardari signed the 'Action in Aid of Civil Power Regulation, 2011', which provided a new framework for the detention of insurgents in the Federally and Provincially Administered Tribal Areas. This allowed the security forces to take, hold and process detainees captured during conflict. It also provided for detainees to be transferred to civilian custody for prosecution. But, despite calls by the prime minister to move forward, Pakistan's legislature did not approve legislation aimed at strengthening its Anti-Terrorism Act. Meanwhile, the acquittal rate for terrorist cases remained as high as 85 per cent.[72] This led the military to pursue arbitrary actions against detainees, not all within the ambit of the law.

All this while, the government's draft legislation on the introduction of a National Counter Terrorism Authority or NACTA sat in the Ministry of Interior. Its founding coordinator, Tariq Parvez, a highly trained and effective police officer, resigned in frustration following lack of resources from his ministry. He had also suggested that the NACTA be housed in the prime minister's office so that it could be seen as a national entity in its coordination role that would include both civil and military institutions and the chief ministers of the four provinces of Pakistan. Rehman Malik, the Minister of Interior, wanted to play a key role in supervising NACTA. He offered to share an amended draft with me that made the prime minister the chairman, with the interior minister as vice chair, so that the interior minister would chair the meetings in the absence of the prime minister. I told him that this would not work from the first time that he chaired the meeting in the prime minister's absence. This drafting legerdemain did not work for the military, among others, and the NACTA effectively lay dormant within the Interior Ministry. My own conversations with senior military and intelligence officials led me to believe that shifting the NACTA to the prime minister's office could have elicited military participation and support at high levels.[73] The PPP government failed to

---

Mesopotamia, including the attempt to break the siege of Kut, and in Europe in World War I.

[72] US Department of State, Bureau of Terrorism, 'Country Reports on Terrorism 2011', released April 2012, p. 142.

[73] Shuja Nawaz, *Learning by Doing: The Pakistan Army's Experience with Counterinsurgency* (Washington DC: Atlantic Council, February 2011), p. 20,

move forward on this. It was left to the successor government of Prime Minister Sharif to try to revive the NACTA, but even that government failed to provide it the resources or the central location that would make it most effective. In the 2018–19 budget, for example, NACTA received only Rs 143 million as opposed to its request for over Rs 1.4 billion to implement its remit.[74]

A government that was hamstrung by its coalition partners and survived crisis after crisis was tested by a series of events in 2011 that not only shook it to the core but also raised serious issues about the relationship with the US. Further, the army, which had regained its popularity after years of martial law as the most respected institution in the country, suffered a jolt to its reputation as its popularity dropped from a high approval rate of 86 per cent in 2009 to 77 per cent in 2012 (while still ranked number one), even as Army Chief Kayani trailed Imran Khan and Nawaz Sharif in the popularity ratings of the Pew Poll.[75]

Against this bleak backdrop, a silent drama unfolded as Kayani reached the end of his three-year term. He had begun receiving criticisms from friendly and hostile quarters related to his inability to launch a comprehensive operation against the Taliban and foreign fighters in FATA. Also, there were reports of preferential treatment of businesses with which his brothers were involved without proof of Kayani's personal involvement in any of those deals. Reports circulated about Kayani himself building a real estate portfolio.[76] Most senior military officers invested in subsidized real estate on small monthly

---

http://www.atlanticcouncil.org/publications/reports/learning-by-doing-the-pakistan-army-s-experience-with-counterinsurgency

[74] Qadeer Tanoli, 'Peanuts for NACTA This Year Too', *Express Tribune*, 29 April 2018, https://tribune.com.pk/story/1698044/1-peanuts-nacta-year/

[75] 'Chapter 5. Institutions and Leaders', in *Pakistani Public Opinion Ever More Critical of U.S.*, Pew Research Center, 27 June 2012, http://www.pewglobal.org/2012/06/27/chapter-5-institutions-and-leaders/

[76] While he was DG-ISI, he had begun constructing a retirement home in the DHA near Morgah in Rawalpindi, a modernistic villa on a spur overlooking the Soan river, just below the home of his colleague and successor at the ISI, Lt. Gen. Ahmed Shuja Pasha. It was a very visible and much talked-about house in Rawalpindi. Similarly, his interest in golf led to talk of another home in the middle of a golf course in Lahore. But the critics lacked specific proof of corruption on his part or that he colluded with his brothers in their business

payments via the Defence Housing Authorities (DHA) in different military cantonments. The plots increased enormously in value once the DHA colonies became fully operational, and army officers then sold them to take care of children's weddings and education expenses. Even President Musharraf, who prided himself on his honesty, declared multiple plots when he took over in 1999. The military saw the DHAs as private entities even though serving General Officers Commanding (GOCs) of Divisions in cities that had DHAs and corps commanders had supervisory roles in their management.

Amid these rumours and innuendo, Kayani's tenure was heading to its conclusion. Zardari saw an opportunity and used his prime minister to effectively 'persuade' Kayani to take a full-term three-year extension of his service as army chief till 2016. This caused much dyspepsia among senior officers in the army, who lost out on the chance to be considered for promotion to the two four-star positions that would result from vacation of the senior-most slots in the military on time. Pasha and Kayani also parted ways, as Kayani only got a one-year extension for Pasha at the helm of the ISI.

Ex post, and in the middle of another civil–military brouhaha, the prime minister offered to explain the circumstances surrounding these extensions:

> Prime Minister Yusuf Raza Gilani . . . dispelled the impression of a government–military standoff when he announced on Monday the government had no intention to remove the Army chief General Ashfaq Pervez Kayani and DG ISI Lt. General (retd) Ahmad Shuja Pasha, terming the idea as 'foolish'.
>
> 'Generals are not removed in the middle of a war,' he remarked and added that Kayani or Pasha had never asked for an extension last year, rather it was he who requested them to continue. 'General Kayani is pro-democracy,' the prime minister told a hurriedly-called news conference at the PM House.[77]

---

activities or forced the government to favour them. This issue persisted beyond his retirement.

[77] *News International*, 'I Begged Kayani, Pasha to Accept Extensions: Gilani', 27 December 2011.

The general may have been pro-democracy but not necessarily in favour of the Zardari government, as later events proved. Both Kayani and Pasha left a lasting effect on Pakistani politics and the army, way beyond their tenures, as the actions they took shaped the nature of the army's and ISI's response to domestic and regional crises.

2

Friends or Frenemies?

O' What a tangled web we weave
When first we practise to deceive

—*Marmion: A Tale of Flodden Field*
by Sir Walter Scott, 1808[1]

Pakistan's internal battles, between the civil and the military, and against militancy and terror, were overshadowed by its failing ties with the US. The roller-coaster relationship between the US and Pakistan went through a number of highs and lows during the presidency of Barack Obama, marked by well-meaning attempts to create a new partnership in the region on the one hand and deep distrust of each other's hidden aims and lack of clarity of long-term goals on the other. Equal parts mistrust and co-dependence marked this fraught relationship. And confusion on both sides, as different parts of the establishment in both Pakistan and the US struggled to be the main interlocutor with the other country.

---

[1] Sir Walter Scott began writing his long poem in 1806 after a publisher offered him the grand sum of 1,000 guineas as an advance (a guinea being 21 shillings). The poem is a complicated love story with many twists and turns, and deceptions, much like the modern-day US–Pakistan relationship. It concludes with the battle at Flodden Field. That story, unlike the US–Pakistan story, has a happy ending. The first quarto edition (about 9 ½ x 12 inches) of 2,000 copies priced at one-and-a-half guineas each sold out in one month. Twelve octavo editions (about 6 x 9 inches) then sold out between 1808 and 1825, a roaring bestseller by all accounts.

In 2008, the US was still embroiled in a losing war in Afghanistan, as public opinion at home and casualties in the field were forcing it to consider an eventual withdrawal. Senator Barack Obama, one of the leading Democratic candidates for president, had called Afghanistan the 'good war' and the 'war of necessity', and decried the Bush administration's invasion of Iraq as a mistake and a big distraction from the Afghan theatre of war. But he vowed also to bring the troops home from Afghanistan. Pakistan both feared a vacuum inside Afghanistan if the US were to leave in a precipitate manner and blamed the US invasion and the presence of Coalition Forces as a stimulus for anti-Americanism and insurgency inside Pakistan. It also feared India's growing economic and military ties with Afghanistan as a move to squeeze Pakistan between two hostile entities.

The people of Pakistan were confused by their government and military's visible closeness to the Americans on the one hand and the continuous statements from their leaders against the US's policies in the region as well as increasing US drone attacks inside Pakistani territory.

How Pakistanis View the United States

Consistently Low Marks for the U.S.									
View of U.S.	1999/ 2000 %	2002 %	2003 %	2004 %	2005 %	2006 %	2007 %	2008 %	2009 %
Favorable	23	10	13	21	23	27	15	19	16
Unfavorable	--	69	81	60	60	56	68	63	68
DK	--	20	6	18	18	17	16	17	16

1999/2000 survey trend provided by the Office of Research, U.S. Department of State.
Question 11a.

Source: Pew Global Survey 2009, Chapter 3, http://www.pewglobal. org/2009/08/13/chapter-3-attitudes-toward-the-united-states/

Over the period 2000–2009 the favourability rating of the US had never gone higher than 27 per cent, and that too was in 2006, after the US had helped Pakistan enormously with earthquake relief. In 2009, Pakistan, at 16 per cent favourable view of the US, rested near the bottom of the twenty-four countries surveyed by Pew. 'Most Pakistanis consider the US an enemy, while only about one-in-ten say it is a partner. Distrust of American foreign policy runs deep, and few believe the US considers Pakistani interests when making policy decisions. Moreover, most think that American policy in South Asia favours Pakistan's arch-rival India.'[2]

Yet, and this issue seemed to be overlooked by many news media and analysts of the Pew data, *more than half* of the Pakistanis surveyed wanted improved relations with the US. Little effort was devoted by Pew to unpacking the reasons behind this desire on the part of 53 per cent of the survey's respondents in Pakistan. And it was unclear if US policymakers had even focused on leveraging this Pakistani majority that favoured better relations with their country.

Flashback to Aid that Worked

The answers to this might lie in a short step back into Pakistan's recent history, when a massive 7.6 magnitude earthquake struck in northern Pakistan in 2005, destroying homes and villages in remote mountainous terrain, killing some 80,000 persons and leaving 4 million homeless.[3] Along with others, the US rushed to assist Pakistan in the earthquake relief effort. The US began the relief effort within thirty-six hours of the earthquake. Then Rear Admiral Michael 'Mike' LeFever was a strike force commander on his ship in the Persian Gulf, ferrying Marines to support the Iraqi elections in the Fallujah area. He received a call earlier in the day as they sailed through the Straits of Hormuz, asking him if he had watched the news of the earthquake in Pakistan. Six hours later, he got another call from his boss, Vice Admiral Dave Nichols: 'Pack your bags. General Vessey (the US Army chief) just talked to Ambassador [Ryan] Crocker.'[4] LeFever was on his way to Pakistan to do a damage-and-aid assessment.

According to LeFever, Amb. Crocker saw the disaster relief 'as a strategic initiative to help Pakistan in their time of need . . . Normally,

---

2   Op. cit. Pew Survey 2009. https://www.pewresearch.org/global/2009/08/13/pakistani-public-opinion/

3   History.com, '2005 Kashmir Earthquake', http://www.history.com/topics/kashmir-earthquake

4   Interview with Vice Admiral Mike LeFever, 27 October 2016.

you are there for 60–90 days. We ended up being there for almost seven months.' The US brought in 1,500 people, a MASH (mobile hospital) unit in Muzaffarabad, a Marine–Navy hospital up in the North West Frontier Province, a Seabee unit of 70–80 persons with its construction equipment, offloaded in Karachi and brought up-country. And helicopters. Initially some helicopters for ferrying relief workers and supplies came in from the war zone in Afghanistan. Later, some thirty helicopters were brought in from the US, and new big Sea Stallions and CH53s from Bahrain. Those thirty-four-odd helicopters, many of them Chinooks, flying seemingly endlessly and helping the people affected by the earthquake, came to be seen as 'Angels of Mercy' by the locals.

A young air force officer on his team, Eliot Evans (now a lieutenant colonel in the Delaware Air National Guard) recalls his own excitement on landing at Islamabad airport in Chaklala from his post at the Standing Joint Force Headquarters of the US Joint Forces Command at Norfolk Naval Station in the Hamptons Road region of Virginia. The JFC had been set up only a year earlier and assigned staff to the combatant commands, as needed. He and his naval officer colleagues, under US Navy Capt. Patrick Hall, had to put up their own tent, near other tents of the Red Crescent Society and other NGOs. The Japanese joined them shortly. They got to work immediately, to prepare for the arrival of equipment from the McGuire Air Force Base in New Jersey. In the meantime, they pitched in to offload supplies from Russia that arrived in large cargo aircraft, but, unlike the organized pallets of the US airlift, the Russians resorted to floor-loading the materials, and the Americans had to help organize the offloaded supplies.

Since it was Ramadan, Evans recalls he found it easier to join his Pakistani colleagues for pre-dawn breakfast or *sehri*. Capt. Hall had made him the liaison with local forces. Being with the Pakistanis at close quarters from that early morning hour allowed him to 'collect whatever information I could get from Pakistan Army officers there to find out what supplies were needed most and what villages needed those supplies'. This unfettered access to each other and the urgency of the humanitarian task brought the Pakistani and American military personnel together in a way that no politician could have imagined.[5] And it led to Evans volunteering to return to Pakistan later when floods struck the country in 2010.

---

[5]   Interview with Lt. Col. Eliot Evans, Washington DC, November 2016.

LeFever had also created a blue baseball-style cap, with the US and Pakistani flags and 'Team Pakistan' embroidered on the peak, for his earthquake relief effort.[6] LeFever called this 'one of the most rewarding events in my career, to be able to help so many'. The key to the success of this mission in his mind was threefold: 'support Pakistan in its time of need, improve US–Pak relations and provide humanitarian relief.' There were no strings attached to this aid. Pakistanis dealt directly with Americans. And the locals benefited directly from the US presence. Clearly this formula worked.

One of the co-authors of a World Bank study of the earthquake relief[7] concluded:

> The Pakistanis who received aid didn't believe there were any strategic motives at play: People overwhelmingly believed that this was assistance offered in the spirit of humanity, rather than a transaction intended to buy hearts and minds. Had the recipients sensed more cynical motives, their positive opinions of foreigners might have been dampened—if not reversed.[8]

The authors of the study concluded that this assistance had a lasting impact on the recipients and their views about those who helped them.

> The results suggest Pakistan's 'trust deficit' is less caused by deep-rooted beliefs and preferences, non-local events such as drone attacks on the Afghan border, or US policy toward Israel. *It's human interactions that change attitudes, and their effects are long term* [emphasis added].

LeFever's experience in Pakistan during the earthquake relief operation fortified that view, though he recognizes that not enough was done to publicize the aid effort. In fact, from a spike in approval rating to 27 per cent in 2006, the US plummeted to 15 per cent shortly after the relief effort

---

[6] I used to keep one of those caps that he later gave me as a souvenir in my office at the Atlantic Council.

[7] Tahir Andrabi and Jishnu Das, 'In Aid We Trust: Hearts and Minds and the Pakistan Earthquake of 2005', World Bank, 2010.

[8] Jishnu Das, 'The Black Hole of Pakistan: Are Billions of Dollars of Aid Going to Waste?' *Foreign Policy*, 7 October 2010.

ended.[9] Pakistan also was keen to send the Americans packing as soon as possible since it was detracting from their own efforts.

But it appreciated the American aid during the floods and handed out the highest civil award of *Hilal-e-Pakistan* (Crescent of Pakistan) to Ambassador Ryan Crocker. Admiral LeFever received the *Hilal-e-Quaid-i-Azam* (Crescent of the Great Leader Mohammed Ali Jinnah). The rest of the team got the appropriately named *Sitara-e-Eisaar* (Star of Altruism). Admiral Mike Mullen was Chief of Naval Operations at the time. LeFever sought his permission to wear his Pakistani decoration. Mullen's comment was, 'Hey, we're going to use this sometime in the future.'

Little was LeFever to know that a few years later, after he had earned his second star as a rear admiral, he would be told by the same Admiral Mullen, 'Pack your bags. You are going back to Pakistan.' This time the mission was not humanitarian, but as Head of the Office of the Defense Representative in Pakistan (ODRP), LeFever was part of a new US strategic policy in the region where Pakistan was to play a key role as an ally in an emerging new approach to the war in Afghanistan under a new American president.

Obama's New Af–Pak Approach

Afghanistan loomed large over the new president Barack Obama's policy discussions soon after he took over in January 2009. He had been thinking about the country and the region during his campaign for the presidency. One report that influenced his thinking was prepared by a team from the Strategic Advisory Group of the Atlantic Council, a bipartisan think tank in Washington DC.[10] The Strategic Advisory Group was co-chaired by the Atlantic Council's chairman, Gen. James L. Jones, former Supreme Allied Commander, Europe (SACEUR), and Kristin Krohn Devold, former Norwegian Minister of Defence.

---

[9]   Richard Wite, 'Does Humanitarian Aid Improve America's Image', Pew Research Center, 6 March 2012.

[10] On 9 January 2009, I formally joined the Atlantic Council as the founding director of its South Asia Center after having been associated with the task force on Pakistan since the summer of 2008.

Make no mistake, the international community is not winning in Afghanistan [emphasis added].[11] Unless this reality is understood and action is taken promptly, the future of Afghanistan is bleak, with regional and global impact. The purpose of this paper is to sound the alarm and to propose specific actions that must be taken now if Afghanistan is to succeed in becoming a secure, safe and functioning state. On the security side, a stalemate of sorts has taken hold. NATO and Afghan forces cannot be beaten by the insurgency or by the Taliban. Neither can our forces eliminate the Taliban by military means as long as they have sanctuary in Pakistan. Hence, the future of Afghanistan will be determined by progress or failure in the civil sector.[12]

These were the opening words of a remarkable thirteen-page report that came out in March 2008 under the lead of the Atlantic Council Chairman, Gen. Jones. (This analysis remained valid a decade later, when President Trump faced a decision on the future US role in the region.) It then presented a succinct analysis of the situation in Afghanistan and Pakistan, and offered practicable ideas for changing the situation. Had it been a voluminous report, it would have likely met the fate of many other such efforts and been left to gather dust on bookshelves in a busy capital city. But it caught candidate Obama's attention and, among other things, produced a meeting with Gen. Jones late in the campaign that led eventually to the selection of Jones as the NSA to President Obama.

Jones was not unfamiliar with Afghanistan. He had come to know the region from his role as SACEUR.[13] He recalled his first encounter as SACEUR in 2003 with the nineteen Ambassadors to NATO over a

---

[11] This attention-grabbing opening sentence is ascribed to Harlan Ullman, an Atlantic Council colleague and military strategist, who is also widely credited with the authorship of the phrase 'shock and awe' popularized by the massive US air attack on Iraq, as an approach to force an enemy to give up without a fight.

[12] *Saving Afghanistan: An Appeal and Plan for Urgent Action* (Washington DC: Atlantic Council, March 2008).

[13] Jones, a veritable poster boy for the Marine Corps, with his statuesque bearing and ruggedly handsome looks, comes from a family of Marines. His father and his uncle were both Marines, and his father's World War II experience in Europe led him to work in Europe for some fifteen years in Paris, where Jones spent his early childhood. He became fluent in French and learned to appreciate not only Europe but also the issues that separated Americans from their French hosts.

weekly lunch that used to be hosted by a different ambassador every week. He had been told this was just a 'social event, to get to know you'. After some welcoming remarks, the British ambassador said to him, 'As host, General, I would like to ask you the first question. And that is, how are you going to get us to Afghanistan?' Nobody had ever said anything to him about NATO going to Afghanistan. But it certainly forced him to focus on the topic in a hurry. He also recalled an exchange with Defense Secretary Donald Rumsfeld when he got his SACEUR appointment, and explained to the Secretary that he did not wish to be the person to switch off the lights for NATO. Rumsfeld told him, 'We may want to re-shape things a bit, but NATO is still very important.'[14]

Against this background, he spent 2003 thinking about Afghanistan and visiting the country, meeting President Hamid Karzai, and working with NATO allies to shape the Coalition presence in Afghanistan. His plan was discussed at the Munich Security Conference in February 2004 with NATO defence ministers. This led to the counter-clockwise deployment in tranches of European national contingents in Afghanistan, starting with the Germans in the north, then others in the south and the west. 'Ultimately the plan was to link up with the US forces in the East.'

He also transformed the NATO mission in Afghanistan by creating a NATO Response Force in the north, an area that had hitherto been a 'sleepy little headquarters', and making the Germans the operational commanders of the NATO mission to Afghanistan. He also visited Pakistan during this period, a country that he had first visited in the early 1980s, as the Marines' military liaison officer to the Senate with Senator John Tower on a congressional visit. As SACEUR he regularly visited Afghanistan and would arrange tripartite meetings with the Pakistanis as well. This allowed him to get to know the Pakistani military high command as well.

After his retirement in 2007, Jones came back to Washington DC and worked on energy issues with the US Chamber of Commerce and became chairman of the Atlantic Council when, according to him, 'to my surprise, President Obama asked me to be his national security adviser in January of 2009'. He said he had met Obama 'may be three times' and told him, 'I'm very worried about the direction that Karzai seems to be taking his country and things he is doing. And I'm extremely worried about Pakistan: the

---

[14]   Interview with Gen. James (Jim) L. Jones, Tyson's Corner, VA, September 2016.

Pakistan military's domination of foreign policy. I had become convinced that the military was running the country, particularly with regard to security, without occupying any position.' He also briefed Obama about the 'difficult dialog[ue] we had had in 2006 about the effectiveness of the [Afghanistan] strategy, particularly [because of] the safe havens that were in Pakistan.'

He recalled that it 'reminded me a little bit about my initial impressions in Vietnam when I was a young second lieutenant infantry officer. Couldn't go north, couldn't go to the west, couldn't go into Laos, couldn't go into Cambodia, couldn't take the fight to the enemy. One of my cardinal rules is that, if you're battling an insurgency you can't give them safe haven. You can't do that.'

Jones saw 'a different replay of the US now going into Pakistan and trying to convince the Pakistan Army that it's in their interest to help us. I left with an uneasy feeling that there was a game being played here that was not in Pakistan's long-term interest, either politically or economically . . . One of the first things we did in the White House in terms of reassessing the Af–Pak strategy, was meeting with the leadership of both countries separately but giving assurances that the US was going to do transformational things in both countries, if in fact, we all agreed on what our respective goals are.'

Easier said than done. Though each side had a vision of what it wished to achieve from this Odd Couple pairing of Afghanistan and Pakistan, two countries that had never seen eye-to-eye since the birth of Pakistan in 1947, they pretended to go along in order to benefit from the massive US economic and military assistance that was expected to head their way. In order to keep that aid flow continuing, leaders in the region continued to dissemble and do their own thing, even as the unlikely alliance crumbled over time.

The Af–Pak approach had a rough birthing. President Obama brought in Bruce Riedel, a retired CIA analyst and Brookings Institution scholar who had been his South Asia policy adviser during the presidential campaign, to conduct a fresh review of the Afghanistan war with a view to coming up with a clearer vision. His co-chairs were supposed to be Gen. David Petraeus, the new CENTCOM commander, Michelle Flournoy from the Department of Defense (DoD) and Richard Holbrooke, Secretary of State Hillary Clinton's favourite troubleshooter, who had successfully shaped the Dayton Accord that ended the three-and-a-half year-long war in Bosnia. Holbrooke had been on the Clinton campaign team when she ran against Obama for the Democratic Party nomination for president. Petraeus had made a name for himself in Iraq, among other things, for reshaping the COIN doctrine of the US Army and for his ability to work well with politicians in Iraq as well as in the US.[15] Lt. Gen. Douglas Lute recalls that his White House team at the NSC was offered to Riedel as administrative support. They convened the group a week after Riedel's arrival in the Eisenhower Old Executive Office Building next to the White House.

Getting this unlikely team to work together was one of the first challenges of the new Obama White House. Defining the remit was an initial issue. Quite rightly, the president wanted a regional approach to the issue, and when the idea of a special representative was first broached, it was seen as one for South Asia as a whole. Holbrooke also preferred the wider remit.

However, India did not wish to be drawn into this circle with Pakistan and opposed the idea successfully. Hence emerged the office of the SRAP that was emulated by the US's allies in the Afghanistan war. The sequencing of those country names created its own dynamic, with the focus being primarily on Afghanistan, and Pakistan seen as secondary to the main effort in Afghanistan. This flawed thought process haunted the relationship for the entire Obama term.

Riedel had been thinking about Afghanistan and Pakistan for some time and had strong views on what needed to be done. In the White House, he was faced with a holdover from the Bush presidency in Lute, who had handled the Iraq and Afghanistan portfolio and had prepared his own report on Afghanistan as part of the transition planning. Lute told me that President Bush asked him to do a report in the summer of 2008 that was presented to the outgoing president in October 2008.[16] Lute was

---

[15]   He had requested the Center for Strategic and International Studies for a report on the FATA, because, as he told Arnaud de Borchgrave of CSIS, it is an area that would be important in his new Area of Responsibility at CENTCOM and that he did not know well. According to de Borchgrave, who brought me in to lead a team to conduct this study, Petraeus wanted a fresh look at the area and ideas for changing the situation on the ground. Our study, *FATA: A Most Dangerous Place*, came out in 2009.

[16]   Interview with Lt. Gen. Douglas Lute on Skype, 28 July 2016, while he was on leave from his position as US ambassador to NATO in Brussels. We also

asked to stay on in the NSC by the new president. According to Lute, Riedel told the White House meeting on the review that he would produce his draft for discussion within a week or so. Lute thought the final report had been produced without any visit to the region and it 'looked a lot like the last chapters of his Brooking's monograph [*sic*]'.[17] Meanwhile Petraeus had his own review in progress (done largely by H.R. McMaster, a legendary officer and strategist, who later became a short-lived NSA to President Donald J. Trump) that came into the White House in January 2009. Another review had been done by the chairman of the Joint Chiefs of Staff (JCS), Admiral Mike Mullen.

In Riedel's view, 'Lute's study was by far the most candid in saying things weren't going well. The two military studies would approach questions like, "Are we losing?" by saying, "We are not scoring a decisive success." [Lute was also famously the author of the '10 Wars' PowerPoint slide deck that reflected the fractured approach to the Afghanistan campaign.]

'But they all were basically on the same wavelength, that we were in deep, deep trouble and really we'd had seven years under the [George W.] Bush administration of giving no priority to Afghanistan, and therefore, everything was being done on the cheap.'

Compounding the difficulty of producing a coherent and cohesive narrative and policy were other factors. As he described this 'cumbersome' situation, Riedel said, 'In fact, there was what I would call a Potemkin Village South Asia team, and then a real South Asia team. But we went through these elaborate charades of getting everyone's input. One of the issues that had separated Senator Obama from Senator Clinton was that he had early on said, "If I get actionable intelligence that there is an Al-Qaeda target I will go after it with or without the support of the government of Pakistan." That was a very thought-through posture, not just something he said off the top of his head. And the "Clintonistas" had pounced on it as an example of his inexperience and rashness.'

Riedel's view of the genesis of the new Af–Pak policy is concise and stark: 'The [Obama] campaign made big of the argument that the

---

spoke after he had retired from his diplomatic assignment. During his stint at the White House, he invited me regularly for discussions on the region and was always open to ideas and suggestions.

17   Bruce O. Riedel, *The Search for Al Qaeda: Its Leadership, Ideology, and Future* (Washington DC: Brookings Institution Press, 2008).

war in Afghanistan was failing, and that, in particular, Al Qaeda had revived dangerously in the Afghanistan–Pakistan border region. What I think happened is that once . . . they got into office, they actually found out that they were not only right, but it was much worse than anything they [had] said. And that the situation particularly with those two elements, the stability of the Afghan government in a war and the rise of Al Qaeda, was much, much more in an advanced stage of falling apart than their campaign rhetoric had made it appear. Many of the holdovers from the Bush administration, particularly in the military and in the intelligence community who were professional people not political people, impressed on them, "We're at a crisis stage. Normal reaction won't work." I think that's when the president's team said, "Who's running the show?"'

Riedel recalled, 'In theory, it was the special representative for Afghanistan–Pakistan, Richard Holbrooke. But, the president had lost confidence in Richard Holbrooke in their first meeting. He came across as very arrogant. He [Holbrooke] made it clear he thought he was smarter than the president. But when pressed, he didn't seem to know very much about South Asia. So there's this kind of combination of two storms. [The] problem really is deteriorating rapidly, and we're not confident we have the right guy in charge. So what's the backup plan? And I think that's when they asked me to come in and do the review.'[18] General Jones also confirmed in a later email exchange with me that President Obama wanted to fire Holbrooke but Hillary Clinton did not agree to do that.

Holbrooke had convened his own briefing session in New York at the Asia Society, where I was invited, among others, to give him a quick update on key elements of the situation in the region. I recall stressing to him the importance of the military intelligence complex in Pakistan since it had established itself as the principal policymaker ever since the formation of the Afghanistan Cell in the period of the Afghan Jihad against the Soviet Union in the 1980s. I also gave him a copy of my newly published book on Pakistan and its army, *Crossed Swords*. Holbrooke had also begun assembling a team of experts from across government and academia, including, among others, Dan Feldman, Vali Nasr, Vikram

---

[18] Interview with Bruce Riedel, 27 October 2016. He consulted me during the review and subsequently, and was willing to accept a number of ideas, not all of which managed to pass through the sieve of the 'bean counters' and others who had final approval of the policies that emerged in due course.

Singh, Mary-Beth Goodman and Barnett Rubin. Some of them had first-hand experience of working in Afghanistan and Pakistan. Others were subject-matter experts on economics, COIN, etc.

Holbrooke himself had served in Vietnam in his early days as a Foreign Service officer, and that experience had imprinted itself on his brain. He evoked great loyalty among his team and carried their ideas to the highest levels in government. In return, most of them revered him. He also had a reputation as a larger-than-life figure who could break bureaucratic barriers. In some ways, he was ideally suited to coordinate activities by demolishing, or at least trying to demolish, the well-fortified silos of the US governmental agencies. But he did not own an official cheque book and had to rely on other sources of funding. He managed to use his considerable diplomatic skills to cajole and coerce others to fund his activities and favourite projects. And in the process, he antagonized others, including the White House staff, who felt it was their primary responsibility to present policy options to the new president. If Holbrooke had been given the pro-counsel role that he thought had earmarked resources, he could well have broken through the mistrust of the Pakistanis. But this was not the case. And he faced a tough and well-established team at the White House that jealously guarded its turf.

Lute maintains that one of the contributing problems was the fact that Holbrooke's 'Terms of Reference were never put in writing. Richard worked a broad mandate, including Iran and Central Asia. It was not a best-defined effort. His presumption was that he'd run the inter-agency process, which is the NSC's job.' Lute told me that he thought it was Gen. Jones's job to demand the definition of responsibilities and that Secretary Clinton ought to have issued the Terms of Reference after an inter-agency review. As Vali Nasr, a Holbrooke adviser and supporter, put it, the SRAP was 'an experiment in what Holbrooke called the "whole of government approach to solving big problems", by which he meant doing the job of the government inside the government but *despite* the government—an idea that for obvious reasons did not sit well with the bureaucracy'.[19] That never crystallized, nor was a Terms of Reference produced, and the result, according to Lute was a 'stormy relationship'.

---

[19] Vali Nasr, *The Dispensable Nation* (Doubleday, 2013), pp. 30–31. Nasr provides a deep and critical review of policymaking in the Obama administration, coloured heavily by his experience in the SRAP Office.

The Bush NSC review 'tried to be balanced between Afghanistan and Pakistan and concluded that US vital interests lay in Pakistan, not Afghanistan. Over the years we had been fixated on Afghanistan when in fact we should have paid more attention to Pakistan,' said Lute. That review called for a COIN approach: no set number of troops, and a cross-governmental approach. It asked USAID on its priorities and execution rates for its projects. 'The numbers were bad,' said Lute. On the military side, the action had shifted to Kandahar and Helmand from the east. Lute felt there were some '10 wars being fought in Afghanistan' in 2009, including, among others, separate efforts by the US, NATO, the Afghan Army and Afghan Police, and White and Black Special Operations forces. All without much coordination. 'This didn't get fixed for another two or three years, till 2010 when Secretary [Robert] Gates rationalized the system under [Gen. Stanley] McChrystal.'[20] In brief, Lute thought the military effort 'became the shiny object' that drew all the attention, leading to a missed opportunity to take advantage of the political side. For example, 'we were not ready to approach Pakistan on the Taliban'. The lack of a centre of gravity in decision making in the war in Afghanistan affected how Pakistan viewed the situation and its own relations with different elements of the US government.

Riedel seemed to agree with the Lute analysis on the domination of the military in the Afghan policy debate. 'So the report's main conclusion, I think, is pretty simple on this, which is we had to build up an Afghan Army and we had to pay for it, and in the interim, American and NATO forces would have to fight the war for some period of time until the Afghans were ready. What that period of time would be would only be determined by events on the ground. When the president did his second review, of course, he put in the timeline.'

Was it wise for Obama to announce the timeline for beginning of withdrawal of US forces from Afghanistan when he did in his West Point speech in December 2009? Riedel does not think so. I agree, for many of the same reasons and also because it went against previous experience of the Soviet Union in the region and failed to recognize the nature of the local tribal system. Riedel said it was 'an artificial timeline,' and, 'I don't think it was wise at all. I think it was a compromise to achieve a political solution inside the Democratic Party rather than a strategy. The left of the

---

[20] Lute interview.

party—particularly the vice-president—more or less wanted to abandon the Afghan war. They never said it in those terms, but they wanted to abandon the Afghan war. The president recognized that was irresponsible, but he wanted to give them something and particularly what he wanted to give them was a timeline and promised an early departure.' Yet Riedel concedes that Obama was in a tough spot: 'Part of him was quite sympathetic to the left's argument that we should just get out. I think if he could have done so, he would have done so. But I think in the end, he's a responsible leader, and he realized that would be an irresponsible approach. And contrary to what he was hoping in 2009 and for several years after, he's now leaving office leaving the war with a substantial American presence for the future as far as we can see.' Plus, of course a NATO presence, so it is not simply America's War.

Riedel also puts some historical perspective on the latest Afghanistan war. 'We are in the unusual position, as the United States of America, of having fought the same war twice from opposite sides.' In the 1980s, we figured out how to bow down a superpower [the Soviet Union] by using a sanctuary in Pakistan. In the twenty-first century, we've been the superpower, and the enemy has a sanctuary in Pakistan. And we're now realizing just how impossible it is to win at war if the opponent has a sanctuary. Now, the drone operations targeted the Al-Qaeda part of that sanctuary, but they never really targeted the Taliban part of the strategy. We've only really had one drone attack on a Taliban target . . . and it was this year [2009]. And so far, that looks like a one-off. All of which gets to the question of the third part of the whole strategy, what to do about Pakistan and how to engage with the Pakistanis.' The idea of sanctuary held American thinking in its grip, even when they understood that the Haqqanis were a relatively small part of the internal Afghan insurgency. It poisoned the US–Pakistan relationship.

He believes that 'the Obama administration inherited the policy on Al-Qaeda and Afghanistan that was not working, in fact, heading towards losing. They inherited from Bush, no policy on Pakistan. Bush had had a policy on Pakistan, and it was Musharraf: backing Musharraf to the hilt. Even when they began to increasingly suspect Musharraf was playing a double game with them, they just stuck with Musharraf. In fact, in the last days of Musharraf, I know that [VP Dick] Cheney told Bush in a small group meeting that, "Abandoning Musharraf would be the functional equivalent of abandoning the Shah in 1977 and '78." And that's how Cheney at least, had framed the picture.' What Cheney failed to produce was a counterfactual view of Iranian history, and in the twenty-first-century Pakistan's history. The US did not show the stamina to continue supporting an autocrat, no matter how close to the US administration, against his own army and people. As in 1979 Iran, the US ended up on the wrong side of local history.

Both Lute and Riedel seemed to agree with the thrust of Holbrooke's push for greater attention to Pakistan. But, as Nasr writes, the US military and intelligence policy was on a different track from the State Department. 'The Pentagon, for its part, had a war to win and wanted Pakistan's help to finish off the Taliban.' The Pentagon and CIA's goals were 'predictably narrow in scope and all terrorism focused . . . but their constant pressure on Islamabad always threatened to break up the relationship.' Nasr termed their tone as 'pugilistic' in their talks with Pakistan, but he maintains they 'bore no responsibility for the outcome'. He recalled Holbrooke shaking his head and saying, 'Watch them [the CIA] ruin this relationship. And when it is ruined, they are going to say, "We told you, you can't work with Pakistan!" We never learn.'[21] Neither the US nor Pakistan was a unitary actor. Both divided their efforts to suit domestic purposes.

Pakistan's unwillingness or inability to share all they knew about Afghanistan and the Afghan Taliban with their American counterparts remained a serious stumbling block in the relationship and figured in the crafting of Obama's Afghanistan policy. A senior White House official reportedly was heard to repeat a familiar joke that has been applied to other nationalities in other situations: 'When do you know the Pakistanis are lying? Their lips are moving!' Feeding this negative view of Pakistan was the Afghan President Hamid Karzai and the powerful voice of the head of Afghan National Directorate of Security or NDS, Amrullah Saleh, a former aide to the slain Tajik leader Ahmed Shah Massoud.

The White House arranged for both Pakistani and Afghan teams to visit Washington DC during the period when the Riedel review was being prepared to seek their inputs on the way forward and to converse with each other in the presence of the Americans. As Riedel recalls, the Pakistanis got a message that they 'were too important for us not to engage with. I think Musharraf was counting on that. He had an exaggerated sense of his ability to talk to Bush and get away with it.' This 'certainly led to a lack of candor in dealing with us'.

---

[21]   Nasr, *Dispensable Nation*, pp. 82–83.

Riedel recalls asking the Afghans during one bilateral: 'Who is our enemy in Afghanistan and where is their headquarters?' As expected, he says, Saleh answered this by stating that 'the enemy is the Afghan Taliban ... and their headquarters is in Quetta, and we've already passed on this information to you 1,000 times! Why are you asking the same question over again?' The next morning Riedel asked the Pakistani delegation the same question. This time it was Lt. Gen. Ahmed Shuja Pasha, the DG ISI's turn to speak. 'He gave a long exposition about Afghan tribal and ethnic politics and the Pashtun sense of having unfairly been removed from power and on and on. So after he made his exposition, I asked him, "General, what is your opinion of the Quetta Shura?" So he sits up, turns to his aide behind him who brings a briefcase up. The briefcase is put on the table. He opens the briefcase, takes a folder out, puts the briefcase back. Quite a show. Opens the folder and says, "I anticipated that you would ask this question. There is no such thing as the Quetta Shura." And he closes the file. And it was really a quite a remarkable moment because it was clear there was going to be no candour on a very important issue. I would say that that characterized the Kayani era. Mullen tried very hard. So did the various CENTCOM commanders, but they never opened the door to a conversation that was really candid. And I think that when Osama bin Laden was finally found, the administration basically said, "Well, we tried, we're done!"[22] Riedel also recalls one moment at the dinner for both Afghan and Pakistani teams when the exchanges between both Pasha and Saleh became heated enough that 'I thought, if I don't take these two men into another room, they're going to start hitting each other ... no hitting each other in the War Room!'

Against this backdrop, the key person in the crafting of the Af–Pak policy was Obama himself, a thoughtful, professorial person who had had exposure to Pakistan at a very early stage in his life when his mother would take him along to the country for her consultancy trips for USAID. Later, at Occidental College in California and then at Columbia University in New York, he befriended and roomed with Pakistanis and had even visited Pakistan as a young man. Some White House staff recall his interest in and affection for Pakistan reflected in the questions he would ask during the early meetings. Gradually, this changed to disinterest and a more detached view of the situation, as he clarified US interests in the region.

---

[22] Riedel interview.

His style was deemed 'Socratic' and 'very professional and deliberate' and 'studious'. He insisted on reading much of the background material given to him. At one stage during the review exercise, a senior White House official told me that Obama had some 16,000 pages of intelligence analysis available to him. He feared that the president would want to read every one of those pages!

The Soviet Union's Example

At that point, I sent over to this friend at the White House the minutes of the Soviet Union's Politburo meeting of 13 November 1986, where Mikhail Gorbachev got the Politburo to discuss and approve a withdrawal plan from Afghanistan. Among the leading lights of the Soviet Union at that time at this meeting were Andrei Gromyko, Eduard Shevardnadze, Anatoly Dobrynin and Marshal Sergey Akhromeyev. I highlighted some key elements of the discussion since it seemed to me that many basic issues that confronted the Soviets in 1986 remained unresolved for the Americans in Afghanistan in 2009 and that President Obama might profit from seeing how Gorbachev had handled the issues.

Gorbachev warns at the outset of the meeting: 'We have been fighting in Afghanistan for six years. If the approach is not changed, we will continue to fight for another 20–30 years.' At one point Gromyko emphasizes, 'In one word, it is necessary to pursue a political settlement. Our people will breathe a deep sigh if we undertake steps in that direction. Our strategic goal is to make Afghanistan neutral.' Marshal Akhromeyev announces at one point, 'There is no single piece of land in this country which has not been occupied by a Soviet soldier. Nevertheless, the majority of the territory remains in the hands of the rebels . . . The whole problem is the fact that military results are not followed up by political [actions] . . . We have lost the battle for the Afghan people . . . We need to look for a way out . . . We must go to Pakistan.' The resolution to exit Afghanistan two years hence was passed at that meeting, but it was not announced, as Obama announced his exit plan to the world in December 2009 at West Point.[23] The Soviets were smarter than the Americans in executing their

---

[23] CPSU CC Politburo transcript (excerpt), 13 November 1986, http://digitalarchive.wilsoncenter.org/document/111599

exit strategy. They kept their plans close to their chests and they involved the neighbouring states.

Bruce Riedel thinks President Obama must have read that Politburo minute, but had to make a political compromise, and chose a policy that fit that need. The basic flaw in the relationship with Pakistan stemmed from the initial approach to crafting an Af–Pak policy and an Af–Pak dialogue by looking at the region through the Afghan prism.

Riedel, who is often seen as very critical of Pakistan by most observers, especially the Pakistanis, had a different view of the relative importance of Pakistan in the emerging policy of the US in the region. He says he never liked the term Af–Pak. 'I remember saying to Richard Holbrooke shortly after we became partners . . . "Do you realize," I said, "Richard, how most Pakistanis regard being called Pakis? Do you know that they think that's a lot like the N word in America?" He looked at me horrified, and I thought, *Nobody ever told you this before?* I always thought if you were going to have a policy, you should have a South Asia policy and put all of this into a coherent goal. But if you weren't going to do that, it should be the Pak–Af policy. Recognizing that one country is significantly bigger in every way than the other. If you pursued it from an Af–Pak policy, you were always seeing Pakistan solely from the Kabul dimension, which undermines the self-importance of Islamabad.

'In one of my lectures that I give [frequently], I keep telling people: "Try to imagine Pakistan not sitting in South Asia. Physically take Pakistan out of South Asia and just look at it. It's a country of close to 200 million people now. It will have 300 million people in our lifetime. It has a proven nuclear weapons programme. It has a huge military, bigger than it needs probably. It has powerful soft power as a Muslim country. It is a country which . . . actually has had real elections in which power has transitioned from one elected government to another . . . Compare that to Egypt, Saudi Arabia, Algeria, you name it, and you would recognize that if we were thinking about the ten most important countries in the world for the United States in the next decade ahead, Pakistan would clearly belong. But unfortunately, because it is in South Asia, it falls into a chasm between India and Iran in which it seems to be lost and passed over.'[24]

This seemed to be the issue that afflicted the US's view of Pakistan in the region. Further, there was a clear and abiding lack of a centre of gravity

---

[24] Riedel interview.

for decision making on Pakistan. The White House wished to call the shots. But the CIA, the Pentagon and, to some extent, the Department of State had their own angles and tried as much as they could to carry on parallel dialogues.

Direct trilateral discussions between the US, Pakistan and Afghanistan were few and far between. The Bush administration had given undue importance to Hamid Karzai, and frequent video-conferences with the US president allowed him to bypass local commanders and the diplomatic staff at will. Once Musharraf had lost his gloss, conversations with him were also limited. Hence, the White House chose to prepare for a tripartite with Karzai and Zardari in Washington on 6 May 2009. Zardari brought over his son, Bilawal, and, contrary to all official protocol, had him seated on his left, across from the US president and his team.[25]

Vice-President Joe Biden prepared for this trilateral exchange, among other things, by meeting with a small group of think-tank representatives at his home the evening before, where he went through his briefing book while seated at his dining table and peppered us with questions late into the evening about Pakistan and Afghanistan. He got some very frank opinions, including some very pointed criticisms of Pakistan's 'double game', and took copious notes. He also shared his own private views with some of us on the fragile state of democracy in both countries and the retrograde system of hereditary political parties in Pakistan.

Obama clearly needed the willing support of both leaders as he prepared his own transition from Afghanistan, even if it meant increasing the US military and financial commitment. Speaking at the conclusion of the meetings the next day he was upbeat about the tripartite dialogue, the second of a new series:

> I'm pleased that these two men—elected leaders of Afghanistan and Pakistan—fully appreciate the seriousness of the threat that we face, and have reaffirmed their commitment to confronting it. And I'm pleased that we have advanced unprecedented cooperation between Afghanistan and Pakistan on a bilateral basis—and among Afghanistan, Pakistan, and the United States—which will benefit all of our people.

---

[25] A very senior White House official recalled to me how Zardari explained to him that he was grooming Bilawal to take over Zardari's seat. This astounded the US official.

He also outlined the immediate goals:

> Now there's much to be done. Along the border where insurgents often move freely, we must work together with a renewed sense of partnership to share intelligence, and to coordinate our efforts to isolate, target and take out our common enemy. But we must also meet the threat of extremism with a positive program of growth and opportunity. And that's why my administration is working with members of Congress to create opportunity zones to spark development. That's why I'm proud that we've helped advance negotiations towards landmark transit-trade agreements to open Afghanistan and Pakistan borders to more commerce . . . Within Pakistan, we must provide lasting support to democratic institutions, while helping the government confront the insurgents who are the single greatest threat to the Pakistani state. And we must do more than stand against those who would destroy Pakistan—we must stand with those who want to build Pakistan. And that is why I've asked Congress for sustained funding, to build schools and roads and hospitals. I want the Pakistani people to understand that America is not simply against terrorism—we are on the side of their hopes and their aspirations, because we know that the future of Pakistan must be determined by the talent, innovation, and intelligence of its people.[26]

This was a theme that he returned to later that year, by when another review of the Afghan War had been done, looking at more specific needs and actions. In his address to the cadets at West Point, he shared publicly his plan to exit Afghanistan in due course, even while he announced a surge of military troops. But there was no parallel major civilian surge in Afghanistan, nor a well-wrought and well-funded plan to engage with Pakistani civil society. All this despite engagement with members of the think-tank corps in the White House on 18 November 2009, when Ben Rhodes and other senior White House staff sought views on what the president ought to emphasize in his West Point speech. As we exited the meeting, Rhodes asked if I could send some ideas for the speech.

---

[26] Remarks by the president after trilateral meeting with President Karzai of Afghanistan and President Zardari of Pakistan, 6 May 2009, The White House, Office of the Press Secretary, https://www.whitehouse.gov/the-press-office/remarks-president-after-trilateral-meeting-with-president-karzai-afghanistan-and-pr

My suggestion in an email a week later to the person who had arranged the meeting for Rhodes was for Obama to declare that the US would engage directly with civil society in both countries and not tie itself to any single individual or institution. I found out later that, among others, Secretary Clinton had pushed for the same approach. Hence, it was a pleasant surprise to hear Obama declare in his West Point address the following words:

> In the past, we too often defined our relationship with Pakistan narrowly. Those days are over. Moving forward, we are committed to a partnership with Pakistan that is built on a foundation of mutual interest, mutual respect, and mutual trust. We will strengthen Pakistan's capacity to target those groups that threaten our countries, and have made it clear that we cannot tolerate a safe haven for terrorists whose location is known and whose intentions are clear. America is also providing substantial resources to support Pakistan's democracy and development. We are the largest international supporter for those Pakistanis displaced by the fighting. And going forward, the Pakistan people must know America will remain a strong supporter of Pakistan's security and prosperity long after the guns have fallen silent, so that the great potential of its people can be unleashed.[27]

Pakistan had changed dramatically. Its population had grown enormously, it was largely youthful, with the vast majority below twenty-five years of age, fairly literate, and had a politically active civil society that was well connected with the globe. Afghanistan too was urbanizing rapidly and the cell phone revolution had produced its own challenges for a government that attempted to rule by fiat.

The Surge

During the West Point speech, Obama spoke about the completion of a second review of Afghanistan, based on the experience since his

---

[27] Remarks by the President in Address to the Nation on the way forward in Afghanistan and Pakistan, The White House, Office of the Press Secretary, 1 December 2009, https://www.whitehouse.gov/the-press-office/remarks-president-address-nation-way-forward-afghanistan-and-pakistan.

inauguration and the surge of 30,000 troops. But, he also announced that eighteen months later, US troops would begin withdrawing from Afghanistan while attempting to build up the capacity of the Afghan forces. This statement of intent negated the surge of troops that Obama announced. As a US Special Forces major from the post at Khost told me later, 'We had convinced a number of local chiefs to come over to our side. The day after the speech, they came in and said to us, "You are leaving!" No amount of explanations by us could persuade them to remain on our side!'

Hidden in the words addressed by Obama to Pakistan was a threat that the US would not tolerate threats from 'safe havens' in Pakistan. The surge itself was a validation of the plan of the new commander of the International Security Assistance Force (ISAF) in Afghanistan, Gen. Stanley McChrystal. In a sixty-six-page report to Defense Secretary Robert Gates, McChrystal had presented a range of 30,000–40,000 troops needed to 'win' the battle in Afghanistan. This report, which was leaked in September, had put the president in a difficult position with his new commander. McChrystal was the tenth commander of the forces in Afghanistan since the invasion in 2001, a fact that in itself reflected the difficulty of prosecuting a coherent and cohesive strategy of war against the Taliban when the leadership kept changing. (Indeed, the average tenure of the seventeen-odd commanders of forces in Afghanistan up to the appointment of Gen. Mick Nicholson was thirteen months, according to Joseph Collins of the National Defense University, Washington DC.) But Obama conceded the military's request and then stayed the course till the end of his tenure. McChrystal had succeeded Gen. David D. McKiernan who had spent barely one year as commander of ISAF, but lost the confidence of the Pentagon and the president in being unable to turn the tide of the war or to introduce innovative tactics.

McChrystal brought to the regional war a well-honed skill as a special operations leader in Iraq and Afghanistan. He had begun in Afghanistan in 2002 as chief of staff to Joint Task Force 180, then spent a year at the Pentagon before becoming commander of Joint Special Operations Command or JSOC focused primarily on operations in Iraq. He transformed JSOC into a highly efficient and effective force that led among other things to the tracking and death of Abu Musaab Al Zarqawi, the Al-Qaeda commander in Iraq. Between 2002 and 2008, he spent part of the time in Afghanistan and kept up with developments there till he was appointed head of ISAF in June 2009. He thought the war effort initially was incoherent because it was a new effort. By the time he took over as ISAF commander, he thought it was 'incoherent' on several levels.

'First, I thought that the progress that you would have expected by the government of Afghanistan was not as good as it should have been. They had deep political divisions but maybe more damaging below the national [level], the competence of the technocrats to deliver governance was very, very low. Almost nonexistent. [And] high levels of corruption.' He found the coalition of forty-six nations that was aiding them adding to the confusion. 'Many had come to do peacekeeping and then found that it had gone more violent so that there was at least differing views on what the mission was and how it should be prosecuted.

'There were five division-equivalent areas, regional commands, and they were all fighting in a different world with a different strategy, [with] really very little connection. Then in the external relationship, the relationship of the US particularly, with Pakistan, with Iran, there were all the players coming at it with their own interests at hand. As a consequence, there was very little confidence on anybody's part of the direction that this was going to take. Many people were playing [with] a cautious wait-and-see attitude, and that uncertainty . . . just pervaded everything.'[28] He discerned a visceral hatred for Pakistan among the Afghans. And the Pakistanis, civilian and military leadership, wanting Afghanistan to succeed, but at the same time 'there was also a contradictory effort to stop them. It was simultaneous, dialectic,' said McChrystal.

Though he got along very well with the Pakistani Army chief, Gen. Kayani, McChrystal felt that it was important that two persons who were key to making the cooperation work across borders had to connect better than they had in the past. These two were Kayani and Karzai.

'I asked both of them if they'd be willing to meet, and they said that they would be willing to meet with me there and without other Americans there. That was uncomfortable for me because I had to go back up my chain of command because I wasn't a diplomat, and there was a possible perception that I was overstepping my bounds, but I got approval from Secretary Gates and support from the White House to bring [them] together [in] a meeting.'

---

[28] Interview with General Stanley McChrystal, Alexandria, VA, 19 December 2016.

Kayani came to Kabul for the meeting and McChrystal recalls both Karzai and Kayani tried hard to make the relationship work. The rapport was 'tentative and cautious', but McChrystal felt they had committed to changing the relationship in that first and then a second meeting.

But like his predecessors and others who followed him, there was deep distrust with the Pakistanis, stemming largely from the inability of Pakistan to staunch the infiltration of Afghan Taliban, particularly the Haqqani Network, into Afghanistan from Pakistani territory. The Americans presented evidence of these infiltrations to the Pakistanis, and were met with blank stares. A senior American officer explained this: 'It was frustrating because we would present evidence, clear evidence, and they would simply deny the evidence or just ignore it. Just as it was laid out they would just ignore it, and so on the one hand we had this constant growing case that said that the ISI and parts of the Pakistani military were clearly facilitating [the Afghan Taliban.]' A senior Pakistani Army officer, now retired, explained one reason why the Pakistanis loyally stuck to the Haqqani Network: They had facilitated the evacuation of ISI personnel and their 'friends' from Kunduz in the north of Afghanistan soon after the American invasion. Ironically, the US is reported to have agreed to the airlift to support Musharraf.[29] It is unclear exactly what role the Haqqanis could have played in this airlift. But ISI field operatives reportedly used this alleged debt owed to the Haqqanis in convincing successive DGs of the ISI to continue to shelter the Haqqani leadership inside Pakistan, even when the Haqqanis had established sanctuaries inside Afghanistan. The ambivalence of these field operatives continued to bedevil the US–Pakistan relationship.

All this while there were attempts at coordinated actions on both sides of the Afghanistan–Pakistan border with parallel operations to clear territory and prevent the escape of militants from one side to the other. Such operations took place in Bajaur and Mohmand, for example. But they were the exception, not the rule, and they rested on the ability of local commanders to communicate and collaborate. They were not a part of an ingrained or well-established policy.

At the same time, Pakistan made the case that it was losing large numbers of their military in the fighting inside FATA. McChrystal recalls,

---

[29] Seymour Hersh, 'The Getaway', *New Yorker*, 28 January 2002, http://www.newyorker.com/magazine/2002/01/28/the-getaway-2

'General Kayani took me to a wall, and he showed me the Pakistani general officers who'd been killed in the fights against Al-Qaeda and the Taliban, and it was real. It wasn't trumped up. He asked me how many American generals had been killed, and of course I knew the answer was zero. The point he was making was Pakistan had lost more soldiers, more generals.' That part of the Pakistani case was real.

On his part, Kayani had a counter-narrative for the lack of ability to move, especially against the Haqqani Network in North Waziristan. To his mind, the Americans had promised that they would move troops into the east, and then they shifted their focus to the south. He recalled 'losing his cool' with Gen. John Allen at one point when instead of US forces on the Afghan side Allen promised to provide Afghan forces that were still being trained. Thus, he really did not have the American anvil to the Pakistani hammer. Although there were smaller operations in the north, in Mohmand, for example, where there were parallel and successful activities, the big effort in North Waziristan never materialized. For him, the Pakistan operation was a question of 'not if but when'. And he kept waiting for more troops. Kayani was also worried about opening up a long front deep into the hinterland since the Taliban had had links with the Punjabi Taliban and other jihadi groups. After the completion of military operations in Swat and Malakand, the Pakistan Army did have a substantial force of close to 40,000 collected in North Waziristan but they did not move to clear the territory till much later, by which time Kayani had retired. His successor Raheel Sharif had little hesitation in acting against the militants in FATA including foreigners who had made FATA their global training ground and headquarters.

The reality was the lack of a clear aim in moving Pakistani forces into FATA and the inability to recognize the sentiments that gave birth to the TTP. Pakistan also failed to prevent the nexus of its Punjabi militants with both Al-Qaeda and the TTP and Afghan Taliban.

A Pakistan argument to counter the US complaints was that the Coalition could have stopped the Haqqanis and other infiltrators once they crossed into Afghanistan. Why didn't they do that? McChrystal's response was that the attacks did not simply emanate from North Waziristan alone but were a network effort all over Afghanistan. He did confirm a key element of the debate that had earlier been presented to me by a senior US official in the White House—that only some 10 per cent of all attacks inside Afghanistan were by the Haqqani group, 90 per cent were from other sources.

McChrystal recalls arguing with Karzai to go after the insurgency to which Karzai responded: "'We don't have an insurgency.' I said, 'I think you do.' He goes, 'No. We've got external terrorism.' I said, 'No, you don't. You've got a little of that.' But he said, 'If we say it's an insurgency, the West will leave us. They'll say it's an internal Afghan problem, and we need the West to stay.' That was an interesting perspective, but I think that the 90/10 number's actually about right.' He then added: 'Having said that, the fact that Pakistan offered a sanctuary cannot be overstated as value' to the insurgency.[30]

Unfortunately, McChrystal did not have the time to alter radically the situation on the ground, nor the mindset of the chief Afghan and Pakistani protagonists. He left the country abruptly and under a cloud, following a story in the *Rolling Stone* magazine where he and his staff were portrayed as being disrespectful of their civilian higher command, including the president and vice-president. Obama fired him.[31]

The US continued to prosecute the war on a short-term basis, attuned to domestic considerations. It changed commanders too quickly, and it failed to convince its Pakistani allies of the importance of helping seal the border on a regular basis. It also failed to adequately equip the Pakistanis with the equipment that would afford their troops protection as well as mobility to conduct operations in difficult terrain against a highly mobile enemy. The Pakistanis and Afghans failed to connect, or coordinate their actions. Distrust marked that relationship too.

At the higher level of command, the White House was struggling to find rapid solutions for a conflict that demanded patience and a longer-term investment in the economic and political stability of Afghanistan. Rotation of the military leadership became the norm. The Afghan theatre of war was fast becoming the Graveyard of Commanders. And the US–Pakistan marriage was heading towards Divorce Court.

---

30 McChrystal interview.
31 Michael Hastings, 'The Runaway General', *Rolling Stone*, 22 June 2010.

3

2011: A Most Horrible Year!

As 2011 dawned, the bleak domestic situation began mirroring Pakistan's external relationships. Specifically, US–Pakistan relations suffered enormously after the 2010 floods despite the massive US help in the recovery efforts, and despite the infusion of $500 million from the KLB funds for Pakistan's flood relief at the insistence of Amb. Richard Holbrooke. A high-level strategic dialogue involving the civil and military leadership of Pakistan had begun with the US. A number of groups were working to find solutions to problems at the sectoral level, well beyond the battlefield. But the basis of a strong partnership had yet to be laid. And the disunity on both sides in terms of relations with the other country began to be reflected in the responses to mini-crises.

The year 2011 produced a convergence of negative events that magnified these problems. 'The drone wars, the outing of two CIA chiefs of station by the Pakistani intelligence, the death of Osama Bin Laden and . . . a scandal called "Memogate" about US–Pakistan relations which threaten(ed) to bring down the Zardari government. And the bad news is there's no floor in sight.' That was the summary description by Bruce Riedel, a leading US intelligence analyst and adviser to President Obama on his Af–Pak policy.

Riedel, JCS Chairman Admiral Mike Mullen and I were on a report by Jackie Northam for National Public Radio's programme 'All Things Considered' in December 2011, which reflected on that watershed year. The programme carried a segment from Admiral Mullen's testimony before the Senate Armed Services Committee when he declared unequivocally, 'The Haqqani network [of the Afghan Taliban operating out of sanctuary in North Waziristan], for one acts as a veritable arm of Pakistan's Inter Services Intelligence Agency.' Mullen had till that point been Kayani's principal interlocutor and advocate in the US. He made a total of twenty-six trips to Pakistan and treated Kayani as a friend. Yet his despondence and sense of betrayal, reflected in Kayani's unkept promise to launch operations against Afghan Taliban in Pakistani territory, led to a break in that relationship. Pakistan also lost support on Capitol Hill. However, this did not change, as I added in that programme, the underlying reality of 'co-dependency [with Pakistan], particularly for the next two years for the US in Afghanistan. But in the longer run too, the United States cannot afford to alienate a country of 185 million at such a strategic location.' As the host Robert Siegel declared, 'The two countries are nominal allies, but the events of 2011 has [sic] severely frayed ties between Washington and Islamabad.'[1]

One reason for the disconnect was the difference in the declared and undeclared strategic aims of the US and Pakistan in the region. The other was a basic flaw in US calculations that assumed that Kayani, under pressure or by force of US argumentation, would forsake his own country's perceived interests in favour of what he saw as US short-term interests. Kayani feared the possibility of opening a domestic front against the network of Afghan Taliban and local militants that would extend all the way into the hinterland, particularly into the Punjab. Although his successor was to launch a major clean-up campaign in FATA later, the Afghan Taliban were never a major target of those operations, though depots and training sites of the Taliban and other foreign fighters were eliminated by the Pakistani military operations. The US and some Pakistani sources maintained that leaders of the Afghan Taliban were evacuated and relocated first into the settled areas and then other parts of FATA in advance of the clean-up operations in North Waziristan. There was also no operation against the Afghan Taliban in the borderlands of Balochistan.

Mullen had invested heavily in the Kayani relationship. A studious man with an ability to connect to others, Mullen relied heavily on his ability to measure and persuade his partners in the war against terrorism across the globe. He was not wont to hyperbole. Yet, when he was asked to contribute to a profile of Kayani in *TIME* magazine's list of 100 most influential persons in 2011, he wrote a gushy paean that would haunt his reputation in later years:

---

[1] 'Tense U.S.–Pakistan Relations Mark 2011', *All Things Considered*, National Public Radio, 29 December 2011.

I don't remember all the details of my first meeting with General Ashfaq
Kayani, the Pakistan Army's Chief of Staff. But I do remember thinking,
Here is a man with a plan, a leader who knows where he wants to go. He
seemed to understand the nature of the extremist threat inside Pakistan,
recognized that his army wasn't ready to meet that threat and had already
started working up solutions.

So far he's done everything he told me he would do. He said he
would provide the Frontier Corps with material support and strong
leaders. He did it. He said he would send more Pakistani army troops
to the northwest border region. He sent nearly 2,000. He said he would
use those troops to go after alQaeda and extremist groups in Bajaur and
the Swat Valley. They have mounted several operations in just the past
few months.

There's much more to do, of course. But I also think it's important
to look at what Kayani hasn't done. For starters, he hasn't let the army
meddle in politics. Kayani helped foster a peaceful outcome to last year's
constitutional crisis, but he did it in a way that was totally in keeping
with his military responsibilities. He also hasn't let tension over the
involvement of Pakistan-based militants in the Mumbai terrorist attacks
spin out of control.

General Kayani, 57, commands an army with troops fighting in what
President Barack Obama has rightly called the 'most dangerous place in
the world'. He's lost more than 1,000 soldiers in that fight. He knows the
stakes. He's got a plan.[2]

Kayani had a plan, but the cautious general played his cards characteristically
close to his chest. He kept Mullen and the Americans stringing along on
a promise to move against the Taliban ensconced in North Waziristan
and other parts of FATA. He frequently hinted at impending operations
to visitors from the US (including me). Among US military circles there
was reference to 'real time' and 'Kayani time'; the latter had a built-in lag.
Kayani certainly had some valid concerns: he did not have enough troops
initially. That constraint ended after the Swat operations when he was
able to redirect substantially more troops to North Waziristan. He was

---

[2] Admiral Mike Mullen, 'Ashfaq Kayani', *TIME*, 30 April 2009,
     http://content.time.com/time/specials/packages/printout/
     0,29239,1894410_1893847_1894215,00.html#

also cautious about moving against the Haqqani Network that his own intelligence field operatives favoured due to their past connections and obligations. He also feared that moving against the Haqqanis might force them into alliances with other insurgents in FATA. Finally, he feared extending a front from the Western border into the Punjab hinterland. Many of the Punjabi Taliban continued to infiltrate into Afghanistan, according to some reports, via North Waziristan, and were also franchisees of Al-Qaeda. But Kayani also had some valid grievances. The US kept moving the goal posts of its game in Afghanistan. And for some reason, Mullen and some others operated under the mistaken belief that Kayani might act in response to their request and pressure even if it went against Pakistan's interests.

Kayani felt that he needed a more organized and powerful force on the Afghan side of the border to help squeeze the Taliban. He and his officers often referred to the more than 1,000 Pakistani posts along that border, while the Afghan posts, they maintained, numbered close to 100. These numbers were not verifiable. As recently as January 2018, Pakistani officers visiting Washington were citing over 900 Pakistani posts compared with 250 Afghan posts. Finally, Kayani bemoaned the lack of US resolve to enhance its presence in the east of Afghanistan rather than shifting its focus to Helmand and Kandahar in the south.

Cooperation continued with the US on other fronts. The search for Al-Qaeda operatives in Pakistan continued, quite successfully. The Ground Line of Communication (GLOC) with Afghanistan was kept operational, though from time to time, for political reasons, it would be interrupted. Throughout this period the Air Line of Communication (ALOC) was never interrupted, allowing the US to use Pakistani air space to fly battlefield and logistical support missions to forces in Afghanistan from aircraft carriers and bases in the Gulf. Unbeknownst to his compatriots, Kayani also sought and received drone support for surveillance and other purposes.

US drones used Shamsi Base in Balochistan as one launch site. Al Jazeera English obtained photographs of US and Pakistani officers with drones being readied for launch at an airbase in Pakistan. I was shown these photographs and managed to use Google to match the runway alignment and buildings to identify the base as Shamsi. The legality of US drones crossing the border from launch sites in Afghanistan was another open question. The US never acknowledged the drone operations till late in the

Obama period. I recall receiving an email in 2009 from an air force office in the Pentagon that mentioned the drone programme and immediately getting another message asking that the previous message be deleted. A replacement message was sent out minus the reference to the drone programme! The US position was that drone operations against militants were preventive actions, and that FATA was 'ungoverned space', hence attacks inside FATA were legal. The Pakistani government and military from the president downwards played along with this charade.[3] Indeed, a senior military officer confirmed to me during a visit to Pakistan Army headquarters the presence of Special Operations Command (SOCOM) personnel inside North Waziristan to assist in targeting Afghan militants inside Pakistani territory.

The Americans were not totally relying on Pakistan's alliance and support, though such support was not 100 per cent. Through an active programme to recruit both witting and unwitting assets inside the Pakistani establishment, civil and military, they penetrated into the state structures to gather information, influence decision making and to infiltrate operatives into Pakistan not only to track Afghan terrorists but also to track Pakistan's own nuclear programme and assets and its intelligence apparatus. The nuclear programme created nightmares for US decision makers who feared that Pakistan might willingly or accidentally allow other countries or non-state actors to gain access to nuclear technology or weapons, with uncontrollable consequences for regional or global security.

A particular target of their operations against non-state actors were the militant jihadi outfits that were based in the Punjab and that had been allied with Pakistani intelligence in their operations against India. In FATA, British, French and German efforts continued to identify and counter jihadi and terror networks and training operations. At one point, the German intelligence agency, known by its initials BND, was reported to have 'lost' track of 200 native Germans somewhere in FATA. The French defence ministry arranged for selected young men from FATA to come to Paris for training before being re-infiltrated back into FATA.[4]

---

[3] Shuja Nawaz, 'Drone Attacks inside Pakistan: Wayang or Willing Suspension of Disbelief?', *Georgetown Journal of International Affairs* 12, no. 2 (Summer/Fall 2011): 79–87.

[4] European sources to author. In the French case, a French scholar, Mariam Abou Zahab, who knew FATA well, saw and spoke with persons whom the scholar knew from her academic work in FATA.

Western agencies worked together in their quest for Al-Qaeda and against terror networks that might operate in the West.

The year 2010 witnessed the height of US financial flows to Pakistan, overt and covert. In that fiscal year, overt US appropriations for Pakistan totalled $4.3 billion, including security assistance, economic assistance, and Coalition Support Fund (CSF) reimbursements. Covert help and assistance in kind added to the amounts received by Pakistan from the US.[5] Those were heady days of the partnership between the US and its non-NATO ally Pakistan. But mistrust lay below the surface. The financial flows began diminishing after 2010.

Well-targeted efforts by US intelligence agencies helped create a network of local assets as well as American male and female agents in place through cover appointments at the US embassy and other offices inside Pakistan. Pakistani intelligence acted as a break against the issuance of visas, especially from the embassy in Washington DC, where President Zardari had sent his close ally Husain Haqqani as ambassador. After the US complained about delays in issuing visas, Amb. Haqqani was given special permission to issue visas speedily without resorting to clearance by the ISI. Amb. Haqqani insists that despite that presidential authority, he kept the Defence Attaché, then Brig. Nazir Butt, in the loop, since the DA was the principal link to the ISI.[6] The military and its supporters in Pakistan insist that more than 2,000 visas were issued in a relatively short period by Ambassador Haqqani. He provided figures that indicated a downward trend from 3,784 in 2009 to 3,555 in 2010. But the Abbottabad Commission on the death of Osama bin Laden provided data from the Pakistan embassy in Washington DC that contradicted the Haqqani figures and showed an increase in visas issued during his tenure, from 3,242 visas issued by the embassy in 2009 to 4,422 issued in 2010.[7] The contention of the commission and many in official Pakistan was that the US government was creating a huge embassy in Islamabad and using that expansion as an excuse for sending spies into the country. According to Pakistani officials, they would delay sending lists to the Embassy of US officials needing visas

---

[5]   Alan Kronstadt, Congressional Research Service.

[6]   Interview with author.

[7]   Abbottabad Commission report carried by Al Jazeera, p. 216, https://assets. documentcloud.org/documents/724833/aljazeera-bin-laden-dossier.pdf.

and then would amend lists at the last minute to insert new names after agreement in principle had been obtained for issuance of visas.

In fact, the infiltration of US spies had begun much earlier under the CIA's Art Keller. 'During the "surge" of CIA officers into Pakistan beginning in 2005 and 2006, when Art Keller was deployed to the tribal areas, American spies arrived in Pakistan in a desperate search for clues about Osama bin Laden and stretched the normally accepted rules of international spycraft.'[8] As a former US intelligence officer told me, the US had penetrated many Pakistani agencies. The normally paranoid Pakistanis were justified in their suspicions about their allies. Some Americans understood this situation very well.

Early in the spring of 2011, I was sharing a cab ride from an event at the US Institute of Peace with former CIA Director Michael Hayden. He told me that he had been asked to write a piece on Lt. Gen. Ahmed Shuja Pasha, the head of the ISI, for *TIME* magazine's annual issue of 100 most influential persons. 'What should I write?' he asked. Noticing our Pakistani driver, I evaded the question during the short ride. When we got out downtown near our respective offices off K Street, I told him not to write what Admiral Mullen had written for *TIME* about Gen. Kayani. Surprisingly, he said he had not read that piece. I recall saying to him that Pasha saw himself as a super patriot and he would do whatever he could to preserve Pakistan's secrets and its objectives regardless of US wishes. Pasha, as DG military operations (DGMO), had been the architect of the army's strategy against the Pakistani Taliban and he was very committed to his approach to fighting terrorism that affected Pakistan directly. He also relied heavily on his operatives inside FATA, who were from the area and in many cases ambivalent about their loyalties to their tribal kin and their ISI superiors in Islamabad. Pasha had no significant prior intelligence experience but became a hands-on spymaster, which put him at the centre of a number of controversial events in 2011 and beyond. Perhaps too much of a hands-on guy and too ready to leap into action himself.

This is what the astute Gen. Hayden produced for *TIME* magazine:

Within weeks of Lieut. General Ahmed Shuja Pasha's becoming head of Pakistan's top intelligence agency, ISI, in 2008, terrorist attacks

---

8   Mark Mazzetti, *The Way of the Knife* (New York: The Penguin Press, 2013), p. 281.

in Mumbai seriously roiled already stressed US–Pakistani relations. Pasha, 59, has grown progressively more suspicious of US motives and staying power. The arrest of a US government contractor in Lahore has led to acrimony. And larger changes in Pakistan—the growth of fundamentalism, nationalism and anti-Americanism—have squeezed the space in which any ISI chief can cooperate with the US. Pasha, a Pakistani patriot and American partner, now must find these two roles even more difficult to reconcile—and at a time when much of US counterterrorism success depends on exactly that.[9]

That paradoxical situation was exactly what challenged Pasha as 2011 dawned.

The Raymond Davis Affair

The 'US Government contractor' that Hayden alluded to was Raymond Davis, thirty-six, who had hit the headlines after killing two persons on 27 January 2011 on a busy street in Lahore, the bustling provincial capital. Davis was kept in custody in Lahore awaiting trial and a verdict, after admitting that he acted in self-defence. Meanwhile, the US and Pakistan sparred over the nature and role of Davis's assignment in Pakistan. He was released on 16 March 2011 after a murky deal for payment of 'blood money' to the families of the persons he had killed. His story was a fascinating saga of a mercenary spy, one of many contractors who followed the money trail into America's wars abroad, driven by a mixture of patriotism and the lure of relatively high 'danger money' compared with regular soldiers.[10]

Born in the coal country of South West Virginia in a 'blink and you miss it' small town named Big Stone Gap, Davis had a hard-scrabble existence.

---

[9]   *TIME*, 21 April 2011, http://content.time.com/time/specials/packages/article/0,28804,2066367_2066369_2066316,00.html

[10] According to a leading employment agency in the United States, the average US Special Forces soldier makes some $67,326 a year. Indeed.com, 'Soldier Salaries', https://www.indeed.com/salaries/Military+Special+Forces+Soldier-Salaries. A Congressional Research Service report in 2006 calculated that it cost nearly $400,000 to keep a US soldier in the field in Iraq. Later, figures ran from $600,000 to $1.3 million a year. Civilian contractors ran around $200,000 or less. See: Raymond Davis and Storms Reback, *The Contractor* (Dallas, TX: BenBella Books, 2017), p. 23.

His coal-miner father was badly injured when a 700-lb rock broke his back in three places. After graduation, Davis tried unsuccessfully to join the Marines. Finally, an army recruiter tested him and suggested he become an army field medic. At eighteen, he made it to Fort Benning, Georgia, to be trained. Some four years later, he got into training to become a member of the elite Special Forces, but an injury to his lung sidelined him and forced him on to a disability temporary retirement list. He then moved to Lexington, Kentucky, with his girlfriend and fellow 82nd Airborne Division soldier, Rebecca, and enrolled in a course at Eastern Kentucky University entitled 'Asset Protection and Security'. By the time he healed from his injury, the Special Forces did not want him back in its active ranks, so he quit and entered the world of security contractors.

Davis's first overseas assignment was in 2004 with DynCorp International, a major US government contractor, in Afghanistan, serving, among other things, with a team of bodyguards for President Hamid Karzai at a salary of $600 a day, earning himself the sobriquet of 'Crossbones'. This was his call sign when he landed up as a security 'contractor' in Pakistan, at the US Consulate in Peshawar, the embassy in Islamabad and then in the consulate at Lahore over the period 2009–2011.

Davis was originally issued a short-term visa to enter Pakistan in 2008 by the embassy in Washington on passport number 910013853.[11] This was a single-entry three-month visa. Amb. Haqqani states the visa was issued in 2008 before he was appointed ambassador. In the routine, the Department of State was the one sending lists of US officials for whom visas were requested. 'His first visa was issued in 2008 before I took over. Last was a renewal issued in Islamabad. When we checked after his case came to light in January 2011—there was no record of his visa application in the embassy. Someone felt embarrassed enough to remove the record,' stated Haqqani in his exchange with me.[12] (The embassy confirmed to me that it does not keep paper records of visa applications for more than five years. However, electronic materials are retained.) He also said, based on what he was told but could not confirm, that Davis travelled on two different passports, and his first visa was issued in 2008 on a separate passport. He was right. The final visa was issued on 14 June 2010 and was a two-year 'Official Multiple Entry' visa on passport number 910105240, different from the one he had

---

[11] Confirmed by the Embassy of Pakistan, Washington DC.

[12] Interview with me.

used for his first visa in 2008.[13] This visa was issued by the Government of Pakistan in Islamabad, not by the embassy in Washington. It may be that Davis got visas extended or reissued in Pakistan by the Ministry of Interior after he got his first visas in Washington DC, using the earlier passport. The ministry failed to catch his use of different passports for different visas.

Another earlier visa, in fact, was issued on 15 September 2009 by the Embassy of Pakistan in Washington DC, and was for a single visit for the period ending 15 December 2009. The passport number is the same as the one on which the last two-year visa was issued in Islamabad, presumably by the Ministry of Interior. A page in the same passport indicates that Davis had entered the country on 18 October 2009. He exited Pakistan on 15 December 2010. Clearly, the Americans were doing what they did best. Try one source in Pakistan, and if that failed, try another. People were always ready to oblige them.

Pakistan remained a divided country. The civilians and the military were unable to coordinate or agree on how to handle the American influx of staff for their growing embassy and consulates. To facilitate their visas, the prime minister of Pakistan reaffirmed the 'existing visa policy for official US visitors to Pakistan' in a note from the principal secretary to the prime minister, Nargis Sethi, a secret memorandum dated 14 July 2010 and copied to the Secretary Interior. Under this policy,

> . . . the ambassador is empowered to issue entry visas for restricted periods to US officials, who have been recommended in writing by the concerned US authority, i.e. the Department of State and [on] whose duly completed applications forms, it is clearly indicated for what purposes they intend to travel to Pakistan.

---

[13] Images carried by Dawn TV and *Dawn* newspaper. And confirmation of passport numbers by the Pakistan embassy in Washington DC, https://www.dawn.com/news/607801/pakistan-intelligence-confirms-davis-is-cia-guy and 21 February 2011; https://www.google.com/search?q=DAWN+TV+and+DAWN+newspaper,+Raymond+Davis+passport+images&rlz=1C5CHFA_enUS555US555&source=lnms&tbm=isch&sa=X&ved=0ahUKEwiOvvjkr9rjAhUPtlkKHduiAXUQ_AUIEigC&biw=1544&bih=935#imgrc=1YFUuuhtWs4ymM:

Going beyond that authority, the prime minister decided that 'the ambassador to Washington will be empowered, with immediate effect, to issue visas valid up to one year without the embassy having to refer each such aforementioned application to the concerned authorities in Pakistan'. The ambassador was instructed to issue such visas 'under intimation to the prime minister's office in Islamabad'. In effect, the ambassador would bypass the normal channel of the ISI and the JCS directorate. This note was clearly issued a month after Davis's first visa was issued in Washington DC.

On the same passport, Davis entered the country on 14 August 2010, exited on 31 August 2010, returned on 26 September 2010, exiting on 15 December 2010, and finally re-entered on 20 January 2011, a week before that fateful day in Lahore. There are no explanations available from Washington for the reason for these frequent and short visits.

During his ninth and last trip to Pakistan, on 27 January 2011, Davis left the US Consulate's guest house in Lahore's Scotch Corner that lies just off the Mall Road, near the crossing of Canal Bank Road and before Aitchison College, where he lived with his team. He headed out into the city, by his own account, 'to survey the route I'd be taking someone three days later'.[14] He drove down The Mall, the main thoroughfare that connected the military cantonment to the City Centre, then got on to Jail Road, heading to Ferozepur Road. Nearing Mozang Chowk, a major intersection, he came to a stop in heavy traffic. After a few minutes, he says he noted a motorcycle pull up about 10 feet ahead of him. On it were two young men identified later as Faizan Haider, the driver, and Mohammad Faheem, the pillion. Davis recalls that he saw Faheem turn and draw a pistol from his waistband. Davis's training kicked in immediately. 'As soon as I saw the gun's muzzle moving in my direction, I unclicked my seatbelt and started to draw the gun I was carrying in a waistband beneath the front of my shirt,' wrote Davis in his book about the incident.[15] He gripped his brand-new Glock 17 and began firing shots rapidly through the windshield at Faheem and Haider, killing both in a matter of seconds. Then he holstered his weapon, got out of the car, fetched his camera from the 'go bag' where he kept his tools and began taking photographs of

---

[14] Davis and Reback, *The Contractor*, is the source of the description given by
      Davis himself of that day and its events.

[15] Ibid.

the men he had just shot. He says he did not run to avoid shattering the apparent calm around him, despite the shooting. Plus the consulate was 3 miles away. And his car was stuck in traffic. Davis identified the weapon that Faheem had tried to use as a Soviet Tokarev, a deadly weapon that is quite common in Pakistan. He then went back into his car, locked its doors and radioed his base to seek assistance.

The US Consulate staff had tried to reach the scene of the incident, but missed Davis who had moved on to the police station in the meantime. In their rush to get there, they had taken a one-way street in the wrong direction, running over a motorcyclist and killing him in the process. They scrambled back to the diplomatic anonymity and immunity of the consulate and were never traced or brought to trial. Davis was caught by the police and handed over to the military who took him to Lahore's military cantonment.

The Davis affair became an instant diplomatic row between the US and Pakistan. The US position was that Davis was a diplomat. Pakistan did not agree. Interestingly, in his book, Davis states bluntly: 'I was enlisted to protect State Department personnel. Did this make me a diplomat? Of course not.'[16] (This may be purposeful misinformation to muddy the trail of his affiliation with the CIA or some other spy agency.) The paperwork supported Pakistan's position. He was not on the foreign ministry's list of accredited diplomatic staff, especially given his affiliation with the consulate in Lahore. The US embassy attributed that to bureaucratic mistakes at their end. This debate over Davis's status created a mini-war inside Pakistan. The PPP Foreign Minister Shah Mehmood Qureshi insisted Pakistan stick to its position and try Davis.

The US decided to go to the mat to extricate Davis, even getting President Obama to call him 'our diplomat'[17] and invoking international conventions to provide cover for him.

---

[16] Ibid., p. 90.

[17] President Barack Obama for the first time today stepped into the international firestorm surrounding the US official accused of shooting two men in Pakistan, calling Raymond Davis 'our diplomat' and urging his release on the grounds of diplomatic immunity. See: Jake Tapper and Lee Ferran, 'President Barack Obama: Pakistan Should Honor Immunity for "Our Diplomat"', abcnews, 15 February 2011, http://abcnews.go.com/Blotter/raymond-davis-case-president-barack-obama-urges-pakistan/story?id=12922282

> We've got a very simple principle here that every country in the world that
> is party to the Vienna Convention on diplomatic relations has upheld in
> the past and should uphold in the future, and that is, if our diplomats
> are in another country, then they are not subject to that country's local
> prosecution,' Obama said in a press conference today. 'We expect
> Pakistan, that's a signatory and recognizes Mr. Davis as a diplomat, to
> abide by the same convention . . . I'm not going to discuss the specific
> exchanges that we've had [with the Pakistani government], but we've
> been very firm about this being a priority.[18]

Of course, Pakistan had never publicly recognized Davis as a diplomat.
The president should have known that. The mood in the White House
was not very pro-Pakistan at the time, among other things, because of
growing evidence that Osama bin Laden was likely hiding in Abbottabad in
northern Pakistan. Qureshi, who had had differences with his government,
eventually resigned and joined the Opposition PTI. But Pakistan proceeded
to allow the case to go to the Lahore High Court to determine Davis's
status before he could be tried for murder.

The US took a big gamble by getting the president to declare Davis
a diplomat. But the Geneva Conventions do not support the Obama
statement, as an independent UK analyst pointed out:

> Full diplomatic immunity is enjoyed only by 'diplomatic agents'. Those
> are defined at Article 1(e) of the Vienna Convention as 'the head of the
> mission or a member of the diplomatic staff of the mission'. Helpfully
> the diplomatic staff are further defined in the preceding article as 'having
> diplomatic rank'. Those ranks are an ascending series of concrete titles
> from third secretary through to ambassador or high commissioner. Davis
> did not have a diplomatic rank.
>
> But there is a second category of 'administrative and technical
> staff' of a mission. They enjoy a limited diplomatic immunity which,
> however, specifically excludes 'acts performed outside the course of
> their duties'. (Vienna convention article 37/2.) Frantic off-the-record
> briefing by the state department reflected widely in the media indicates
> that the US case is that Davis was a member of technical staff covered
> by this provision.

---

[18] Tapper and Ferran, 'Pakistan Should Honor Immunity'.

But in that case the US has to explain in the course of precisely which diplomatic duties Davis needed to carry a Glock handgun, a headband-mounted flashlight and a pocket telescope. The Vienna convention lists the legitimate duties of an embassy, and none of them need that kind of equipment.[19]

Further, Pakistani senior ex-military sources told this analyst that there was no note appointing Davis as embassy or consulate staff. 'If the note exists, why have the Americans not produced it?' he asked.

Pakistan's fractured political power structure added to the muddle. The PPP government wanted to appease the Americans. The military, and especially the DG-ISI Gen. Pasha, were less wont to yield to US demands. Pasha made an initial attempt to get CIA Director entre nous to confirm Davis as a spy. Panetta, who was hawkish on the bin Laden matter, refused to confirm Davis as a CIA agent. Pasha was turned off by this behaviour and allowed the case to proceed in Lahore. Caught between these opposites, Amb. Munter tried to find the middle ground and seek a way out. Amb. Haqqani, who had had been educated at an Islamic school in his early years, claims he came up with the possibility of invoking Sharia law to allow payment of blood money to the victims' families. Munter does not recall this idea originating from Washington.[20] In any case, Davis's incarceration continued. The trial proceeded in fits and starts. Complicating the use of the Sharia gambit under the rubric of Diyat (*Diyya* in Arabic) was the US injunction against paying any money as ransom, which was how the US viewed this issue. That was the public position. Behind the scenes, Pasha, seeing an opportunity to resolve the lingering dispute, worked to oil the wheels of justice. Rumours swirled about who provided the funds. Some attributed the largesse to Malik Riaz, a celebrated and highly successful real estate developer with strong ties to the military and almost all political parties. But that was never confirmed publicly.

Regardless, nearly four months after Davis was jailed, a deal was struck. At one point in mid-February, Senator John Kerry, the chairman of the Senate Foreign Relations Committee, also arrived in Pakistan to

---

[19] Craig Murray, 'This CIA Agent Is No Diplomat', *Guardian*, Opinion, 28 February 2011, https://www.theguardian.com/commentisfree/cifamerica/2011/feb/28/cia-agent-diplomat-pakistan-raymond-davis

[20] Author interview.

help with the deal. Notably, drone strikes inside Pakistan were suspended during that period.

On 16 March, the court that was hearing the jurisdictional case before proceeding to trial of Davis for murder was instantly transformed into a Sharia court under Pakistan's schizoid legal system. Davis was given a quick rundown of what was happening by US Consul Gen. Carmela Conroy, who had been his main interlocutor throughout the case.[21] Eighteen family members representing both victims and the wife of one of the Davis victims, who had reportedly committed suicide soon after her husband's killing, filed in, some teary-eyed. Each signed a piece of paper that confirmed that they forgave Davis for the murders at Mozang Chowk. Each person received $130,000. Davis was a free man heading for a flight to Kabul.

At Lahore airport, a Cessna airplane with Amb. Munter on board waited. Also on board was a doctor from the consulate, whom Davis knew, and who would also examine him before he left the country. Munter had been receiving texts from Pasha during the court proceedings, though it is unclear if Pasha was actually in the courtroom, as some accounts, including Davis's book, later stated. He could have been simply relaying someone else's reports to Munter. Among others in that relatively small courtroom, there was no one who recalled seeing Pasha there. A senior military officer also confirmed to me that Pasha was not in the court that day. Regardless, Pasha and Munter played a role in Davis's release. Interior Minister Rehman Malik also claimed credit via a governmental group that he convened.

> Mr Malik claimed that the Pakistan Peoples Party (PPP) government and the military establishment had decided not to release Davis till he was acquitted by a court of law. 'A high-level meeting had decided that neither would Davis be deported nor would he be granted diplomatic immunity, and that we would wait for the decision of the court in the matter and no action would be taken through any executive order,' he said, adding that the name of Davis had been placed on the Exit Control List immediately.

---

[21] Ms Conroy was at the Department of State when I wrote this book and agreed to answer written questions. According to her, she provided answers to the Department's Press Office to clear and convey to me. Despite repeated exchanges with her and the Press Office over a period of many months, I was unable to obtain those answers.

He said that later in a meeting at the President House, the then Inter-Services Intelligence director general, Gen Shuja Pasha, had told the political leadership that the Americans wanted to exercise the right of Diyat (blood money) under Islamic law. 'The matter was dealt with the cooperation of the Punjab government, the Ministry of Foreign Affairs and the Ministry of Interior,' he said.[22]

The judgment of the Lahore court gives the necessary though somewhat convoluted background to the case and how, in the absence of a case for murder under the regular penal code, the sharia law was applied and Davis was acquitted and released.[23]

The provincial government of the PML-N tried to downplay its role, not wishing to assist the federal government, which it opposed tooth and nail. The disconnect between them and the central government, and the gap between the civil and military authorities, added to the delay in finding a solution to the Davis problem. On the American side, the CIA and Amb. Munter had had their own tiff over drone attacks. The latter wanted veto power over drone strikes. The CIA resisted and carried the day. The CIA also had the bin Laden matter up its sleeve and was hence unwilling to cede anything to Pasha and the ISI. As soon as Kerry had left Pakistan, the CIA resumed drone strikes. It was back to business as usual. Mistrust and grudging cooperation, all for the short term. 2011 continued to unleash new horrors on the benighted US–Pakistan relationship.

---

[22] Syed Irfan Raza, 'RAW Paid Raymond Davis to Write Anti-Pakistan Book, Says Rehman Malik', *Dawn*, 7 July 2017, https://www.dawn.com/news/1343756.

[23] *Dawn*, 'Court Releases Detailed Judgment in Davis Case', Associated Press of Pakistan report in *Dawn*, Karachi, 19 March 2011, https://www.dawn.com/news/614440.

4

From Tora Bora to Pathan Gali

A major blow to the US–Pakistan relationship occurred when a heliborne force of SEAL Team Six of the US Navy invaded Pakistan on 2 May 2011 from their base in Afghanistan, killed Osama bin Laden in his secret lair in the Bilal Town neighbourhood of Abbottabad, and then took his body and whatever they could of his books, papers and computer systems back to Jalalabad. The bin Laden hideout on so-called Pathan Gali (or Pathan Street) was a short distance from the Pakistan Military Academy (PMA) in Kakul, the prestigious officer training school similar to West Point in the US and Sandhurst in the UK.

It was a long way from Tora Bora in 2001, in the Safed Koh (White Mountain) range straddling the Afghanistan and Pakistan border, the last time that reasonable intelligence had been established of bin Laden's presence in any place. Bin Laden had fled to the network of caves dug into the depths of the Tora Bora after the US invasion of Afghanistan.

Flashback: The First US 'Invasion' of Pakistan

Soon after the terrorist attacks on the US mainland in September 2001, a small team of CIA agents who linked up with local commanders, mainly from the so-called Northern Alliance of Afghanistan, spearheaded the US invasion of Afghanistan. Roughly simultaneously, the US launched a naval expeditionary force designated Task Force 58 or TF58 to provide military muscle to the CIA's smaller and more surgical operations. Under instructions from Vice Admiral Willie Moore, commander, naval forces of CENTCOM/Fifth Fleet, operating out of Bahrain, TF58 was tasked initially to conduct raids in southern Afghanistan. Later the task force was instructed to take and establish a forward operating base or FOB. This

FOB shifted 'back and forth from Camp Rhino (a 6,400-foot-long dirt strip some 400 miles inland) to Khandahar (*sic*) to Herat to Shindad, and back to Rhino'.[1]

The commander of this naval expeditionary force and TF58 was fifty-one-year-old Brig. Gen. James Mattis, a hard-as-nails and highly decorated Marine commander who first had made a name for himself as a colonel in the invasion of Kuwait during the Persian Gulf War. He was the first Marine to command a naval expeditionary force. This expeditionary force established its base in Kandahar, originally under the name of Operation Swift Freedom, but later became part of Operation Enduring Freedom, the name given by Gen. Tommy Franks, the commander-in-chief of CENTCOM, to the invasion of Taliban-controlled Afghanistan as part of the global war on terrorism. Mattis played a key role in the invasion of Afghanistan and rebuilding an abandoned US relationship with Pakistan.

> Afghanistan, a landlocked country, presented an obvious challenge to the amphibious assault forces, but Mattis brokered a secret agreement with the government (sic) of Pakistan to provide landing beaches and access to an airstrip. Task Force 58 was airlifted into Afghanistan in late November 2001 and was instrumental in the capture of Kandahār, a city regarded as the spiritual home of the Taliban.[2]

His task force established itself at FOB Rhino that he refers to as Objective Rhino with an initial force cap of 100, which changed to 1,048, then 1,100, and reached a peak of 1,400.[3] This 'invasion' was aided and abetted by the Pakistan Army and largely kept secret from even the Pakistani foreign office. An interesting backstory to the selection

---

[1]   https://www.strategypage.com/articles/tf58/planning.asp and also Goulding, Vincent, 2011, 'Task Force 58: A Higher Level of Naval Operation.' *Marine Corps Gazette* 95 (8): 38–41., https://www.mca-marines.org/gazette/2011/08/task-force-58-higher-level-naval-operation

[2]   Michael Ray, 'James Mattis', Biography, *Encyclopaedia Britannica*, https://www.britannica.com/biography/James-Mattis.

[3]   Strategy Page, 'Execution: 25 November to 25 December', Strategypage.com, https://www.strategypage.com/articles/tf58/execution.asp. This was an agreement not with the government but with the military. The Foreign Office did not appear to have been consulted nor involved in the tactical details of the cooperation with TF 58.

of this site for FOB Rhino is provided by Amb. Rick Olson, later US ambassador in Pakistan and SRAP.

I arrived in Dubai as US Consul General on 11 August 2001. Exactly one month later, my world changed, as it did for many. Having anticipated that my tour would be dominated by Iran watching, instead it turned out to be all about the War on Terror.

The UAE had been one of three countries that recognized the Taliban regime in Afghanistan (the others were Pakistan and Saudi Arabia). Throughout 2001, this had been a growing source of tension in the bilateral relationship with the US (from 1999 to 2001 I was a political-military affairs officer at Embassy Abu Dhabi, and saw this tension growing firsthand).

As it happened, the crown prince of Dubai (and already *de facto* ruler), Mohammed bin Rashid Al Maktoum had [been in] the United States on 9/11 (in Kentucky to buy horses), so had actually seen the events in New York and Washington from an American perspective. . . .

As part of my informal 'accreditation' in Dubai, it was obligatory to hold a formal meet with MbR. Ordinarily, this involved going to Zabeel Palace, but in the first and as far as I know only break with this protocol, MbR came to meet me at the American Consulate General. I interpreted this to be an act signaling conciliation, and desire for a new relationship with the US. I recall that the meeting was on 17 September 2001, although I could be off by a few days. The Chargé d'Affaires at the US Embassy joined me, because we had just received from Washington the 'You're with us or against us' demarche, and we both felt it was important to deliver this at the highest level. (Worth noting that in addition to being Crown Prince of Dubai, MbR was also UAE Defense Minister.) Although the demarche was sent out worldwide, clearly it applied most especially to three countries: Pakistan, Saudi Arabia and the UAE.

The Chargé. Gordy Olson (yes, same last name, no relation), delivered the stiff demarche, and we received assurances that the UAE and Dubai were indeed with us and supportive of the US War on Terror. Although this was about a month before we invaded Afghanistan and there was no preview in the language of the demarche, the clear implication was that the US would be taking decisive action against terrorism, and one could presume that would involve action in Afghanistan. Toward the end of the conversation MbR said that he owned a piece of land near Kandahar in southern Afghanistan that he used for hunting (presumably, hunting Houbara Bustards with Falcons). He had traveled there frequently and had built an airstrip that could accommodate a C-130 (Dubai Royal Flight had several). If the USG had any use for the strip, we should consider it ours. That is how it came to be that the Marines, under Brigadier General Mattis, landed at what became known as Camp Rhino a few weeks later.

As far as I know, this UAE contribution to the Afghan war effort has never been made public. When I was later US Ambassador to the UAE, I asked Secretary of State Clinton to thank MbR, which she did orally in her first meeting with him, but that may be the only recognition he ever received.

A final note: you will recall that in Steve Coll's masterpiece, *Ghost Wars*, there is a reference to a botched attempt by the USG to kill Osama bin Ladin with a Tomahawk attack (ca 1998-99). The attack was aborted because of the presence of some Emirati royals in Afghanistan at the time. I have always wondered if the group include MbR.[4]

Coll recalls in a message to me, the CIA as having identified the aircraft as Emirati military planes from imagery of their tail numbers. The Marines of TF58 came on ships under cover of darkness, landed at Pasni on the Mekran coast of Pakistan, established a beach-head, and then were transported to the Pasni airfield where they were kept out of sight under aircraft hangars or sheds during the daytime. At night, they were transported by road to Jacobabad, where an airfield had been handed over by Pakistan for the US's Afghanistan operations. From Jacobabad, the Marines were flown to southern Afghanistan to establish their FOB at what was later to become Camp Rhino. A senior Pakistan Army corps commander confirmed to me that a regiment of infantry had been deployed to cordon off Pasni and ensure that no one in Pakistan, except the relevant military officers dealing with Mattis, found out about the Marine 'invasion'. It appears that there was a higher-level agreement by the government (including the civilian foreign minister Abdul Sattar Khan) to cooperate with the United States and facilitate the use of Pakistan as a stopping place for US forces en route to Afghanistan. But the Pakistani Foreign Office was not involved in crafting the details of the tactical

---

[4] Email from Ambassador Rick Olson, 12 May 2019

and logistical arrangements. Those plans were principally implemented by Mattis and the DG Operations, Maj. Gen. Farooq Ahmed Khan, at the JCS headquarters, who worked with the GHQ Military Operations Directorate, the air force, and navy under the Director General Joint Staff and the Chairman Joint Chiefs of Staff Committee. Mattis was later to praise the cooperation of Gen. Khan and the Pakistani military for the success of the Afghan invasion.

According to the official history of TF58,[5]

> The establishment of Intermediate Support Bases (ISBs) in Pakistan was imperative to the success of operations in Afghanistan. Numerous sites were initially assessed for their suitability to support TF 58 operations and three sites—Pasni, Shamsi, and Jacobabad—were ultimately selected. Pakistani military support for TF 58 operations was outstanding. In terms of commitment and professionalism, Major General Farooq and his associates never let the Marines down. Coordination for the use of these sites was an ongoing process, requiring close ties with the CENTCOM liaison cell at the American Embassy in Islamabad, Pakistan. Lt. Colonel Asad 'Genghis' Khan,[6] a Marine liaison officer assigned to Brigadier General Ron Sams, USAF, with his CENTCOM liaison cell provided a critical interface between TF 58 and the Pakistani military for the use of the ISBs in Pakistan. The Pakistani Joint Headquarters Staff trusted Genghis and years of disengagement and distrust were replaced by a warm, supportive, professional and personal relationship. Pakistan's commitment to this effort consisted of over 35,000 Army troops committed to base security, activation of two Navy bases, 7,000 Air Force troops and squadrons and the deployment of frontier battalions along the Afghan–Pakistan border. The Pakistani Government's contribution to combating terrorism was visibly demonstrated throughout OEF [Operation Enduring Freedom].

---

[5] Op. cit. https://www.strategypage.com/articles/tf58/planning.asp and Goulding. See also https://www.armyupress.army.mil/Portals/7/combat-studies-institute/csi-books/the-mattis-way-of-war.pdf

[6] Reportedly a nephew of Air Marshal Asghar Khan, a legendary former Pakistan air chief.

But there were some ground rules for this cooperation.

The Pakistani government placed certain constraints on TF 58 throughout the operation, adding a level of complexity to the impending mission. These constraints reflected the Pakistani desire to conceal its support of US military operations and to control the information released to the public due to the volatile nature of its internal politics. One restriction required TF 58 to conduct all ship-to-shore and air movement into and out of Pakistan during hours of darkness. Others involved the movement and staging of equipment and personnel required to support the FOB seizure, at sites in Pasni, Shamsi, and Jacobabad.[7]

There was still a lingering lack of trust between the Pakistani military and civilians, and this affected the sustainability of the US–Pakistan relationship. It was guided by exigencies. Despite all this, the Pakistani military pulled out all stops for their US military counterparts to facilitate the invasion of Afghanistan.

As the history of TF58 states:

Pasni, located on the coast of Pakistan, provided both access from the sea and the air. Movement occurred from the Amphibious Ready Group (ARG) to a Beach Landing Site (BLS) under the cover of darkness for subsequent ground movement to Pasni airfield, approximately an hour's drive away. Upon arrival at the airfield, the Pakistanis placed restrictions on the amount of equipment allowed at Pasni at any given time and required that personnel ashore maintain a low profile during the day (initially many of them remaining confined inside hangers). Despite the restrictions, without the cooperation and willingness of the Pakistani government to open Pasni in support of TF 58 operations, the assault into Afghanistan would not have been possible.[8]

Once the US invasion of Afghanistan had gained its foothold and achieved its early objectives, Mattis wrote to Gen. Farooq Ahmad Khan to thank him.

---

[7] https://www.strategypage.com/articles/tf58/planning.asp

[8] Strategy Page, 'Planning: 6 November to 24 November 2001', https://www. strategypage.com/articles/tf58/planning.asp

We both recognize that there would have been no successful Marine operations in southern Afghanistan without your adroit orchestration of support for Task Force 58.

Committing my Naval forces into a fight over 300 miles from the seas required the assistance that you willingly and professionally provided.[9]

These sentiments were echoed by the commanding officer of the 22D Marine Expeditionary Unit K.F. McKenzie a month later. Maj. Gen. Robert J. Elder, Jr, of the Combined Air Headquarters US Air Force, also wrote to Farooq Ahmad Khan in December 2003 to acknowledge that 'Working side by side [with Pakistan] has been vital to the success of Coalition air operations in Afghanistan'. Lt. Gen. Paul T. Mikolashek, Commanding General, Coalition Forces Land Component Command, in February 2002, and Lt. Gen. David W. Barno of the Combined Forces command, Afghanistan, heading Operation Enduring Freedom, capped off the US appreciation for Pakistan's role in a letter to Farooq Ahmad Khan in 2004.[10]

Key to this close collaboration was Mattis, the commander of TF58. Mattis was never one to sit tight and stay within the lines of his original remit. After all, his chosen call sign for the Afghanistan invasion was 'Chaos!' When he heard that Al-Qaeda remnants, perhaps including bin Laden, had retreated into Tora Bora with its high peaks and deep valleys, he reverted to his study of early American history and especially the battle to capture the legendary Native American chief, Geronimo. He first told me the story of his plan to capture bin Laden in Tora Bora during one of his visits to my office at the Atlantic Council in Washington DC. At that time, he said he knew that I would not use the material without permission. Later, he confirmed it in a formal interview and allowed me to repeat his story. Characteristically, he put it succinctly: 'I had the plan, basically, to seal off—it was in one of two valleys, do that much. So, seal off the two valleys and move against them. And with the line of sight outposts, basically, he [Osama bin Laden] wouldn't have gotten away.'[11] Mattis would have encircled bin Laden in Tora Bora and then tightened the noose to capture or kill him. This had been the approach

---

[9]   Brig. Gen. Mattis letter to Maj. Gen. Farooq Ahmed of 22 February 2002.

[10]   Letters from US officers to Maj. Gen. Farooq Ahmad Khan.

[11]   Interview with Gen. Mattis, October 2016.

in the Geronimo campaign of 1886, and, as I told Mattis, similar to what the British Indian Army did in the North West Frontier warfare in India: establish line-of-sight heliograph posts on the high ground and thereby dominate the rugged terrain.

Mattis laid out the plan to his superior in Tampa on the telephone, making the case for speed and stating that he had the Marine force ready to encircle and capture or kill bin Laden. He was told to drop the idea since the CIA and Northern Alliance commanders had made local arrangements with tribal allies to stop bin Laden from escaping into the Pakistani borderlands or to kill him in the process. According to one report, Mattis yelled his disappointment at his superior and with some choice words slammed the phone down.[12]

Despite Mattis's plea to Gen. Tommy Franks at CENTCOM, and repeated urgent requests for troops from the CIA team leader Gary Bernsten to encircle and capture Bin Laden, CENTCOM did not respond. Berntsen recalls Hank Crumpton at CIA headquarters telling him, 'You need to remember that even though you work for me, any time Gen. Franks tells you he needs something or wants something done, you do it immediately and then inform me. We have to be married to CENTCOM.' Berntsen's reply was, 'We fight together or die separately.'[13] Yet, Berntsen's own request for Rangers to be dropped behind bin Laden's hideout to cut off their escape route to Pakistan was refused, and the CIA redacted the segment dealing with that request from his book.[14]

Bin Laden survived, as the hugger-mugger approach of the tribal surrogates that the CIA had hired dissolved in chaos. He melted away into the Pakistani borderland. Had Mattis's plan for Tora Bora been accepted, it is highly likely that the bin Laden story would have ended in those remote mountains, seriously damaging the future development of Al-Qaeda, as well as obviating the huge and expensive US intervention in

---

[12] Typically discreet, Mattis refused to divulge the identity of his superior or the exact language used with the officer in Tampa, citing it as a 'classified communication'. Others identified the recipient of Mattis's call as Gen. Tommy Franks.

[13] Gary Bernsten and Ralph Pezzulo, *Jawbreaker: The Attack on Bin Laden and Al Qaeda* (New York: Three Rivers Press, 2005), pp. 75, 287.

[14] Ibid. Confirmed also by Duane Evans in an interview with the author.

Afghanistan and the region. It took another ten years for bin Laden to be eliminated, and billions of dollars of expenditure on a never-ending war, with thousands of Afghan, Pakistani and American casualties.

In some ways, the debacle of Tora Bora reflected the confusion about US goals as well as the internal organizational battles that affected the progress of the war in Afghanistan.

The CIA had taken the lead with its insertion of six teams into Afghanistan, loaded with hard cash and relying on their contacts with tribal chieftains in the north, west and south. Operating under their codenames of Alpha, Bravo, Charlie, etc., they sought to energize and organize the local resistance to the Taliban while the military prepared to move larger numbers of troops into the fight.

Team Echo and then Team Foxtrot ended up in the southern part of the country, in the heavy Pakhtun belt, aiming to secure the Taliban 'capital' Kandahar. TF58, the Naval Expeditionary Force under Mattis, meanwhile, headed to Helmand and their FOB Rhino. (The joke among US Army types was that the Marines chose that site in Helmand then and later only because it was the end of the range of their heli-lift capacity.) Foxtrot team leader Gary Schroen described one conflict within the CIA. Islamabad CIA Station chief, Robert Grenier, was seen by Schroen as 'loudly beating . . . the Pakistani drum song—that focusing on the north and concentrating our military efforts against the Taliban forces there would allow the Tajik Northern Alliance to capture Kabul and sweep across the northern half of Afghanistan'.[15] This would leave the Pakhtuns fragmented and militarily weak.

Pakistan would have preferred the US bombing to hold the Taliban fighting in the north while bombing them over time, allowing the Pakhtuns to rally in the south and giving them a greater advantage in a post-Taliban Afghanistan. Then, Hank Crumpton, at CIA Headquarters, asked Schroen to invite SOCOM to send a team to assist the Panjshiris. This after Schroen states he had been begging and pleading for SOCOM to send troops! 'We had limited communications with the outside world, and only indirect contact with CENTCOM or the other military commands' involved in the invasion of Afghanistan, recalls Schroen. In his view, the

---

[15]   Gary C. Schroen, *First In: An Insider's Account of How the CIA Spearheaded the War on Terror in Afghanistan* (New York: Ballantine Books, Presidio Press, 2006), p. 146.

infighting among the Special Operations components led to delays in entering the fight. Nowhere in his account does Schroen acknowledge or explain the role of TF58 or Special Forces operations in tandem with the CIA's teams.

Even after the initial bombing had begun, Grenier in Islamabad protested the lack of progress as well as the 'political disappointment' while making the case for cooperating with the Pakistani intelligence under the new leadership after the firing of pro-Taliban Lt. Gen. Mahmud Ahmed. Indeed, Duane Evans, the eventual team leader of Team Foxtrot, recalls also that Grenier had tried to name one of his own staff to lead Team Foxtrot since that officer knew Gul Agha Sherzai, the local Pakhtun leader whom the CIA was trying to use to infiltrate and capture Kandahar.[16] Evans claims that Foxtrot entered Kandahar on 7 December 2001, the first team inside the Taliban stronghold. Within two days, Team Echo had brought Karzai into Kandahar. And then Evans recalls travelling outside the city to get Sherzai's fighters to hand over the airport to Mattis's expeditionary force.[17]

Grenier reserved his best shot for the Marines: 'Fortunately, rather than moving north to create mayhem as we had feared, the Marines had sat on their haunches at Camp Rhino and done nothing.'[18] Mattis, who is one of the best-read generals around, despite his reputation as a profane and rough Marine, had already jabbed at the dapper Grenier, who arrived at Kandahar airport in a spiffy blazer: 'You must be the best-dressed man in Kandahar.' Grenier retorted, 'Well, sir, I was planning to pay a call on the headmaster of Kandahar Prep and thought I should dress appropriately!' The Marines did not think this was the CIA's war to fight and win. The CIA did not think the military alone would account for the victory.

In all this confusion, Bin Laden escaped. The 'necessary war' became an unending one.

---

[16]   Duane Evans, *Foxtrot in Kandahar: A Memoir of a CIA Officer in Afghanistan at the Inception of America's Longest War* (El Dorado Hills, CA: Savas Beatie, 2017), pp. 71–72.

[17]   Ibid., pp. 142–43.

[18]   Robert L. Grenier, *88 Days to Kandahar—A CIA Diary* (New York: Simon and Schuster, 2015).

Picking Up bin Laden's Trail

Pakistan had earlier tried to set up a commando team with US help to track and capture bin Laden in Afghanistan. But this ISI-led team was disbanded after Musharraf took over the government of Pakistan, largely because the main architect was Lt. Gen. Ziauddin Khwaja, the ISI chief whom Nawaz Sharif had chosen to replace Musharraf as army chief. The Pakistanis also believed that the US would take unilateral actions via drones or otherwise if they found Al-Qaeda targets inside Pakistan. The attack on Damadola in FATA to get Zawahiri, the Al-Qaeda second-in-command, was one such effort. Musharraf also believed bin Laden was sick and dying.

The US set up a unit to track bin Laden, but the trail had gotten cold, as their target went off the grid by not using electronic communications and employing human cut-outs to receive and carry his messages. A small team of female analysts at the CIA carried the torch though, and devoted thousands of hours to their dogged pursuit of bin Laden. The CIA had already infiltrated many agents into the country since 2004. The third floor of the US embassy in Islamabad where the CIA agents maintained their offices was a busy place. More than trying to track their target, agents were in place to subvert the loyalties of Pakistanis in civil and military positions, or even retired officers of the military, who might have useful information that could fill in the pieces of the jigsaw puzzle of the hunt for bin Laden.

Among these was a Lt. Col. Eqbal Saeed Khan of ISI,[19] who had once been in Military Intelligence and commanded the MI's 408 Battalion in Rawalpindi. His son from his first marriage, Shaheryar (known as Sherry), was an aide-de-camp to President Musharraf and continued to work with him after Musharraf left office. Saeed himself was commissioned in the 24th War Course into the Pakistan Army and joined 44 SP (self-propelled) artillery regiment, Musharraf's regiment. He did his intelligence staff course in 1993, and his colleagues recall him being 'a bright guy and lively company'. He was well known by his nickname of Bailee, a Punjabi word equivalent to 'buddy' in English.[20] He was reportedly retired prematurely

---

[19] This was confirmed by a retired senior officer of the ISI. He spells his name as Eqbal but documents use the common spelling Iqbal.

[20] Information from a former colleague of Col. Saeed. One of Saeed's names in his later life in the US was Bailey Khan.

by the army chief for dealing in fake currency.[21] Another report has him being passed over for promotion to brigadier and then prematurely retired. There were many such disgruntled former intelligence officers. Military promotion boards were ruthless in sifting through the candidates and intelligence officers often did not stand a chance against regular army officers who had served with many army commanders who then sat on promotion boards.

Many of these retired intelligence officers became security contractors. Some took on religion and joined jihadi outfits whom they had once monitored or controlled, including Al-Qaeda and Lashkar-e-Taiba. This was also fertile recruiting territory for the CIA. Col. Saeed, who ran a security firm in Islamabad, may have been responsible for providing logistic and surveillance assistance to the Americans in tracking and locating movements related to what turned out to the final lair of bin Laden in Abbottabad. Col. Saeed's office in Abbottabad is reported to have been used as a listening and staging post. He is reported to have been recruited by Lt. Col. Hafeez, his predecessor at the helm of the 408 Intelligence Battalion, who had been hired by the US, and according to one report was even in the US team that CIA Director George Tenet brought to a meeting with Gen. Kayani.[22]

According to another senior retired ISI officer, Saeed may have been rewarded by the Americans for having kept mum about the final stages of the search for bin Laden's hideout in Abbottabad. Another retired brigadier was also prominently mentioned in assisting the search for bin Laden, but no formal inquiries in Pakistan have been shared with the public.[23] Indeed, the Abbottabad Commission that was set up by Pakistan to investigate the raid that killed bin Laden appeared to clear Col. Saeed.[24] And a very senior

---

[21] Azaz Syed, *The Secrets of Pakistan's Wars against Al Qaeda* (Narratives, Pakistan 2015), pp. 137–38. My brother General Asif Nawaz was then the army chief.

[22] Ibid., p. 138.

[23] This information was confirmed by a senior army officer and a former DG-ISI. After the Abbottabad raid, Saeed and his immediate family disappeared. He relocated to the San Diego area in California. Attempts to reach his son were unsuccessful. See also, Syed, *Secrets of Pakistan's War.*

[24] The Director General Military Operations at the time, Major General Javed Iqbal, later a three-star, was in charge of the Abbottabad Commission proceedings as a representative of GHQ Pakistan Army. In 2018, he was arrested, charged, and convicted for espionage for an unnamed country

military officer who spoke with me about a brigadier implicated in that case also indicated that they had not found much on him. The brigadier was not mentioned in the report.

Yet, Col. Saeed suddenly decamped from Pakistan immediately after the raid on Abbottabad, leaving behind an empty home in the DHA at Morgah, days before his child's high-school exams and even as his second wife was reported to be recuperating from a medical procedure.[25] The house was then disposed of by the manager of his security firm, according to a former colleague of the colonel. He is living in San Diego, California, owns a $2.4-million home under his own name and also operates under the name Bailey Khan, a Western variation of his nickname Bailee in Pakistan. In May 2018, photographs emerged of the colonel and his wife enjoying their new life. A white BMW convertible with California licence plates is visible in some of the photos of the dapper colonel.

The US had a vast array of human and technological expertise to try to track bin Laden. Among these, the National Security Agency, from its perch in Maryland outside Washington DC and networks with intelligence agencies around the globe, captured electronic communications from all over the world. The National Geospatial Intelligence Agency on its new campus[26] just off I-95, south of Washington DC, kept its eyes peeled via satellites on targets in war zones and in neighbouring countries to evaluate

---

and sentenced in a secret military court to effectively fourteen years of rigorous imprisonment; https://www.reuters.com/article/us-pakistan-military-spying/pakistani-army-general-given-life-sentence-on-spying-charges-idUSKCN1T021C. He had been very helpful to me as DGMO in understanding Pakistan's counterinsurgency campaign and later in discussing Army Chief General Kayani's paper for the tenth anniversary of 9/11 for the NATO meeting in Seville.

[25] A Pakistani journalist claims Col. Saeed's wife was recovering from plastic surgery when his family was evacuated. Incidentally, the wife of Dr Shakeel Afridi had also planned plastic surgery, according to a US source, which was the reason why he demurred when he was offered to be evacuated following the Abbottabad operation. Ironically, the marriage did not survive his tribulations. US pressure continued to press for his release, possibly in exchange for some Pakistanis held for breaking US sanctions related to weapons systems or Dr Afia Siddiqui, another Pakistani prisoner in the US.

[26] The offices and cafeteria of this agency resemble a college campus: lots of young men and women, a virtual United Nations of national origins, in constant discussion, soaking up information from visiting scholars and think-tank

developments as quickly as possible and help analysts at the CIA and other agencies triangulate information on friends and enemies alike. Bin Laden became one of the targets of the combined searches by these and other agencies of the US.

The first CIA unit tasked to track and capture bin Laden was set up in 1996 under Michael Scheuer, a bearded and intense man who named his unit Alec Station, after his son, and provided a constant stream of reports and analyses to the CIA from his operation close to CIA headquarters in Langley, VA. He left the unit and the agency in 2006 after writing a scathing bestselling book on US policy called *Imperial Hubris*[27] under the nom de plume Anonymous. His cover was soon blown and he went public with his critiques in open and private fora.[28] His website[29] began to serve as his primary launchpad for ideas that often excoriate official Washington. As a recent post explains: 'Wasted lives, limbs, and dollars are three of the main characteristics of the US government's military interventionism overseas.' Robert Grenier, who had been CIA station chief in Islamabad at the time of the invasion of Afghanistan, and later headed the Counter Terrorism Center, was seen as a proximate cause of the departure of Scheuer, as Grenier sought to reorganize the search for bin Laden within a global strategy.

While the US focused attention on bin Laden, as did the Afghan NDS, there did not appear to be a major effort on the Pakistan side with its primary focus on domestic terrorism and insurgency. An abortive attempt to create a special team of commandos to try to track and capture bin Laden created under DG-ISI Ziauddin Khwaja was disbanded soon

---

experts and assessing photographic intelligence to add value to human intelligence from sites of interest.

27 Anonymous, *Imperial Hubris: Why the West Is Losing the War on Terror*, Washington DC, Brasssey's Inc. 2004.

28 We appeared together in a number of such forums, including on a programme with Fareed Zakariya for CNN. I always found Scheuer provocative and interesting, though his strong views on Israel and radical ideas to foment a Shia–Sunni war in the Muslim world alarmed and enraged many in the US establishment. In 2014, he reportedly married a woman named Alfreda, who is often mentioned as the inspiration for the female lead of the movie *Zero Dark Thirty* on the killing of bin Laden. Alfreda is reported to have worked for Scheuer at Alec Station in the early days of that unit.

29 http://non-intervention.com/; Michael Scheuer's website operates under the motto 'Foreign Policy Independent of All, Under the Influence of None'.

after Gen. Khwaja was removed from the army by Gen. Musharraf, after Prime Minister Sharif tried to install Khwaja as Musharraf's successor as army chief in 1999. It appeared that Pakistan did not wish bin Laden to be found on its soil, and the story peddled by officialdom in Islamabad was that he was either dying or dead or had fled to some other country. The ISI's Counter Terrorism Wing made its own effort to track terrorists operating inside Pakistan and at one point is reported to have requested the CIA to provide satellite surveillance of a house in Abbottabad that had aroused their suspicion.[30]

The US search persisted and gained ground after 9/11. The US provided frequent information to Pakistan, but none of those leads produced anything tangible. A story told by President Musharraf at a dinner in suburban Maryland was one such dead-end tale. Someone had photographed a tall bin Laden–like figure sitting in an open Jeep in Chitral, often described as a likely hiding pace for bin Laden. This intelligence was shared by US officials with Musharraf who then deputed his people to track down the occupant of that Jeep. Kudos to the Pakistani intelligence team, they actually located the individual, who turned out to be Yaqoob, an Afghan from Khost, who resembled and liked to dress like Osama bin Laden. Yaqoob was found across the Afghan border in Khost and brought to meet Musharraf. He was a virtual doppelganger of the Al-Qaeda leader. The ISI released him with a sizable payment and told him to keep his mouth shut.[31]

Musharraf was clear on where things stood in the search for bin Laden.

[T]he search for Osama bin Laden has gone completely cold, with no recent intelligence indicating where he and his top lieutenants are hiding.

More than three years after al Qaeda's attacks on the World Trade Center and the Pentagon killed almost 3,000 people, Musharraf insisted that Pakistani forces are still aggressively pursuing the world's most notorious terrorist. But he acknowledged that recent security force

---

[30] Shaukat Qadir, *Operation Geronimo: The Betrayal and Execution of Osama Bin laden and Its Aftermath* (Amazon Kindle. 2012). Qadir, a retired brigadier in the Pakistan Army, was given carefully monitored access to the bin Laden hideout in Abbottabad after the raid and access to some materials by the ISI.

[31] Syed, *Secrets of Pakistan's War*, pp. 71–72.

operations and interrogations have been able to determine only one fact—that bin Laden is still alive.

'He is alive, but more than that, where he is, no, it'll be just a guess and it won't have much basis,' Musharraf said in an interview with *Washington Post* editors and reporters.[32]

Later he and others in Pakistan would opine that perhaps bin Laden was dead.

Former FBI Special Agent Brad Garrett who had been involved in tracking and capturing Aimal Kansi, the killer of CIA staff in Langley VA, had a clear notion of how to work with the Pakistanis in this quest. He suggested using Pakistani muscle but maintaining a 'unilateral American operation', and putting out a 'sizable cash reward'.[33]

Meanwhile, presidential candidate Barack Obama, a fresh senator from Illinois, delivered a well-crafted speech at the Wilson Center in Washington DC that outlined his position on the search for bin Laden and other terrorists:

> If we have actionable intelligence about high-value targets and President Musharraf won't act, we will . . . I will not hesitate to use military force to take out terrorists who pose a direct threat to America.[34]

This was more than campaign rhetoric and was later to inform his decisions once he became president. On 2 June 2009, Obama issued an order to the director of the CIA, Leon Panetta, that included the following sentence:

> In order to ensure that we have expended every effort, I direct you to provide me within 30 days a detailed operational plan for locating and bringing to justice bin Laden.[35]

---

[32] Robin Wright and Peter Baker, 'Musharraf: Bin Laden's Location Is Unknown', *Washington Post*, 5 December 2004.

[33] Peter L. Bergen, *Manhunt* (Crown Publishers, New York. 2012), p. 88.

[34] Ibid., p. 110.

[35] Ibid., p. 116.

Pakistan, a frontline state once more, in an Afghanistan war, became a huge target for the US, and every effort was made to flood agents into the country from then onward. Strengthening that view was the series of attacks or aborted attacks on US targets by persons trained in Pakistan, including an Afghan Najibullah Zazi[36] and Pakistani Faisal Shahzad.

Secretary of State Hillary Clinton had her own very clear idea of where Pakistan stood regarding the Al-Qaeda and Taliban leadership.

On a fence-mending visit to Pakistan in 2009, she

> . . . strongly suggested . . . that some Pakistani officials bore responsibility for allowing terrorists from Al Qaeda to operate from safe havens along this country's frontier.
>
> 'I find it hard to believe that nobody in your government knows where they are, and couldn't get to them if they really wanted to,' she said to a group of Pakistani journalists. 'Maybe that's the case; maybe they're not gettable. I don't know.'[37]

This new focus on the search for bin Laden and other terrorist leaders led to the rejuvenation of the JSOC under Gen. Stanley McChrystal. JSOC had grown to 4,000 personnel after 9/11, with its own drones and intelligence operations. McChrystal's intelligence specialist in the early days was a Col. Michael Flynn,[38] whom he sent to Iraq to learn the ropes of battlefield intelligence operations. Later, McChrystal would take him to Afghanistan. McChrystal created a virtual network of expertise via video conferencing to capture analyses and data speedily

---

[36] Zazi's indictment contained a prominent quotation from my report for CSIS, 'FATA: A Most Dangerous Place', to establish the role of that border region as a training ground for terrorists.

[37] Mark Landler, 'Clinton Challenges Pakistanis on Al Qaeda', *New York Times*, 29 October 2009, http://www.nytimes.com/2009/10/30/world/asia/30clinton. html?mcubz=3

[38] Flynn later gained notoriety as a short-lived NSA for President Donald J. Trump, having severed ties to McChrystal in the meantime.

across the globe. And he personally sat in on many intercontinental video conferences.[39]

When McChrystal moved on to command troops in Afghanistan, he was succeeded by Vice Admiral William McRaven, a veteran of the JSOC wars inside Iraq, where, among other things, he had led Task Force 121 that hunted down and captured Saddam Hussein in 2003. By 2009, McRaven had been shifted from Iraq to Afghanistan by Gen. David Petraeus, then commander in Afghanistan. In the process, he increased Special Operations missions in Afghanistan from 200 a year in 2008 to well over 2,000 a year by 2010.[40]

Behind the scenes, a small group of female CIA analysts laid the ground for the tracking of bin Laden. The basis of their work was a paper entitled 'Inroads' that listed four pillars for the search: first, locating the courier network that bin Laden used to communicate with his organization; second, contacts with his family members; third, communications with senior Al-Qaeda persons; and fourth, outreach to the media.[41] This grid served as a guide for their persistent work, and all incoming intelligence fell into their framework. Pakistani information became an unwitting element of this search process.

According to an interview given by former DG-ISI Ahmed Shuja Pasha to Pakistani journalist Azaz Syed:

> Months before the [Abbottabad] operation, the Americans would routinely request the data of surveillance of different mobile phone numbers from the ISI. Two of these numbers were of the Kuwaiti brothers [the Pakistanis who had lived in Kuwait and who were hiding bin Laden] . . . About 18 people were tasked to tap and monitor the special telephone numbers . . . The ISI routinely shared Americans (*sic*) the data they requested. Little did the ISI know that the shared data would lead to the most-wanted man of the world. Pasha spoke very little

---

[39] McChrystal was often seen in the Kabul headquarters as he connected with the Friday Afghanistan Theatre Video Teleconferences at the Pentagon. I recall him asking me questions when I was invited to present at that forum.

[40] Bergen, *Manhunt*, p. 165.

[41] Ibid., p. 90.

about this topic, saying 'most of the times (*sic*) these [phone] numbers were silent'.[42]

The Americans were triangulating information from their interrogations of Al-Qaeda leaders, often captured with Pakistani help inside Pakistan, with electronic intercepts by their own array of eavesdropping technologies and systems and the ISI's local interception of targeted and suspected Al-Qaeda cell phones. The CT cooperation between the Americans and their Pakistani counterparts continued to be a key element in this search, even if the Pakistanis did not benefit from feedback from their American partners.

The US focus began to sharpen on the cut-outs used as couriers between Al-Qaeda leadership. Numerous references to a courier named Al Kuwaiti sparked their interest in the brothers who had once lived in that Gulf kingdom and also worked for bin Laden. ISI intercepts importantly helped prepare that case. The brothers identified by the CIA as Abu Ahmed Al-Kuwaiti and Tariq (real name: Abrar) became the focus of the CIA's attention as the conduits for bin Laden's communications with his far-flung network. Abu Ahmed was in fact Arshad, a Pakistani born in a village near Kohat, Pakistan. He had been the contact for Abu Faraj Al Libi also, especially in the period when bin Laden was moving between different hideouts inside Pakistan proper.[43]

In fact, bin Laden had moved into a safe house in Shangla in Swat and then into a home in Haripur, not far up the road from Abbottabad, reportedly also near a sensitive Pakistani security site (most likely a nuclear weapons storage location).

Interestingly, Amrullah Saleh, the head of the Afghan security service NDS, is reported to have sent a warning to Pakistan that bin Laden was hiding in that general area, near Mansehra, a short distance from Abbottabad. Pakistan maintained it could not confirm that intelligence. Eventually, a decision was made by Al-Qaeda to have Arshad purchase different tracts of land in the Bilal Town area near Abbottabad and combine them into a single plot. Bin Laden drew a sketch of the outline of the house within a house that would shelter him and his family, as well as the Pakistani brothers who were his keepers and couriers. The site was considered safe since it was far from the battlefront. Also, it turns out the

---

[42] Syed, *Secrets of Pakistan's War*, p. 114.

[43] Qadir, *Operation Geronimo*, p. 9.

ISI did not have a permanent presence there till after Al Libi was tracked to that town in the Nawan Shehr neighbourhood, not far from Bilal Town. The ISI team later grew in size. In February 2011, a terrorist Umer Patek, alias Jaffer Alawi, a.k.a. Hisyamein Alazein (of Kuwaiti origin), implicated in the Bali bombing, was captured near Abbottabad. But even this did not raise the alarm at ISI headquarters about a more important Al-Qaeda presence in the area.

In addition to the ISI presence, there is also an MI detachment in Abbottabad. After the raid, it emerged that some questions about the origins and background of these brothers had been raised by ISI investigators who were trying to verify their antecedents and contacts in Mardan (where they had a home at one time), Charsadda and Peshawar, but these got lost in the maw of the Pakistani bureaucracy. The ISI was tracking Arshad's movements though, and established that he travelled once a month to Peshawar and bought medicines. It was during this period of inquiry that the ISI requested satellite surveillance by the CIA of the house on 'Pathan Street' in Bilal Town.[44]

The Americans had meanwhile zeroed in on the house with the unusual architecture. It had a wall within the outside wall and windows that looked away from habitations in the neighbourhood. Using their extensive network of local agents, they began surveillance of the house, supplemented by aerial surveillance. A separate local operation was launched to use a Pakistani doctor, Shakeel Afridi, and his team to try to get DNA evidence from the inhabitants of the mysterious house on Pathan Gali under the guise of a health campaign that was wrongly attributed later to an anti-polio campaign. It is not clear if he succeeded. The betting began in Washington on who lived there and on the chances that this was bin Laden. McRaven's team was brought into the picture and saw it as a routine operation, except that it involved penetrating deep into a non-NATO ally's country and exiting safely after completing the search-and-destroy mission.

This was a serious concern if the Pakistanis were to engage with the US force during or after the raid was over and tried to arrest them. According to a member of the SEAL Team Six, 'When President Obama was presented with that possibility, he nodded his head and said, "That's interesting." Then he looked at the Air Force Chief of Staff and said, "What do you

---

[44] Qadir, *Operation Geronimo*, p. 13.

need to rain hell on Pakistan—because my guys aren't surrendering to anybody."[45] If true, that was the clearest signal about Obama's intentions regarding Pakistan when it came to capturing or killing bin Laden. Separately, according to a senior US official, Obama had told his senior colleagues that he would not fight Pakistan over the Taliban. He stuck to that despite being under US military pressure.'[46]

The story of the raid has by now become part of popular lore. Fact and fiction have intermingled. Some by accident. Some by design, to create misinformation and to protect the innocent and the not so innocent. A Hollywood movie that conflated various events unconnected with the raid (including an attack on the movie heroine analyst as she drove from her home on to the street in Pakistan)[47] also served to further obfuscate reality.

In short, the US story was that the raid began in Jalalabad, Afghanistan, using stealth helicopters. An intermediate drop site in Kala Dhaka was used as a staging post for reserve helicopters. A senior Pakistan Air Force officer confirmed that to me. Two helicopters, Dash 1 and Dash 2, were to get to Abbottabad in the middle of the night around midnight. One was supposed to drop some members of SEAL Team Six outside the house to guard the

---

[45] Robert O'Neill, *The Operator: Firing the Shots That Killed Osama Bin Laden* (Scribner, New York. 2017), p. 290. This book was cleared by the CIA but it does not certify all the details as accurate in such clearances.

[46] Senior Obama administration official to author.

[47] Many years earlier, on 26 August 2008, the US principal officer in Peshawar, Lynne Tracy, had been targeted by gunmen as she drove out of her home. She managed to escape the attack and backed into her garage, unhurt. Tracy was a devoted diplomat who had chosen to extend her assignment in Peshawar, starting in 2006, beyond the normal one-year posting, and had established very powerful relationships with Pakistani society figures in Peshawar. She regularly wore local clothes (salwar-kameez and dupatta). I interviewed her for my report on COIN efforts of Pakistan in the border region. Later, she became a senior official at the NSC in the White House and then Deputy Chief of Mission in Moscow. *See*: Farhan Bokhari, 'U.S. Diplomat Safe after Pakistan Attack', CBSNews.com, 26 August 2008, https://www.cbsnews.com/news/us-diplomat-safe-after-pakistan-attack/; Tracy was given the Secretary's Award for Heroism in 2009. See: U.S. Department of State, 'Present Secretary's Award for Heroism to Lynne Tracy', 7 December 2009, https://2009-2017.state.gov/secretary/20092013clinton/rm/2009a/12/133238.htm

perimeter and the rest on to the roof. The perimeter team included Robert O'Neill, two snipers, a machine gun operator, a dog handler, and Cairo, the Belgian Malinois dog,[48] plus an interpreter. The other chopper was supposed to land in the courtyard and its team was to force its way into the compound. The aim was to kill bin Laden and take his body back to Afghanistan. In the event, one of the stealth helicopters crashed while landing, though without any injuries to the SEAL team members. Team members rappelled into the courtyard of the house from the other.

Despite losing one helicopter in the ingress operation, the SEAL team managed to achieve its objective without any casualties. Bin Laden was shot and killed. His wife was injured and left for dead. Bin Laden was photographed, identified, and a message sent to superiors in Afghanistan and those huddled in a small room at the White House:

Geronimo EKIA!
(Geronimo being the code name for bin Laden's capture or killing, and EKIA being the initials for Enemy Killed in Action.)

Mission accomplished, the helicopters headed back to Afghanistan, where bin Laden was properly identified and then a decision was made to transport his body to a US aircraft carrier that then buried him at sea.

O'Neill, who claimed to have fired the shots that killed bin Laden, saw the CIA female analyst who had briefed them on bin Laden and took her over with his point man to see bin Laden's body. 'As I watched her look him over, I was just thinking, *This is historic. Here's her life's work. She just found the most wanted man in history. There he is. It's all her doing. What's she going to say?* Stone-cold, stone-faced, she said, "Uh, I guess I'm out of a fucking job." And then she walked away.'[49] That is what happened in real life. In the movie *Zero Dark Thirty*, the analyst walks away quietly and tears up only when she boards a C-130. Reality was far more dramatic.

---

[48] Cairo had been severely wounded in an operation in Afghanistan when he was shot by a Taliban fighter he had chased up a tree. Somehow he managed to survive and make it into the history books during the Abbottabad raid. See: O'Neill, *The Operator*, pp. 261–62.

[49] O'Neill, *The Operator*, p. 317.

The Plot Thickens

As is usual in such cases, involving intelligence agencies and secretive governments, the story of the Abbottabad raid became complicated and messy once the operation was completed. Questions arose regarding possible Pakistani collusion with American forces as well as the timeline of events of that fateful night of the attack. When did Pakistan Army leadership find out about the raid? How did they react?[50]

Wider issues arose: How could the American forces penetrate deep into Pakistani territory without being detected? Who was to be held responsible for such dereliction of duty to protect the borders of Pakistan? Given the seemingly perpetual chasm between the civil and military inside Pakistan, could the raid be used to assert civilian supremacy over the military?

The American narrative was that Pakistan was unaware of the raid because the Pakistanis could not be trusted. In Pakistan, the Land of Conspiracies, this was seen as a smokescreen to help protect Pakistani collaboration. Providing fuel for such thinking were articles in the US and UK media indicating that US helicopters had used the Special Services Group training base near Tarbela as the final jumping-off point for the raid on Abbottabad.

'From Ghazi Air Base in Pakistan, the modified MH-60 helicopters made their way to the garrison suburb of Abbottabad, about 30 miles from the center of Islamabad,' wrote Marc Ambinder for the *Atlantic* on 2 May 2011. He halved the distance to Islamabad, unless it was a calculation of the direct map distance as the crow flies. But clearly, he had been privy to some inside information, adding,

> In an interview at CIA headquarters two weeks ago, a senior intelligence official said the two proud groups of American secret warriors had been 'deconflicted and basically integrated'—finally—10 years after 9/11. Indeed, according to accounts given to journalists by five senior administration officials Sunday night, the CIA gathered the intelligence that led to bin Laden's location. A memo from CIA Director Leon Panetta sent Sunday night provides some hints of how the information was collected and analysed. In it, he thanked the National Security Agency and the National Geospatial Intelligence Agency for their help. NSA

---

50   Marc Ambinder, 'The Secret Team That Killed Osama bin Laden', *Atlantic*, 2 May 2011, https://www.theatlantic.com/international/archive/2011/05/the-secret-team-that-killed-osama-bin-laden/238163/

figured out, somehow, that there was no telephone or Internet service in the compound. How it did this without Pakistan's knowledge is a secret. The NGIA makes the military's maps but also develops their pattern recognition software—no doubt used to help establish, by February of this year, that the CIA could say with 'high probability that bin Laden and his family were living there'.

Ambinder also recalled in a separate conversation with me[51] that he was suddenly being approached by officials offering to connect him to intelligence analysts who could provide background information on the raid. Hollywood also was being fast-tracked. A movie under way called *Tora Bora*, by Mark Boal and Kathryn Bigelow, was suddenly shelved in favour of a new film entitled *Zero Dark Thirty*. The producers were given access to CIA headquarters and also a walking tour of the NCTC so they could get a sense of the surroundings in which US intelligence experts work. They even ended up being invited to the tent on the CIA grounds where Director Panetta lauded the work of his Agency in the raid on Abbottabad, though it was unclear, according to the CIA Inspector General's (IG) report, who had invited them and whether the event was 'classified' or not.[52]

In any case, the end result of the movie of the raid was a mish-mash of reality and fiction, patching together different pieces from different sources and time periods. Either wittingly or unwittingly, Hollywood ended up creating a new reality of how the raid was conducted and how it eluded Pakistani defences and detection.

I asked Gen. Kayani if he knew that bin Laden was hiding in Abbottabad. His response was direct and crisp: 'Did we know? Of course we did not know. Even the Americans did not know, when they came. It was a shot in the dark. All phone conversations were captured by the

---

51   Telephone conversation with Marc Ambinder, 28 February 2018.

52   An interesting footnote related to the gifts that Bigelow passed on to her CIA contact, a woman who was given a 'pair of Black Tahiti Pearl earrings' that were handed over by the CIA officer. On examination by an expert it turned out they were not real pearls but painted objects and the metal was not precious. They were not even worth a formal appraisal, being valued at $60 or $70. Other 'gifts' included dinners and a bottle of Tequila. *See*: https://www.scribd.com/book/279621337/CIA-ZDT-wm

United States. They came to the conclusion that we did not know.'[53] The Pakistani military did establish afterwards the fact that bin Laden's family was there, based on DNA testing and the body of bin Laden's son.

The American story of trailing the bin Laden courier 'was not disinformation' according to Kayani. But he stated unequivocally that there was 'no walk-in'. Admitting this would have indicated a chink in his armour. But how then to explain the defection of Col. Eqbal? He maintained that there had been intelligence-sharing with the Americans. The ISI gave a lead for the courier. The US developed the lead but 'they kept us in the dark'. Referring to a retired officer as an 'old timer who lived in Islamabad', and who reportedly walked into the US embassy, Kayani said this man had never seen Osama bin Laden. It is not clear how that was established. But Islamabad is rife even today with detailed stories about the walk-in episode.

Kayani regretted that the American raid 'created a bad environment'. He told Admiral Mullen, when the latter called him to inform him of the US action: 'If you had shared with us, we would have done it as a daylight two-hour operation. You could have monitored it "live".' Even if this meant 'incurring the wrath of Al-Qaeda. You should have trusted me.' Kayani maintains that the raid 'ruined the US–Pakistan relationship'. It also ruined his personal relationship with Mullen, who went on the war path against the ISI and Pakistan to denounce the ISI and pronounce the Haqqani Group as a 'veritable arm of the ISI'. A lesser-known coda to this incident was a private meeting that the two had, at Mullen's instigation, in Spain, prior to Mullen's testimony against the ISI on Capitol Hill. Each of them continues to hold the other in high regard.

Timeline of Events of that Fateful Night

The gossip mill in Islamabad churned out various timelines for what happened in Abbottabad that night, and who knew what at what time. Adding to the churning was an attempt by the DG-ISI, Lt. Gen. Pasha, to privately brief selected journalists. In his telling, he was the one who first called Kayani.

---

[53] Interview with General Ashfaq Parvez Kayani at his home in Rawalpindi, 26 February 2016.

Kayani recollects that he heard first from the Military Operations Directorate at General Headquarters. The DGMO called to report that a 'ball of fire' had erupted in Abbottabad following a helicopter crash. 'I asked him: what type of helicopter?' Kayani suggested that the DGMO check with the DG Aviation at Dhamial, near Rawalpindi, about any night flights. He got a rapid reply: 'None of ours.' Kayani suspected that it could have been 'a sneak raid on an SPD [Strategic Plans Division, Pakistan's nuclear weapons agency] facility nearby'. He immediately made a call to the air chief ACM Rao Suleiman Qamar (noting that the chairman of the JCS was absent). 'I gave him an executive order within five minutes of the DGMO's call. Scramble F-16s and anything that is coming in or out, shoot them down!' Soon after, Sargodha airbase scrambled F-16s. Then Kayani says he called SPD. He recalls speaking to Pasha later. 'He informed me about Osama being there.' It is unclear how Pasha came to that conclusion. The F-16s missed the exiting American helicopters, probably because of the delay in the Pakistani reaction and because they may have been directed to the nuclear facility rather than Abbottabad itself. At that point, the Pakistani forces did not know for sure if the ingress had come from Afghanistan or India.

At 3.30 a.m., Kayani was informed that a secure line had been set up by the US embassy so he could speak with Admiral Mullen. 'Mullen was the first to confirm the capture and killing of Osama bin Laden. He told me he was speaking from the White House and that the intention was to announce the news after twenty-four hours. I told him, "We know it. His family is there. Why wait for twenty-four hours?" He took my recommendation.'

At least one American report of this conversation raises the possibility of Pakistani foreknowledge of bin Laden's hiding place. Mike Morell, the deputy director of the CIA, confirms that there 'was discussion of possibly waiting till the next day, when we would have preliminary DNA analysis, or even the day after, when the final DNA analysis would be completed'. But 'that all changed when Admiral Mike Mullen, the chairman of the Joint Chiefs, called his counterpart [*sic*] in Pakistan, Gen. Ashfaq Kayani. *Before Mullen could say anything, Kayani told Mullen that we had gotten Bin Laden. With this, and with the certainty that the news would start getting out, the president felt it safe to make his announcement to the world* [emphasis added].'[54]

---

[54] Mike Morell and Bill Harlow, *The Great War of Our Time* (New York, Boston: Twelve, 2015), p. 169. After President Obama spoke, Morell gave a press backgrounder on the intelligence that led to the conclusion that bin

However, Kayani by that time had received reports from Abbottabad about the attack and the people who were killed or wounded in the target house. So, he could have surmised that bin Laden was the intended target.

A slightly different timeline emerged later when select Pakistani journalists were briefed by Pasha, among others, on the raid. Najam Sethi of the *Friday Times* reported:

> Shortly after reports of a helicopter mishap in Abbotabad hit the media around 1.20 a.m., not so far away in Rawalpindi, the DG-ISI was woken up by a phone call about a crashed helicopter. He called his people to ask: 'Is it ours?' After a brief check, he was told, 'No sir, it's not ours.' He called up DG-MO. 'Is it yours?' After a brief check he was told, 'No sir, it's not ours.' He called up his boys and told them to rush to the scene of the incident. He also called up the COAS Gen. Kayani to brief him. [Note that Kayani states he first heard from the DGMO.] The COAS called up the top military man in Abbotabad who ordered forces to rush to the area. The COAS also called up the PAF Air Chief. The Air Chief checked, explained that radar hadn't picked up any intruders, and ordered two F-16s to scramble. When the ISI team arrived at the compound, they reported the burning wreckage of the chopper and the markings on its fin. They reported three dead men and one woman. They reported a wounded woman who spoke Arabic and halting English, and two other women who were unharmed. They noted there were sixteen children aged six to eight years approximately. The woman said she was OBL's wife, along with two other women, and confirmed that OBL and his family had been living in the compound for six years. She said the Americans had attacked them, killed OBL and taken his corpse. Soon thereafter, the army arrived to seal off the area and whisk away the occupants and dead bodies in the compound.
>
> Around 3 a.m., Admiral Mullen called General Kayani, and CIA Chief, Leon Panetta, called DG-ISI, General Pasha. They explained the nature of the operation and why it had been kept a secret from them. President Obama called President Zardari at 7 a.m. to acquaint him with

---

Laden was in Abbottabad. Mike Vickers of the DoD briefed the journalists on the raid itself. This may have been the briefing that Marc Ambinder cited in his article on the raid for *The Atlantic*.

the facts. They thanked the Pakistanis for providing the initial clues that led the CIA to the compound.[55]

Those clues were the transcripts of wiretaps of conversations in Arabic between someone in Nowshera and later Peshawar, Waziristan, and finally the bin Laden Compound in Abbottabad and someone in Saudi Arabia that the ISI shared with the CIA in 2009 and 2010. The information and location data in those wiretaps allowed the CIA to hone in on the compound and find bin Laden.

Kayani was 'bitter' against both Mullen and the NSA, Jim Jones. He recalled how, after the attempted bombing of Times Square by Faisal Shahzad, he had written a note to them warning against any strikes inside Pakistan. He said he signed the note so that it would be shown to President Obama. There was bitterness on both sides.

One of the first senior Americans to sense the Pakistani anger at the invasion and raid of Abbottabad was SRAP Marc Grossman. Pakistan had been his first foreign service posting in 1977–79 and retained a special place in his heart. He was in Kabul the night before the raid, getting ready to head to Islamabad for a core group meeting with his Pakistani counterparts, when he heard from William Burns in Washington: 'Stay where you are. Don't go to Pakistan!' His US Air Force aircraft was parked overnight in Manas Transit Centre near Bishkek in Kyrgyzstan for security reasons. After about an hour, Burns called Grossman back: 'We've changed our minds. Someone has to go right now to Pakistan and explain, and in public!' Grossman had to alert the aircraft crew to get ready for a flight to Kabul en route for Pakistan. An hour later, Burns called again to ask, 'How come you are not there yet?' Grossman recalled with a smile that Washington thought 'it was an Eastern [Airlines] Shuttle that we were going to catch: Washington, Boston, Washington.' But he managed to fly to Islamabad in the morning.

There he saw the first Pakistani reaction, from the senior leadership and the Foreign Office. He recalled saying to himself, 'This is fantastic!' Everybody seemed to welcome the killing of bin Laden. Congratulations were being showered on the Americans for this action. 'And then boom! It wasn't twenty-four hours before they decided they wanted to be the victims of this and not stick with their first statement.' Grossman was not clear

---

55 Najam Sethi, 'Operation Get OBL', *Friday Times*, 6–12 May 2011.

who on the Pakistani side drafted and who approved the first statement. Minister of State for Foreign Affairs Hina Rabbani Khar told me that the first statement had been drafted jointly by Foreign Secretary Salman Bashir and DG-ISI Pasha. It was released to the public by the Foreign Office spokesperson Tehmina Janjua.[56]

The text of that first statement is worth reading carefully. It does not object to the raid. Nor does it claim Pakistani collaboration in the raid, though it gingerly hints at 'extremely effective intelligence sharing arrangements' with other agencies '. . . including that of the US'. It appears to condone the US action and celebrates the raid as 'a major setback to terrorist organizations around the world'.[57]

Ambassador Cameron Munter, who had landed in the country in 2010 and had had to deal with a number of prickly situations from the outset, including the capture of Taliban leader Mullah Baradar and then the Raymond Davis fiasco, also recalled that in the core group meetings with Kayani and Pasha almost the first words out of their mouths on the raid were 'Congratulations!' He then noted, 'If they were trying to be deceptive, they were wonderful actors!' His conclusion was that they were genuinely

---

[56]   Interview with Hina Rabbani Khar, 21 February 2016.

[57]   *PR. NO.150/2011*
       Date: 02/05/2011
       Death of Osama bin Laden
       In an intelligence driven operation, Osama Bin Ladin was killed in the surroundings of Abbottabad in the early hours of this morning. This operation was conducted by the US forces in accordance with declared US policy that Osama bin Laden will be eliminated in a direct action by the US forces, wherever found in the world.
           Earlier today, President Obama telephoned President Zardari on the successful US operation which resulted in killing of Osama bin Ladin . . .
           Pakistan has played a significant role in efforts to eliminate terrorism. We have had extremely effective intelligence sharing arrangements with several intelligence agencies including that of the US. We will continue to support international efforts against terrorism.
           It is Pakistan's stated policy that it will not allow its soil to be used in terrorist attacks against any country. Pakistan's political leadership, parliament, state institutions and the whole nation are fully united in their resolve to eliminate terrorism.
       Islamabad 02 May 2011

surprised by the discovery of bin Laden in Abbottabad. According to him, 'Kayani was very concerned about reactions from the army.'[58]

Grossman met with the core group and then remembers being put before 'a very large and hostile group of press, with people jumping up'. The main thrust of the local media was denial of the raid as reality. 'It's not true. This is like the moon landing. You did this. Disney did this. It was done in a studio. You have him. He is alive. You are going to use him against us some day.' The normally soft-spoken Grossman leaned forward, grabbed the podium and said crisply: 'Listen to me. He's dead. We did it. That's good. Next question.'[59]

Meanwhile, the Pakistanis had released a longer statement on the raid that hinted at their role in the search for bin Laden, and distanced themselves from assisting the raid itself. Unwittingly, the statement also acknowledged Pakistan's clear inability to protect its borders and civilian installations as opposed to military and security installations. In words that reflected the legalese of diplomacy, the statement stipulated that the raid could not serve as a precedent for other similar actions. 'The Government of Pakistan further affirms that such an event shall not serve as a future precedent for any state, including the US. Such actions undermine cooperation and may also sometime constitute threat to international peace and security.'

PR. NO.152/2011
Date: 03/05/2011
Death of Osama bin Ladin—Respect for Pakistan's Established Policy Parameters on Counter Terrorism

The Government of Pakistan recognizes that the death of Osama bin Ladin is an important milestone in fight against terrorism and that the Government of Pakistan and its state institutions have been making serious efforts to bring him to justice.

However, the Government of Pakistan categorically denies the media reports suggesting that its leadership, civil as well as military, had any prior knowledge of the US operation against Osama bin Ladin carried out in the early hours of 2nd May 2011.

---

[58] Skype interview with Ambassador Cameron Munter, 15 July 2016.
[59] Interview with Ambassador Marc Grossman, 16 November 2016.

Abbottabad and the surrounding areas have been under sharp focus of intelligence agencies since 2003 resulting in highly technical operation by ISI which led to the arrest of high value Al Qaeda target in 2004. As far as the target compound is concerned, ISI had been sharing information with CIA and other friendly intelligence agencies since 2009. The intelligence flow indicating some foreigners in the surroundings of Abbottabad, continued till mid April 2011. It is important to highlight that taking advantage of much superior technological assets, CIA exploited the intelligence leads given by us to identify and reach Osama bin Ladin, a fact also acknowledged by the US President and Secretary of State, in their statements. It is also important to mention that CIA and some other friendly intelligence agencies have benefitted a great deal from the intelligence provided by ISI. ISI's own achievements against Al Qaeda and in War on Terror are more than any other intelligence agency in the World.

Reports about US helicopters taking off from Ghazi Airbase are absolutely false and incorrect. Neither any base or facility inside Pakistan was used by the US Forces, nor Pakistan Army provided any operational or logistic assistance to these operations conducted by the US Forces. US helicopters entered Pakistani airspace making use of blind spots in the radar coverage due to hilly terrain. US helicopters' undetected flight into Pakistan was also facilitated by the mountainous terrain, efficacious use of latest technology and 'nap of the earth' flying techniques. It may not be realistic to draw an analogy between this undefended civilian area and some military / security installations which have elaborate local defence arrangements.

On receipt of information regarding the incident, PAF scrambled its jets within minutes. This has been corroborated by the White House Advisor Mr John Brennan who while replying to a question said, 'We didn't contact the Pakistanis until after all of our people, all of our aircraft were out of Pakistani airspace. At the time, the Pakistanis were reacting to an incident that they knew was taking place in Abbottabad. Therefore, they were scrambling some of their assets. Clearly, we were concerned that if the Pakistanis decided to scramble jets or whatever else, they didn't know who were on those jets. They had no idea about who might have been on there, whether it be US or somebody else. So, we were watching and making sure that our people and our aircraft were able to get out of Pakistani airspace. And thankfully, there was no engagement with Pakistani forces. This operation was designed to minimize the prospects, the chances of engagement with Pakistani forces. It was done very well, and thankfully no Pakistani forces were engaged and there were no other individuals who were killed aside from those on the compound.'

. . . Notwithstanding the above, the Government of Pakistan expresses its deep concerns and reservations on the manner in which the Government of the United States carried out this operation without prior information or authorization from the Government of Pakistan.

This event of unauthorized unilateral action cannot be taken as a rule. The Government of Pakistan further affirms that such an event shall not serve as a future precedent for any state, including the US. Such actions undermine cooperation and may also sometime constitute threat to international peace and security . . .

Islamabad 03 May 2011[60]

Pakistan had a deep-rooted fear that the bin Laden raid might not only set an unwelcome precedent for future raids against Pakistan's nuclear assets and facilities, but also give India ideas for similar pre-emptive or punitive raids. Especially once India had the advanced technologies and aircraft that allowed the US raiders to evade and elude detection or interception by Pakistan's relatively less advanced air force and air defences.

Freefalling Relationship

US–Pakistan relations then went into freefall, but both sides wanted the dialogue that had begun in earnest the previous year to continue. When President Obama had decided to send his SRAP, Marc Grossman, to Pakistan to mend the fraying ties, the CIA's deputy director, Mike Morell, was with him. In a one-on-one meeting at DG-ISI Pasha's home in Chaklala, Morell got an earful from his intelligence counterpart. 'Pasha explained to me that the United States and particularly CIA had deeply embarrassed Pakistan. I clearly understood this. He explained that the embarrassment was twofold: one, embarrassment for his service because it had not found bin Laden, and two, embarrassment for the Pakistani military because it could do nothing to stop such a raid deep in its country.' Morell reminded Pasha of the location of the hideout, near Pakistan's

[60] 'Pakistani Foreign Office Issues Longer Statement after bin Laden Raid', *Newsline*, 3 May 2011, http://newslinemagazine.com/pakistani-foreign-office-issues-longer-statement-after-bin-laden-raid/

military academy, and of President Obama's public statement that 'if we found Bin Laden we could come and get him'. Yet Morell assured Pasha that 'while I knew that neither he nor the most senior officials in Pakistan had been aware of his presence in Abbottabad, it was impossible at some level to dismiss the notion that some Pakistani security officials at some level might have been aware of his presence'. Despite this contretemps, the discussion turned towards the future, and Pasha himself drove Morell to meet Kayani at the latter's home to continue that discussion.[61]

Inside Pakistan, the initial anger was against the military for having failed to protect Pakistan's borders. Kayani, concerned about the rank-and-file reaction, undertook a series of five Town Hall–style meetings around the country. A senior commander, who was there, remembers at a training school in Nowshera a young officer standing up and declaring that he was ashamed that day to be wearing the army uniform, as a reaction to the failure to intercept the American raid. Kayani reportedly went silent for a moment and then whispered that he shared that sentiment.[62]

A closed-door session of parliament was called that was to be briefed by the DG-ISI, the DGMO and the Deputy Chief of Air Staff Operations, though Minister of State Khar recalls that only Pasha spoke. Kayani sat in the visitors' gallery, as parliamentarians initially demanded answers. Pasha informed them that there had been no complicity in the attack but that there had been failure to detect the raid. This 'incompetence defence' became the accepted narrative to justify Pakistan's inaction. Pasha also informed the parliament that he had offered his resignation to the army chief and the prime minister. This gave an edge to some hostile members of the assembly. But it

---

[61] Op. cit. Morell, pp. 172–73. Morell's security detail was caught unawares of this move. They had to scramble in the dark streets of Rawalpindi to chase the car being driven by Pasha to the gates of the Army House, where the security detail leader had to talk his way into the compound to ensure that his ward, Mike Morell, was safe.

[62] Private communication from a now retired senior Pakistani general. Pasha, who had earlier spoken with me on a number of issues, recently did not respond to written requests for information and avoided a promised face-to-face interview. He did deny forcefully having given any interview about bin Laden to two British co-authors, Cathy Scott-Clark and Adrian Levy, for a book entitled *The Exile* (Bloomsbury, 2017).

prompted others to come to the aid of the military. Khar thought this may have been a planned action. Whether this was an orchestrated move or not, the debate turned then from an indictment of the guardians of the frontiers to the cursing of Pakistan's American 'friends' who had infringed Pakistan's sovereignty. This became the narrative of the day. No one asked for or got the resignations of Pasha or Kayani, or anyone in the civilian hierarchy. Instead, the parliament called for a commission to investigate the Abbottabad incident and report back.

Clearly, Pakistan continued to shield the reality of its CT operations from scrutiny by the people and their elected representatives. Though it helped capture Al-Qaeda operatives, based on US intelligence, there were few, if any, verifiable actions taken to track down and capture or kill Al-Qaeda leaders and Afghan Taliban leaders inside Pakistan.

Abbottabad Commission

The Abbottabad Commission was announced in June 2011 and its president was Justice Javed Iqbal. Members included Abbas Mohammed Khan, a retired IG Police, Ambassador Ashraf Jehangir Qazi, then DG, Institute of Strategic Studies, Lt. Gen. Nadeem Ahmed (retd) and Cabinet Secretary Nargis Sethi.

Key elements of the remit of the commission were:

*   Determine the nature, background and causes of lapses of concerned authorities, if any, and
*   Make consequential (*sic*) recommendations.[63]

As a result, Pakistan went through yet another frustrating exercise in getting to the truth, following a national disaster. Over a period of nearly one year—from 11 July 2011 to 25 May 2012—the Abbottabad Commission 'held 52 closed door hearings, conducted 7 field visits, examined 201 witnesses, and held numerous brainstorming sessions among its members'. It also

---

[63] Leaked early draft of the Abbottabad Commission Report, reportedly authored by Amb. Ashraf Jehangir Qazi, published by *Al Jazeera* on its website: *Al Jazeera*, "'Document:' Pakistan's Bin Laden Dossier', 8 July 2013, http://www.aljazeera. com/indepth/spotlight/binladenfiles/2013/07/201378143927822246.html; While the recommendations were the result of the proceedings, they failed to be of 'consequence' in the larger order of things in Pakistan's politics.

benefited from documents and publications as well as reports from other agencies. Among these, 'The Pakistan Army Board of Inquiry informed the Commission that the stealth helicopters were probably guided by ground operators who were already in place around the OBL Compound.' Given the statements of the army chief to the author and other information given to Shaukat Qadir and Pakistani journalists, it is worth highlighting some portions of the timeline for events of that raid on 2 May 2011, Pakistan time, established by the Commission:

0115–0130	Quick Reaction Force, mobile units and Police arrive at the scene
0207	COAS Kayani speaks to Chief of Air Staff
0216	Chinook exits, flying straight to Afghanistan
0226	Black Hawk and refueller Chinook exit
0250	F-16 gets airborne from Mushaf airbase (formerly Sargodha airbase)
0300/0310	COAS speaks to the PM Yousaf Raza Gilani and Foreign Secretary
0500	Admiral Mullen calls the COAS [Kayani and Pasha gave an earlier 3 a.m. time for this call]
0645	COAS informs President Zardari

Most of the initial decisions were made by the army, with the air force being drawn into the action by the COAS. (This disconnect between the services in formulating a joint and cohesive policy has been an abiding condition in Pakistan. The air force and navy are seen by the dominant army as merely support services.) The prime minister was informed later on via the Foreign Secretary, and finally the president was informed of the raid. The commission's draft that was leaked to *Al Jazeera* gives a critical insight into the testimonies of senior civil and military officials. It reflects a state of disarray and lack of cooperation among various civil and military institutions at both the local and national level, especially on the counter-intelligence front. Even senior members of the air force sparred with each other on the issue of radar coverage of Pakistan's western approaches.

The ISI that launched its Counter Terrorism section and later expanded it to a 'wing' in 2007 had not originally been tasked for such work but had assumed it would fill the gap left by civilian inaction. It is not clear whether it was the DGCT or the DG, who headed the Directorate S that helped manage the Afghanistan operations, and was the lead agent in the Abbottabad inquiry. Steve Coll gives Directorate S a greater heft in such activities.[64] The DG-ISI reflected on the general lack of confidence in civil competence and the vulnerability of Pakistani officials and members of civil society (especially the media) to bribery and coercion by foreign powers, such as the US. He also, in effect, confirmed the emerging ISI role in policing or arresting individuals, both actions that were not in the agency's original remit, when he responded to one question by the Commission by stating that only those people feared the ISI who had reason to fear it.[65]

The Commission also exposed the lack of development and growth of strategic thinking among the military, especially in the formulation of a current and effective defence policy. No wonder that the leak of the initial draft of the Commission's report led to the sealing of its work and nothing more was seen or heard about it. No final report. Nor a hint of the dissenting report that was reportedly written by Amb. Qazi. Many years later, Justice Iqbal, the president of the Commission asked that the report be released. But too many skeletons were stuffed into that cupboard. Like many similar commissions of inquiry, the Abbottabad report was put into deep cold storage. Clearly, the Pakistani state and its military did not trust its general populace or its ability to face the truths that exposed their weaknesses.

But the awful year, 2011, that produced such deep fissures in the US–Pakistan relationship, still had more surprises in store, even as Pakistan faced internal challenges of its own, produced by both man and Nature.

---

[64] Coll, *Directorate S*.

[65] The Supreme Court had taken cognizance of the role of intelligence agencies in the disappearances of individuals from civil society. Some of these persons had eventually been produced in court. In more recent times, unexplained disappearances of bloggers were alleged to have been linked to intelligence agencies, especially when some of the missing persons were produced in court following judicial orders.

5

Internal Battles

Even as Pakistan was reeling from the invasion of its territory by US Navy SEALS, three weeks later, on 22 May, roughly a dozen gunmen launched a brazen attack on PNS Mehran, a naval base in Karachi, ostensibly to avenge the killing of bin Laden. Some ten military personnel were killed and twenty wounded, and two US-supplied surveillance airplanes and a helicopter on the base were destroyed. A sixteen-hour battle ensued before Pakistani forces recaptured the base after killing four of the attackers, according to early reports. PNS Mehran had seen an earlier attack near its front gate when a bus carrying naval personnel was attacked on 28 April. So, security ought to have been at a higher level. Yet, the attackers not only managed to penetrate the base, they also took hostages and held the security forces at bay for a long time. The Pakistani Taliban claimed responsibility.[1]

Yet, five days later, Syed Saleem Shahzad, an intrepid bureau chief for *Asia Times Online* in Pakistan, wrote an article challenging the official story. Headlined 'Al-Qaeda Had Warned of Pakistan Strike', the article alleged that the attack was not by the TTP or its affiliates but by Al-Qaeda, and resulted from the failure of talks between the authorities and Al-Qaeda on the release of Al-Qaeda sympathizers whom the military had uncovered and taken into custody. He alleged that the military had been penetrated by such elements and cited an anonymous military source:

---

[1] *Dawn*, 'Terrorists Attack Navy Airbase in Karachi, Destroy Three Aircraft', 22 May 2011, http://www.dawn.com/news/630878

'Islamic sentiments are common in the armed forces,' a senior navy official told Asia Times Online on the condition of anonymity as he is not authorized to speak to the media.

'We never felt threatened by that. All armed forces around the world, whether American, British or Indian, take some inspiration from religion to motivate their cadre against the enemy . . .,' the official said.

'Nonetheless, we observed an uneasy grouping on different naval bases in Karachi. While nobody can obstruct armed forces personnel for rendering religious rituals or studying Islam, the grouping [we observed] was against the discipline of the armed forces. That was the beginning of an intelligence operation in the navy to check for unscrupulous activities.'

The official explained the grouping was against the leadership of the armed forces and opposed to its nexus with the US against Islamic militancy. When some messages were intercepted hinting at attacks on visiting American officials, intelligence had good reason to take action and after careful evaluation at least 10 people—mostly from the lower cadre—were arrested in a series of operations.

'That was the beginning of huge trouble,' the official said.

Shahzad went on to report:

Within a week, insiders at PNS Mehran provided maps, pictures of different exit and entry routes taken in daylight and at night, the location of hangers and details of likely reaction from external security forces.

As a result, the militants were able to enter the heavily guarded facility where one group targeted the aircraft, a second group took on the first strike force and a third finally escaped with the others providing covering fire. Those who stayed behind were killed.[2]

This story and the release of Shahzad's book, that detailed infiltration by the militants into the military and alleged links between the ISI and militant organizations, created a public furore and may have raised hackles inside the security services. Shahzad had earlier been approached by the

---

[2] Syed Saleem Shahzad, 'Al Qaeda Had Warned of Pakistan Strike', *Asia Times* (online), 27 May 2011, http://www.atimes.com/atimes/South_Asia/ME27Df06.html?sms_ss=facebook&at_xt=4dde264f700949a3%2C0

ISI to retract a story on 25 March stating that bin Laden was on the move inside Pakistan and hinting at knowledge of Pakistani intelligence about his movement.

> The next morning, he got a phone call from an officer at the I.S.I., summoning him to the agency's headquarters, in Aabpara, a neighbourhood in eastern Islamabad. When Shahzad showed up, he was met by three I.S.I. officers. The lead man, he said, was a naval officer, Rear Admiral Adnan Nazir, who serves as the head of the I.S.I.'s media division.
>
> 'They were very polite,' Shahzad told me. He glanced over his shoulder. 'They don't shout, they don't threaten you. This is the way they operate. But they were very angry with me.' The I.S.I. officers asked him to write a second story, retracting the first. He refused.
>
> And then Admiral Nazir made a remark so bizarre that Shahzad said he had thought about it every day since. 'We want the world to believe that Osama is dead,' Nazir said.
>
> Bin Laden was still alive, his whereabouts presumably unknown, when that conversation occurred. I pressed Shahzad. What did they mean by that?
>
> He shrugged and glanced over his shoulder again. 'They were obviously trying to protect bin Laden,' he said. 'Do you think the I.S.I. was hiding bin Laden?' I asked him.
>
> Shahzad shrugged again and said yes. But he hadn't been able to prove it. (The I.S.I. calls this claim an 'unsubstantiated accusation of a very serious nature.')[3]

Nine days later Shahzad disappeared. Two days after that, his badly tortured body was found in a canal near Jhelum. The *New York Times* reported, 'Obama administration officials believe that Pakistan's powerful spy agency ordered the killing of a Pakistani journalist who had written scathing reports about the infiltration of militants in the country's military.' But the *Times* added: 'In a statement the day after Mr. Shahzad's waterlogged body was retrieved from a canal 60 miles from Islamabad, the ISI publicly denied accusations in the

---

[3]   Dexter Filkins, 'The Journalist and the Spies', *New Yorker*, 19 September 2011.

Pakistani news media that it had been responsible, calling them "totally unfounded".'[4]

The ISI said the journalist's death was 'unfortunate and tragic' and should not be 'used to target and malign the country's security agency'. Much later, when I asked a senior Pakistani intelligence official about this murder, he said he had no idea who had done it. 'Why did you not investigate it in that case, since the ISI was being blamed for it?' I asked. His answer was a shrug.

The government came under intense pressure from the journalist community to investigate Shahzad's murder. On 16 June 2011, 'the government accepted the demands of journalists and announced the formation of the commission. Headed by Justice Saqib Nisar, the Commission's other members are Justice Agha Rafiq, Additional IG Punjab Investigation, President of the Pakistan Federal Union of Journalists (PFUJ) and the Deputy DIG Federal Police. The commission will complete its report in six weeks.'[5] From the outset it was mired in controversy since only the Supreme Court Chief Justice can form and announce such a commission. Regardless, the Commission completed its work and issued a 146-page report in January 2012 that offered many suggestions on how to fix the 'systemic causes of tensions between [intelligence] agencies and the media', but failed to identify either the motive or the likely suspect behind the murder of Shahzad. Many journalists testified to receiving threats from or being harassed by intelligence agencies. However, both the 'Military Intelligence [which normally operates only on military matters and is housed in army headquarters] and Intelligence Bureau' simply notified the Commission that they had nothing to do with Shahzad's murder and were not questioned further.

The ISI's written testimony and replies to the Commission's questions pointed to Al-Qaeda as the likely suspect, and hinted at an American link given what they thought was undue interest in the case from 'President Obama to every man worth a name in the US [who] felt disturbed. Was he [Shahzad] a pawn who could be used at appropriate time to further use the

---

4   Jane Perlez and Eric Schmitt, 'Pakistan's Spies Tied to the Slaying of a Journalist', *New York Times*, 4 July 2011.

5   Agence France-Presse, 'Inquiry Commission Formed to Probe Saleem Shahzad's Murder', 16 June 2011, https://www.geo.tv/latest/24526-inquiry-commission-formed-to-probe-saleem-shahzads-murder

US Objectives and create a wedge between establishment [the euphemism in Pakistani parlance for the military and its intelligence agencies] and other segments of society?' Brig. Zahid Mehmood Khan, of the ISI's Sector Headquarters, central Islamabad, who delivered some of the ISI rebuttal against charges that his agency was implicated in the murder, also pointed to Shahzad's contacts with other intelligence agencies from India and the UK.[6] Not surprisingly, the Commission was unable to implicate the ISI. This murder, like many other disappearances and highly public assassinations in Pakistan's history, remained unsolved.

It also left an unresolved issue in the fractured relationship between the US and Pakistan and reflected poorly on the lack of ability of the civilian administration in Islamabad at safeguarding the citizens of Pakistan. It also underlined the gap between the government and the autonomous military establishment to which the government had outsourced security issues. Indeed, the PPP government itself felt constantly threatened by the coercive potential power of the military, as other events in 2011 indicated.

Memogate

Compounding the difficulties for the Zardari government and especially in its awkward relationship with the military was the emergence of a newspaper column in October 2011 by a Pakistani American businessman, Mansoor Ijaz, that exposed a 'plot' involving the Zardari government's envoy in Washington DC, Husain Haqqani. Ijaz alleged that 'a senior Pakistani diplomat' had asked him to convey a message to senior Obama administration national security officials in the form of a memorandum. The aim of the memorandum was to get the US government to intervene and prevent Pakistan's military from moving against its civilian government in the immediate aftermath of the Osama bin Laden assassination. This was to become known in the media as Memogate, an issue that was not fully resolved in the Pakistani courts but provoked a debate that continues to this day.

Nearly five months after the Abbottabad raid that killed bin Laden, and just weeks after Admiral Mike Mullen, the outgoing chairman of the

---

6   Salman Siddiqui, 'Saleem Shahzad Murder: Commission Report Points Out Everything, but the Murderers', *Express Tribune*, 13 January 2012. https://tribune.com.pk/story/320957/saleem-shahzad-commission-report-released/

US JCS, had given his farewell testimony to the Senate Armed Services Committee, Ijaz, who had been pronouncing on Pakistani and regional issues on broadcast and print media for some years, published an article in the *Financial Times* of London that alleged that fear of an impending coup by the army in the aftermath of the bin Laden raid led Zardari to send a message via the unsigned memorandum on 9 May to Mullen.

The memorandum offered a change in Pakistan's security structure and stance in return for a strong message from Mullen to Gen. Kayani to desist from any move to upend the Zardari government. Specifically, the memorandum, which Ijaz charged was the work of Haqqani, stated that Zardari was willing to offer his American counterparts, among other changes, 'a new national security team that will eliminate Section S of the ISI [variously known as S Wing or S Directorate] charged with maintaining relations with the Taliban, Haqqani Network, etc. This will dramatically improve relations with Afghanistan.' Ijaz's opinion piece stated that 'Pakistanis are not America's enemies. Neither is their incompetent toothless civilian government . . . The enemy is the state organ that breeds hatred among Pakistan's Islamist masses and then uses their thirst for jihad against Pakistan's neighbours and allies to sate its hunger for power.' His target was the ISI.[7] Haqqani stated to me that the first he knew of the memorandum was when the Ijaz article appeared in the media, something that Ijaz challenges.

Ijaz used his friend Gen. Jim Jones, NSA to President Obama, as the conduit to pass on the message to Admiral Mullen. Gen. Jones confirmed this to me in an interview and recalled that he had come to know Ijaz in Europe when Jones was at NATO as SACEUR. He said he had even asked Ijaz to accompany 'a very large delegation to Afghanistan . . . We became friends'. Jones recalls getting the Ijaz memo at the White House and since it was 'mostly military, I sent it over to Mike Mullen with a note. Frankly I didn't think twice about it until this thing blew up. Mike Mullen by then [when the note came to light] was retired. He called me and he said, "Do you remember anything about this?" I said, "Yeah. Mansoor gave me this message. It sounded very strange."' To refresh Mullen's memory, Jones says he rummaged in his files and found the memo and sent it again to Mullen in his retirement home in Annapolis, Maryland. Mullen said that he had not acted on the memo.

---

7   Mansoor Ijaz, 'Time to Take On Pakistan's Jihadist Spies', *Financial Times*, 10 October 2011.

After the memo became public, and media frenzy ensued in Pakistan to understand its origins and authenticity, Ijaz claimed that Zardari's ambassador, Husain Haqqani, in Washington DC, was the instigator of the memo and had planned to use Ijaz as the cut-out in conveying the message to the US military command. Jones defended Haqqani in his deposition during the subsequent Pakistani Supreme Court inquiry, saying that he believed the memo to have originated with Ijaz. That ended his relationship with Ijaz.[8] Haqqani challenged Ijaz's veracity and credentials. He says he had known Ijaz since 2002 but had only met Ijaz twice before this Memogate affair. He also said that he was in regular contact with Mullen and others in the US government and did not need a conduit to relay messages to them.

Ijaz offered me details of their long-standing correspondence dating back to July 2000 and frequent interactions by BlackBerry PIN-based messages, including inviting Haqqani to speak at an Afghan charity event he hosted in New York City, and Haqqani arranging a private one-on-one meeting for Ijaz with Zardari in May 2009 when the president visited Washington for the first time. Haqqani responded that most messages cited by Ijaz were from him to Haqqani and none referred to the memo. Ijaz's email records showed that more than half of their eighty-two email exchanges (forty-four) during the period July 2000—May 2011 were from Haqqani to Ijaz, the balance from Ijaz to Haqqani. According to Haqqani, official records of Zardari's Washington visit did not show Ijaz as having met the president, nor did any of the Pakistani presidential staff, including military personnel, confirm such a meeting. Ijaz presented me an email from him to Haqqani of 6 May 2009 thanking him for arranging his meeting with Zardari and apologizing that 'it was not my best briefing performance'. Haqqani responded from his BlackBerry the same day: 'Do not worry. You have started a relationship. Will try and sched (*sic*) new meeting too.'

The Commission set up by the Supreme Court insisted that Haqqani appear before it in person, which Haqqani refused to do, citing security concerns. Thus, the Commission depended primarily on Ijaz's account. Ijaz provided the court with numerous friendly messages exchanged with Haqqani over an extended period of time that led the court to accept Ijaz's contention of a long-standing friendship. Haqqani maintained that Ijaz

---

8   Interview with Gen. Jim Jones, Tyson's Corner, VA, September 2016.

had put forth unconnected emails and text messages exchanged over a decade as evidence of a close relationship that did not exist. Ijaz stated that he had in fact met Haqqani face-to-face at different events, times and places some seven or eight times since 2000. Ijaz's BlackBerry was examined by forensic experts to back his claims of frequent communications with Haqqani. Haqqani's BlackBerry was not made available for examination by forensic experts.

In his presentation of evidence to the Supreme Court of Pakistan, Ijaz appended the covering email[9] from him on Monday 10 May 2011 to Jones with which he had attached two versions of the memo, one in Word format and the other a pdf. He referred to earlier telephone discussions of that day on Pakistan and its relations with the US.

> I am attaching herewith a document that has been prepared by senior active and former Pakistani government officials, some of whom served at the highest levels of the military intelligence directorates in recent years, and as senior political officers of the civilian government. This document has the support of the president of Pakistan, I have been informed one hour ago.

Ijaz also stated in the covering memo to Jones that he was considering the use of two alternative channels to convey the same message to Mullen—Senator Tom Daschle and Secretary of the Navy Ray Mabus, to ensure that Mullen had the document in time before Mullen was to meet 'certain key Pakistani officials at the White House on Wednesday'. Ijaz did not name Haqqani nor refer to his role in the drafting of the memo at the time. Ijaz maintains that his reference to 'senior political officers of the civilian government' was an oblique reference to Haqqani. He referred to two Pakistani officials in the past tense as having 'served'. Ijaz explained to me that reference to these officials who had served in past positions in the Pakistani government and military was based on information Haqqani had allegedly provided to him when Ijaz pressed him about the source of certain points to be included in the memorandum. He also explained to me that by mentioning others were part of the effort, he was helping camouflage Haqqani's direct role in the drafting of the memorandum as Haqqani had

---

9   Copy of email of 10 May 2011 from Ijaz to Jones, provided by Mansoor Ijaz directly to me at my request.

told Ijaz he was under constant ISI surveillance and they knew when he met senior US officials and would connect any event, such as a call from Mullen to Kayani warning against a coup, to any of his prior meetings with Mullen.[10] Haqqani described this as evidence that Ijaz decided to blame him as an afterthought, once the ISI got interested in his memo.

The case took on added import once the DG-ISI Lt. Gen. Ahmed Shuja Pasha entered the picture and proceeded to meet Ijaz on 22 October at the Park Lane Intercontinental Hotel, room 210, in London, a room arranged by the ISI. Pasha and Ijaz followed safety protocols by removing the batteries of their cell phones and putting them in a drawer near the table where they sat. Pasha had brought a notepad to the meeting, as had Ijaz. Ijaz also brought his computers and BlackBerry device containing the exchanges with Haqqani.

Haqqani questioned the very occurrence of the meeting between Pasha and Ijaz as suspicious. 'Why did Ijaz write about something he had agreed to do in secret, if indeed he had been asked to do it? Why was he so ready to meet with the ISI, which he had described as the font of evil, to spill the beans about a "plot" of which he had become part to stop that evil?' asked Haqqani. Ironically, both protagonists were on record as being suspicious and critical of the ISI and its role in Pakistani politics. Both favoured civilian supremacy.

According to Ijaz's witness statement for the Supreme Court Commission:

> After being seated face to face at a small dining table, Gen. Pasha opened the meeting by stating his purpose in asking to meet me. He made clear he was not there to interrogate but rather to understand with evidence supporting my statements what exactly had happened in the days in question. He made clear he was in London with the consent of the army chief, Gen. Kayani.[11]

---

10   Telephone interview with Mansoor Ijaz in Europe from my home in Alexandria, VA, 14 December 2016. Subsequently, I had several telephone conversations with him to clarify issues related to this episode. I also spoke with Husain Haqqani on the telephone and met him once during December 2016 to receive documents related to the case and to clarify issues.

11   Witness statement of Mansoor Ijaz before Supreme Court Judicial Commission.

Over the next four hours, Ijaz states, Pasha asked questions or looked at the BlackBerry messages exchanged with Haqqani and other material that Ijaz provided, or showed on his laptop. Pasha also read the memorandum that had been sent to Mullen via Jones. According to Ijaz:

> Gen. Pasha read the Memorandum itself in about three or four minutes, demonstrated surprise and dismay—at times disgust and disappointment—over the content of the document. He did not ask a single question about the content of the document other than if I was willing to divulge the names of the others besides Haqqani that he had told me were to be part of the new national security team. I did so with the caveat that I did not believe either [Gen. Jehangir] Karamat [the former army chief and ambassador to the US] or [Maj. Gen. Mahmud Ali] Durrani [the former ambassador to the US and NSA] knew anything about the plan to deliver the Memorandum, the contents of the Memorandum or the mindset of Haqqani and those behind him in dreaming up the scheme.[12]

President Zardari asked Haqqani to return to Islamabad amidst media furore over the alleged memo and turned down Haqqani's offer to resign, saying, in Haqqani's recollection, 'If you don't come, that will make our government look weak, and the government will be dispensed with.' Haqqani initially stayed with Zardari and was taken to a meeting at the prime minister's house on 22 November 2011, where Zardari, Gilani, Kayani and Pasha were present. Haqqani's presence in the meeting 'lasted no more than 10 minutes'. And he says he was asked to explain what had happened. 'It's all untrue,' said Haqqani. Kayani, who did most of the talking, according to Haqqani, then asked him if he would sue Ijaz. Haqqani says he explained that he was not mentioned in the memo and a defamation suit would mean that all Haqqani's 'relations, and documentation . . . about the military etcetera, could be subject to discovery requirement under law'. Haqqani says he was talking about the conviction a few weeks earlier of the president of the Kashmiri American Council (KAC), Ghulam Nabi Fai, who had been accused by the FBI of working as an unregistered agent of the

---

12 Op. cit. Witness statement of Mansoor Ijaz.

ISI.[13] (Fai pleaded guilty on 7 December 2011 and exposed a wider scheme involving other 'straw donors' who allegedly helped him funnel money acquired from the government of Pakistan and the ISI to influence US politicians.)[14] Ijaz maintains that a secret fund that his lawyer later brought

---

[13] Kim Barker and Habiba Nosheen, 'The Man behind Pakistan's Spy Agency's Plot to Influence Washington', *Pro Publica*, 3 October 2011, https://www.propublica.org/article/the-man-behind-pakistani-spy-agencys-plot-to-influence-washington

[14] US Department of Justice, Office of Public Affairs, 'Virginia Man Pleads Guilty in Scheme to Conceal Pakistan Government Funding for His U.S. Lobbying Efforts', 7 December 2011, FBI Archives, https://archives.fbi.gov/archives/washingtondc/press-releases/2011/virginia-man-pleads-guilty-in-scheme-to-conceal-pakistan-government-funding-for-his-u.s.-lobbying-efforts

Today, Fai admitted that, from 1990 until about July 18, 2011, he conspired with others to obtain money from officials employed by the government of Pakistan, including the ISI, for the operation of the KAC in the United States, and that he did so outside the knowledge of the U.S. government and without attracting the attention of law enforcement and regulatory authorities.

To prevent the Justice Department, FBI, Department of Treasury and the IRS from learning the source of the money he received from officials employed by the government of Pakistan and the ISI, Fai made a series of false statements and representations, according to court documents. For example, Fai told FBI agents in March 2007 that he had never met anyone who identified himself as being affiliated with the ISI and, in May 2009, he falsely denied to the IRS on a tax return for the KAC that the KAC had received any money from foreign sources in 2008.

In addition, according to court documents, Fai sent a letter in April 2010 to the Justice Department falsely asserting that the KAC was not funded by the government of Pakistan. Later that year, Fai falsely denied to the IRS that the KAC had received any money from foreign sources in 2009. In July 2011, Fai falsely denied to FBI agents that he or the KAC received money from the ISI or government of Pakistan.

In fact, Fai repeatedly submitted annual KAC strategy reports and budgetary requirements to Pakistani government officials for approval. For instance, in 2009, Fai sent the ISI a document entitled 'Plan of Action of KAC / Kashmir Centre, Washington, D.C., for the Fiscal Year 2010,' which itemized KAC's 2010 budget request of $658,000 and listed Fai's plans to secure U.S. congressional support for U.S. action in support of Kashmiri self-determination.

Fai also admitted that, from 1990 until about July 18, 2011, he corruptly endeavored to obstruct and impede the due administration of the internal

up in the proceedings of the Supreme Court's inquiry commission was separate from the ISI's funds and came under the ambassador's purview.

Haqqani was asked to wait for the group's decision. An hour after the group meeting, Zardari came back and said to him: 'We have decided that you should resign.' Haqqani says he had a resignation already drafted since 16 November 2011 and handed it over.

The matter did not end there, however. The Chief Justice of Pakistan, Iftikhar Muhammad Chaudhry, accepted petitions by Opposition leader Nawaz Sharif and several others, barred Haqqani from leaving the country, and decided to investigate the entire affair. It took some time after that for Haqqani to get permission to exit Pakistan on 31 January 2012, that too after then US Senator John Kerry's intercession, among others, on his behalf. He has not gone back since then. The ISI has not shared its findings, nor has there been any public investigation of the other senior retirees mentioned in the discussions surrounding Memogate.

An interesting side plot to the Memogate saga emerged, surrounding the dismissal of Lt. Gen. (retired) Naeem Lodhi, the defence secretary, at the time that Memogate reached the Supreme Court.[15] Lodhi was still serving as a three-star in the army in late 2011, when he describes a visit to him, before the Memogate issue and the resulting civil–military spat erupted in public view via the Supreme Court's proceedings in Pakistan. His visitor was a course mate from the 50th PMA Long Course and Lodhi's fellow Army Engineers officer, Lt. Col. Hassan Saleem Haqqani. The colonel was the elder brother of Amb. Husain Haqqani. Col. Haqqani passed him a message from his brother to the effect: 'Husain says I'm sorry

---

revenue laws by arranging for the transfer of at least $3.5 million to the KAC from employees of the government of Pakistan and the ISI.

According to court documents, Fai accepted the transfer of such money to the KAC from the ISI and the government of Pakistan through his co-defendant Zaheer Ahmad and middlemen (straw donors), who received reimbursement from Ahmad for their purported 'donations' to the KAC. Fai provided letters from the KAC to the straw donors documenting that their purported 'donations' to the KAC were tax deductible and encouraged these donors to deduct the transfers as 'charitable' deductions on their personal tax returns. Fai concealed from the IRS that the straw donors' purported KAC 'donations' were reimbursed by Ahmad, using funds received from officials employed by the ISI and the government of Pakistan.

[15] Telephone interview with Lt. Gen. (retd) Naeem Lodhi, 10 March 2018.

and I want to come and call on GHQ [army headquarters]. I am ready to accept whatever they say. We'll do whatever they say.' Lodhi says he had no idea what this was about, not having been briefed about the details of the Memogate issue. He says he called Gen. Kayani's office and asked if he could see him that afternoon and also asked if Gen. Pasha of ISI could be invited to the army chief's office in Rawalpindi for the same meeting. 'I delivered the message. They both exchanged a glance, thanked me', but did not say anything further about the cryptic message from Ambassador Haqqani. So, Lodhi says he left Kayani's office. Little did he know how he would be drawn later into the vortex of the Memogate inquiry.

Haqqani categorically denies that he sent a message to Gen. Kayani: 'No message was sent by me to K. None whatsoever. And there was no question of an apology. I met K and P only at the PM House in the presence of PM and President. That was all. I have no idea what Lodhi sb. [sahib] is referring to.'[16] Gen. Pasha did not respond to a request to confirm this incident. Indeed, this was not brought up in the subsequent proceedings related to this case in Pakistan. Lodhi later became a caretaker minister in 2018. Surprisingly, this information did not figure in any of the public investigation of Memogate.

The Parliamentary Committee on National Security had been charged on 28 November 2011 by the prime minister to investigate the Memogate issue at the 'highest level'.[17] The Supreme Court via a judicial commission set up a month later also asked for statements from Kayani and Pasha. Those statements were sent to Lodhi, in his role as the defence secretary, in sealed envelopes. He said that he sent those sealed envelopes via a dispatch rider to the Attorney General with the instructions that if the Attorney General was not available, to hand them to the Registrar of the Supreme Court. That was indeed the final outcome, and the statements from Kayani and Pasha ended up directly in the Supreme Court's hands.

That became the basis of the complaint of the civilian government against its defence secretary. Prime Minister Yousaf Raza Gilani wanted to know why Lodhi had passed the statements directly to the court instead

---

[16]   Communication to author, 10 April 2018.

[17]   Munizae Jahangir, 'Parliamentary Committee on National Security to Investigate the Scandal: PM', *Express Tribune*, Pakistan, 28 November 2011, https://tribune.com.pk/story/298746/parliamentary-committee-on-national-security-to-investigate-the-scandal-pm/

of via the government. The parliamentary committee asked for his views on the Memogate issue. Though he had not read the Kayani or Pasha statements, Lodhi says he responded that he had nothing to add to what the two senior military officers had conveyed. He was then summoned to the prime minister's camp office (attached to the PM's residence), at 8 a.m. on 12 January 2012, an unusual hour for a meeting. He informed Pasha of the invitation. At the PM's camp office, he saw the Secretary of the Ministry of Interior, the Secretary, Law and Justice, the Secretary, Foreign Affairs, and the Principal Secretary to the PM, Khushnood Akhtar Lashari. Lashari gave him a legal stamped paper that had been pre-typed with a statement for the Supreme Court. Lodhi began to read the document. Lashari said to him there was no need to read the document. Lodhi says he responded that he needed to know what he was being asked to sign. That document said in effect: 'Now that a high-powered Parliamentary Committee has been formed, no other forum should investigate Memogate.' Lodhi says, 'I refused to sign. Lashari said to me, "Do you know the consequences of not signing?" They [then] connected me via telephone to the Attorney General, who wanted to know why I was not signing. I told him that I came from the army, where even a captain would refuse to sign a document that was not his personal statement.'

Lodhi left the PM's office and informed both Kayani and Pasha of the incident. Later that evening, he heard on the news that he had been relieved of his position as defence secretary. Having only taken over on 28 November the previous year, he had one of the shortest tenures in that post. His replacement was Nargis Sethi, who had served in various important positions in government and in the PM's office.

Lodhi's firing prompted an exchange of verbal fire between the government and the military. The ISPR Directorate, the publicity arm of the military, denied that the army chief and the DG-ISI acted 'unconstitutionally and illegally' while filing their replies in [the] memo issue, and noted that Mr Gilani's allegations [of misconduct by the military and the Defence Secretary] could have 'very serious ramifications with potentially grievous consequences for the country'.

Beyond that, ISPR said:

The responses by the respondents [Kayani and Pasha] were sent to the Ministry of Defence for onward submission to the Honourable Supreme Court, through Attorney General (Law Ministry) . . . Responsibility for moving summaries and obtaining approvals of competent authority thereafter lay with the relevant ministries and not with the respondents.[18]

On 30 December 2011, a Judicial Commission of Inquiry had been set up to determine the origins of the memo based on Mansoor Ijaz's assertions. The Commission's hearings continued until the middle of 2012 and it issued a detailed report generally upholding Ijaz's version of events, citing him as a 'credible witness' whose credibility Haqqani had sought unsuccessfully to undermine.[19] The Commission refused to accept Haqqani's testimony by video link from overseas, the means by which Ijaz had offered his account. It wanted him to appear in person in Islamabad.

Haqqani reportedly had agreed to return to Pakistan if asked to do so by the Supreme Court when he was allowed to leave in January 2012. Later, he refused to do so, citing concerns about his safety in Pakistan.

According to Haqqani,

My lawyer conveyed our decision to boycott the Commission's proceedings in May 2012, having cooperated with it until then, after it refused to let me record my evidence by videolink and refused to accept any of the documents and material submitted by us.

We did not participate in the forensic examination even though the Secretary of the Commission wrote to us two days before the examination informing us of his choice of forensic examiner. We also objected to the examination being conducted at the Pakistan High Commission instead of a Forensic lab or research facility.[20]

Some months into the Commission's proceedings, in May 2012, Ijaz's lawyer, Akram Sheikh, a former president of Pakistan's Supreme Court Bar Association alleged that a secret fund of approximately $8 million had been created at the National Bank of Pakistan's DC branch under Ambassador Haqqani's control at the Pakistan embassy in Washington. This funding, it was alleged, came from the Pakistani treasury, and was being used to pay

---

[18] *Dawn*, 'Defence Secretary Naeem Lodhi Sacked', 12 January 2012, https://www.dawn.com/news/687507

[19] Supreme Court of Pakistan's Judicial Commission Report, issued June 2012, pp. 111–12, Section 25.

[20] Email to author.

certain Americans for unknown reasons and services. According to Ijaz's lawyer, the fund was reportedly authorized by President Zardari.

Ijaz believes that the political fund could have been used to undermine the integrity of the US political system. This secret fund was subsequently the subject of an in-camera session of the Commission. In the Commission proceedings, it is alleged that cash withdrawals were made from this National Bank of Pakistan (Washington DC branch) account in amounts just less than the $10,000 US Treasury reporting threshold. The Commission found that only some $1.7 million was left in this account when the Memogate affair exploded on the scene and Haqqani was recalled. Ijaz's lawyer spoke publicly of this operation and after reports in the media at least one of the non-Pakistanis challenged his assertions publicly.[21] A number of simultaneous articles in US media defended Haqqani and challenged Ijaz's credentials and claims of past activities in resolving conflicts around the globe.

Haqqani says the so-called secret fund was a perfectly legal Special Service account with different auditing requirements and Ijaz's lawyer invoked it only to justify the testimony presented to the Commission.

---

[21] *News International*, 'David Frum Denies Receiving Money from Pakistan Embassy', 30 May 2012, in which he stated,

On Wednesday, Google Alerts brought me a piece of startling news: A lawyer speaking to a tribunal of the Supreme Court of Pakistan had accused me of acting as a paid agent of the government of Pakistan.

No, seriously, that's what the man said.

Frum was responding to a reported statement of prominent SC lawyer Akram Sheikh who, it was reported, had 'claimed in a statement that Pakistani Embassy provided funds to Harlan Ullman and David Frum for damage control after the memo controversy.' In his response Frum wrote on CNN.com he was so taken aback by the claim that he telephoned Sheikh to ask whether it was true. 'We had a short but intense exchange.' He said given that charges against him have gained a hearing inside Pakistan, some kind of answer seems due. Frum wrote: 'Where is the fake evidence? The forged check, the bogus wire transfer, the suborned courier? Money always leaves a record.' He said Mansoor Ijaz, the Memogate character, told the Memo Commission that he had sued me for libel. He quoted Ijaz as telling the Commission: 'In view of the fact Mr Frum defamed me, my lawyers in Washington informed him that if he does not retract, I will be taking legal action against him.'

https://www.cnn.com/2012/05/28/opinion/frum-pakistan-accusation/index.html

Haqqani challenged Ijaz's claims as a secret, private negotiator in official matters, referring, among others to a CNN article against Ijaz.[22] Ijaz presented me with correspondence authored by leaders of Sudan and Kashmiri separatists which were transmitted by him to US legislators, President Bill Clinton and others, as well as other material to support his claim of having attempted to bring Sudan and the US together in the fight against terrorism and specifically against Al-Qaeda, as well as his efforts to bring India and Pakistan together on Kashmir. These included, among other things, an article co-authored with a former US ambassador to Sudan.

The Commission completed its work regardless and submitted its findings. No legal cases emerged from this imbroglio nor was there any evidence of an official US government inquiry into the matter of the secret fund and its operation in a US-based bank on the part of the US Treasury or the Federal Bureau of Investigation.[23]

Weighing all the conflicting evidence and attacks by the protagonists on each other's credibility, the Supreme Court Commission concluded that the 'Memorandum' 'was authentic and Mr Haqqani was the originator and architect . . . [He] sought American help, he also wanted to create a niche for himself making himself indispensable to the Americans.' It then proceeded to criticize his behaviour and the motives of the government. Specifically, the Commission characterized Haqqani's actions as 'acts of disloyalty to Pakistan that contravened the Constitution of Pakistan'. And it criticized the government for appointing him ambassador, when he had

---

[22] Peter Bergen and Andrew Lebovich, 'What's Behind the Furor in Pakistan?', CNN, 25 November 2011, http://www.cnn.com/2011/11/24/opinion/bergen-memogate-pakistan/

[23] Harlan Ullman, the other non-Pakistani allegedly named in the Supreme Court proceedings, wrote an article rebutting Ijaz's allegation in the Pakistani newspaper *Daily Times*. This was reproduced on the Atlantic Council website. Ullman was associated with the Council as a senior adviser. I was then director of the Council's South Asia Center. Ullman was close to President Zardari and Benazir Bhutto and had spent some time travelling to Pakistan, including on a fact-finding trip with me and others on a report on a comprehensive US policy for Pakistan, which was issued in early 2009. Ijaz had been a member of the Atlantic Council Board of Directors and was on the task force that produced the 2009 report, sponsored by then senators John Kerry and Chuck Hagel.

... chosen not to live in Pakistan . . . held no property or asset in Pakistan, held no money (save a paltry amount) in a Pakistani bank, but despite having no obvious ties to Pakistan was appointed to the extremely sensitive position of Pakistan's ambassador to the USA, and in addition to being paid a salary and accompanying emoluments was handed a largesse of over an amount of two million dollars a year.[24]

Haqqani described the Commission's findings as 'one-sided and politically motivated', and wondered why, if its findings were true, no legal or criminal proceedings were initiated against him or anyone else. According to him, the army had overreacted to Ijaz's claims and the Commission helped close the matter without further embarrassment. The Supreme Court later described the Commission's report as an 'opinion' that required further adjudication.[25] Haqqani, who had left the country with a pledge to return if needed by the court, refused to do so because of security concerns. It appears that none of the institutions at the centre of this affair wished to pursue the matter further. As a legal footnote, Haqqani's lawyers pleaded with the Supreme Court to recognize that the commission of inquiry had been set up outside the pale of the law since the law invoked by the Supreme Court's Chief Justice to set it up had expired some years earlier! That plea was never heard. In 2018, the Government of Pakistan began attempting to issue an Interpol Red Warrant for the arrest and repatriation of Haqqani. That effort stalled.

Haqqani became the only casualty of the battle between the military and the civilian leadership after being sacrificed by his patron President Zardari. He had become a key adviser of Bhutto and Zardari after having

---

[24] Report of the three-judge judicial commission of the Pakistan Supreme Court to investigate Memogate, headed by Justice Qazi Faez Isa, and including Justices Mushir Alam and Iqbal Hameed-ur-Rehman, 4 June 2012, https://pakistanconstitutionlaw.com/detailed-order-in-memo-gate-case/
https://www.washingtonpost.com/world/pakistani-probe-finds-former-ambassador-husain-haqqani-was-behind-memo-seeking-us-help/2012/06/12/gJQAtaSpWV_story.html?utm_term=.d2b05d1bf71f

[25] 'During today's proceedings, the bench remarked that the commission had only expressed its opinion and not declared Haqqani a traitor.' See: Agence France-Presse, 'Memo Commission Didn't Declare Husain Haqqani Traitor: SC', Geo.tv, 12 July 2012. https://www.geo.tv/latest/79498-memo-commission-didnt-declare-husain-haqqani-traitor-sc

been allegedly spurned by Musharraf, whom he then subsequently opposed vehemently from his academic perch in Boston University. His book, *Pakistan: Between Mosque and the Military*,[26] was seen by the military as a diatribe against that institution. In it he outlined his thesis that the military and the Muslim clerics had been in partnership since independence, though the strong evidence was of a patron–client relationship till the period of Zia-ul-Haq, when the relations became closer. After Zia, the military again changed tack away from close quarters with the mullahs. Surprisingly, when Zardari nominated Haqqani as ambassador, the military did not veto his appointment, though the ISI routinely vetted all such appointments. Haqqani had met the DG-ISI at the time and had called on then President Musharraf before taking up his post. In fact, he even won an extension after visiting Gen. Kayani and convincing him that he could serve the military's interests in the US too. But the civil–military distrust was mutual and deep and proved to be the cause of his eventual removal from Pakistani politics.

The army was also feeling vulnerable, having narrowly survived a successful terrorist assault on its main headquarters in Rawalpindi. And it had long harboured deep suspicions that Haqqani may have helped the American Congress draft specific conditions in the KLB legislation pertaining to civilian controls over the Pakistani military. Haqqani's difficult position as Zardari's man in Washington as well as the country's ambassador led him to defend Pakistan and its military in public. Sotto voce, he sometimes hinted at the internal tensions inside a military-dominated polity, even in his public discussions. Under one plausible but unproven scenario, he could have encouraged the production of the Ijaz memorandum as a way of helping strengthen Zardari's hand against the military. But the maladroit and incomplete handling of the inquiry by the ISI chief and the lack of forensic evidence from Haqqani's BlackBerry, as well as the need to keep under wraps the nature and purpose of the special Pakistan embassy account helped quash the inquiry without a clear conclusion.

There was further collateral damage too. In June 2016, while in the US, Haqqani publicly parted ways with the PPP, as did his wife,

---

[26] Husain Haqqani, *Pakistan: Between Mosque and Military* (Carnegie Endowment for International Peace, Washington DC 2004).

Farahnaz Ispahani, who had been a PPP parliamentarian and also media spokesperson for the president. 'PPP spokesperson Farhatullah Babar, in a statement, said his party does not agree with Haqqani's opinion or analysis and connecting his work with the PPP is wrong.'[27] This led to Ispahani tendering a public resignation from the party. Pasha, who had earlier been subjected to a sometimes harsh and unusual grilling in parliament after the Abbottabad raid, also did not stay long in his post, having been given only a one-year extension as DG-ISI. He later moved to the United Arab Emirates reportedly as an advisor before returning to his home in Rawalpindi. Kayani's final years as army chief were also rife with rumours and innuendo about corruption charges associated with his brothers' business dealings. No one, it seems, neither in the army nor in the civilian government, came out the winner in this affair. No one in power appeared willing to pursue the case to a conclusion. Memogate further deepened the distrust between the two institutions of the state and between the US and Pakistan. Pakistan continued to muddle through its crises.

27   Mateen Haider and Raza Khan, 'PPP Disowns Husain Haqqani', *Dawn*, 24
     June 2016.

6

Salala: Anatomy of a Failed Alliance

'In war, truth is the first casualty.'[1]

Before it came to a close, the watershed year 2011 had another surprise up its sleeve for Pakistan and its US 'partners'. An exchange of fire on the night of 25–26 November, in the Pakistan–Afghanistan borderlands, between Pakistani and US forces, led to an unrelenting US aerial attack for nearly two hours on two isolated Pakistani posts named Volcano and Boulder at a place named Salala. These prominent posts were on a ridgeline on the western shoulder of a desolate mountain range in Mohmand Agency of the FATA of Pakistan, facing Kunar (also spelled Konar) province of Afghanistan. The Pakistani troops were supposed to be monitoring the border for incursions by Pakistani Taliban and allied Swati rebels who had fled to sanctuary in Afghanistan after the army's clearing operations in Swat and Malakand. Under the terms of the US–Pakistan arrangement, as allies, these posts were also supposed to stop the flow of militants fighting the Coalition and Afghan forces into Afghanistan from the Pakistani

---

[1] Variously ascribed to Aeschylus, US Senator Hiram Johnson (1866–1945) and, among others, the edition of the *Idler* magazine from 11 November 1758, which says, 'Among the calamities of war may be jointly numbered the diminution of the love of truth, by the falsehoods which interest dictates and credulity encourages.' (The last reference courtesy of Andy Ward in the *Guardian*.) See also Arthur Ponsonby's *Falsehood in War* (1928), also available as *Falsehood in War Time: Containing An Assortment of Lies Circulated Throughout the Nations During the Great War*, Kessengir Publishing, reprint, paperback, Whitefish Montana, USA, 2010, and Phillip Knightley, *The First Casualty* (New York: Harcourt Brace Jovanovich, 1975), staring down at me from my bookshelf.

side. There were no indications of major Afghan Taliban infiltration from Mohmand Agency into Afghanistan. In fact, US sources indicated that there was no substantive US or Afghan 'governance or development activity in Maya Village [opposite Salala] since 5 October 2011 because of an absence of ANA (Afghan National Army) or coalition military presence'.[2] Generally, the US footprint had almost disappeared from this area of Afghanistan as the US/ISAF interest shifted to the South.

By the time the firing ceased that night, twenty-four Pakistanis had been killed by American forces and another thirteen wounded. The dead included two officers and twenty-two soldiers. Significantly, there were no US or Afghan casualties.

This attack, one in a number of such attacks by Coalition Forces on Pakistani military positions, represented the failure of the partnership between the US and Pakistan in a most glaring manner, fuelled by years of mistrust. The very first major instance of American boots on the ground inside Pakistani territory was in a village Musa Nika near Angoor Adda in South Waziristan on 3 September 2008. This attack, aimed at capturing or killing an alleged Taliban facilitator, was conducted by US Navy SEALS and followed a major Pakistan offensive in Bajaur Agency that displaced a large number of civilians and fighters from Bajaur to the southern agencies of FATA. At least twenty persons were killed in this raid. It also followed a meeting between the new Pakistani army chief Gen. Ashfaq Parvez Kayani and his prospective DG-ISI Lt. Gen. Ahmed Shuja Pasha with Admiral Mike Mullen, the chairman of the JCS of the US, in the Indian Ocean on the American aircraft carrier *USS Abraham Lincoln*. Pakistan denied that 'hot pursuit' raids were discussed or agreed to at that meeting.[3] Other US incursions via helicopters occurred from time to time. Interestingly, Steve Coll's definitive *Directorate S* does not mention the attack on Angoor Adda or other US cross-border raids.

The attack on Salala provoked anger and recriminations on the Pakistani side, and awkward and seemingly reluctant attempts to express regret but not to apologize from the American side. The relationship went into a tailspin. The ground lines of communication into Afghanistan were

---

[2]   Final report on Salala attack by Brig. Gen. Stephen Clark (Unclassified), CENTCOM, December 2011, p. 10.

[3]   Candace Rondeaux and Karen De Young, 'US Troops Crossed Border, Says Pakistan', *Washington Post*, 4 September 2008.

closed by Pakistan. Parliament took umbrage at what it considered to be American high-handedness in dealing with Pakistan, and got into reviewing and debating the situation. It took some four months for the issue to be laid to rest. Unresolved in terms of assignment of fault or punishment, one more painful episode was thus added to Pakistani memory banks about the overbearing attitude of the American 'friends', while on the American side many on the ground in Afghanistan and in the White House thought it was an overdue lesson for the Pakistanis for being duplicitous and non-compliant non-NATO 'allies' over a long time. On Pakistan's side, this was the beginning of the end of a misbegotten misalliance in which it, as a junior partner, had to suffer American pressure to 'do more' and be rewarded with snubs and abiding distrust. Yet, the story of Salala has never been fully told nor understood by either the Americans or the Pakistanis.[4]

What Happened? The American Story

On the day of the Salala attack, Gen. John Allen, the commander of ISAF and former deputy commander of CENTCOM under Gen. David Petraeus, was on a visit to Rawalpindi, accompanied by Maj. Gen. James B. Laster[5] and Maj. Gen. John W. Nicholson,[6] to meet with his Pakistani counterpart, Army Chief Gen. Ashfaq Parvez Kayani and his colleagues

---

[4] Salala garnered one paragraph in Coll's *Directorate S*, p. 626.

[5] A Marine, Laster was then head of joint operations at ISAF Joint Command. Later he was promoted to lieutenant general and made director, Marine Corps Staff, in the Pentagon.

[6] Later appointed commander of US Forces in Afghanistan, Nicholson had deep experience in Afghanistan, commanding troops in the south and also helping manage the war effort. From December 2010 to January 2012, he served as Deputy Commanding General for Operations of US Forces Afghanistan and Deputy Chief of Staff for Operations of NATO's ISAF where he was responsible for operations, planning and assessments of ISAF's comprehensive COIN campaign waged by roughly 140,000 troops from fifty nations in partnership with the Afghan government, Afghan National Security Forces and interagency partners. https://www.eastwest.ngo/sites/default/files/COM%20LANDCOM%20Biography%20JAN27.pdf. An interesting footnote to his genealogy is an alleged link to Maj. Gen. Nicholson who helped quell the Indian Mutiny of 1857 and to whom an obelisk monument sits next to the Grand Trunk Road between Rawalpindi and Hasan Abdal.

at General Headquarters. Among other things, they had discussed recent and ongoing operations in Afghanistan, especially in the border regions abutting Pakistan. Notably, Operation Sayaqa, an Afghan commando operation guided and supported by US forces to clear suspected 'enemy' forces from the village of Maya, a few miles from the Pak–Afghan border inside Afghanistan, was not mentioned by the Americans although both, and most certainly Maj. Gen. Laster, had been briefed on the operation and had suggested alterations in the plan. Pakistani military sources at General Headquarters indicated that,

> Detailed research about pre- and post Salala incident and overall environment leading to events of 26 Nov 2011, indicate that no info on Op SAYAQA either through formal memos / CONOPs [Concept of Operations] or interactions was shared with Pakistan. On 25 Nov 11, ISAF senior leadership visited MO Dte, [Military Operations Directorate] shared info (story boards) on two ops (Op Sarhad Khamana and Op Shamsheer).[7]

The later Pakistan statement on the investigation of the Salala attack reflected this view.

Gen. Allen recalls being woken later during the night by an assistant to be informed that: 'We'd had a firefight and there were Pakistani casualties.' He was heading soon after to the airport in Chaklala to catch his Gulfstream back to Kabul.

'As we were driving to the airport, I'm getting call after call. First it's four dead. Then it's twelve dead, and . . . by the time I get to the airport, it's over twenty dead.' Allen called Kayani to offer his condolences. 'I said, I don't know what happened. I'm going to find out what happened. Please accept my sincere condolences and you know this was not intentional.' Kayani's response was crisp, recalls Allen. 'You have no idea what's happened here. I've lost my ability to manage our relationship now.'[8]

The fraught US–Pakistan relationship was not faring well at that time. Accumulated anger and mistrust on both sides led to a by-the-book

---

7   Statement provided by Pakistan Army HQ via Lt. Gen. (retd) Ishfaq Ahmed, former DG Military Operations at GHQ at the time of the Salala attack. Military-style abbreviations in original spelled out in full here.

8   Author interview with Gen. John Allen, August 2016, Washington DC.

approach and unilateral actions resulting from a major tragedy such as the Salala attack. Upon the advice of the army chief, Pakistan immediately shut down the GLOC. The ALOC remained open, allowing the US to continue to prosecute its war in Afghanistan, albeit at a much higher cost. Clearly, Pakistan was not seeking a total break in the relationship.

In Washington DC, the White House wanted quick answers. A senior official there told me immediately after the attack that the president wished to receive an initial report within a week. But, CENTCOM commander Gen. James Mattis had decided to follow strictly prescribed US military procedures and commissioned an investigation on Monday, 28 November, by Brig. Gen. Stephen Clark of the US Air Force, in conjunction with a five-person NATO team from Joint Force Command Brunssum in Europe, led by Canadian Brig. Gen. Mike Jorgensen. Clark, a command pilot with over 3,500 flight hours in eight different fixed-wing aircraft, was director of plans, programmes, requirements and assessments for Air Force SOCOM. Mattis asked that the final report be delivered by 23 December. This meant that Obama would have to wait for a final report. At the same time, it gave both sides a chance to cool things down.

Pakistan Army headquarters confirmed that a request to Pakistan for 'participation in the inquiry was received verbally through ODRP (Office of the Defense Representative in Pakistan, Lt. Gen. Ken Keen) as indicated to BG Stephan Clark in Gen. James Mattis' memo ordering [the] inquiry. Pakistan chose not to be part of an inquiry, since it was "not mandated to affix specific resp[onsibility], within ISAF".[9] In other words, Pakistan did not trust the purpose of the inquiry.

The Firefight

The attack on Salala emerged out of Operation Sayaqa, under which an Afghan National Army commando company, supported by US Army Special Forces, was to attack and neutralize insurgents operating in the Maya Valley, especially in Maya village in the Khas Kunar District of Kunar Province of Afghanistan. The concept of operation for this operation was defined as a shaping operation in support of Regional Command-East's objective to neutralize the capability of insurgents to freely operate in the Maya Valley. According to Gen. Clark's investigation report, the troops

---

9   Pakistan Army GHQ statement.

were supported by two Chinook heavy-lift utility helicopters, two AH-64D Apache Longbow attack helicopters, one AC-130H/Spectre gunship, two F-15E Strike Eagle multipurpose fighter aircraft and one MC-12 Liberty turbo-propeller, Intelligence, Surveillance and Reconnaissance aircraft. An estimated twenty-five to thirty insurgents were reported to be present in Maya village. On 5 October, four rocket-propelled grenades had been fired upon a CH-47 helicopter about to land near Maya village. The concept of operation was shared with Maj. Gen. Laster on 22 November. He asked that the helicopter landing zone north of Maya village be moved further away from the border and to confirm the location of Pakistani border posts. The landing zone was moved to 1.3 km north of Maya village (the objective) and 2.3 km from the Pakistan border. According to the Clark report, a map of the known Pakistani border points was provided to Maj. Gen. Laster the next day indicating the changed landing zone and known Pakistani border points. Notably, the declassified Clark report carried Figure 2 indicating the landing zone, the objective and the Afghan border, but not the 'known locations' of Pakistani check posts.[10]

The ground forces assembled at the landing zone at 2206 hours local time on 25 November, and proceeded to their objective along 'goat trails' in a very rugged terrain into a valley that opened up to the ridgeline to the east where the Pakistan border was located. It was a moonless night so the US forces employed their night-vision goggles with infrared capabilities. They split up into two elements in order to approach Maya village from two sides.

At 2309 hours, they reported heavy machine gun fire 'right over their heads' from a position identified by the AC-130H gunship and MC-12 helicopter crews on the 'eastern ridgeline' in the 'vicinity of the Pakistan border', roughly 3,000 metres above Maya village. Within minutes, 'accurate mortar fire' was reported, effectively separating the two coalition force elements. The ground force commander called back to his higher headquarters for confirmation that there is no Pakistani military in the area because he identified the fire as coming from the ridgeline that he identified as the border. In addition, the Joint Terminal Attack controller requested a 'show of force' from the F-15E 'to demonstrate a credible

---

[10] This account is based on the final declassified Clark report and the transcript of Brig. Gen. Clark's teleconference from Hurlburt Field, FL, of 22 December 2011.

military presence'. The F-15E flew at high speed and low altitude over the ridgeline from where the fire was emanating, dispensing flares. The AC-130 gun ship also dispensed flares. Suddenly, the dark quiet valley was filled with the sound of the low-flying aircraft, and the AC-130 dropped its flares 'effectively illuminat(ing) the entire valley'. The aircraft could now see the 'machine gun nest' on the ridgeline. But the machine gun and mortar fire did not cease. According to Clark, the ground force's immediate headquarters came back at the same time to say that 'there is no Pakistani military in the area'. This was the first in a series of witting or unwitting 'miscommunications' surrounding this incident. In fact, Regional Command East, the higher-level headquarters, had communicated, 'We are checking with the BCC (Border Coordination Centre), but we are tracking no Pak mil in the area.'

The Ground Force Commander then directed the AC-130 to attack the positions from where the fire was being conducted. This attack lasted six minutes. But at 2344 hours, fire was emerging from what were described as 'rudimentary bunkers', and both the gunship and the helicopters attacked those sites till 'approximately' midnight.

All this while, Pakistani liaison officers attached to ISAF were making frantic telephone calls to their regional command contacts to say that their forces were coming under fire. The American liaison officers demanded specific location information and the response was, 'You know where it is because you are shooting at them.' Further, RC-East asked the 'battlespace owner' and the Nawa BCC to share with the Pakistani liaison officer at Nawa BCC only 'general' location information rather the specific latitude and longitude coordinates, 'for security reasons' that were not specified. Clark blames this on an atmosphere of 'mistrust'.

Notably, his report does not identify who issued this command at RC-East, nor did it propose any action against that individual for withholding information that could have halted the attack on the Salala posts. Compounding the confusion, Clark found that the 'individual who received that information put it into his computer. Unfortunately, he had his overlays configured incorrectly.' He conveyed the incorrect location, some 14 km away from the actual firefight, to his Pakistani liaison officer, who told him there were no Pakistani forces at that particular location.

Finally, a third firefight occurred at 0040 hours that lasted till 0100 hours in another area on the ridgeline slightly north of the first site.

By 1 a.m., it became clear that there was indeed Pakistani military in the area, and the firing was stopped.

The chief of the ODRP, Lt. Gen. Ken Keen, normally was supposed to be given information on near-border operations in advance. The concept of operation for Sayaqa was not shared with him. Again, there is no explanation in the Clark report as to why this happened or if it was ordered by someone at RC-East or higher up the US command chain. He was first notified by his ISAF liaison officer about the attack at Salala at about 1.20 a.m., 'after the actual engagement had ended'. Keen had, in fact, been informed by Pakistani authorities after the first US air attack on the Pakistani border post. According to the Clark report, the ISAF liaison officer at the ODRP informed the Night Director of the IJC's Combined Joint Operations Centre of the incident at 0035 hours. At 0120 hours, that person updated Maj. Gen. Laster and US Army Brig. Gen. Gary Volesky, Deputy Commander Maneuver at RC-East. [On page 4 of the Clark report this time is given as 0115 hours.] Laster then contacted RC-E and directed them to de-escalate the situation without further delay. The report does not indicate if Laster briefed Gen. Allen immediately, with whom he was in Islamabad at that time.

Notably, the Clark report does not indicate Laster or Nicholson's Pakistan location at the time of the attack. Pakistani sources indicate that both were accompanying Gen. Allen on 25 November for his visit to Pakistan. They had briefed the Pakistani DGMO, Maj. Gen. Ishfaq Nadeem, on ISAF 'operations in another zone but, as the Pakistanis noted later, chose not to share anything about an operation opposite Salala which was to happen the same night and so close to the border'.[11] During the night, Laster, who had been briefed about the operation in advance and contributed to its planning, asked the ISAF liaison officer at ODRP to connect him to Maj. Gen. Nadeem 'in an attempt to defuse the situation'. He then informed US Army Lt. Gen. Curtis Scaparotti of the incident, and Gen. Allen was informed en route to Islamabad airport.[12]

---

[11] 'Pakistan's Perspective on the Investigative Report Conducted by BG Stephen Clark into 26th November 2011 US Led ISAF/NATO Forces Attack on Pakistani Volcano and Boulder Posts in Mohmand Agency', 23 January 2012, https://www.ispr.gov.pk/front/press/pakistan.pdf

[12] Clark report, p. 14.

Pakistan's Reply

As expected, Pakistan was shaken by the deaths of two officers and twenty-two soldiers, and the wounding of thirteen others at their two border posts named Volcano and Boulder. The military response was swift and decisive. The army chief called the IG Frontier Force (FF) in Khyber Pakhtunkhwa at 9 p.m. on 26 November, and ordered the GLOC to Afghanistan to be shut down. He then called Prime Minister Gilani in Multan and requested him to return from his son's wedding so that Pakistan could coordinate its response to the American attack.[13] Kayani believed that the GLOC closing would be temporary and was a means of getting the Americans to focus on this issue at hand. He said he conveyed this to the government. The government appears to have had a different view of the length of the blockade imposed by Kayani.

Foreign Minister Hina Rabbani Khar was the point person in contacts with the US government. Early on the morning of 27 November, she called Secretary of State Hillary Clinton to complain about the attack and said that it 'negates the progress made by the two countries on improving relations'. Pakistan also lodged a protest with Afghanistan and urged its neighbour to prevent future air strikes from its territory. Khar recalled that Clinton shared 'her deepest sympathies' at the loss of Pakistani lives. Later, both Clinton and Secretary of Defense Leon Panetta issued a joint statement offering 'their deepest condolences for the loss of life', and they supported 'fully NATO's intention to investigate immediately' the attack on Salala.[14]

Khar remembered that 'the Military was not very strong on what our reaction should be. We [the civilian government] were ready to close down the door.' She said she 'warned Kayani that if we don't take a strong position the message you would give to the US is that they can do what they want'. The civil and military leadership were in agreement on the lack of usefulness of an American apology, though they continued to press for it. 'What does it do for us?' Kayani agreed with Khar. He said, 'It will

---

[13]   Author interview with Kayani, February 2016.

[14]   Karin Brulliard, 'Pakistani Officials Say Alleged NATO Attack Kills 24 Soldiers', *Washington Post*, 27 November 2011, https://www.washingtonpost.com/world/pakistani-officials-say-alleged-nato-attack-kills-at-least-12/2011/11/26/gIQA2mqtxN_story.html?utm_term=.471e5621260f

go in the dustbin!'[15] But she reckoned that Kayani wanted to get more out of the Americans on the GLOC, while the civilians wanted to take a firmer position. Initially, the two sides were together. Later Khar said the government wanted to open the GLOC but the army delayed. This runs counter to Kayani's narrative and even to the public record.

The government took the issue to parliament. On 2 December 2011, the prime minister and relevant cabinet ministers and officers of the armed forces appeared before the Parliamentary Committee on National Security and gave a comprehensive briefing on Salala as well as the coordination mechanisms with the US, ISAF and NATO, including agreed Standard Operating Procedures. Foreign Minister Khar briefed the committee on 12 December and presented the recommendations of the Pakistani envoys conference held in Islamabad on 12 December. The committee was also briefed on extant agreements on cooperation between Pakistan and the Coalition in Afghanistan, but was not shown the actual documents.[16] The defence secretary was asked by the committee to get the response of the 'stakeholders' connected with the Ministry of Defence (MoD) to these recommendations. On 24 December, the defence secretary informed the committee that the 'stakeholders' concurred with the recommendations and also offered his ministry's views as well as the texts of various agreements signed with the US, ISAF and NATO. The committee then formulated its draft recommendations and on 5 January sought institutional responses from both the ministries of foreign affairs and defence. Their views were taken into account five days later. The finance ministry's views were also sought on the economic impact of the situation and its consequences. The committee finalized its report on 11 January 2012, containing sixteen main and twenty-four sub-recommendations that were conveyed to the Speaker of the National Assembly and the prime minister on 12 January 2012. (One member, Senator Prof. Khurshid Ahmed of the Jamaat-e-Islami [JI], later resigned from the group on 24 January.)

After reiterating Pakistan's sovereignty and the need for an independent foreign policy, the committee reaffirmed Pakistan's 'commitment to the elimination of terrorism and combating extremism in pursuance of its national interest'. It also demanded an 'unconditional apology from the US' for the 'unprovoked' attack on Salala and asked that 'those held

---

[15] Author interview with Hina Rabbani Khar, Lahore, 21 February 2016.

[16] A senior foreign office staff member confirmed this.

responsible . . . should be brought to justice'. It also demanded that parliament should approve 'any use of Pakistani bases or airspace' and that all agreements be put in writing. It also recommended that the original Memorandum of Understanding of 19 June 2002 with the Ministry of Defence of the UK and Ireland acting as the Lead Nation for ISAF be revisited and the ten-year agreement with the US on Acquisition and Cross-servicing of 9 February 2012 should be renewed with terms that respect 'the territorial integrity and sovereignty of Pakistan'. A laundry list of rules and regulations pertaining to the transit of supplies for Afghanistan via Pakistan then followed, reflecting the wide range of participants and their affiliations, as well as guidelines for relationships with other countries in the region.[17]

An examination of some of the US–Pakistan agreements shows that they were produced in opaque Pentagonese by lawyers for the US military, and mid-level Pakistani MoD officials signed them, probably without understanding the details of the texts that gave the US open access to Pakistani routes and services and little in return. As a former senior Pentagon official told me later, often, senior Pentagon officials had trouble understanding these legal texts!

The Pakistan Military Response to Salala

Within a few days of the attack, the Pakistan Army had prepared its own immediate report on the incident that it shared via a detailed briefing for selected journalists. The briefing was presented on 29 November 2011. I heard about this presentation and contacted a senior member of the military high command to see if I could get a copy, provided it was not classified. I received a copy almost immediately and was told later that it had been cleared at the highest level. I then asked if I could share it and was told I could. In my conversations with senior White House officials, I discerned that they were still waiting for details of the incident from the US military. I immediately shared the Pakistan military briefing with a

---

[17] Report of the Parliamentary Committee on National Security on guidelines for revised terms of engagement with USA/NATO/ISAF. See also: Web Desk, Zahid Gishkori and Huma Imtiaz, 'Nato Attack: Parliamentary Committee Says Pakistan Should Demand Apology', *Express Tribune*, 20 March 2012, https://tribune.com.pk/story/352546/nato-attack-parliamentary-committee-says-pakistan-should-demand-unconditional-apology/

senior White House official so that the Pakistani perspective was available in Washington, even as the DoD conducted its own investigation.

Later, a version of that Pakistani brief was shared with US journalists in Washington by the Pakistan embassy. But B.G. Clark denied having taken any of these presentations or media reports on them into account, when asked by Eric Schmitt of the *New York Times* on 22 December 2011. He did not refer in his report or in the news conference to having seen the official Pakistan military briefing that was available to the White House within days of the Salala attack. 'Unfortunately we did not have Pakistani participation in this investigation,' he said. When Schmitt pressed as to why the US had not sought to redirect questions based on media accounts of the Pakistani version of events to Pakistan, Clark was emphatic: 'The direction I was given. I had very specific things to look at and things that we could take into account.' Clearly, the Pakistani point of view as presented by the media was out of bounds for the report he issued. Also out of bounds was any recommendation for punishments as a result of the investigation.[18] The Clark report failed to explain why Operation Sayaqa had been kept from the ODRP as well as the BCCs where Pakistani officers were stationed, raising the question that this could have been a planned diversion to 'punish' the Pakistanis for their sins of omission or commission related to the interdiction of Afghan Taliban attacks from Pakistani territory.

The Pakistani military briefing laid out in detail the background to the recent operations of the Pakistan Army in Mohmand Agency and the coordination mechanisms with Coalition Forces/ISAF. It listed the use of Centrixs (Combined Enterprise Regional Information Exchange System), email and commercial line and cell phones. In addition, there were personal contacts between senior Pakistani liaison officers at CENTCOM headquarters in Tampa and CENTCOM senior staff, including Gen. Mattis. GHQ Pakistan Army was connected via its Military Operations Directorate with 11 Corps in Peshawar and its formations in the Afghanistan border region as well as with Regional Command East and the BCCs in Afghanistan. The US ODRP was also serving as a connection between Islamabad and Kabul and Islamabad and Washington. The mandate for all these coordination systems, according to the Pakistani presentation, was to 'communicate shared situational awareness of border activities to include

---

[18]   Clark media briefing, 22 December 2011.

surveillance, intelligence, force dispositions and movement in order to de-conflict and coordinate operations against militants.'

A key slide in the Pakistani military presentation identified 'Mutually Agreed SOP for Operations Close to Border.' The Clark report makes no reference to any agreed SOPs nor does it address the list of SOPs that the Pakistani military shared with the world.

The SOPs were:

- Sharing of detailed information about impending operations regardless of size.
- In case fired upon, immediate sharing of information about point of origin to the other side. Responsibility to take action, if confirmed, is of the country from where the fire is originating.
- In case of operation, request for blocking position/complimentary (*sic*) operations on the other side of the border.
- Immediate cessation of fire by both sides when communications established.

All this information was presented by Pakistan before the Clark report was issued. Clark ignored it.

Within a month of the Clark report being made public, and in the absence of any sharing by the US and NATO with Pakistan of a draft of the public report or its classified version, a more detailed Pakistani response was issued. This response raised some key issues related to the events leading up to the Salala incident, the environment, and coordination mechanisms.

The Pakistani report[19] referred to a series of earlier incidents involving attacks on Pakistan military posts in the border region by US/ISAF forces. There were at least four recorded attacks between June 2008 and July 2011 before the deadliest attack at Salala. A total of eighteen Pakistani soldiers were killed and ten injured in these four attacks. One of these four attacks was on Ziarat Post in the area close to Salala on 17 June 2011. The first attack was on 10 June 2008 at Goraprai Post in Mohmand Agency when 'an unprovoked aerial strike' killed eleven Pakistani soldiers and injured seven. The second attack was another air strike on 30 September 2010 in Kurram Agency at Kharlachi Post when two US helicopters killed three soldiers and seriously injured three. The third incident, as mentioned

---

[19]   Op. cit. Pakistan Army report.

earlier, was at Angoor Adda in South Waziristan Agency, when mortar and artillery fire erupted.

According to the Pakistani narrative on Salala, 'Despite repeated contacts with ISAF, including Lt. Gen. (LG) Ken Keen and Maj. Gen. (MG) Laster and activation of other coordination mechanisms, the fire which was proving fatal continued for several hours resulting in the *Shahaddat* [martyrdom] of four Pakistani soldiers.' COAS Gen. Kayani had to intervene personally with Chief ODRP Lt. Gen. Keen, and warn that he would order 'an enhanced level of response' before the firing was stopped. The Pakistani report stated that the resulting inquiry by US/ISAF of the Salala attack and other similar incidents 'failed to hold anyone accountable'.

Separately, a senior Pakistani general involved in border operations for many years stated in a private communication to a senior US military counterpart that the Salala attack was 'the eighth attack on our troops by friendly troops. We have lost a total of 72 troops to our allies. Only 5 of these 8 incidents have been enquired into and none of these enquiries has ever given closure to these events.' He also stated that, 'There has never been a single incident of our [Pakistani] troops ever causing casualties through such friendly fires/activities.'[20]

The Pakistani military pointed out that the Clark report acknowledged that there had been no Coalition or ANSF presence in the area of Operation Sayaqa for some time. Meanwhile, Pakistan had been experiencing infiltration of terrorists from Konar province. Pakistan maintained that 'since September 2011, no crossing from Pakistani side from Mohmand Agency into Afghanistan had taken place'.

Regarding the two Pakistani posts of Boulder and Volcano, the Pakistani report used Google maps to indicate their location relative to the Afghan border and the village of Maya as well as the landing zone north of the village. Photographs of the two posts support the Pakistani claim that each of the two posts constructed two months prior to the attack was located on top of barren mountain ridges with clearly visible bunkers on the ridgeline. They were in the line of sight of Maya village and would have been visible to attacking aircraft and ground troops, especially once flares had been deployed.

---

[20] Private email exchange between a senior Pakistani general and his American colleague in Afghanistan.

Commander 11 Corps Lt. Gen. Asif Yasin Malik, who was responsible for the region on the Pakistan border, arrived at the battered posts the next morning. He was livid at what he saw at Volcano and Boulder and later at the Clark report. He termed the Clark report 'a cover up'. According to him: It was,

> . . . all a cover up. There was a five foot Green and White [Pakistan flag] flying even after the raid, as I was the first one to land in the morning. They [The Americans] had refused a joint investigation. The Red Neck [his angry characterization] pilots actually hunted down the soldiers as they fled the terror of gunships. In fact two of the bodies were found nearly two thousand feet below in a nullah [a dried gully] behind the post. They even intercepted a relief patrol coming to the help of the beleaguered post. All of these [Pakistani] troops were in combat uniforms. As far as location of posts is concerned the US side did not update their maps while locations were updated regularly by LOs [Liaison Officers]. Actually this post was hindering a TTP gathering on Afghan side preparing to attack Pakistani positions. Mohmand has a history of large-scale attacks from Afghan side, some times as large as 200/250. In one incident they even took prisoner 26 FC personnel.[21]

The occupants of the bunkers were in fact not FC but regular Pakistan Army soldiers of the 7 Azad Kashmir Regiment, belonging to 77 Brigade of I Corps, based in Mangla and inducted from their home base at Kharian (near Kashmir) into Mohmand in 2011 to deal with the surge of infiltration from Kunar province. This brigade took over the area in Mohmand and from 26 Brigade in Bajaur that had been deployed for two years. The 77 Brigade continued to monitor the border and manned forty-eight posts on the Pakistani side, while, according to Lt. Gen. Tariq Khan, former IG Frontier Corps (FC) and at that time commander I Corps, there were only twenty-nine posts manned by the Afghan National Army in that sector. Since there was no strong US/ISAF or Afghan National Army or Afghan Border Police presence across the border, they assumed that any movement was by potentially hostile elements on the move into Pakistani territory. The Pakistani report stated:

---

[21]   Communication via email from retired Lt. Gen. Asif Yasin Malik, 16 January 2018.

This is true for both ISAF and Pakistan Military for entire Area of Responsibility of ISAF's Regional Command East (RC-E) and that of Pakistan Military's 11 Corps. Fire is also carried out on *suspected movement(s)*, such fire is called 'speculative fire'. On any given night *several* Pakistani posts, if any when deemed necessary carry out speculative fire.

The Pakistan military maintained that there had been US/ISAF ground activity 'in and around Maya village' prior to 26 November supported by aircraft, and that 2–3 US/ISAF aerial platforms, including ISR aircraft, fighters, helicopters and drones, operated opposite Mohmand Agency on a daily basis. It did not indicate if it had shared the location of the two newly constructed posts named Boulder and Volcano with US/ISAF, but assumed that 'it is inconceivable that these or any other Pakistani Posts in the area were/are not known to US/ISAF.' The Pakistan military blamed the USD/ISAF commanders for not briefing Pakistani military colleagues at GHQ Rawalpindi about Operation Sayaqa, though both Maj. Gen. Laster and Maj. Gen. Nicholson had been involved in the formulation of the concept of operation for Sayaqa. If this was not a witting omission on their part, the Pakistani military maintained that in the planning phase of Sayaqa US planes should have conducted an ISR sweep of the area that would have identified the Pakistani posts. Further, the concept of operations was not formally shared with the Nawa BCC and the Pakistani liaison officer at that post, having been provided by 'an interested third party' that is not identified by B.G. Clark. Nor, as stated earlier, was the concept of operation shared with ODRP in Islamabad.

Regarding the actual exchange of fire, there appeared to be a wide gap between the US and Pakistani versions. The Pakistani military stated that their speculative fire was aimed at a spot 'only 400 metres from Volcano Post, a location which was already registered and which lay almost 1.5 to 2 kilometres away from Maya Village, and in a different direction' from the US/ISAF patrol. The US/ISAF ground force was approaching from a landing zone to the north of Maya Village and heading to the village itself from two directions. 'There is no chance that this fire could have landed even close to US/ISAF GF [Ground Force], let alone being effective.' They maintain that the Pakistani fire could not have provoked 'self defence ROE (Rules of Engagement)'.

There is a clear disconnect between the two narratives. If the US/ISAF troops were far north of the area of speculative fire from Volcano, at whom were the Pakistanis directing their speculative firing? Further, if the Pakistanis were using night-vision goggles, they must have identified the infrared lights in use by the US/ISAF that were ordered switched off by local commanders during the exchange. There are no reports of Pakistani Taliban insurgents using IR devices or night-vision goggles. So, both the US/ISAF troops and the Pakistanis could have ruled out insurgent 'hostiles' as the source of ground-based firing. If the firing was really 'accurate' as described by Clark, why were there no casualties on the US/ISAF side? These issues have not been addressed by Clark, nor in the Pakistani report on Salala. Against this background, the Pakistani narrative challenged the description of the use of force by US/ISAF as proportionate or justified. The attack lasted between ninety minutes and two hours, and involved helicopters, a gunship and fighter aircraft, aided by ISR aircraft. The Pakistanis maintained that after the initial speculative fire, the post personnel were firing in defence mode on the attacking aircraft rather than at the ground force, as alleged in the Clark report.

Poor coordination of information and prohibition against sharing accurate information about the Salala attack with Pakistani liaison officers also came under criticism from the Pakistani military. The Clark investigation report also accepted at face value unverified reports from Afghan Border Police sources that 'insurgents have been wearing PAKMIL uniforms to move freely across the border'. This despite the fact that the investigating team was unable 'to safely travel to the villages on either side of the Afghanistan–Pakistan border that were near the area of the incident'. The investigating report referred in part to capture of 'multiple sets of *salwar kameez* (traditional style dress) made from PAKMIL uniforms'. This the Pakistani military dismissed as 'an unconvincing attempt to cover the US/ISAF attacks by giving a misleading impression that Pakistani soldiers on Volcano and Boulder posts may well have been mistaken by US/ISAF to be anyone else'. In any case, the personnel from 7 AK Regiment of the regular army would not have been wearing traditional salwar-kameez uniforms that are normally associated with the FC. They were in regular Pakistan Army combat uniforms.[22] The possibility remains that the Salala attack was retributive in nature by US commanders who had long served in Afghanistan and lost men to actions they associated with Pakistan-backed

---

[22] Even the FC is now wearing regular uniforms and adopts the traditional garb only for ceremonial occasions.

Afghan Taliban. If so, there should have been evidence presented of prior infiltration from Pakistan in that region. There was none in the Clark report.

Beginning of the End of the Alliance

In many ways, Salala marked the beginning of the end of the Pakistani alliance with the US that had been revived after 9/11. Pakistani Army Chief Gen. Kayani, a quiet man not given to histrionics, issued a very strong command to his troops following Salala, echoing some of the anger and the calls for correction of coordination and cooperation between Pakistan and US/ISAF forces.

In a Command Communique on the 'Acts of Aggression by NATO/ ISAF' in both English and Urdu signed by him in the traditional Islamic-green ink used by Pakistani military and civil leaders, Kayani first praised the soldiers of 7 AK Regiment for doing whatever they could against the US/ISAF attack on Salala. He absolved the Pakistan Air Force since the 'breakdown of communications with the affected posts' prevented the air force from being engaged. Then he ordered that his Command Communique be read out at all regimental durbars (formal gatherings) and posted on regimental information boards:

> I want to re-emphasize and leave no ambiguity in the Rules of Engagement for everyone, down the chain of command, especially the Unit/Sub Unit Commanders. When under attack, you have the full liberty of action to respond employing all capabilities available at your disposal. This would require no clearance at any level. Army will continue to provide the resources as required, on the ground.

Under the pall of Salala, both the civil and military exchanges between Pakistan and the US continued, but in fits and starts. The White House resisted making an apology despite suggestions, among others, from the US embassy in Islamabad. But the damage had been done. US assistance to Pakistan began a steady decline from the heights of 2010. The cumulative damage to the relationship of the Raymond Davis incident, the attack on Abbottabad, the Memogate scandal and then Salala was added on to the institutional memories on both sides of the fractured Afghan border. US military commanders who had grown up fighting the war in Afghanistan through multiple deployments and lost comrades at different levels to Taliban attacks blamed Pakistan for abetting or condoning Afghan Taliban activity and providing them safe haven in Pakistani territory. There was little direct communication or coordination at tactical levels on the border between Pakistani and US/ISAF officers or soldiers. There were no joint border patrols or posts. The BCCs were few and far between, and as the Clark Report showed, the BCCs were open to manipulation of information.

The mistrust between the US and Pakistan was deep, and a symptom of the real underlying disconnect between their different regional strategies and objectives, especially as they related to Afghanistan. At the command level, American officers, who had access to detailed intelligence of contacts between Pakistani intelligence and some Afghan Taliban groups, such as the Haqqanis, were inherently suspicious of Pakistani actions and intent. Pakistan did little to allay these concerns. There was also little communication or trust between Afghanistan and Pakistan. And there was little that the US could do to mend the broken relationship with Pakistan at that stage in its war in Afghanistan. At best, the US could patch things up to tide itself over to the exit plan envisaged by President Obama.

It took some effort, especially on the part of Foreign Minister Khar and her colleagues, with some understanding on the part of the army chief. On the US side, Secretary Clinton chose to take the responsibility. On 3 July, she sealed the deal after speaking with Khar on the telephone.

I once again reiterated our deepest regrets for the tragic incident in Salala last November. I offered our sincere condolences to the families of the Pakistani soldiers who lost their lives. Foreign Minister Khar and I acknowledged the mistakes that resulted in the loss of Pakistani military lives. We are sorry for the losses suffered by the Pakistani military. We are committed to working closely with Pakistan and Afghanistan to prevent this from ever happening again.

As I told the former prime minister of Pakistan days after the Salala incident, America respects Pakistan's sovereignty and is committed to working together in pursuit of shared objectives on the basis of mutual interests and mutual respect.

In today's phone call, Foreign Minister Khar and I talked about the importance of taking coordinated action against terrorists who threaten Pakistan, the US, and the region; of supporting Afghanistan's security, stability, and efforts towards reconciliation; and of continuing to work together to advance the many other shared interests we have, from increasing trade and investment to strengthening our people-to-people ties. Our countries should have a relationship that is enduring, strategic, and carefully defined, and that enhances the security and prosperity of both our nations and the region.[23]

An important announcement though for many, these may have just been empty words.

Kayani had wanted to retrieve a bad situation arising out of Salala. Closing the GLOC was a minor victory for him. But his transactional relationship with the Americans was not to produce full fruit. He failed to launch a much-promised clearing operation against the Pakistani and Afghan Taliban in the borderlands. He was in a constant tussle with the civilian government that wished to have its own relationship with the Americans, whom they saw as their own political insurance against a military takeover. Yet, the Pakistani politicians were unable to assert civil supremacy or back it up with good governance.

On his part, Gen. Mattis had anticipated that Pakistan might use the shutdown of the GLOC as a strategic move of some kind. He appreciated the fact that Kayani had kept the ALOC open even while the GLOC was suspended. But Mattis saw Kayani's move as 'a mistake with [the civilian] leadership adding fuel to the fire. They then lost control.' He maintained that 'we were vulnerable on the logistics lines, so we put together the Northern Distribution Network . . . I don't think they realized that we'd put the Northern Distribution Network together and tested it over the preceding year . . . just out of concern for this sort of action.'[24] The overflights to Afghanistan, after the initial invasion in 2001, were just that. No landings in Pakistan. So the Pakistani public was not aware of them. (By 2018, Pakistani military commanders were referring to over 2 million such flights since 2001.)

ISAF commander Gen. Allen, who had a high regard for Gen. Kayani, calling him 'one of the greatest strategic thinkers I've ever seen' [perhaps in

---

23   Associated Press, 'Text of Clinton Statement on Pakistan', *San Diego Union Tribune*, 3 July 2012, http://www.sandiegouniontribune.com/sdut-text-of-clinton-statement-on-pakistan-2012jul03-story.html

24   Author interview with Gen. Mattis, 2016.

a surfeit of fulsome praise], also spoke about the alternative to Pakistan as a means of supplying the war in Afghanistan.

> We spun up perhaps one of the greatest airlifts in the wake of the Berlin Airlift. I had about sixty days of supplies in all the critical components that I needed. I had them not because of Pakistan but if Iran got shut down and we lost air space control. I needed to be able to fight sixty days. This airlift was so big and so huge that by the time Pakistan opened the ground line of communications, I had over 100 days of supplies. They'd not only failed at starving me out, they weren't really influencing the nature of the campaign.[25]

True, but at what cost? The US airlift was hugely expensive, as explained below.

What Pakistan failed to take into account was that the US had the money and was prepared to pay for setting up and using a Northern Distribution Network to bring supplies into Afghanistan rather than cave in to Pakistani demands. It had in fact begun using that transportation system in previous years. US Transportation Command had begun investigating a network of ships, rail and other surface means of transportation of supplies from Europe to Northern Afghanistan.

> In 2009, fuel and non-lethal cargo began shipping along the NDN and eventually military equipment also began to flow on these routes. The complexity of the routes and the purposefully wide range of countries involved made the cost of transportation over these new routes more expensive and the time to traverse them generally longer than what was observed over the PAKGLOC, but these routes provided a critical fallback position in case of a loss in access to the Pakistan routes. The extra time and costs (which were approximately double what the costs for cargo on the PAKGLOC) incurred to use the NDN were accepted as a necessary cost of doing business to make sure that the coalition did not leave thousands of deployed troops without a logistics network to support them in the case of a falling out with Pakistan. By March 2010, the Commander of USTRANSCOM reported to Congress that while

---

[25]   Author interview with Gen. Allen, August 2016.

the PAKGLOC remained the primary route (50%), 30% of supplies were now flowing on the NDN with approximately 20% flowing by air.

. . . While the PAKGLOC was closed, coalition forces shifted their supply lines to the NDN to the maximum extent possible and by February 2012, 85% of fuel flowing into the theater was traversing the NDN along with a much larger share of other cargo. This shift and expansion led to costs of approximately $100 million per month along the NDN during the closure as opposed to around $17 million before it. However, those costs were dwarfed by the approximately five times the cost per pound that it would cost to shift all that cargo to airlift.[26]

As Secretary Clinton stated when she announced her apology to Pakistan over Salala:

Foreign Minister Khar has informed me that the ground supply lines (GLOC) into Afghanistan are opening. *Pakistan will continue not to charge any transit fee* [emphasis added] in the larger interest of peace and security in Afghanistan and the region. This is a tangible demonstration of Pakistan's support for a secure, peaceful, and prosperous Afghanistan and our shared objectives in the region. This will also help the United States and ISAF conduct the planned drawdown at a much lower cost. This is critically important to the men and women who are fighting terrorism and extremism in Afghanistan. Foreign Minister Khar has informed me that, consistent with current practice, no lethal equipment will transit the GLOC into Afghanistan except for equipping the ANSF.[27]

The US had meanwhile begun withholding payment of CSF to Pakistan, especially for the period when the GLOC was blocked.

Other than some face-saving, Pakistan failed to gain any leverage from the closing of the GLOC, despite US difficulties in activating the NDN, and in the face of Russian influence in Central Asia that was forcing the closure of their airbase in Manas. Pakistan failed to renegotiate the terms

---

[26]   Greg Grindley, 'Mitigating Supply Chain Risk: What the Military Does and You Should Too', Llamasoft, 11 October 2017, https://www.llamasoft.com/ mitigating-supply-chain-risk-military/

[27]   Clinton apology. Associated Press, 'Text of Clinton Statement on Pakistan', *San Diego Union Tribune*, 3 July 2012, http://www.sandiegouniontribune. com/sdut-text-of-clinton-statement-on-pakistan-2012jul03-story.html

for the use of both the ALOC and the GLOC, an inexplicable failure on the part of both its military and the government. The ALOC remained free of overflight charges, even though it was the only way for the US to bring to bear its air power from bases in Diego Garcia and the Gulf. Much later, perhaps too late in the game, in 2018, Pakistani military officers took to mentioning the nearly 2 million overflights in support of the US war effort in Afghanistan. At the commercial charge for such overflights, US aircraft traversing nearly 500 nautical miles of Pakistani airspace would have a value of some $1.3 billion. Not that the US Congress or administration would have willingly handed over this payment ex post. But, it could have been a bargaining chip, one that the Pakistani leadership never deployed.

The 'Good Soldiers'

Beyond the economics and weaponry of the war, there was a human element. Despite the atmosphere of mistrust that pervaded the relationship among Afghan, American and Pakistani commanders, there were some who had forged personal relationships of trust and deep respect. Theirs were not relationships based on expediency or caricature of the 'other'.

As Salala unfolded, the pain of the unfortunate loss of allied lives was reflected in a series of email exchanges between two senior American and Pakistani officers who had served together and established a level of trust that was not common. The American officer wrote to his Pakistani counterpart about Salala:

> I feel compelled to tell you how heartsick I am at the loss of soldiers that I respect, made even worse because this loss was by our own hand. This is the antithesis of everything I have been trying to do for Pakistan since 2005. My mission was to help you and yours, not cause harm . . .
>
> I still carry the burden from the June 2008 and the September 2010 incidents. We should have learned more and insisted on implementing the lessons learned to preclude fratricide ever again. I am being told that Pakistan cleared the fires, but if we did not know where the border posts were, we should have.

His Pakistani friend responded with details about the failures that accumulated during the Salala attack, summing it up thus: 'All liaison systems failed. All communications broke down. This has become a pattern. A Coalition patrol [was] influenced and misled by Afghan Intelligence.' This Pakistani general personally refused to participate in any inquiry into Salala 'since I am certain it would lead to nothing. No procedural, operational, or coordinative measures will be taken; just as I am certain that these incidents will continue and we [the Pakistanis] will always be blamed.' He feared that 'the relationship will be governed more by those who never really wanted this to work. This war can easily be won and the US can even now exit with honour. I hope this is understood since that can only happen with Pak–US military cooperation and no other way.' He blamed the asymmetrical relationship between the US and Pakistan. In other words, this was a true misalliance, a marriage between unequal partners.

His American counterpart blamed the growing perception on the US side of the

> ISI relationship with militant groups intent on killing our soldiers on the Afghan side of the border . . . The help guys like you need and deserve is watered down to meaningless crap because of the chilling effect of our perceptions . . . But I make the distinction between those in the intelligence world and the good soldiers manning the line and doing their duty as they know it. I respect them, because I see myself doing the same thing.[28]

The abiding question was whether the 'good soldiers' would triumph over those who were ensnared by expediency or be compromised by their dependence on the other side. The reality was that Pakistan and the US lost political space in the process, and this was exacerbated by the internal struggles on both sides. Pakistan in particular faced a worsening of the communication and coordination between the politicians and the soldiers.

---

[28]   Private email exchanges between a Pakistani and an American senior officer.

7

Mismanaging the Civil–Military Relationship

Pakistan meanwhile headed into a political mess, with growing distrust between the civil and the military and declining US interest in Pakistan's needs or role in the region. The domestic security situation was deteriorating, with a rise in terrorist attacks. The powerful military was loath to give the civilians the driver's wheel, particularly when it came to traversing the terrain of security and foreign policy. This made it harder for the Americans to influence events in the country, except via the military. Internally, the Zardari government had managed to make some critical changes in Pakistan's political systems, including the devolution of powers from the presidency to the prime minister and shedding ministries from the federal government to the provinces. On paper, it managed to restore Pakistan to some semblance of the federal system envisaged in the 1973 and earlier constitutions. It achieved a major success in the completion of the work of the National Finance Commission after eighteen years of trying to apportion federal revenues among the provinces. Even the mighty Punjab shed some of its share to the other less economically advantaged provinces. However, it failed to properly prepare for this devolution, and acrimony and chaos ensued as the provinces were unable to cope with their new responsibilities.

Against this background, the country headed to fresh elections. This was a landmark for Pakistan. The first potentially peaceful transfer of power from one elected government to another was a major political milestone. The electorate had meanwhile weighed the tenure of the PPP and the provincial governments carefully. As had the military. Yet the latter carefully avoided getting involved in the process except to provide security, as needed.

Mutual distrust between the military and the government persisted throughout the PPP tenure. Both Zardari and his interior minister Rehman

Malik, according to WikiLeaks revelations, feared a military coup. Zardari also feared he would be assassinated.

At one point he said he had instructed his son Bilawal to name Zardari's sister Faryal as president.[1] According to a February 2009 US embassy memo, Zardari told Bilawal that if Zardari was assassinated, Bilawal should name the president's sister, Faryal Talpur, as president. COAS Gen. Ashfaq Parvez Kayani told US ambassador to Pakistan Anne Patterson that Faryal would be a better president than Bilawal. The memo notes that 'embassy officers have been very impressed with Talpur'. UAE's Foreign Minister Abdullah bin Zayed told US Special Representative Richard Holbrooke in January 2010 that Zardari had asked Zayed to convey a request to the UAE president that Zardari's family be allowed to live in the UAE in the event of his death.[2]

Rumours flew at the slightest whiff of an impending coup. One such incident involved the quick dash by a shaken Zardari to Dubai after being presented evidence by the DG-ISI Pasha on 5 December 2011 on what was later called Memogate.[3] This was followed by another public spat between Prime Minister Gilani and the army, when he summarily fired his defence secretary, a retired three-star general, Naeem Khalid Lodhi, in January 2012, replacing him with Nargis Sethi, a civilian. Both the ministries of defence and defence production had gradually become military fiefdoms, with the army chief effectively nominating or, in the case of President and Army Chief Musharraf, seconding military officers to both ministries. This removed the civilian hierarchy from decision making related to military masters.

> Mr Lodhi, who retired from the army last March and became defense secretary in November, became embroiled in a controversy last month after he submitted a statement in the Supreme Court on

---

[1] Saba Imtiaz, 'Pakistan: WikiWreaks Havoc', Express Tribune, 2 December 2010, http://tribune.com.pk/story/84795/pakistan-wikiwreaks-havoc/

[2] WikiLeaks, 'Re: Compilation of Pak Related Wikileaks Stuff', 21 February 2013, https://wikileaks.org/gifiles/docs/10/1039592_re-compilation-of-pak-related-wikileaks-stuff-.html

[3] Issam Ahmed, 'Rumors of "Silent Coup" as Pakistan President Zardari Heads to Hospital', Christian Science Monitor, 7 December 2011, http://www.csmonitor.com/World/Asia-South-Central/2011/1207/Rumors-of-silent-coup-as-Pakistan-President-Zardari-heads-to-hospital

behalf of the Defense Ministry, saying that the civilian government had no operational control over the Inter-Services Intelligence Directorate, Pakistan's powerful spy agency. Saying that Mr Lodhi had overstepped his authority, Mr Gilani objected to the blunt statement, a public acknowledgment that while the intelligence services are technically answerable to the prime minister, they are widely perceived to act independently of civilian control.[4]

The civilian Sethi was eventually replaced by former Peshawar corps commander, Lt. Gen. (retd) Asif Yasin Malik in July 2012. He continued his tenure even after the new administration of Prime Minister Sharif came into power and retired in July 2014. Malik, an independent-minded professional, maintained his autonomy during his tenure, especially when his ministry was assigned to a part-time minister, Khawaja Asif, during the Sharif term, who rarely came to the defence ministry and who concurrently ran the power ministry, according to a senior ministry official. (Asif, a product of the cadet college at Hasan Abdal, a leading feeder school to the PMA, had also publicly castigated the military in his speeches in the National Assembly when he sat in the Opposition benches. This the army never forgot and it limited its direct interaction with him.) Malik notably also rebutted a claim by his former military boss, Musharraf, when Musharraf claimed that he had the support of the Pakistan Army and also when he wished to leave Pakistan for medical treatment abroad. This was done, after Musharraf had returned to wage political battle in Pakistan, against the advice of the military, and become embroiled in court cases galore.

> In a strong rebuff to former military ruler Pervez Musharraf, Defence Secretary Lt General (retd) Asif Yasin Malik said on Tuesday that the army had no stake in the treason indictment of the former president . . .
>
> 'Pakistan Army has no connection with the trial of former army chief Pervez Musharraf in the special court,' Malik told the media soon after attending the meeting of the National Assembly Standing Committee on Defence and Defence Production.

---

4   Salman Masood, 'Secretary's Ouster in Pakistan Adds to Tensions with Army', *New York Times*, 11 January 2012, http://www.nytimes.com/2012/01/12/world/asia/firing-of-pakistans-defense-secretary-raises-tension-with-army.html

The military, according to him, has no interest in the trial. He also pointed out that there are no servicemen present on the judicial panel that heads the special court constituted to try the former president.

The defence secretary said he was unaware that Musharraf had sought army's help to get himself out of the legal mess. Last month, during an interview, Musharraf claimed that he had the backing of the country's powerful army in the case. The military, however, remained silent on the comment made by its former chief.[5]

All this despite the popular perception that it would side with its former chief, Musharraf, if the civilians used his trial to envelope the military into court critiques of the workings or role of the military. Musharraf used this latent military sentiment to try to bring the military on to his side whenever he could. He did this by issuing statements that claimed his continuing and deep-seated support within the military.

From the outset, the PPP government, following the example of earlier civilian governments, including those of Prime Minister Sharif, routinely outsourced various governance functions to the military, showing such deference to the army chief in particular that the general public began accepting a bipolar system of rule in the country, even when democracy ostensibly was being practised. To maintain a semblance of civilian oversight, civilian defence ministers were appointed from time to time, most of whom had little knowledge or interest in defence matters. No cadre in the civil service was created to specialize in managing defence operations or budgets or to work with their military counterparts to jointly craft policies and systems that would benefit the military and the country as a whole. The defence minister under the PPP government was a businessman, Chaudhry Ahmed Mukhtar, who remained a virtual ghost during his tenure, while the retired military officers ran the ministry.[6] He

---

5   *Express Tribune*, 'No Love Lost: Army Has No Stake in Treason Trial, Says Defence Aide', 8 January 2014, https://tribune.com.pk/story/656278/no-love-lost-army-has-no-stake-in-treason-trial-says-defence-aide/

6   I recall getting a message from a US journalist from the Rawal Lounge for VIPs at Islamabad airport that the journalist was interviewing US General David Petraeus, commander CENTCOM, as he left Pakistan after one of his many visits. Across the aisle from him was Defence Minister Mukhtar. The amused journalist noted that they had not acknowledged each other and seemed to not even recognize each other.

was dismissed along with the prime minister when the Supreme Court disqualified Gilani's government in 2012. He came into the limelight once when he reportedly confessed to an Indian TV channel that senior military and civilian leaders knew of Osama bin Laden's presence in Abbottabad, though it seems more likely he did not fully comprehend the question and his answer related to their efforts to find the Al-Qaeda leader.[7]

The military's hands were full anyway, as it faced not only a growing Indian presence on its eastern border but also a rise in militant attacks on it and on the softer civilian targets inside Pakistan. Pakistan ranked third in the Global Terrorism Index behind Iraq and Afghanistan. There were some 2,345 fatalities resulting from terrorism in 2013, a 13 per cent increase over the previous year.

> Over 60 per cent of fatalities were from bombings and explosions and around 26 per cent from firearms. A quarter of targets and deaths were against private citizens, with police accounting for 20 per cent of targets and deaths. The deadliest attacks were against religious figures and institutions which, on average, killed over five people and injured over 11 per attack.[8]

Despite these killings, many religious leaders were challenging the war against militants, and the head of the JI even wondered if soldiers killed in the fight were *shaheed* (martyrs). The powerful military issued a strong statement against that view. The JI removed its errant leader Munawar Hussain.

Politically, the PPP government suffered a setback when the Supreme Court disqualified Prime Minister Gilani on 19 June 2012, effectively removing him from office on 26 April when the Court had convicted him of contempt for refusing to open a case of corruption against Zardari. He was succeeded by Raja Pervez Ashraf, who too was ordered on 12 July to reopen the Swiss graft case against Zardari. The government refused and

---

[7]   Manoj Gupta, 'Pakistan Ex-Defence Minister Ahmed Mukhtar Drops Political Nuke Bomb, Says Osama bin Laden Was Their "Guest"', CNN-*IBN*, 13 October 2015, http://www.news18.com/news/world/pakistan-ex-defence-minister-ahmed-mukhtar-drops-political-nuke-bomb-says-osama-bin-laden-was-their-guest-1151478.html

[8]   Global Terrorism Index, http://www.visionofhumanity.org/sites/default/files/Global%20Terrorism%20Index%20Report%202014_0.pdf

managed to pass a new law to protect the prime minister, but the Supreme Court struck down that law. On 18 September, Prime Minister Ashraf said he would not stand in the way of the revival of the old graft case against Zardari.

The terrorist threat at home was highlighted by a brazen attack in Swat on 9 October on a bus carrying schoolchildren, when an activist for girls' education, Malala Yousafzai, fourteen, was shot in the face and left for dead by the TTP. The US steadily increased its drone attacks inside Pakistani territory. It ushered in the new year with a flurry of seven strikes in the first 10 days of 2013.

Zardari's increasingly feeble government came under fresh pressure from civil society when a fiery cleric from Canada, Tahir-ul-Qadri, led his followers in shutting down the capital Islamabad in January. Soon after that, the Supreme Court ordered the arrest of the new prime minister, Ashraf, on corruption charges. The head of the national anti-corruption body refused to follow the Supreme Court's instructions. The PPP government hobbled across the finish line of its five-year term in March 2013 and preparations began for fresh elections on 11 May.

Before it handed over power, it had the opportunity to craft a new trade relationship with its neighbours, India and Afghanistan. The American influence led to a partial transit trade deal with Afghanistan, but that trade stopped at the Indian border and therefore did not yield great results. The military had given tacit approval for trade talks, but, as Foreign Minister Hina Rabbani Khar explained, they were held back by the army from declaring India a Most Favoured Nation (MFN).[9] Kayani's explanation was that India had to be engaged on a wide range of issues.[10] I challenged that approach by arguing with him that his 'all or nothing at all' approach effectively stopped the trade talks from gaining traction and bearing fruit. Ishrat Husain disputes the Khar explanation, citing the signed approval by the defence secretary of the note prepared by the trade minister, Khurram Dastgir, to give India MFN status and to phase out by 2012 even the negative list for imports from India.[11] Under pressure from the Punjabi agriculture lobby in the waning days of his term, President Zardari and the PPP dithered on the MFN decision and thus Pakistan lost

---

[9] Interview with Hina Rabbani Khar, Lahore, 2016.

[10] Conversation with me in his office at GHQ, Rawalpindi.

[11] Conversation with author, August 2018.

a golden opportunity to reset its relations with India and Afghanistan as a regional trade hub. During this period, the US was improving its trade and investment relations with India, while Pakistan faded in comparison.

Civil–Military Disconnect

The PPP government's relationship with the military was burdened by historical memories. The military tended to accumulate its grievances, real as well as imagined, regarding the party of Zulfikar Ali Bhutto and his daughter, Benazir Bhutto. The elder Bhutto had wished to cut the military down to size, demoting the commanders-in-chief of the services to chiefs-of-staff. But, he failed to understand that their power stemmed from their disciplined and organized institutions, while the political party that he headed, not unlike other political parties, tended to be fractured and weak, especially on governance. Moreover, the much-vaunted quest for democracy continued to be undermined by the behaviour of political leaders. Family rule was the order of the day. Civilian leaders failed to empower the people who elected them time and again, and they failed to deliver on the promise of economic development.

Under President Zardari, the PPP tried to maintain a smooth relationship with the military. Appeasement was the principal tool. Avoidance of confrontation with the military was in fashion, while fearing the military's potential to create political waves. Meanwhile, the general perception was that the PPP leadership was intent on cutting down the opposition while accumulating wealth through surrogates. The military watched all this with a keen eye.

According to Hina Rabbani Khar, there was a 'perennial trust deficit, not unlike earlier governments'. The relationship 'detonated' with 'Memogate', when the military's worst fears about the use of the civilian government's American relationships were fed by the possibility that the Pakistani ambassador in Washington was conniving with Americans to undercut the security establishment inside Pakistan. Khar believed that 'the military role [on the domestic political scene] was very large. Any whisper from them created ripples.'[12]

Her own government contributed to its difficulties when crises erupted. For example, when the Raymond Davis case exploded,

---

[12]   Interview with Hina Rabbani Khar, Lahore, February 2016.

the central government was content to let the ISI and the Punjab government (under the Opposition PML-N) do the heavy-lifting. Similarly, on the perennial issue of drone strikes that provoked much anger among the general population of Pakistan, the PPP's public stance was one of outrage, but it conveyed a different, more accepting message to the Americans in the US embassy in Islamabad and in Washington. Conceded, it attempted to reduce or end the use of drones by the US in Pakistani territory. It also attempted to take control of targeting and management of drone strikes. As did the military. But it appeared that they never tried to coordinate their efforts to that end. A key divisive issue remained the US position that the ISI continued to support extremist Islamists inside Pakistan and maintained ties to the Afghan Taliban, even while professing to be a US ally.

Khar did not recall any discussion with the president or the prime minister on drones. In fact, much to the surprise of the civilian government, the air chief gave a public statement about the ability of the Pakistan Air Force to shoot down drones if the government gave it the order to do so. (This matter was also discussed in the Abbottabad Commission Report and fuelled the debate about civil and military cooperation, or lack thereof.) This statement was made soon after a meeting of the Defence Committee of the Cabinet where he had not raised this issue at all. The Foreign Office stated after the Salala incident that its persons would sit in on meetings of foreign representatives with the COAS and other military leaders. The military resisted, according to Khar. At no time was the Foreign Office apprised by the military that they were 'colluding with the Americans on drones'.[13]

She recalled that when the UN Special Rapporteur wanted to come to study collateral damage caused by drone strikes, the military informed the government that 'we will be exposed on the issue of collateral damage by both the military and drones'. Ambassador Zamir Akram took a strong position in favour of the UN study. But it came to naught. The military refused to cooperate or participate in the inquiry. Interestingly, in the negotiations with the Americans, a senior US official told me that Khar was often seen as reflecting the military's talking points. Domestically, it suited the military to control the public discourse on US drone attacks.

---

[13]   Interview with Hina Rabbani Khar, Lahore, 2016.

Zardari's party and government ran out of steam as the nation went to the polls in 2013. Nawaz Sharif, the self-styled 'Lion of the Punjab', managed to roar back into office for the third time. Despite fears on the part of many analysts that there would be another weak coalition government, the PML of Nawaz Sharif got 188 seats out of a total of 340 in the National Assembly, according to the Election Commission of Pakistan, and 216 out of 300 in the Punjab, establishing itself as a majority party with no need to form a coalition. This was a substantial jump from the ninety-two seats it had won in 2008. Its nearest rival was the PPP Parliamentarians (the official successor of the PPP of old) with only forty-six National Assembly seats, a huge drop from the 125 seats it had garnered in 2008. The PPP had a large majority in Sindh, with seventy-one out of 129 seats. Imran Khan's PTI won thirty-three National Assembly seats and a majority of thirty-seven of 102 seats in Khyber Pakhtunkhwa, where it could form a coalition government, while the PML-N sat in Opposition. The PTI had boycotted the 2008 elections because it suspected fraud. The oldest and most established Islamic party, the JI, won only four seats, while the Jamiat Ulema-e-Islam won thirteen seats in the National Assembly.

Some 84 million Pakistanis went to the polls in 2013, accounting for 55 per cent of the registered voters. This was an increase of some 4 million voters. Overall, the PML-N gained 1,48,74,104 votes, followed by the PTI with 76,79,954 votes, and the PPP with 69,11,218 votes. Independents got 58,80,658 votes, while the Muttahida Qaumi Mahaz, a largely Karachi and Sindh-based party, got 24,56,153 votes.

Balochistan, as usual, had a very mixed bag of results. The PML got nineteen out of the seventy-two seats, with the Pakhtun Milli Awami Party getting fourteen; the National Party, a social democratic party of the Centre-Left variety, got ten seats; and independents got nine. Dr Abdul Malik Baloch became the first provincial chief minister who was not from a traditional tribal chief background. He formed a coalition government with support from the Sharif government at the Centre. The PPP formed the Sindh government. The PTI, for the first time ever, formed a government in KP. In many ways, this was a historic election, with no national party emerging, nor a broad base for the PML-N victory at the Centre.

With this substantial victory under his belt, Sharif was able to form a Central government without being dependent on squabbling or blackmailing coalition partners. Also as the major party in the Punjab, with its nearly 50 million voters, it had a strong grip on the political scene, except the senate that was still in the hands of its political foes, including the PML-Q that formerly backed Musharraf, and the PPP. But he had a fractious political system to deal with, and pressures from abroad and at home continued to mount.

Changed Spots?

Immediately, speculation arose about the change expected in Sharif's behaviour. Some opined that he had learned from his previous stints in government and would alter his method of rule, especially given his lack of political breadth in the provinces. Others averred that he would be much more careful, in dealing with the military, drawing them into decision making in a way that kept them from alienation, and would avoid creating internal power-sharing crises. The more forward-leaning commentators looked for Sharif 3.0 as a newer and updated version of the self-destructing premier of the past. He did not meet their expectations.

Politics as family business did not change with the change in government. Like the PPP, the PML-N government was formed on the bases of personal ties and loyalties, with the party being treated as a fiefdom for the ruling family. Sharif's brother, Shehbaz Sharif, continued to be the chief minister in the Punjab. His older teammates became the Inner Cabinet, including the *Chaar Pyaarey* or Favourite Four who were seen to be closest to him. Among them, his brother Shehbaz, the activist chief minister of the Punjab, spent an inordinate amount of his time in Islamabad. Others were Ishaq Dar, his finance minister and also relative by marriage of their children; Khwaja Asif, who was given the powerful energy portfolio and later the defence ministry too; and Chaudhary Nisar as interior minister and purportedly unofficial liaison with the military. Nisar's late brother Iftikhar had been a friend of Musharraf and was key in recommending Musharraf for the post of army chief when Sharif parted ways with Gen. Jehangir Karamat in 1998.

A second tier of faithfuls included the Planning Minister Ahsan Iqbal and Information Minister Pervaiz Rashid. The cabinet met infrequently. However, most decisions were made by the Inner Cabinet, but not as a group. The prime minister preferred private bilaterals. And the Inner Cabinet members did not get along with each other. The decisions would then be conveyed by an all-powerful civil servant, as in the past, from within the burgeoning bureaucracy of the prime minister's office. Sharif also brought into decision making his daughter, Maryam Safdar, who was married to his former aide de camp, who had left the army as a captain. She was also given responsibility, till a court forbade it, for the Prime Minister's Youth Programme. One of the most experienced old hands, Sartaj Aziz, was given the title of Adviser for Foreign Affairs and rank of minister, but not the autonomous title of Minister of Foreign Affairs, an inexplicable snub for one of the most faithful and competent members of the party. A minister of state for the same ministry was appointed. He was Tariq Fatemi, a former diplomat and another loyal Sharif adviser during the days of exile. And when the opportunity came to elect a president, the titular head of state, Sharif ignored Aziz, who would have been a popular and very competent choice, and brought in a nationally unknown individual from Sindh: Mamnoon Hussain,[14] thus ensuring that there would be no likelihood of any dissent from that quarter. Even the faithful Fatemi was sacrificed eventually to salvage a freefalling relationship with the military.

The NSC was handed over to Aziz, but rarely met and did not function effectively, nor was it given the resources and staffing to operate effectively. The Defence Committee of the Cabinet met rarely. Late in the day, an NSA, Lt. Gen. (retd) Nasser Khan Janjua, was appointed, but he was not given a clear mandate nor resources to tackle the growing issues related to internal and external security. He focused initial attention on relations with India largely through his back-channel sessions with his Indian counterpart, and, when that went into cold storage, he was asked by the prime minister to review the National Action Plan (NAP) against militancy and terrorism. There was no real secretariat to provide materials for discussions. As a result, on national security issues, the military and the ISI had the upper hand in terms of preparation of ideas and getting their agenda approved. Kayani continued to operate directly with the PM on a one-on-one basis, bypassing the chairman of the JCS as being redundant to the process. Every now and then, the chairman of the JCS committee stepped in to clear misunderstandings between the prime minister and the army chief. The meetings rarely produced debate. Contentious issues would be left unresolved and misunderstandings grew over time as participants

---

[14] This remarkably honest man admitted publicly at Cadet College, Hassanabdal, that he had never gone to school. *Dawn*, 'I Have Never Gone to School, Says President Mamnoon', 22 December 2016, http://www.dawn.com/news/1303732

took back their own interpretations of what had been agreed. In many ways, there was little substantive change in the system of decision making from the PPP government, with the military given free rein to craft its plans and pursue them, with little civilian input or oversight.

Dawn Leaks

One public spat between the civil and the military emerged after an incident in October 2016 known as the Dawn Leaks.

> It all started when the *Dawn* journalist Cyril Almeida 'broke confidential minutes' of a meeting among the government and military officials on the 'national action plan' in which the civilians reportedly apprised the military of mounting international pressure for more action against armed groups.
>
> The civilian government's representatives at the meeting gave warning that Pakistan could face international isolation if the security establishment did not take the recommended course of action and what followed suit was the hornet's [*sic*] nest in the military ranks.
>
> Almeida's exclusive story came against a backdrop of mounting border tensions between India and Pakistan following a claim by the Indian government of a cross-border 'surgical strike' by their [forces] on September 18.[15]

The military took great umbrage at the public airing of these differences and pushed the government to take action against the culprits.

> On Oct 10, the then chief of Army staff General Raheel Sharif called on Prime Minister Nawaz Sharif to discuss matters pertaining to national and regional security. During the meeting, they termed the 'fabricated news story' against the national security.[16]

---

[15] Azhar Khan and Baseer Ahmed, 'What Are the "Dawn Leaks"? A Look into Pakistan's Headline-Making News Scandal', arynews.tv, 2 May 2017, https://arynews.tv/en/what-are-the-dawn-leaks-a-look-into-pakistan-infamous-news-scandal/

[16] Khan and Ahmed, 'What Are the "Dawn Leaks"?'.

Almeida was pressured to divulge his sources but properly held his ground. The matter would not die down. The government sacrificed a pawn with the resignation of the information minister, Pervaiz Rasheed. An inquiry commission was set up, but its report was leaked too, leading the military spokesman to publicly reject the 'notification' under which the prime minister approved the commission's findings. Following further pressure from the military, the Minister of State of Foreign Affairs Tariq Fatemi was also let go. Sharif had saved himself, for the time being.

In fact, a senior government official who was at the meeting said there were two meetings. One on Monday, 3 October 2016, that did not have any military members present. And the other on Tuesday that was the NSC as a whole, including military officials. This official characterized the tone of the meeting as cordial, resulting in agreement to send the DG-ISI and the NSA to each provincial capital to convey instructions to proceed against all militant groups. This is disputed by others who maintain that in fact the DG-ISI was at the Monday meeting and that is where there was a sharp exchange between the chief minister of the Punjab and the DG-ISI about some militant groups that were being protected by the military. (Civil servants, even after retirement, are loath to take a position counter to the military, fearing retribution, especially as it relates to post-retirement appointments to head research institutes or ambassadorial appointments. Not without good reason.)

According to the non-official account of the meeting reported by *Dawn*, the issue of Kashmir had arisen after the death of Burhan Wani, commander of the militant Kashmiri separatist group Hizbul Mujahideen, at the hands of Indian forces. The government had sent emissaries around the world to make Pakistan's case on Kashmir and on behalf of the right of self-determination for the Kashmiri people. The feedback from these visits reportedly was not as positive as expected. Even the Turks and Chinese had expressed reservations on Pakistan's stance. This issue snowballed in the discussion. Another issue behind the scenes was the possibility of a further extension for the army chief. Nawaz Sharif was reported to be against that. Also under debate were the cases against persons suspected of militant or terrorist activities. The courts argued that cases were being presented without sufficient preparation and forensic evidence, making it difficult for courts to base judgments on the law of the land. Moreover, overcrowding of court cases made swift justice a rare commodity. In this impasse, whoever had greater potential coercive power triumphed.

Sharif also had to contend with an endless political campaign to unseat him, more often than not led by the PTI's populist leader Imran Khan. Khan's resort to sit-ins or dharnas added a new wrinkle to Pakistani politics. Reports that the ISI head Lt. Gen. Zahir-ul-Islam was abetting the plans for putting pressure on the prime minister to keep him on the back foot added to the confusion of 'who was doing what to whom' but, 'with what effect?' The rumour mills also spoke of a former DG ISI assisting Khan in planning his protests in the heart of Islamabad. Sharif continued to run the country, focusing on his agenda for infrastructure and energy and large deals with China, Qatar and Turkey, among others. Security was left largely to the military, except when the military's operational interests overlapped with Sharif's ideological base, especially in central and southern Punjab. As usual, he showed quiet patience and waited out his military opponents.

Choosing a New Chief

Kayani's term was ending in 2013 and his corps commanders were getting more agitated by the lack of active support for their COIN efforts and for legal and other issues from both the government at the Centre and in the provinces. Sharif waited till near the end of the Kayani term to announce his successor rather than doing it in advance and preparing the way for a smooth transition in which the new chief would be involved in promotion and posting decisions that were pending before the handover occurred.

A number of strong contenders were available to Sharif to select the next chief. But his reluctance to reside his trust in ex-commandos and ex-ISI persons for the powerful post of COAS may have led him to prevaricate and then select Raheel Sharif, whom Kayani had virtually sidelined by removing him from an operational corps, the mainstay of Pakistan's conventional defence against India's land forces in the Ravi–Chenab corridor of the Punjab, and assigning him to the post of IG Training and Evaluation (IGT&E) at GHQ. Raheel Sharif had earlier been commandant at the PMA, before becoming commander of the Gujranwala Corps that Kayani had strengthened with the addition of the armoured division based in Kharian. Kayani had confided in me during one of our GHQ conversations that this was his conventional check against any Indian 'cold start' move into Pakistan, referring to the much-talked-about

Indian plan to rapidly ingress Pakistani territory to capture key locations and make Pakistan sue for peace.

Curiously, during that period, when Raheel Sharif was heading the Gujranwala Corps, Kayani did not appoint him to lead one of the forces in the army's major war game where Foxland (read: India) invades Blueland (read: Pakistan) along the lines of Cold Start. He chose commander I Corps, Lt. Gen. Tariq Khan from Mangla, to lead Foxland, and Lt. Gen. Zubair Mahmood Hayat, a relatively new and hence junior corps commander and former Kayani aide, as commander of Blueland. As a brigadier, Hayat had served as Kayani's private secretary. Blueland had the full complement of the current corps commanders, except I Corps that had a division commander substituting for its corps commander, Tariq Khan, who was commanding Foxland forces. The war game was to last five days. But it ended after two days, highlighting performance issues in executing the defence plans rather than a weakness of the doctrine. That provided much food for thought for the subsequent field exercises under the rubric of *Azm-e-Nau* when the new military doctrine was tested, apparently successfully, and thus validated.

Gen. Sharif took over as IGT&E at a time when the Pakistan Army Doctrine was released via his new outfit. However, this doctrine had been prepared under Kayani and marked a subtle shift from a sole focus on India to looking at internal threats also. Sharif was not the author of this doctrine. But, earlier at the PMA in Kakul, he had transformed the curriculum to introduce anti-insurgency training as a key part of the new system. He showed me with great pride an indoor electronic firing range that he had imported from Germany, where he had attended a junior officers' course and then served an attachment before returning to PMA as adjutant in October 1986.[17] Most of his cadets were proceeding to FATA for action immediately after being commissioned. He created a new physical course to prepare them for irregular warfare and also changed military exercises to use religious zealots as enemies in Tactical Exercises without Troops (TEWTs).[18]

Though he had not fought in FATA, unlike a number of his senior colleagues, Raheel Sharif was well prepared to act when it was needed. It

---

[17] When my late brother, then Maj. Gen. Asif Nawaz, was commandant of PMA.

[18] Nawaz, *Learning by Doing*.

helped also that he had name recognition. His late brother Maj. Shabbir Sharif had been awarded a posthumous *Nishan-e-Haidar*, the nation's highest military honour, in the 1971 conflict with India, and his uncle, Maj. Raja Abdul-Aziz Bhatti, had also won the same award in the 1965 war with India. His father had served as a major in the Pakistan Army.[19] It helped that he was a Punjabi. Ethnic backgrounds mattered, especially to this prime minister. Nawaz Sharif had a built-in wariness of Pakhtuns. A Pakhtun president, Ghulam Ishaq Khan, had fired him once. Another Pakhtun, Gen. Abdul Waheed, had forced him into resigning once. The only Pakhtun in the mix for the COAS slot was Lt. Gen. Tariq Khan, who had made a name for himself in FATA and was very popular with the troops. But he also spoke his mind. And no one in the prime minister's Punjabi inner circle spoke out for him. Moreover, he was being portrayed as the 'American candidate' since he had served with CENTCOM and had good relations with his US counterparts at both CENTCOM and SOCOM. This was a horrible and unfair mischaracterization of a professional general who was a strong-minded nationalist. Prime Minister Sharif put his trust in his namesake general.

Same Page, Different Books?

But it seemed that history was to repeat itself. The prime minister and his coterie assumed they had the new army chief on their side in the crafting of a timetable for tackling the militancy inside the country. They miscalculated the reactions of the new chief. Unlike Kayani, who weighed things over a period of time before acting, the new chief acted with alacrity soon after taking over and responded with full force when militants in North Waziristan killed a number of soldiers in an ambush. This rejuvenated the spirits of the more than 40,000-strong force that had been posted in that

---

[19] Raheel Sharif's father, Maj. Rana Muhammad Sharif, was in the Signals Corps and served in Rawalpindi with my late father-in-law, Lt. Col. J.D. Malik, Commanding Officer, GHQ Signals Regiment, when my uncle, Brig. Muhammad Zaman Khan, was the director of the Signals Corps. Raheel Sharif was born during the family's stay in Rawalpindi. Shabbir Sharif attended our school, St. Mary's Cambridge School on Murree Road, Rawalpindi, before the family moved away to Lahore where both brothers attended St. Anthony's School.

agency of FATA in a wait-and-see mode. I had observed earlier during my own visit to the area that,

> In North Waziristan, the land of the Ahmedzai Wazir and the Daur tribes, and home also to the Haqqani group of the Afghan Taliban, the army adopted what a senior military officer derisively called a policy of *sitzkrieg*—meaning, sitting in camps without any aggressive actions. The army described its passive stance as 'dominating space'.[20]

Junior officers that I spoke to, especially those commanding troops who had been killed by TTP insurgents, including those being given shelter by the Haqqani group, were resentful of the inaction against all Taliban ('good' or 'bad') in their territory.

Nawaz Sharif had tried a peace dialogue with the militants before Kayani's retirement in 2013. That effort fizzled out. Attacks on the military in FATA prompted the new chief to seek action with civilian support. Discussions began between the military and the government on a comprehensive move against the militants in FATA, starting with North Waziristan, which had been spared action under Kayani. Apparent agreement on such an operation had been reached when the prime minister suddenly announced in parliament in the new year a fresh effort to broker peace with the militants:

> Addressing a session of the National Assembly after a span of six months, Sharif said the government wanted to give peace another chance.
>
> The premier announced the constitution of a four-member team—comprising his Adviser on National Affairs Irfan Siddique, veteran journalist Rahimullah Yusufzai, former ambassador and expert on Afghanistan affairs Rustam Shah Mohmand and former ISI official Maj. (Retd) Amir Shah—to holds talks with the militants.
>
> He said that Interior Minister Chaudhry Nisar Ali Khan would assist the committee.
>
> Sharif also called on the militants to observe a ceasefire in the televised speech. He said that he would personally supervise the performance of the committee, adding that he was sincerely trying to restore peace in the

---

[20] Nawaz, *Learning by Doing.*

country and expressed his hope that the other side would reciprocate in a similar manner.[21]

A chill descended on civil–military relations after this surprise move.

The so-called peace talks between Prime Minister Sharif's representatives and surrogates for the TTP broke down roughly a month later when the Taliban executed twenty-six Pakistani soldiers who had been taken captive in 2010 in retaliation for army killings in FATA.[22] The army immediately launched action against the militants, bringing in the air force to hit selected targets. The new army chief was not willing to talk things out nor did he fear the after effects of a counter-strike against the militants.

In retaliation the TTP carried out an attack on Karachi airport's Jinnah Terminal in June that year. The TTP spokesman Shahidullah Shahid called the so-called peace talks a 'tool of war' for the government. '"We carried out this attack on the Karachi airport and it is a message to the Pakistan government that we are still alive to react over the killings of innocent people in bomb attacks on their villages," the TTP spokesman said.'[23]

The tempo of the battle picked up after the Karachi attack, and a full-scale clearing operation *Zarb-e-Azb* (or 'sharp and cutting strike' and named after the Prophet Muhammad's sword in two famous battles of early Islamic history) was launched on 15 June 2014.

The two Sharifs were clearly not on the same page, or even if they were, they were obviously consulting different books. But now the army was in the driving seat and, as many of its leaders were to say later about their efforts, they were determined to take the operations to 'their logical conclusion'. The conclusion was often left undefined, though there were powerful hints that they would follow the evidence to the political sponsors of militancy and terror inside Pakistan, in all provinces. This proved to be mere rhetoric, as later events indicated till late in the Sharif tenure. The

---

[21] *Dawn*, 'PM Sharif Announces Another Push for Peace Talks with Taliban', 29 January 2014, http://www.dawn.com/news/1083531

[22] Maria Golovnina and Amjad Ali, 'Peace Talks between Pakistan and Taliban Collapse after Killings', Reuters, 17 February 2014, http://www.reuters.com/article/us-pakistan-taliban-idUSBREA1G0MP20140217

[23] *Dawn*, 'TTP Claims Attack on Karachi Airport', 9 June 2014, http://www.dawn.com/news/1111397

only logical exclusion appeared to be the removal of the Sharif family from
Pakistani politics. Nothing was done to disarm the Punjabi militant groups,
including those that operated against India. Zarb-e-Azb did manage to
dislodge all militants from their bases and training grounds inside FATA,
especially in the final TTP redoubt of North Waziristan. But it did not
end the insurgency, as promised by the army chief. Nor could it, without
ancillary civilian actions in Pakistan proper. And rumours persisted,
fuelled by US allegations, that the Haqqani group and its leadership had
been spirited out of North Waziristan first to Tank, in the settled areas
bordering the FATA, and later to safe houses in or around Islamabad,
while their operations moved to bases in Kurram Agency, closer to Kabul.

Then occurred another of those seminal events in Pakistani history that
sparked a national outrage and movement. The Taliban attacked the Army
Public School in Peshawar on 16 December 2014—invading a soft target
in the heart of the military cantonment and slaughtering children and their
teachers in a brutal manner. They left 141 dead. Pakistan as a whole was
shocked by the temerity and the wantonness of this attack.[24] Not only had
the Taliban penetrated the military's territory, they had targeted yet again
and with horrible effect the children of the military officers and men that
were waging war against them in the borderlands.[25]

National Action Plan

Faced by this horrific tragedy in Peshawar, the prime minister hastily
assembled his own team and announced on television a NAP to fight
terrorism and militancy.[26] The NAP emerged after a long gestation period
for a National Internal Security Policy that had been launched earlier by

[24] BBC, 'Pakistan Taliban: Peshawar School Attack Leaves 141 Dead',
16 December 2014, http://www.bbc.com/news/world-asia-30491435

[25] An earlier attack on the mosque in Westridge, a military suburb of Rawalpindi
had killed 40 person, including the son of the Peshawar corps commander
fighting the militants in FATA, https://www.theguardian.com/world/2009/
dec/04/militants-attack-rawalpindi-mosque-pakistan

[26] Anup Khaphle, 'Pakistan Announces a National Plan to Fight Terrorism,
Says Terrorists' Days Are Numbered', *Washington Post*, 24 December 2014,
https://www.washingtonpost.com/news/worldviews/wp/2014/12/24/
pakistan-announces-a-national-plan-to-fight-terrorism-says-terrorists-days-
are-numbered/?utm_term=.b6362d358f8a

the Ministry of Interior and that went into a number of iterations but failed to get traction, especially from the military establishment. A key element in the NAP and the preceding National Internal Security Policy was the NACTA that had been created neither with adequate resources nor the desirable and necessary strategic base in the prime minister's own office to allow it to operate effectively. It remained relegated as a sub-unit of the Ministry of Interior and could not take effective charge of its national remit. Soon wags began referring to the NAP as the National In-Action Plan. Even the military courts that were set up for two years to conduct faster trials were unable to fully dent the huge backlog of cases or complete the prosecution of politically connected figures whom they considered to be involved in fomenting militancy and terrorism at the behest of their political masters.

My own nine-month review of the NAP and the civil–military nexus came to the conclusion that the battle against terrorism and militancy is long-term and demands a greater cohesion among the country's civil and military elites than has been evident so far:

> If Pakistan fails to follow through on its promised war against violent extremism, it will invite pressure and interference from powerful forces in the region. This could create conditions of external conflict with a growing and extremely powerful, and also nuclear-armed, India to the east, and an Afghanistan emerging from its decades-long internal wars but now with a large army of some 350,000 that may be tempted to assert its influence in the porous border region. Iran, too, would not countenance unrest on its border with the Pakistani province of Balochistan, a traditional hotspot in Pakistan–Iran relations.
>
> Internally, the failure of the state to assert control over its own territory will continue to spawn the growth of numerous religion-based militant organizations, supported by internal and external actors. A Lebanon-like situation could emerge in Karachi and elsewhere, with open interference in sectarian conflict from external forces, especially Saudi Arabia and Iran. The end result could well be sectarian, ethnic, and rural–urban fights that could challenge the ability of Pakistan's 500,000–strong military to effectively control these internal wars in the absence of adequate and effective civilian structures and policing capacity.
>
> Pakistan's immediate enemy appears to be within the country. Its survival depends on a clear victory, changing the landscape that

nurtures organized militancy, and changing its ideological narrative by removing the overwhelming influence of Islamic extremists from its education and political system. Pakistan must also build a strong and viable economy to bolster its security. The campaign will be long and arduous, and cannot rely on military might alone; it will rest importantly on the ability of Pakistani political leaders and civil society to muster support from the general population to reshape the country's priorities and recast the socio-political compacts that have defined the country since independence in 1947.[27]

My nine-month study, based on many interviews with key players and civil and military experts in Pakistan identified a number of areas where the NAP needed to be improved and supported with much greater sharing of COIN resources by the military with its civilian counterparts. Until the civilian side becomes the frontline force, the military will be unable to take the battle effectively to the militants, especially inside Pakistan's growing cities. And the military also has no tools to tackle the socioeconomic issues that spawn radicalization. Nor does it know how to reshape the educational systems to remove decades of obscurantist Islamist dogma that seeks to divide rather than unite the population of Pakistan. By focusing attention, among other things, on Karachi, I also highlighted the importance of the urban battlefield, if this war was to be won inside Pakistan. By 2017, the NAP had effectively died down, as Nawaz Sharif's political battles took their toll on his famously short attention span. It continues to receive lip service.

The internal warfare continued in 2014 and 2015 with both weapons and words. The fiery cleric from Canada, Tahir-ul-Qadri, who tends to drop in on the scene at critical political junctures, continued to press the government and launched a sixty-five-day sit-in in Islamabad in August, as the country prepared for its Independence Day in 2014. A parallel demonstration by Imran Khan and his PTI was scheduled. The aim was to topple the Sharif government. But with no overt support from the military or from other political parties, those efforts failed.

---

[27] Shuja Nawaz, *Countering Militancy and Terrorism in Pakistan: The Civil– Military Nexus*, United States Institute of Peace Special Report (Washington DC: USIP, 2016), http://www.usip.org/sites/default/files/SR393-Countering-Militancy-and-Terrorism-in-Pakistan-The-Civil-Military-Nexus.pdf

Sharif came under fresh attack as the Panama Papers listing offshore companies owned by a global array of famous personalities came to light. Among the 259 Pakistanis named as owners of offshore accounts in the British Virgin Islands, the Cook Islands and Singapore, via a firm named Mossack Fonseca, were the two sons and daughter of Prime Minister Sharif. The leaks alleged that 'while he was in Opposition, Mr Sharif's children raised a £7 million loan from Deutsche Bank against four flats in London's Park Lane owned by offshore companies based in the British Virgin Islands'.[28] This gave fresh fodder for the loud and rambunctious media in Pakistan on the one hand and Sharif's political opponents on the other, as court cases continued to drag on in an attempt to link him with financial skulduggery. Sharif denied any direct connection with offshore firms. But failed to convince the Supreme Court that ended up disqualifying him from membership of the National Assembly. This, in turn, led to his removal as prime minister.

Changing the Military Leadership

As 2015 ended and 2016 rolled around, and the highly popular army chief Gen. Raheel Sharif entered his final year in office, a fresh issue arose: whether Sharif would give his namesake army chief an extension so he could continue the battle against militancy and terrorism that he had so vigorously prosecuted. The affable general had struck a chord with the public imagination. Though he had his critics within the military and outside, especially of the overblown publicity given to him by the military PR wing, there was no stench of corruption from him or his family. No hints of cronyism either. Placards and banners began sprouting in different cities asking Raheel Sharif to stay on, as if it was his choice alone, amid strong suspicions that the military PR outfit was behind the campaign. The prime minister continued to maintain a stony silence.

The general complicated matters somewhat by releasing a statement early in 2016 via his Tweet-happy head of the ISPR Directorate, then Maj. Gen. Asim Bajwa: 'I don't believe in extension and will retire on the due

---

[28] *Dawn*, '259 Pakistanis Named in Fresh Panama Papers Leak,' 10 May 2016, http://www.dawn.com/news/1257275

date.'[29] In other words, he planned to go home on 30 November that year. The chairman of the JCS was also to retire a day before him. But this did not end the speculation, nor the efforts by interested parties to stir up the pot of rumours and back-room deals, much like the period surrounding the Kayani extension. Numerous press reports hinted at a deal in the works, including speculation by some that a one-year extension might be offered to the general to allow another 'favourite' of the prime minister to become eligible for the army chief's slot. (This one-year extension is always used as a trial balloon by Pakistani politicians. It surfaces in the final year of the army chief's term and then dies down after public debate.) Even diplomatic circles were awash in these rumours and speculations. A usually reliable senior foreign diplomat in Islamabad told me how the prime minister's family and inner circle was pressing him to retain the army chief but the PM was holding out.

Raheel Sharif had by then also become a prisoner of his own propaganda machinery. The ISPR directorate had become virtually a publicity arm of the army alone and spent an inordinate amount of time and effort on projecting the role of the army chief himself. Its seemingly unfettered resources allowed it to contract with private enterprises in the Pakistani media to project not only the work of the military in its fight against terrorism and militancy but also publicize the image of its peripatetic army chief. It also used its clout to get regulatory agencies to rein in critics of the military, according to former ISPR officers. The chief also promoted the DG-ISPR from major general to lieutenant general, a rare promotion for someone in the PR wing. This publicity wave of the army chief created pushback among younger officers. According to one report, at one session at a training institution, Raheel Sharif was asked about the extraordinary projection of the COAS and the credit given to him alone while forgetting the earlier original operations as well as sacrifices of the army as a whole.[30]

Meanwhile, public discussion began about the succession order and the likely chances of different candidates.

---

[29] Baqir Sajjad Syed, 'Gen Raheel Sharif Puts Speculation to Rest, Says Will Retire on Due Date', *Dawn*, 26 January 2016, http://www.dawn.com/news/1235421

[30] A senior military officer, who was there, confirmed this story for me.

The four senior-most officers turned out to be coursemates from the 62nd PMA Long Course at in Kakul, with their seniority based on their rank order at the time they were commissioned in 1980! In other words, they were co-equals, except for this antique and artificial differentiation of their class rank. It has always been the prerogative of the constitutional appointing authority (currently the prime minister) to select the army chief, other services chiefs and the chairman of the JCS Committee. Seniority may play a role, but their recommendations are not binding. However, a prime minister under pressure may be able to use seniority as an excuse for his or her decision.

The top ranking of the four candidates was Lt. Gen. Zubair Mahmood Hayat, who had served as personal secretary to Kayani, then commanded a division in Sialkot, a corps in Bahawalpur, and headed the SPD (responsible for Pakistan's nuclear arsenal and planning). He had then moved to the GHQ as CGS, but had never served in a battlezone on the western frontier. Next in order was Lt. Gen. Ishfaq Nadeem Ahmed, a former division commander in the Swat operation, DGMO, CGS, and then corps commander in Multan. Ahmed was seen by many military observers as the most qualified and battle-tested commander. He was followed by Lt. Gen. Javed Iqbal Ramday, who was commanding the Bahawalpur Corps and earlier had been president of the National Defence University (NDU), He had also commanded a division in Swat and had been injured by sniper fire while flying in a helicopter during that operation.

Finally, there was Lt. Gen. Qamar Javed Bajwa, the IGT&E at GHQ (the same post that Raheel Sharif occupied before he was elevated to army chief). Bajwa, like Raheel Sharif before him, had not served in FATA in the most recent conflict but had commanded the largest corps of the army, X Corps, based in Rawalpindi and commanding an area that encompassed all of Kashmir and the Northern Areas. He had served as a major in the Northern Light Infantry on the LOC in Kashmir, as well as the Force Commander Northern Areas in the same region as a major general. He attended the Army Command and Staff College in Canada and took a summer management course at the Naval Post-Graduate School in Monterey, California. He was a graduate of the NDU in Pakistan. As a major general, he also had been commandant of the School of Infantry and Tactics in Quetta that had been transformed by his predecessor, Maj. Gen. Agha M. Umer Farooq, and then by him, from a conventional training establishment to one that focused increasingly on irregular warfare. It now catered for all arms and not just the infantry.[31] Bajwa's earlier education had been in Rawalpindi at the Sir Syed College and then Gordon College.[32]

Unlike the pool of candidates at the time Kayani left, none of the top four candidates had served in senior positions in the ISI, a particular bugaboo of Nawaz Sharif. But the local rumour mill churned out an allegation that Bajwa was an Ahmadi, a group that had been declared non-Muslim during the elder Bhutto's tenure. His marriage to the niece of a famous Ahmadi general and war hero, Eftekhar Khan Janjua, was cited as proof for this allegation. To his credit, the prime minister chose not to disqualify him on these grounds. He was probably also made aware that Bajwa's father-in-law, a retired general, had declared himself to be a Sunni while he was in service. This bogus allegation against Bajwa continued to haunt him during his term, especially when his extension became disputed.

Each commentator who speculated on the PM's decision brought to the discussion of the selection of the next army chief his or her own set of biases and assumptions. Did the general have battle experience? Was he related to the prime minister's family in some way? Did he have a strong tribal background and following? Would he speak his mind or get along with the PM by going along with him? It became clear that all the contenders were from the Punjab, a criterion that seemed close to the prime minister's heart. Many a prediction by the 'experts' turned out to be wrong.

Why the prime minister delayed his announcement, given the clear choice before him from a good crop of candidates, remained a mystery. He waited till the last couple of days before the changeover, announcing on 28 November that Gen. Bajwa would take over as the sixteenth army chief of Pakistan, while the senior-most, Gen. Hayat, would become chairman of the JCS committee, his titular superior, but with little real power over the

---

[31] I spent time at the Infantry School, its old name that is still used by many, while researching the Pakistan Army's COIN experience, including sitting in seminars and attending a field exercise without troops in the countryside. It was impressive to see that both students and instructors had seen war in FATA and the focus of the training was on understanding the enemy as Islamists who had deviated from religious teachings and were distorting the message of Islam. The discussions were rooted in battlefield reality, not textbooks.

[32] He grew up in Rawalpindi and is the first graduate of these two schools to become army chief.

troops. Only the then prime minister knows why this choice was made. One can only speculate that he selected a professional who might be least interested in politics and had not been talked about as a strong contender. From all accounts, this created a smooth transition at the helm of the Pakistan Army at a critical juncture in its history.

But the honeymoon with the new army chief did not last long. Nawaz Sharif soon came under fire from the judiciary and found himself being disqualified from being prime minister since he was found wanting in terms of the constitutional requirements of good character. This emerged from the investigation into the so-called Panama Papers where he was alleged to have been employed by a company owned by his son in the UAE even while he served as the prime minister, and having failed to disclose that 'employment', though there was no proof that he had actually availed himself of the remuneration from that position. His party alleged that this was a collusive action on the part of the army and the judiciary. Even then, Sharif could not bring himself to identifying the army by name, referring to *'Khalai Makhlooq'* or Space Aliens as the motive force behind his ouster. He was then brought to trial for having failed to satisfy the courts on the ownership of flats in London and, along with his daughter and son-in-law, convicted and sentenced to jail. Shahid Khaqan Abbasi, a technocratic political leader, was brought in to head the ersatz government that remained in power for the remainder of the government's five-year term, while Sharif continued to pull the strings on all major issues.

Against that sorry backdrop, fresh elections were called that eventually produced victory for the 'non-politician' Imran Khan and his PTI in July 2018. Sharif's family members and favourites were trounced comprehensively at the polls, as were the other major parties. Meanwhile, the US relationship continued to slide as American assistance began to dwindle and desperation seemed to set in among the leaders in Washington DC about a failing war effort in Afghanistan. Pakistan came into the crosshairs, becoming a scapegoat and suffering the consequences of aid cutbacks.

8

US Aid: Leverage or a Trap?

Foreign aid is an excellent method for transferring money from poor people in rich countries to rich people in poor countries.

—Peter Bauer[1]

In the waning days of the Muslim League government of Nawaz Sharif's party and the early days of the new army chief, Gen. Qamar Javed Bajwa, the US–Pakistan relationship began heading south in a hurry. Already, the US posture on South Asia had evolved in favour of India as the principal strategic partner of the US in the region reflected in the so-called pivot to the Pacific in the waning days of the Obama administration. That tack had built on the Bush administration's earlier civil nuclear deal that Obama would need to implement, howsoever slowly, given Indian's recalcitrance and sclerotic bureaucracy. Moreover, India's huge economy and a return to positive growth was making it a massive importer of arms on the global stage. This had defence firms in the US salivating uncontrollably. Effectively, the Americans had succeeded in de-hyphenating India and Pakistan, though they were forced to employ Pakistan in dealing with the Taliban in Afghanistan. They did so with a certain pent-up anger at what they saw as Pakistan's 'double game', while imposing greater constraints on what could be provided to Pakistan by way of aid and reimbursements for its assistance in the failing war effort.

---

[1] Mohammad Samin, 'Afghanistan's Addiction to Foreign Aid', *Diplomat*, 19 May 2016, https://thediplomat.com/2016/05/afghanistans-addiction-to-foreign-aid/

The arrival of a new US president in the form of Donald J. Trump, a populist of no firm political leanings prior to his campaign for the Republican Party nomination, added to the growing contumely from the White House for Pakistan and many other Muslim nations that did not appear to toe the US line. A seventy-year-old relationship that involved deep links between the two countries in the area of politics, economics and defence was suddenly being questioned in both the US and Pakistan. A blame game ensued that did not appear to serve the purpose of either side, particularly since it was cast in the context of a losing US and coalition campaign in Afghanistan. The unending war in Afghanistan was testing the stamina of the new US president and the US Congress and public in supporting the embattled and divided Afghan National Unity Government.

Trump had promised during his campaign to close out the US military campaign in Afghanistan. But he readily acceded to his military's demand for a slight increase in the total number of US forces in Afghanistan, accompanied by a small increase in allied forces, to become more aggressive trainers and advisers of the Afghan forces against a rampant Taliban. By devolving responsibility to his new Secretary of Defense, James Mattis, Trump retained the right to change his mind at short notice if domestic politics demanded it. Or if the US suffered massive casualties at any point and provoked the ire of the population at home. The US military fervently believed that the only reason the Taliban remained undefeated was because they, and especially their leadership, had sanctuary in the borderlands in Pakistan. Each new commander promised to turn things around and proclaimed that his forces were 'turning the corner'. So many corners had been turned that they came back to the starting point a number of times. But it seemed Washington had little sense even of recent history. And firing commanders assuaged the angry or disappointed president, whoever it was.

Pakistan believed it had done enough to clear the border areas of militant training grounds and sanctuaries and that it could not afford to alienate the Pakhtun tribals who comprised the Afghan Taliban. It saw them as potentially less hospitable to a surging Indian presence in the region, and especially in Afghanistan. The Haqqani Network, previously based in North Waziristan and later believed to be headquartered in Kurram Agency, were identified by the US forces as the main instigators of high-profile attacks in Kabul. Meanwhile, the Taliban leadership, known as the

Quetta Shura, was reported to be using Balochistan and even Karachi as its base.

Perhaps under the influence of his new and aggressive NSA, Lt. Gen. H.R. McMaster, who favoured relations with India, the 'sworn enemy' of the Pakistanis, President Trump took a strong anti-Pakistan turn. McMaster argued with Chief of Staff Reince Preibus over the need to give a grand welcome for India PM Narendra Modi, including a weekend at Camp David. Modi wanted to go to Camp David and have dinner, bond with Trump. 'It's not in the cards,' Preibus told McMaster. 'We're just going to do dinner here. It's what the President wants.'

'What the fuck?' McMaster blew up. 'It's India, man. It's fucking India.' He understood the strategic importance of India, a sworn enemy of Pakistan. Modi got a 'no-frills' White House cocktail reception instead.[2]

But, after his NSC briefing by McMaster's team during the Christmas break, President Trump got McMaster's message and captured the essence of the complaint against Pakistan in a Tweet on New Year's Day 2018.

'The United States has foolishly given Pakistan more than 33 billion dollars in aid over the last 15 years,' Trump tweeted on Monday morning, 'and they have given us nothing but lies & deceit, thinking of our leaders as fools. They give safe haven to the terrorists we hunt in Afghanistan, with little help. No more!'[3]

He conflated aid with reimbursements under the CSF given to Pakistan to cover its expenses in aid of the war in Afghanistan. But so did every other American leader.

Interestingly, eight years earlier, these were the same factors identified by Pakistani Army Chief Gen. Ashfaq Parvez Kayani in describing how the US viewed this relationship in a famous note that he had handed to President Obama during a White House meeting in October 2010.[4] So, this was not news to the Pakistanis. But it was not something they wished to hear from the new American president.

---

[2] Bob Woodward, *Fear: Trump in the White House* (Simon and Schuster, New York, 2018), p. 146.

[3] Dia Hadid, 'Tensions Rise between US and Pakistan after President Trump's Tweet', NPR, 2 January 2018, https://www.npr.org/sections/parallels/2018/01/02/575056954/tensions-rise-between-pakistan-and-u-s-after-president-trumps-tweet

[4] See next chapter for details.

Pakistan immediately rejected the Trump assertion but chose not to retaliate by cutting off US access to Afghanistan by land and air. Blocking the air route would have effectively closed US support for the land war in Afghanistan but it would have created an immediate rupture in the relationship between the two so-called allies. Pakistan was caught on the back foot though, since it had not taken any proactive steps to forestall US action in the whole year since Trump took office. Wishful thinking, and a belief that the US would come around to Pakistan's point of view, in order to benefit from Pakistan's strategic location, coloured the Pakistani calculations. It chose to take a methodical and measured approach to responding to Trump. But the US and its allies began to tighten the screws, after some years of patience on the part of President Obama, who, according to a senior White House adviser on the region, 'repeatedly and steadfastly refused to address the US grievances': (1) The release of Dr Shakeel Afridi, who was jailed by Pakistan, though he had helped in the search for bin Laden; (2) 'Talibexit', or the reconciliation with the Afghan Taliban that would allow the US to exit Afghanistan with some honour; and (3) nuclear issues, including the steady development of long-range nuclear-capable missiles, as well as so-called tactical nuclear weapons.

The Pakistani approach to Trump's broadside against Pakistan was muted, almost non-existent. It ran counter to US–Pakistani history, especially as it is understood in Pakistan.

Historical Ties

Both Pakistan and the US have had their own reasons for establishing an alliance since Pakistan became an independent state in 1947. Indeed, the US was the superpower ally of choice for Pakistan as it looked for security against a larger and actively hostile neighbour India to its east. The Pakistani fear that the avowedly secular but predominantly Hindu India would throttle the newborn Muslim state of Pakistan was founded on the narrative that India pressured, with the active connivance of the British Governor General Lord Mountbatten, the Hindu ruler of the Muslim-majority state of Kashmir to accede to India. The delay by the ruler of Kashmir in announcing his accession led to an incursion from Pakistani tribals with support from some second-tier Pakistani officers at army headquarters. The government and the Pakistan Army (still under command of British officers at the upper ranks) were late into the battle for Kashmir, while India had already airlifted troops into Srinagar.[5] An unfinished war ensued. The subsequent subdivision of Kashmir into areas controlled by India and Pakistan was the cause of continuous conflicts. India also ceased the transfer of military and other assets to Pakistan under the term of independence from British rule. India and Pakistan shared the Indus River basin and the five rivers of the Punjab (a Persian word meaning five rivers). 'Eight months after Partition . . . India decided to cut off the flow of some of these waters from the Pakistani canals in order to divert them into its own parched areas.'[6] Pakistan's India Paranoia Syndrome became an abiding condition as a result of these actions.

The US needed partners in a global and regional alliance against the spread of the influence of the Soviet Union. Pakistan became a more than willing partner in that alliance that tied together Turkey and Pakistan, and to some extent Iran, to protect Middle Eastern oil against the Soviets. So, military needs became the bedrock of the alliance between Pakistan and the US, based on Pakistan's strategic location and its professional armed forces that were arguably among the best in the Muslim World. The US was fully aware that Pakistan's expanding military and equipment needs were designed for use in defending itself against India. But it needed an alliance in a Cold War in which India ostensibly had chosen to take the path of neutrality while consummating military deals with the Soviet Union and, initially, political ties with China too. Later, as the first and only Muslim nuclear-armed state, Pakistan acquired additional heft. The US persisted in the Pakistan relationship with its eyes wide open. Pakistan took full advantage of that. Now that was being held against Pakistan by a combative new US president with limited knowledge of and interest in history or foreign policy.

The perennial question that was asked over the decades is what appeared in a *New York Times* editorial in 2015, when the Obama administration decided to withhold aid to Pakistan: 'Is Pakistan Worth America's Investment?' The nub of that editorial was:

---

[5]   See chapter 'The First Kashmir War' in Shuja Nawaz, *Crossed Swords: Pakistan, Its Army, and the Wars Within* (Oxford University Press, 2008, 2017), also published in the *Indian Review*.

[6]   'India and Pakistan: An Atlantic Report', *Atlantic*, November 1960, https://www.theatlantic.com/magazine/archive/1960/11/india-and-pakistan/306376/

Since 9/11, the United States has provided Pakistan with billions of dollars, mostly in military aid, to help fight extremists. There are many reasons to have doubts about the investment. Still, it is in America's interest to maintain assistance—at a declining level—at least for the time being. But much depends on what the money will be used for. One condition for new aid should be that Pakistan do more for itself—by cutting back on spending for nuclear weapons and requiring its elites to pay taxes.

Doubts about the aid center on Pakistan's army, which has long played a double game, accepting America's money while enabling some militant groups, including members of the Afghan Taliban who have been battling American and Afghan troops in Afghanistan.[7]

Behind this accountant approach to aid was the obvious calculation that the purpose of US aid to Pakistan was to get military help in fulfilling the strategic aims of the US in the region. But it was also based on the view that US aid was a major determinant of Pakistan's economic development and financial stability. This was a false assumption, based on an inaccurate assessment of Pakistan's own economic resources, its access to other sources of funding, its regional strategic calculations and needs, and the US inability to remember its own historical relationship with Pakistan. To wit, the US got the most of the relationship when it did not overtly tie strings to its aid to Pakistan and when it helped make Pakistan stronger as an economy and polity. As a corollary to this approach, the US laid the grounds of mistrust among the Pakistani people (separate from their government of the hour) when it supported autocrats and dictators who were more than willing to feign friendship with the US and thus garner US approval.

The *New York Times* editorial missed the mark on two points by positing that aid could be used 'as a cudgel to extract better performance from the government in its fight against terrorism'. An experienced and empathetic South Asia hand with deep ties to Pakistan, Andrew Wilder, wrote about the securitization of aid to Pakistan in a study of the earthquake relief:

Security objectives have always had a major influence on US foreign assistance to Pakistan. Aid flows have therefore oscillated wildly based

---

7 Editorial Board, 'Is Pakistan Worth America's Investment?' *New York Times*, 9 January 2015.

on whether Pakistan was a 'frontline state' or a 'forgotten state'. The
resulting feast or famine of aid has undermined the effectiveness of
US development assistance to Pakistan (Wilder, 2009). It has also
contributed to an image in Pakistan of the US as a 'fair-weather friend'
whose aid programmes have much more to do with buying or renting
influence, especially with the Pakistan military, and promoting US
security interests, rather than helping Pakistanis . . . this approach is
based in part on misplaced faith in the effectiveness of development aid
in promoting US security interests.[8]

As Nancy Birdsall, an experienced development economist from the World
Bank who later headed the Center for Global Development in Washington
DC, countered, there were two arguments against the common American
view of economic aid to Pakistan:

> The first is that America's $500 million a year of 'economic' aid brings
> any leverage. Compared to the Pakistani government's own budget of
> around $30.7 billion annually, $500 million is a pittance. Threatening
> to withdraw this money, which is designed, for example, to increase
> access to schooling or provide minimal access to energy in the interests
> of job creation is unlikely to persuade the Pakistani government to
> do a better job of, say, raising taxes on its insider elites or improving
> its own education systems. No doubt the civilian government would
> like to raise taxes and spend more on schooling; no doubt it has
> difficulty doing so because of its own internal politics, and because the
> army will take first dibs on any additional domestic revenue. *But the
> United States' ability to influence this through its economic aid is minimal*
> [emphasis added].
>
> Second is the assumption that the purpose of the American
> 'economic' or development aid is leverage. In fact the purpose is to
> invest in democracy and economic opportunity in Pakistan, in the
> interests of prosperity and stability there. The military aid to Pakistan
> may provide a vehicle for dialogue with the army which may or may

---

8   Andrew Wilder, 'Aid and Stability in Pakistan: Lessons from the 2005
     Earthquake Response' in *Disasters* (Blackwill Publishing)., online, 16
     September 2010, https://onlinelibrary.wiley.com/doi/abs/10.1111/j.1467-
     7717.2010.01209.x

not be thought of as 'leverage' in the fight against terrorism. The development aid is about investing in making Americans more secure in a dangerous world; Americans will be more secure when Pakistan, a nuclear power, is itself more secure, prosperous and democratic. Development aid has the additional benefit of reflecting America's values and generosity as well as its security and commercial interests. Conflating development aid with military is a dangerous trap that we should try to avoid.[9]

Indeed much of the history of the early US intervention in Pakistan and my own analysis of this relationship supports Wilder's and Birdsall's arguments. The most effective US assistance involved creation of human capital and institutions that allowed Pakistan to take on economic management at a much higher level than most developing countries. The export of knowledge and technology that introduced the Green Revolution in Pakistan (and India), as well as the path-breaking work of the Ford Foundation and the Harvard Advisory Group in helping set up the Planning Commission of Pakistan and train Pakistan's stellar crop of internationally acclaimed development economists,[10] was much valued in Pakistan, and not seen as an attempt to influence Pakistan for political purposes. Funding for the Mangla and later Tarbela dams, and the US support for the World Bank to assist India and Pakistan in agreeing on the Indus Basin Treaty did more to avert war and secure the peace in the region than any direct aid from the US. Similarly, provision of wheat under the PL480 programme allowed the US to dispose of its wheat surplus while giving Pakistanis access to a very visible form of US help.

The US also helped Pakistan acquire its first nuclear training and research reactor for the Pakistan Institute of Nuclear Science and Technology (PINSTECH) at Nilore in 1965. It also helped provide seed money via USAID for the Lahore University of Management Sciences, the Institute of Business Administration in Karachi and development of the Forman Christian College in Lahore. The US also helped set up important

---

9   Nancy Birdsall, 'Aid to Pakistan Is Not Leverage', Center for Global Development, Washington DC, 27 January 2015, https://www.cgdev.org/blog/aid-pakistan-not-leverage

10   Professor George Rosen, *Western Economists and Eastern Societies: Agents of Change in South Asia 1950–1970*, Johns Hopkins Studies in Development, 1 April 1985.

agriculture universities in Pakistan to support its Green Revolution. There was no visible quid pro quo involved in these actions as was also the case of US aid to Pakistan during natural disasters such as catastrophic floods or earthquakes (mentioned in detail in earlier chapters).

Both the US and Pakistan failed to recall these earlier successes and focused instead on the failures and the negative spin-off from their more recent partnership. As a result, even high officials were wont to provide caricatures of the relationship, ascribing evil motives to the other side. Distancing the general Pakistani population from the debate and engagement on issues also provided an opportunity for nationalistic and religious elements inside Pakistan to muster public discontent with the US relationship.

The focus then would turn on to failures. These included, among others, the US involvement in the Afghan Jihad that ousted the Soviet Union from Afghanistan. Pakistan took on the role of facilitator. The US provided the funding, along with Saudi Arabia. The US also helped design Islamic school curricula for use in Afghan refugee camps to prepare for and recruit warriors in the jihad. Cheap weapons imported for the jihad leaked into Pakistani society, leaving behind the so-called Kalashnikov Culture that became the bane of Pakistani existence.

> The US also had a large part to play in the spread of the madrassahs in Pakistan. Under President Jimmy Carter, the US established a $500 million fund to prepare Mujahideen to fight against the occupying Soviet forces in Kabul. This figure eventually increased to $4 billion and the project was given the title 'Operation Cyclone.' It primarily aimed at promoting Jihadi culture in Pakistan, and the establishment of Islamic seminaries was an integral part of the operation.[11]

The Saudis and other funders continued to support the madrassahs in Pakistan after the US decamped from Afghanistan and the region in 1990, placing Pakistan under sanctions for developing nuclear processing

[11] Ali Riaz, 'Global Jihad, Sectarianism and the Madrassahs in Pakistan', IDSS, August 2005, cited in: Paul M.P. Bell, 'Pakistan's Madrassahs: Weapons of Mass Instruction?', March 2007, Naval Post Graduate School, Monterey, CA, http://www.dtic.mil/dtic/tr/fulltext/u2/a467143.pdf

facilities, something that had been ignored by US officialdom through a 'willing suspension of disbelief'.[12]

The Aid Strategy

The invasion of Afghanistan in 2001, following the 9/11 attacks on the US by Al-Qaeda, was a military plan. Economics was given a back seat till quite late in the game. As a result, security and aid became intertwined, with aid becoming a junior partner in the process.

Both Afghanistan and Pakistan became the recipient of US aid. Afghanistan received a much larger quantum of assistance, producing the equivalent of the Dutch disease in that war-torn country: when too much money becomes available, it creates its own problems. Corruption ensued, and the results of the investments were hard to identify or measure. Pakistan had been a recipient of US assistance for many decades. But it was a flow with many peaks and valleys. The earliest peaks had been in the Cold War period of the 1950s up to the mid-1960s, when US aid stopped with the advent of the Indo-Pakistan war of September 1965. Pakistan was then under a military autocrat, General, later Field Marshal, M. Ayub Khan. The second peak occurred in 1980 and lasted till 1988 when another military dictator, Gen. Zia-ul-Haq, who had usurped power in 1977, had at first been ostracized but then became an indispensable ally against the Soviet Union in the Afghan jihad. When the Afghan conflict ended with the departure of the Soviets, aid dried up under the pretext of sanctions for Pakistan's nuclear activities. The third major peak of US aid flows reoccurred from 2002 onwards when another hitherto-shunned military usurper, Gen. Pervez Musharraf, suddenly became a friend of the US in the Global War on Terror of President George W. Bush.[13]

---

[12] I recall this term being ascribed to Samuel Taylor Coleridge in our BA English Literature class at Gordon College, Rawalpindi, under Professor V.K. Mall, the principal, whose PhD dissertation had been on William Wordsworth, another Romantic poet.

[13] *Beyond Bullets and Bombs: Fixing the US Approach to Development in Pakistan,* Reports of the Study Group on a US Development Strategy in Pakistan, Center for Global Development, Washington, DC, June 2011. I was a member of this study group and helped present its findings.

History of US Obligations to Pakistan, millions US$(2011)

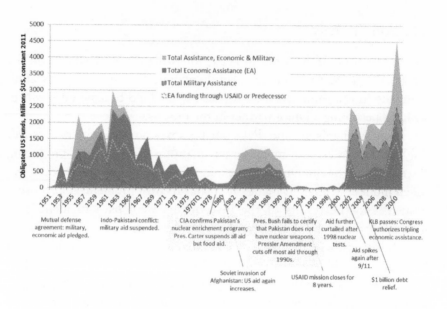

Source: US Overseas Loans and Grants, 'Obligations and Loan Authorizations' (aka the Greenbook). For the years 2002–2011 we have added data on CSF spending to the military assistance category; while CSF is not technically foreign assistance, it has constituted the bulk of military assistance to Pakistan during the post-9/11 period. Source for CSF amounts is 'Direct Overt US Aid Appropriations and Military Reimbursements to Pakistan', prepared for the Congressional Research Service by K. Alan Kronstadt.

Between 1951 and 2011, the US obligated some $67 billion dollars to Pakistan, according to the Center for Global Development. The driving force behind much of this aid was US global or regional security needs. In the period FY 2002–FY 2009, that is, immediately after the Afghan invasion, only 30 per cent of the aid was for economic purposes. The rest was security-related. This general trend continued, even as the overall amount of aid and financial flows trended downward after FY2010. Pakistan ranked fourth in terms of overall foreign assistance from the US, at 3.4 per cent of total US aid, well behind Afghanistan, which received 26.1 per cent of aid. It was ranked fifth in economic assistance with 3.2 per cent of such aid, again well behind Afghanistan which accounted for 8.4 per cent of economic aid. It also ranked fifth behind Afghanistan in military aid at 3.8 per cent, with Afghanistan leading the pack at 57.5 per cent.[14]

This was ironic, since in the eyes of the vice-president of the United States, Joseph Biden, Pakistan ranked much higher on the value chain for the US. Biden was visiting Kabul two months after the 2008 elections.

> As Karzai urged Washington to help root out Taliban sanctuaries in Pakistan, implying that more pressure needed to be exerted on Pakistani leaders. Biden's answer stunned Karzai into silence. Conveying the views of Barack Obama's incoming administration Biden stated: 'Mr President, Pakistan is *fifty* times more important than Afghanistan for the United States.[15]

If only others in the US administration and Congress saw things as clearly as Biden! There was little strategic vision behind the US policy in the region. It lurched from year to year, from commander to commander. The military called the shots.

Pakistan's Accounts of US Aid

The Pakistanis kept close watch on the nature and quantum of US aid, using financial legerdemain in the Ministry of Finance to employ US financial flows as a fungible source for supporting its Balance of Payments. Interestingly, this attracted the attention of both the Pakistan Army, which complained that it was not getting the entire amount allotted for its operations and the US Congress. Former State Bank Governor, Ishrat Husain, disputes this, since the SBP would capture all the transferred dollars, and deposit the rupee equivalent into the relevant military accounts.

Tables 1 and 2, based on US data provided to the Ministry of Finance of Pakistan, give a panoramic view of US financial flows to

---

14 Ibid.

15 Mark Mazzetti, 'The Devastating Paradox of Pakistan', *Atlantic*, March 2018 cited in Coll's *Directorate S*.

Pakistan over the period 2001–2011 and then beyond 2012, including the requirement for FY2019. In the first period, 2001–2011, the trend is upwards. In the second period from 2012 onwards, the trend was declining. Indeed, aid stopped in 2018 following President Trump's Tweet.

Overall, in the first period ending 2011, the total flow was $22.29 billion, while in the period 2012–2015 it was only $15 billion. Civilian assistance during the first period, up to 2011, was $7.626 billion, compared with only $3.296 billion in the second period and dropping to a projected $226 million in FY2019. Meanwhile, military assistance dropped from $3.405 billion to $1.72 billion from the first to the second period. CSF that were not aid but reimbursements for Pakistani expenditures in support of the US-led military operations in the region totalled $8.650 billion in the first period, dropping to $4.574 billion in the second period ending 2016 and were projected to drop to $336 million in 2019, by which time President Trump had stopped all payments to Pakistan. An abiding concern in the US was that no one had a clear idea where the US funding was going and what effect it was producing inside Pakistan as well on the US war effort. Congress took the lead in launching a critique of the US lack of a clear strategy for Pakistani aid.

Table 1. The Upswing: US Assistance to Pakistan 2001–2011
(US$ Millions)

Programme	FY 2001	FY 2002	FY 2003	FY 2004	FY 2005	FY 2006	FY 2007	FY 2008	FY 2009	FY 2010	FY 2011	Total
Civilian Assistance	100	699.5	275.1	306.0	387.6	539.2	576.4	506.8	1366.0	1726.7	1143.4	7626.7ᵉ
O/W-Budget Support		600.0	188.0	200.0	200.0	200.0	200.0		229.0	320.0		2137.0
Security and Military Assistance	77.0	176.5	257.2	112.4	340.8	342.6	333.0	406.2	428.1	493.1	439.2	3405.9b
Other than Military Assistance		220.0			8.0	47.3	62.8	109.8	561.0	743.0	863.0	2614.9
CSF (Reimbursement of Pakistan's Expenditure)		300.0	847.2	753.1	830.5	1073.3	893.4	1002.6	912.9	1294.0	743.2	8650.1
Grand Total	177.0	1396.0	1379.5	1171.5	1566.9	2002.4	1865.6	2025.4	3268.0	4256.8	3188.8	22,297.6

Source: A. Wajid Rana, former Secretary, Ministry of Finance of Pakistan, based on US Data.

Table 2. The Downswing; US Assistance to Pakistan 2011–2018
(US$ Millions)

Programme	Total 2001–2015	FY 2012	FY 2013	FY 2014	FY 2015	FY 2016	Total 2001–2016	FY 2017 Actual	FY 2018 Req	FY2019 Request
Civilian Assistance	7716.7	1067.0	834.0	608.0	561.0	226.0	11012.7	222.5	211.25	222.5
O/W–Budget Support	2137.0	–	–	–	–	–	2137.0	–	–	–
Security and Military Assistance	3405.9	396.0	353.0	353.0	320.0	310.0	5137.9b	285.05	133.5	113.5
Other than Military Assistance	2614.9	453.0	8.0	18.0	23.0	12.0	3128.9	–	–	–
CSF	8881.0	688.0g	1438.0	1198.0	700.0h	550.0h	13455*.0	h	h	h
Grand Total	22,618.5	2604.0	2633.0	2177.0	1604.0	1098.0	32734.0	507.55	344.5	336.0

Additional CSF in FY2013 and FY2014 = $1118.

Source: A. Wajid Rana, former Secretary, Ministry of Finance of Pakistan, based on US Data.

Notes for both tables:

a.   This funding is 'requirements-based'; there are no pre-allocation data.

b.   Includes $312 million 'global train and equip' funds for FY2006–FY2009 as authorized by Section 1206 of the National Defense Authorization Act (NDAA) for FY2006, within which $100 million from the FY2008 and FY2009 funds went to train and equip Pakistan's paramilitary FC.

c. Congress authorized Pakistan to use the FY2003 and FY2004 ESF allocations to cancel a total of $1.5 billion in debt to the US government. Also includes $17 million in Human Rights and Democracy Funds from FY2002–FY2007.

d. P.L.480 Title I (loans), P.L.480 Title II (grants) and Section 416(b) of the Agricultural Act of 1949, as amended (surplus agricultural commodity donations). Food aid totals do not include freight costs.

e. Includes $286 million in Development Assistance appropriated from FY2002–FY2008.

f. CSF is Defense Department funding to reimburse Pakistan for logistical and operational support of US-led military operations; it is technically not foreign assistance. Figures in the CSF row reflect *actual payments by appropriation year* and not appropriations themselves.

g. The FY2013 NDAA disallowed reimbursements to Pakistan for the period of FY2012 during which the US military's GLOC and ALOC across and over Pakistan to Afghanistan were closed by the Pakistani government (November 2011–July 2012).

h. The FY2015 NDAA authorized up to $1 billion in additional CSF to Pakistan, $300 million of which was subject to Haqqani Network–related certification requirements that cannot be waived by the administration. The FY2016 NDAA authorizes another $900 million, with $350 million ineligible for waiver. The FY2017 NDAA authorizes a further $900 million, with $400 million ineligible for waiver. In August 2016, the Pentagon announced that certification for FY2015 would not be forthcoming. A decision on FY2016 certification was pending.

Congressional Critique

A report from the House Committee Oversight and Government Reform, Subcommittee on National Security and Foreign Affairs, Majority Subcommittee Staff,[16] chaired by Rep. John F. Tierney, criticized the poor tracking of US flows once they reached Pakistani hands.

Specifically examining the flow of CSF, the Tierney report was also sweeping in its criticism of aid to Pakistan which had become 'the third largest recipient of United States military and economic support' by 2008.

According to this report,

> . . . much of this financial support has been ad hoc, lacking suitable accountability, arguably ineffective in some respects, and not guided by a long-term strategic plan. Problematic are the military reimbursements to the Pakistani military by means of presidentially supported and congressionally appropriated Coalition Support Funds.

It went on to state that

> . . . there is a credible critique that the program looks like a rental arrangement designed to get Pakistan to undertake operations in the United States' rather than Pakistan's interests.

In other words, congressional critics, rather than Pakistani leaders were seeing Pakistan as a hired gun!

Reviewing CSF payments under three headings—accountability, effectiveness and diplomatic strategy—the Tierney report found the US approach wanting on all fronts. The report suggested reducing the total quantum of CSF payment, reducing it

> . . . back to the relevant Pakistani military components under the current Coalition Support Funds program. This should be examined, and if there

---

[16] 'US Coalition Support Funds to Pakistan: From Ineffective, Unaccountable Reimbursements to a Long-Term, Strategic Relationship', Washington DC, 25 September 2008. Report of House Committee Oversight and Government Reform, Subcommittee on National Security and Foreign Affairs, Majority Subcommittee Staff. Washington DC.

is excess funding once the program is phased out into more appropriate long term, strategic funding platforms, this excess funding should be redirected to these other critical bilateral priorities:

- Establish significant funding to support Pakistan's efforts to enhance law enforcement and justice-sector capacity, something increasingly seen as vital.

- Provide robust funding for education, health, energy, economic, and institution-building that is delivered in a manner that would be visible and meaningful to all segments of the Pakistani populace. It should be a high priority to fund the 'democracy dividend' proposed by Senators Joseph Biden (D-DE) and Richard Lugar (R-IN) to the new democratically-elected Pakistani government and serve as a powerful signal that the United States does, in fact, favor democracies.

The Tierney Report then added a need for a policy shift that never took place in the decade that followed:

Now is the time to fundamentally rethink the complexion of the US relationship with Pakistan, including the various flows of financial support. It is now more than seven years after 9/11 and beyond time for the US to shift from temporary reimbursement and assistance programs to a strategic relationship with Pakistan, its institutions, and its people.[17]

Even the Trump administration failed to come up with a viable and sustainable plan to replace the old arrangement with one that would serve both the US and Pakistan's interests, without blowing up the relationship.

Overall, in 2011, the US provided $1.3 billion, some 30 per cent of total foreign development assistance, to Pakistan, followed by soft loans from the World Bank's International Development Association, and Japan, at 21 and 14 per cent respectively.[18] It also provided indirect assistance via the Asian Development Bank and the IMF in which the US had huge shares. (China meanwhile pledged assistance, largely in the form of loans, worth $850 million.) Yet, the US–Pakistan relationship remained distrustful

---

[17] 'US Coalition Support Funds', a.k.a. 'Tierney Report'.

[18] Center for Global Development, 'Aid to Pakistan by the Numbers', September 2013, www.cgdev.org/page/aid-pakistan-numbers

and constantly verging on collapse. This was largely due to the lack of a coherent and cohesive overall approach to Pakistan, with the military leading the way to satisfy its tactical aims, and Pakistan's ability to play US needs to advantage by doing just enough to keep the flows coming while fulfilling its own regional objectives, especially vis-à-vis Afghanistan. It did so with practised ease, taking advantage of inherent weaknesses in the US aid system and the lack of a centre of gravity in decision making on foreign relations, especially with Pakistan. By 2016, the US share of ODA to Pakistan had fallen to 19 per cent, behind IDA and ahead of other bilateral donors. It totalled only $703 million out of a total of $3.640 billion ODA.[19]

The creation of the SRAP caused some confusion. This office lacked resources to back up its many proposals for the region. But it managed to cajole others to provide the funding it needed to get things done in Pakistan. The Department of State's regional South Asia Bureau had little direct input into relations with Pakistan. So, decision making gravitated to the seventh floor and Deputy Secretary Tom Nides for a while, as he dealt directly with the Pakistani Finance Minister Hafeez Shaikh, among others, to lay the ground for sustained dialogue and to troubleshoot.

In the White House, David Lipton, a former IMF economist who had worked on the Russia bailout at the Fund, knew Pakistan well and kept tabs. He later took that experience back to the IMF when he was made deputy managing director. Mary Beth Goodman on the Holbrooke team was the economic guru there, and later handled the Pakistan economic portfolio at the White House. At Treasury, David Cohen played a big role on the threat financing side and travelled to Pakistan frequently. Neal Wolin represented Treasury at the Deputies meetings in the White House. But surprisingly Treasury did not get visibly engaged on macroeconomic policy issues in Pakistan.

These personalized contacts did not make up for lack of institutional mechanisms. The US Treasury had the resources available directly as well as through the international financial institutions where the US had a major share. But State and Treasury rarely coordinated. It fell to the NSC staff at the White House to bring Treasury into the game. Deputy Secretary Wolin was one key figure given the Pakistan portfolio, as was

---

[19]   OECD Credit Reporting system, Table DAC 2a, July 2013.

Vice-President Biden.[20] It is unclear what role, if any, the CIA had in the discussions of economic or military assistance to Pakistan or how such aid could be better deployed to meet the US war aims in the region. The main weight of managing aid flows fell to a much weakened and transmogrified USAID. It was now largely a contracting agency and lacked the heavyweight economic expertise of the past.

Issues at USAID

Traditionally, the Agency for International Development or USAID had a key role in formulating strategy for economic assistance. Its staff could discuss economic policymaking with Pakistan's best and brightest on an equal footing. But, over time, US foreign aid became primarily a tool for foreign policy, not development policy in recipient nations. It had had a formidable presence in Pakistan until the sanctions of the 1990s led to the diminution of its work and disbanding of the Pakistan hands from USAID and the wrapping up of AID operations in Islamabad.

After the 1999 coup, Pakistan came under even stricter sanctions and USAID effectively ended its presence there. But USAID had become a shadow of its former self, even in Washington. Its leadership had very few, if any, development economists at the helm. Afghanistan was a major magnet for resources and attention and this affected staffing and the selections of experts who knew that country better than they did Pakistan. Moreover, it was now a subsidiary of Department of State. As one senior USAID official told me: 'You have a military that is interested in what they are interested in and that influences what State's going to be interested in.' In essence, State and USAID became tools of the DoD, whose vast resources overshadowed the money available to State and within it to USAID.

Programmatic decisions at USAID were left to the country director and his staff. But the strategy was based on a higgledy-piggledy approach, with little direct input from Washington. Largely due to the increasing security issues, it became difficult to staff the Islamabad office with long-term experts who knew the country and would establish relations not only

---

[20] He sought out analysis of Pakistan's economy and politics from the think tank world, including briefings by me at his home and in the White House before key meetings on Pakistan.

with those in the capital but also with those in the provinces, where the real development project work was to be done.

When Gregg Gottleib arrived in Pakistan in 2012, he was the first director to sign up for a two-year stint. Some of his staff continued to sign up for multi-year stints, as did some regular State personnel. But the challenges were manifold. AID was rebuilding its operations in Pakistan. Since 2008, it had had to deal with a new US administration and an expanded aid programme. The AID staff essentially had to 'jam $1.2 billion into a machine that really managed $100, $150, maybe $200 million [a year]'. The money started stacking up. A major reason on the US side was the need to follow the long and detailed project identification and approval procedures designed for more 'normal' country environments while operating in a country that had enormous security issues and urgent needs. As Gottleib put it:

> You have to maintain all the elements of a mission as if you were in Malawi, a relatively peaceful country, rather than Pakistan, a country in a security crisis zone. I think we ended up with a whole lot of mistakes because we tried to rush into this. Plus we had the disadvantage of Holbrooke [the SRAP] saying 'Now give half your money to the local organizations.' Which in itself isn't bad. But you can't give a group that's been managing a million dollars $40 million, right? We ended up with a number of programs that basically didn't work.

The tussle between State and AID continued to bedevil AID operations too. As a junior partner in Pakistan, AID officials had to listen to the Coordinator for Aid Programmes in Pakistan appointed by State in August 2009 to assist the SRAP.[21] The coordinator, Amb. Robin Raphel, an old Pakistan hand, knew Pakistan, its movers and shakers and its systems well, but was not a development economist and therefore may have been unable to make the powerful economic case for the types of investments that would lay the ground for sustained and sustainable growth. Going along to

---

[21]   ANI, 'Raphel Appointed Coordinator for Non-Military Assistance to Pakistan', *Thaindian News*, Islamabad, 3 August 2009, http://www.thaindian. com/newsportal/south-asia/raphel-appointed-coordinator-for-non-military-assistance-to-pakistan_100226806.html

get along seemed to be the guiding principle for both the US and Pakistani officialdom.

According to Gottlieb, the mantra was: 'You don't get a billion dollars to do development. You get it to do politics.' Resolving these disputes became a necessary part of AID's mission even before it got involved with its Pakistani counterparts. Raphel got into trouble with her own authorities in later years when news leaked that she was under investigation for having become too close to the Pakistanis and possibly spying for Pakistan. Her security clearance was withdrawn. After a prolonged period of suspense and tension for her and her family, the US government quietly closed its inquiry.[22]

'I give a lot of credit to Ambassador [Rick] Olson,' recalls Gottleib. 'When I got there, we sat down and talked and I said to him "What do you want?" He said, "I want the [in]fighting to stop." Olson gave AID freedom to operate fairly autonomously at the day-to-day level. That quelled the battles with State personnel.

The other issue was the rising expectations of Pakistani counterparts who saw the $7.5 billion promised to Pakistan under the KLB bill over five years as manna from heaven. By their calculations, they were expecting $1.5 billion a year. Only the Pakistan embassy in Washington understood the difference between appropriation and authorization; few inside the Pakistani establishment at home understood the US process. 'From the very beginning it was pretty clear that the $1.5 billion wasn't coming . . . If you look at the appropriations, it started at $1.2 billion and just continued downward . . . You look at the latest one, the 2018 proposed budget $200 million.'[23] This was hard for Pakistanis to comprehend. On the US side, there were complications also. Pakistan would demand faster movement of resources. An estimated $2 billion of the $7.5 billion KLB funds remained undisbursed in 2019.

---

[22] Matt Apuzzo, 'US Ends Spying Case against Former Envoy', *New York Times*, 21 March 2016, https://www.nytimes.com/2016/03/22/us/robin-raphel-spying-case-ends-without-charges-lawyer-says.html. See also Adam Entous and Devlin Barrett, 'The Last Diplomat', *Wall Street Journal*, 2 December 2016, https://www.wsj.com/articles/the-last-diplomat-1480695454

[23] Telephone interview with Gregg Gottlieb from Tufts University, 2018.

Dan Feldman, who had been a long-standing member of the SRAP team and eventually became SRAP himself, performed as the external facing part of the team in the earlier years. He recalls Foreign Minister Hina Rabbani Khar exhorting him to 'Speed this up. You need to brand better. You just need to give it [American aid] to Diamer Bhasha [dam]' and so on. He conceded:

> There are so many things that they were likely right about. But there are also just fundamental barriers to effectiveness from Pakistan . . . First of all, I think the expectations for Kerry–Lugar–Berman were way too high and unrealistic . . . [Further, Pakistan] needed to demonstrate each year that they deserved the appropriation. What were we spending on? How was it being used? And then obviously the [Pakistani] military took such an adversarial position against it at the very outset, which really undercut support for it in the United States at the very beginning.

Feldman added that the question in American minds was: 'If we are going through all this effort to try to move this amount of assistance [Over $1 billion a year], why is the military ginning up acrimony about it?'[24]

There were also debates on the US side about the nature of assistance to be given to Pakistan. Feldman said that Holbrooke favoured 'big signature projects', more infrastructure. Holbrooke's view was, 'Let's get more credit for what we're doing. Let's be up there.' And his vision was, 'Let's build another iconic Tarbela [dam] for the twenty-first century. Turns out, Congress doesn't like big projects like that any more; they become big White Elephants. The US isn't equipped to undertake it . . . So it became more focused on core priority areas; energy being the first one, then some infrastructure, like roads, and economic stabilization programs.' It also shifted to more traditional health and education programmes, leaning towards capacity-building rather than hospitals and school buildings. Feldman recalled a frustrated Holbrooke yelling for more signature projects in his meeting with USAID officials. 'Alex Thier will tell you he was the last person that Holbrooke yelled at before he died!'[25] Thier, an old Afghan hand who had developed strong relationships with Pakistan too,

---

24   Interview with Amb. Dan Feldman, Washington DC, 2 November 2016.
25   Ibid.

was a lawyer who was working as an assistant to USAID Administrator Raj Shah on Afghanistan and Pakistan Affairs at that time.[26]

Holbrooke may have been right. The sustaining symbols of US direct or indirect help for Pakistan in the past had been the signature projects like the Mangla and Tarbela dams and universities. No longer were such projects on the USAID drawing board.

One of the most thoughtful analysts of the Afghanistan and Pakistan scenes in Washington DC remained Andrew Wilder, whose parents were Presbyterian missionaries in Pakistan for forty years (first at Gordon College, Rawalpindi, my alma mater, and then in Lyallpur/Faisalabad; his grandparents were missionaries in south India also). He speaks Urdu, the national language of Pakistan; that immediately gave him a leg up. Wilder offered me a detailed and insightful critique of USAID that may not appeal to his Washington audience or even the Pakistani establishment elite. But it is borne out by my own experience:

Three factors . . . have undermined the effectiveness of USAID programs during the past couple of decades. The first is the assumption that humanitarian and development assistance is an effective tool to 'win hearts and minds' and promote stabilization. Security considerations have understandably always influenced USG assistance levels to Pakistan . . . But while levels of assistance were affected by perceived national security interests, it was not until the past 10–15 years that there was an explicit belief in the power of development initiatives themselves to promote COIN or stabilization objectives, or in the case of KLB [Kerry–Lugar–Berman bill] to help 'win hearts and minds' in Pakistan . . . But there was very little evidence that shows that aid is an effective tool to achieve these objectives, and indeed considerable evidence that development assistance can in fact be destabilizing. In my view, a major factor that has undermined the effectiveness of US assistance efforts in Pakistan in recent years is that we set development projects up to fail because they are judged by the extent to which they buy stability and/or popularity—where they have consistently fallen short—rather than achieving development objectives—where they have often achieved some success.

---

[26] He later headed the Overseas Development Institute in the UK.

A second factor that has undermined the effectiveness of USAID is that it has been pressured into becoming a contracting organization more than a development organization. In the 1960s–1980s USAID had many more sectoral experts with hands-on experience designing and implementing programs in the field, and much more country-specific expertise. This meant that there was much more practical field experience and many more opportunities to develop relationships with key host-nation officials and partners. Over time USAID budget cutbacks along with security considerations forced it into becoming a much more bureaucratic institution focusing on contracting beltway bandits to implement programs that were increasingly designed by USAID officials with less and less familiarity with the countries and issues with which they were working.

The third factor . . . is infatuation with 'metrics' for measuring impact, which for some reason are considered much more rigorous if they are quantitative rather than qualitative. [This] can often result in the tail wagging the dog, with projects implemented because their impact is measurable (e.g., kilometers of roads built in FATA) rather than effective in achieving positive development outcomes. The multiple levels of bureaucracy created to ensure greater accountability has created a much more risk-averse environment that can easily smother the creativity and innovation that are essential to identifying more effective ways to address the daunting development challenges in countries like Pakistan.

Wilder simply does not criticize, he also offered me a succinct cure for what ails USAID:

The root causes of the increasingly ineffective delivery of US development assistance is due to the incentive structures for bureaucracies back in DC. This is where we need more studies done, but even these are unlikely to change the policymaking processes and bureaucratic structures needed to make development assistance more effective as there's not a strong enough political constituency to prioritize reform of US foreign assistance policies and mechanisms. Development assistance in countries like Afghanistan and Pakistan, for example, is really only valued by many policymakers if it is justified in terms of promoting security interests rather than improving development indicators. Aid bureaucracies in aid agencies therefore justify what they do in terms of promoting 'stabilization' and security, even if most of our development efforts aren't successful in achieving these objectives. In the current security-centric environment it's hard to see this change to a point where development assistance is valued for achieving development objectives, where there is more of a proven track record of success. We therefore often set development assistance up to fail by expecting it to achieve something it's not very effective at doing—but it's hard seeing that changing anytime soon.

We also know that longer tours of duties where key development (and diplomatic and military) officials can get to know the local contexts and form relationships would also strengthen the effectiveness of our development (diplomatic and military) efforts, but we nevertheless still only assign US officials for one, or if we're lucky, two-year assignments. We also know that 'Use it or lose it' budgeting mechanisms create perverse incentives to spend money quickly and often ineffectively, rather than reward more prudent budgeting based on identified needs, absorptive capacities, changing circumstances, etc . . . These are just some of the examples of very well-known problems that undermine the effectiveness of USAID and other foreign assistance funding, but despite billions of dollars being spent (and often wasted) in contexts like Pakistan and Afghanistan there is still not sufficient political will to prioritize a foreign assistance reform agenda.[27]

The trouble in Washington was that there were few takers for such longer-term and thoughtful approaches. Everyone, from policymakers in each administration to lawmakers on the Hill, wanted that elusive Magic Key to fix the relationship and transform the losing war in Afghanistan into a victory. They knew that the US–Pakistan relationship was in trouble. Almost every time I testified on the Hill, the chair would ask me what that single thing was that we could do to transform it. My response that it was not a linear but a multivariate equation did not satisfy. The only time I seemed to connect with a House committee was when I quoted the Beatles by saying that 'Money can't buy you love!' or when my friend Ambassador Cameron Munter invoked the Tina Turner Doctrine: 'What's love got to do with it?'

---

[27] Email exchange with Andrew Wilder for this book.

Meanwhile on the Pakistani Side . . .

Adding to the difficulty was the incapacity of the Pakistani civilian establishment, especially following the devolution of powers from the federation to the provinces, to manage development assistance and projects. The Ministry of Finance was keen on aid and other financial flows as a means of resolving some of its Balance of Payments difficulties. Its Economic Affairs Division (EAD) was supposed to be the key liaison with donors. But other than being a post office of sorts, over the years it had not developed the expertise or the mechanisms to track and critically review appropriations, disbursements or expenditures, especially at the provincial level. Even today, its website offers little clue on the quantum and distribution of aid within Pakistan or project specific information. (USAID's updated website is a bit more useful but it does not track projects transparently.) Neither the Ministry of Finance nor the EAD has shown any ability related to convening of development economists and project managers from the provinces to better coordinate the development programme and thereby create a useful feedback loop for the Planning Commission.[28] Parliament, in the meantime, slept its way through the whole process, instead of exercising its right to oversee and question economic policy and development policy and administration.

The Ministry of Finance and EAD also do not have a clear strategy for economic development, largely because that is seen to be the remit of the Planning Commission. These two ministries are often at odds. As a result, the criticism often levelled at Pakistan is that its development agenda is driven by donors.

Some of the most scathing critiques have emanated from a former head of the Planning Commission and former IMF official Nadeem ul Haque. In his blog entitled 'Development 2.0', he takes a verbal scythe to both Pakistani and US aid bureaucracies:

---

[28] This was similar to the conditions that persisted when I went as an adviser to Minister of Planning and Development, Mahbub ul Haq, in the summer of 1982, to help him prepare the strategy for the launch of the Sixth Five-Year Plan for Pakistan. At that time, Planning Commission staff, including division chiefs, had difficulty even making long-distance calls to the provinces to discuss issues or gather feedback from the provinces. Every call had to be approved by the Chief Economist Moin Baqai! On my suggestion, Dr Haq changed that in a heartbeat.

Inept leadership, perpetually looking for shortcuts has been begging for aid for most of our history. The result: problems and debt both pile up while donors do all manner of experiment here and leave a mess behind . . .

They give huge contracts—100s of million dollars—to so called contractors—firms of friends and retired aid officials . . . With so much failure around them, donors are quick to reinvent their narrative. Of course the blame is all on the locals who are seen as corrupt, inept and stupid.[29]

He then goes on to level the oft-repeated charge that much of USAID funds go back to the so-called Beltway Bandits in Washington DC or to other NGOs inside Pakistan. Gottleib pushed back on some of these criticisms. The USAID website actually gives the details of US firms that have been given money for projects in Pakistan. But, Gottleib maintains, NGOs like Save the Children 'had about 2,000 people nationwide in Pakistan and they had only one expatriate. She was a Pakistani with a British passport.' Both sides deserve criticism. The US for having focused overly on the use of aid as a quid pro quo for political support in different parts of the world, and Pakistan for failing to wean itself off the aid dependency that trapped short-sighted governments.

Kerry–Lugar–Berman

For much of the Obama presidency, Kerry–Lugar–Berman became a familiar name, often abbreviated to KLB. A programme for the provision of $7.5 billion in assistance to Pakistan over a period of five years was actually called The Enhanced Partnership with Pakistan Act of 2009. Officially known in Senate parlance as S.1707, this act became better known as the Kerry–Lugar–Berman Act. Congress passed it on 15 October 2010. It authorized the release of $1.5 billion per year to the Pakistan as civilian aid over 2010–14. The formal proposal came from Senators John Kerry (Democrat-Massachusetts) and Richard Lugar (Republican-Indiana). What made it significant was that it signalled a major shift in foreign aid to Pakistan, and it effectively tripled the civilian aid given to

---

[29] 'Advocacy—The New Missionaries', 10 March 2015, Development 2.0—by Nadeem ul Haque, http://development20.blogspot.com/search/label/aid

the country. Democratic congressman Howard Berman, whose name was attached to the bill that the president signed into law on 15 October 2009, had produced his own version of the bill that was merged into the much-shorter Senate version over time and became S.1707.

The genesis of this bill can be traced back to the efforts of then Senator Joe Biden, who was chairman of the Senate Foreign Relations Committee. Biden had been deeply involved in the South Asian region and the war in Afghanistan, especially after the US invasion of Afghanistan. Speaking on 28 January 2004 at the Hearing of the Senate Committee on Foreign Relations (CFR) on 'India–Pakistan: Steps toward Rapprochement', Biden praised the recent meeting in Islamabad of Indian Prime Minister Vajpayee and Pakistani President Pervez Musharraf. They were attempting to change the dialogue between the two adversaries from war to peace:

> If a lasting peace does arrive this time, it will not come in by leaps and bounds, but by a series of careful, measured steps. Steps that are no less courageous for all their care and measure.
>
> A lasting peace must be a peace with honor, one in which all sides are winners. The people of India and Pakistan, and Kashmiris on both sides of the Line of Control, must feel as if their aspirations and their security considerations are fully recognized.
>
> A lasting peace can be facilitated by the United States and other nations, but it cannot be imposed by any outside power. The only peace that will survive will be one forged and negotiated by the parties themselves.[30]

Biden had a bold plan—much bolder than the one that President George W. Bush had presented to Congress. That day he laid the ground for that plan by declaring:

> We in the United States must indeed be prepared to facilitate such a peace. It is in our own national interest, and the interest of the world community. Even if the spectre of nuclear weapons were not part of

---

[30] Senator Biden's opening remarks at the Senate Foreign Relations Committee hearing on 'India–Pakistan: Steps Toward Rapprochement', 28 January 2004, https://www.foreign.senate.gov/imo/media/doc/BidenStatement040128.pdf

the equation, the threat of war in South Asia would be a prospect too dangerous to be ignored.

What can we do to help? That depends what the parties themselves request. India and Pakistan have pledged to reopen bus service between the two main cities in divided Kashmir, and there are suggestions that this will be merely the first step towards more entry points and softer borders. Perhaps we can help with technical assistance, and the expertise we've gained from managing thousand-mile borders to our north and our south.

President Bush has pledged a $3 billion aid package to Pakistan, to be spread over the coming five years. We in Congress will have to consider this proposal very carefully. Questions we'll have to consider include:

– Is this the right figure?
– Should any conditions be attached?
– Is the mix of aid proposed by the President—half for military aid, half for nonmilitary—the right ratio?

This last question is, perhaps, the most important. A Task Force of the Council on Foreign Relations has proposed shifting the ratio from 1:1 to 1:2—that is, keeping the overall aid figure stable, but doubling the percentage that goes for such things as schools and hospitals.[31]

Biden had invited three members of that CFR Task Force, Amb. Frank Wisner, Stephen Cohen of Brookings and Michael Krepon of the Stimson Center, to meet him and his colleagues. The ensuing discussion helped Biden work with his Republican colleague Senator Richard Lugar to come up with what they called the Enhanced Partnership with Pakistan Act 2008. This was designed to further US interests at a 'discount', as Pakistani commentator Mosharraf Zaidi later put it. Coming in at $8.72 per Pakistani, compared with $353 per Iraqi, $114 per Afghan and $22 per Egyptian (no longer denizens of a frontline state in a conflict zone). But there were also certification requirements that the administration would have to satisfy for Congress before monies could be disbursed each year.

Senator Biden's main drafter was Jonah Blank, who was the policy adviser to the Senate Foreign Relations Committee on South Asia and

---

[31] Ibid.

the Near East. Blank, a PhD from Harvard, had extensive first-hand knowledge of the subcontinent. He had lived in Mumbai while studying the Dawoodi Bohra Muslim community that led to a book *Mullahs on the Mainframe*.[32] He learned Sanskrit, the ancient language of India, and Hindi and Gujarati, the language of the Bohras. He also lived in Lahore, while studying Urdu. His aim in coming up with the new legislation was to provide a broad framework for a new US–Pakistan relationship that gave the US Congress some control over how the administration would implement the aid programme. Hence the front-loaded requirements for certification by administration officials. The final draft was relatively concise, but Biden and Blank had not taken into account the bigger size of the House of Representatives and the many different views on how Pakistan needed to be corralled, even while the US was attempting to recast its relationship with a country that many considered a sometime 'ally'.

The lead on the House side went to Congressman Berman. His principal South Asia expert was Jasmeet Ahuja, of Sikh parentage, fluent in both Hindi and Punjabi, who knew South Asia very well and had worked closely with Pakistan. She oversaw the sale of the F-16s to Pakistan as well as parts for its different weapons systems. Ahuja was a Stanford graduate who had also worked on her undergraduate and honours' thesis on the birth of India and Pakistan at the University of Oxford (UK), then worked in the Pentagon, and subsequently at the State Department. She had travelled frequently to Pakistan, building relationships there, before being hired by Congressman Berman to become his South Asia adviser. She also had a close relationship with Pakistani officials, being their point of contact on the Hill. These included the Pakistan ambassador in Washington DC, Husain Haqqani.

Haqqani, who also maintained very close relations with Blank, had a direct line to President Asif Ali Zardari. Haqqani was walking the fine line between representing the wide national interests on the one hand, and the sometime competing viewpoints of the Pakistani military and the civilian president on the other. This led to the widespread perception in some Pakistani quarters that he had been complicit in the front-loading of the certification requirements that became part of the bill to aid Pakistan.

Biden's wishes could not be fulfilled. The 110th Congress ran out of time as a new election took place in November 2008. President Bush

---

[32]   University of Chicago Press, March 2001.

was replaced by President Obama, and Biden moved on to become vice-president, taking with him his foreign policy adviser Anthony Blinken. Blank was left behind to continue to shepherd the Biden–Lugar bill that later became KLB, as Senator John Kerry took over the Senate Foreign Relations Committee. Blank was later to leave the Hill to join the RAND Corporation. Blinken went on to become an influential senior official in President Obama's White House, as the Deputy NSA, and then Deputy Secretary of State.

Ahuja recalls that President Obama signalled that 'getting some sort of a financial package for Pakistan, an economic/military package, was his priority. So we, in the House, started working on what it would look like, knowing full well that the Senate was doing the same.'[33] The champions on the Senate side, according to her, were Senators Kerry and Lugar. 'It was Biden's original bill, so Jonah Blank' was also a champion. On the House side, she identified Congressmen Berman, and Ed Royce, a Republican from California, as the strong partners in the effort. Representative Sheila Jackson Lee, democrat from Texas and chair of the Pakistan Caucus, was 'very involved' in the process.

The resulting effort produced what became the 'Pakistan Enduring Assistance and Cooperation Enhancement Act of 2009' or the 'PEACE Act of 2009' on the House side, and the bill that carried the Biden title except for the coda of 2009 as the new date for the 111th Congress. There were thus two different and separate bills.

Ahuja recalls the process:

> The first bill to come out in that session related to Pakistan was the 'House' version of the bill. The Senate then came out with their initial version of the bill. Their initial version of the bill and what became law are very, very different. The format of the bill, the final law, follows the House format of the bill. I recall there were three different titles of it, for instance, so three separate parts [in the House version], and there were similarly three separate parts in what became the law. Similarly, as I recall, there was no authorization specifically for security assistance, for instance, in the Senate original version, as introduced, but in what become law, as in the House version of the bill, there was

---

[33] Telephone interview with Jasmeet Ahuja in Philadelphia, PA, on 20 April 2017.

in fact security assistance authorized, and what the security assistance would be used for.[34]

Given the many contributions from house members, it was challenging to craft the final draft based upon an 'agreed version'.[35]

In her consultations with the Pakistan embassy, the US embassy in Islamabad, think-tank experts and others, Ahuja was trying to garner feedback. Among these sessions, she recalled a visit by Gen. Ashfaq Parvez Kayani and his entourage to the Hill. The group included the DG-ISI Lt. Gen. Ahmed Shuja Pasha and other senior military officers. Congressman Berman spoke to the army chief,

> ... about some items in it that might be less palatable to General Kayani, and the General said, 'I understand. Essentially democracies are a democracy.' He didn't use those words, but he [said that he] understands how the process works. Berman later repeated this characterization of the bill in an interview with the media and his views were also captured by Ahmed Rashid for the BBC.[36]

Amb. Haqqani had also flagged for the Congressman the areas that 'he thought the military would not appreciate'.

He was right about that. The military chose to come out with a statement that essentially refused to accept the conditions perceived to be inherent in the new KLB bill. The parts that the military took special umbrage at actually did not apply to Pakistan per se, they dealt with the certification requirements within the US system for the administration to assure Congress that Pakistan was on the path to representative and independent civilian rule, free of military control, direct or indirect. Interestingly, Jasmeet Ahuja pointed out that the original Senate bill from the 2009 Session (the original 'Kerry Lugar' bill) S.962 required the Secretary of State to

---

[34] Ibid.

[35] I recall sharing some comments along these lines with Ahuja when she called me from Shannon Airport while on her way back from a whirlwind congressional visit to India. She did not recall that specific conversation, but acknowledged that after the mark-up, the bill was changed. The marked-up version is available online for anyone interested in seeing how it progressed.

[36] Ahmed Rashid, 'Pakistan Civil–Military Ties Hit New Low', BBC News, 16 October 2009, http://news.bbc.co.uk/2/hi/south_asia/8309532.stm

certify that the military: '(3) are not materially interfering in the political or judicial processes of Pakistan'. The original House bill, HR1886, had no such language. The Pakistani military was convinced that Haqqani had helped draft or point the way for US Congressional staffers to tighten the screws on the military via the certification rules.

Indeed, Bill S3263 of 15 July 2008, presented in the second session of the 110th Congress by Mr Biden (for himself, Mr Lugar, Mr Obama, Mr Hagel, Mr Kerry, Mr Casey, Mrs Boxer, Mr Durbin, Mr Carper, Mrs Clinton, Mr Dodd and Mr Whitehouse), which was read twice and referred to the CFR, had a relevant section dealing with certification and waivers.

Section 6 of this original draft Senate bill stated:

(c) Certification The certification required by this subsection is a certification to the appropriate congressional committees by the Secretary of State, after consultation with the Secretary of Defense and the Director of National Intelligence, that the security forces of Pakistan—
(1) are making concerted efforts to prevent al Qaeda and associated terrorist groups from operating in the territory of Pakistan;
(2) are making concerted efforts to prevent the Taliban from using the territory of Pakistan as a sanctuary from which to launch attacks within Afghanistan; and
(3) are not materially interfering in the political or judicial processes of Pakistan.
(d) Waiver The Secretary of State may waive the limitations in subsections (a) and (b) if the Secretary determines it is in the national security interests of the United States to provide such waiver.[37]

This certification requirement levied on the US administration was reproduced in Bill S962 that was presented in the 111th Congress by a fresh cast of characters since former senators Obama and Biden had moved on to higher office. This act was passed by the Senate on 24 June 2009.

Similar certifications requirements were in S1707 that passed Congress on 23 August 2010. Under Section 203:

(c) Certification

---

[37] Govtrack.us, 'S. 3263 (110th): Enhanced Partnership with Pakistan Act of 2008', 26 September 2008, https://www.govtrack.us/congress/bills/110/s3263/text

The certification required by this subsection is a certification by the Secretary of State, under the direction of the President, to the appropriate congressional committees that—

(1) the Government of Pakistan is continuing to cooperate with the United States in efforts to dismantle supplier networks relating to the acquisition of nuclear weapons-related materials, such as providing relevant information from or direct access to Pakistani nationals associated with such networks;

(2) the Government of Pakistan during the preceding fiscal year has demonstrated a sustained commitment to and is making significant efforts towards combating terrorist groups, consistent with the purposes of assistance described in section 201, including taking into account the extent to which the Government of Pakistan has made progress on matters such as—

(A) ceasing support, including by any elements within the Pakistan military or its intelligence agency, to extremist and terrorist groups, particularly to any group that has conducted attacks against United States or coalition forces in Afghanistan, or against the territory or people of neighbouring countries;

(B) preventing al Qaeda, the Taliban and associated terrorist groups, such as Lashkar-e-Taiba and Jaish-e-Mohammed, from operating in the territory of Pakistan, including carrying out crossborder attacks into neighbouring countries, closing terrorist camps in the FATA, dismantling terrorist bases of operations in other parts of the country, including Quetta and Muridke, and taking action when provided with intelligence about high-level terrorist targets; and

(C) strengthening counterterrorism and anti-money-laundering laws; and

(3) *the security forces of Pakistan are not materially and substantially subverting the political or judicial processes of Pakistan* [emphasis added].

Via this bill, Congress also sought under Section 302 semi-annual monitoring reports from the US administration:

(11) an evaluation of efforts undertaken by the Government of Pakistan to—

(A) disrupt, dismantle, and defeat al Qaeda, the Taliban, and other extremist and terrorist groups in the FATA and settled areas;

(B) eliminate the safe havens of such forces in Pakistan;

(C) close terrorist camps, including those of Lashkar-e-Taiba and Jaish-e-Mohammed;

(D) cease all support for extremist and terrorist groups;

(E) prevent attacks into neighbouring countries;

(F) increase oversight over curriculum in madrassas, including closing madrassas with direct links to the Taliban or other extremist and terrorist groups; and

(G) improve counterterrorism financing and anti-money-laundering laws, apply for observer status for the Financial Action Task Force, and take steps to adhere to the United Nations International Convention for the Suppression of Financing of Terrorism;

(12) a detailed description of Pakistan's efforts to prevent proliferation of nuclear-related material and expertise;

(13) an assessment of whether assistance provided to Pakistan has directly or indirectly aided the expansion of Pakistan's nuclear weapons program, whether by the diversion of United States assistance or the reallocation of Pakistan's financial resources that would otherwise be spent for programs and activities unrelated to its nuclear weapons program;

(14) a detailed description of the extent to which funds obligated and expended pursuant to section 202(b) meet the requirements of such section; and

(15) *an assessment of the extent to which the Government of Pakistan exercises effective civilian control of the military, including a description of the extent to which civilian executive leaders and parliament exercise oversight and approval of military budgets, the chain of command, the process of promotion for senior military leaders, civilian involvement in strategic guidance and planning, and military involvement in civil administration* [emphasis added].[38]

These conditionalities reverberated in US–Pakistan history for years to come and were reflected in some of the stringent and muscular tactics of the Trump administration in 2017 and 2018. In 2010 and 2011, they created a political fire storm in Pakistan, pitting the military against the civilian

---

[38] Govtrack.us, 'S. 1707 (111th): Enhanced Partnership with Pakistan Act of 2009', 23 August 2010, https://www.govtrack.us/congress/bills/111/s1707/text

government. Lacking the ability to monitor and manage financial flows effectively, the civilian government may have been secretly pleased to see the Americans shine the light on the issues that highlighted the allocation of funds within Pakistan: by whom? for whom? But the military was suspicious of the civilians, their representative in Washington and the Americans.

Backlash from the Military

As CBS News reported:

> In an attempt to address Washington's concerns over Pakistan's military and its long-suspected ties to hard-line Islamic militants, the bill stipulates that US military aid will be withheld if there is evidence that Pakistan is not helping to fight terrorists including al Qaeda and the Taliban.
>
> The bill also seeks Pakistan's cooperation to dismantle illegal nuclear supply networks by sharing 'relevant information from or direct access to Pakistani nationals associated with such networks.'
>
> . . . The bill also provides for an assessment of the control of Pakistan's civilian government over the powerful military which has ruled it directly for more than half its life since it became independent in 1947.
>
> Apparently stung by such provisions, General Ashfaq Pervez Kiyani (sic), the powerful military chief, on Wednesday met with his top commanders at the Pakistan army's general headquarters in Rawalpindi—a suburb (*sic*) of Islamabad, the Pakistani capital.
>
> 'The forum expressed serious concern regarding clauses impacting on national security,' said the military in a statement after the meeting, acknowledging that part of the discussion was on the Kerry–Lugar bill.
>
> The military further said it was providing the government of President Asif Ali Zardari and Prime Minister Yusuf Raza Gilani who both support the Kerry–Lugar bill with its 'formal input' over the issue. The statement also said it was the parliament that would debate the issue and finally enable the government to respond.[39]

A spooked government dispatched Foreign Minister Shah Mehmood Qureshi to Washington. Ahuja recalled that Ambassador Haqqani

---

[39]   Farhan Bokhari, 'Pakistan Military Riled by US Aid Bill', CBS News, 7 October 2009.

played the role of a facilitator and emollient to get Congress to issue a joint statement, separate from the bill, to allay Pakistan's concerns about infringement of its sovereignty.

But the bottom line in Congress, as reflected in Ahuja's words, was clear. The US continued to go for the 'harder assistance', not just infrastructure such as dams or a bridge, like China.

Ahuja summed up:

> So we believe in democracy . . . the whole freedom agenda of President Bush was to spread democracy, and so part of that is helping, for instance, civilian institutions get legs. Ensuring that the military isn't involved in selecting government, and we hear, and have heard, and continue to hear voices in Pakistan who agree with us, and so we want to, as we say in US parlance, amplify those voices and give them a voice.
>
> That was the intent of the bill. Maybe it's impossible . . . We want to get our hands dirty and help on women's empowerment or women's rights because we think there's profound change that can happen from empowering a mother, a sister, a daughter, but it's not sexy [as a dam] and it's really hard.[40]

Not just hard. But also complicated, since both sides continued to have many different voices and the dialogue was filled with noise. The Government Accountability Office, for example, had prompted the emergence of the KLB legislation by calling for a comprehensive programme to address Pakistan's needs. Other voices had chimed in. The Atlantic Council also published a Task Force report, co-sponsored by senators Kerry and Hagel, and presented by me on the Hill in February 2009 in the Senate Foreign Relations Committee Room, listing many issues that needed to be addressed urgently to create a sustainable partnership.[41] Despite these efforts to transmute the relationship from transactional to strategic, the

---

[40] Telephone interview with Jasmeet Ahuja in Philadelphia, PA, on 20 April 2017.

[41] A photograph taken in the Senate Foreign Relations Committee room in February 2009 shows me presenting the Atlantic Council Task Force report while the Task Force co-chairs Senators Kerry and Hagel listen attentively, chins resting on their hands. And Atlantic Council President Fred Kempe looks on. Kerry and Hagel ended up occupying higher offices later in the Obama term. But neither could effect a massive change in US or Pakistani behaviour.

rifts stayed within each polity and between the US and Pakistan—except for some manner of cooperation between their militaries, though their relationship also was marked by a certain and abiding level of mistrust.

Pakistan continued to operate as an aid-dependent country, living from handout to handout rather than reshaping its economic and political landscape to take into account its natural and human resources as well as its strategic location for economic advantage. The US lacked a strategy for Pakistan that would build its ties with this key South Asian nation on the one hand and help its global aim to contain China's growing influence. It failed to persuade Pakistan to produce a viable and sustainable plan for coordinating receipt and use of US aid to maximum effect. Pakistani civilian governments tended to aim for short-term development expenditures that would yield electoral benefits but not lay the ground for longer-term growth. They also failed to understand or rein in military expenditures to assist the military in improving its internal financial management and to do more with less. Instead, they relied on conniving with donors to send messages to the military. This added to mistrust internally as well as between the US and Pakistan. For its part, the US lost confidence in the civilians and relied heavily on its military partners in Pakistan. But pressure, rather than persuasion, or better still, moral suasion, failed to produce results.

9

Mil-to-Mil Relations: Do More

A persistently nagging theme in US–Pakistan relations, especially in the so-called mil-to-mil relationship between the two militaries, was the US demand that Pakistan 'Do more'. As the Afghan War sank into a quagmire in the first decade of that conflict, the US began to see 'signs that Pakistan may not be a fully willing and effective US partner, and that official Pakistani elements continue to support Afghan insurgent forces'. Indeed,

> . . . during a period of economic and budget crises in the United States, Obama Administration officials and some senior Members of Congress voiced concerns about the efficacy of continuing the flow of billions of US aid dollars into Pakistan, with some in Congress urging more stringent conditions on, or even curtailment of such aid.[1]

US policy took on a catch-as-catch-can approach. Some called it 'kicking the can down the road', a signature criticism of Obama's foreign policy, not just for the Af–Pak region, but also for other wars around the Middle East. By the time President Donald J. Trump was elected, these sentiments bubbled again to the surface. An aggressive foreign policy was the order of the day, launched by a brash and untutored new president who favoured disruption as a tactic and reportedly resisted detailed briefings on complex foreign policy issues.

---

[1]   Susan B. Epstein and K. Alan Kronstadt, 'Pakistan: US Foreign Aid Conditions, Restrictions, and Reporting Requirements', Congressional Research Service, 15 December 2011.

By 2010, President Obama had turned from being actively engaged with Pakistan issues to realizing that it would not be possible to produce a sustainable strategic relationship. His key security policy aides saw him as resigned to a purely transactional relationship from then onwards. (Interestingly, he never once visited Pakistan as president.) The Strategic Dialogue with Pakistan pursued by his team at the NSC and the Department of State sputtered along. But it failed to produce any breakthrough change in Pakistani or US behaviour. The year 2011 proved to be the watershed, not only because of the events that unfolded in Pakistan, but also because it highlighted the misalliance, as US budget constraints forced the US Congress to weigh the placement of further certification requirements on the flow of both civil and military assistance to Pakistan. Pakistan, and especially its military, continued to believe that it remained crucial to the US's strategic calculus in Afghanistan and the region, and that it could leverage its strategic location to good effect. Meanwhile, it chose to avoid taking action against some adherents of militancy and terrorism at home, especially domestic groups that operated against the US in Afghanistan and India, both in Afghanistan and in Kashmir. It had gotten away with this policy for nearly a decade and hoped that the US would continue to give it leeway, as it had done in the past, for tactical reasons.

According to a senior US diplomat with years of experience in the region and Pakistan, 'You can fool the "*gora*" (white guy) most of the time' was the basis of the Pakistani stance. During a conversation, he tested this hypothesis on a DG-ISI, someone who had been trained in the US. After his initial shock and surprise at this direct accusation, the DG-ISI murmured a reluctant and unexpected 'Yes'. The US on its part talked about a strategic approach to Pakistan and the region, but it too continued to behave tactically, shifting its policies and operations frequently and behaving in a transactional manner. It was prepared to look the other way on Pakistani transgressions, in the interest of temporary gains, thus feeding the Pakistani cynicism. It also prosecuted the war in Afghanistan in a manner that defied military logic.

When Gen. John 'Mick' Nicholson took over command in Afghanistan in January 2016, he was the seventeenth allied commander since the 2001 invasion. He had the most experience inside Afghanistan of any of his predecessors. 'In all, Nicholson had spent three-and-a-half years deployed in Afghanistan before he took over command of ISAF, far more than any of his predecessors when they took the top post in Kabul. Between 16 months as a brigade commander in the country's mountainous east, a second year as a one-star general in the south, and a third year as the top operations deputy to the four-star U.S. and NATO commander in the Afghan capital, Nicholson also did an intervening tour supervising the Pentagon's highest-level cell dedicated to the Afghanistan-Pakistan theater.'[2]

He ended his term on 2 September 2018 and was succeeded by Gen. Austin 'Scott' Miller, the eighteenth allied commander.

Afghanistan: One War, 17 Years, 18 Commanders

1.	Lt. Gen. John C. McColl, UK	10 January 2002–20 June 2002
2.	Lt. Gen. Hilmi Akin Zolu, Turkey	20 June 2002–10 February 2003
3.	Lt. Gen. Norbert van Heyst, Germany	10 February 2003–11 August 2003
4.	Lt. Gen. Gotz Gliemeroth, Germany	11 August 2003–9 February 2004
5.	Lt. Gen. Rick J. Hillier, Canada	9 February 2004–9 August 2004
6.	Lt. Gen. Jean-Luis Py, France	9 August 2004–13 February 2005
7.	Lt. Gen. Ethem Erdagi, Turkey	13 February 2005–5 August 2005
8.	Gen. Mauro del Vecchio, Italy	5 August 2005–4 May 2006
9.	Gen. Sir David J. Richards, UK	4 May 2006–4 February 2007
10.	Gen. Dan K. McNeill, USA	4 February 2007–3 June 2008
11.	Gen. David D. McKiernan, USA	3 June 2008–15 June 2009
12.	Gen. Stanley A. McChrystal, USA	15 June 2009–23 June 2010
13.	Gen. David H. Petraeus, USA	4 July 2010–18 July 2011
14.	Gen. John R. Allen, USA	18 July 2011-10 February 2013
15.	Gen. Joseph F. Dunford, USA	10 February 2013–26 August 2014
16.	Gen. John F. Campbell, USA	26 August 2014–28 December 2014
17.	Gen. John William 'Mick' Nicholson Jr., USA	March 30 2016–2 September 2018
18.	Gen. Austin Scott Miller, USA	2 September 2018–

Source: Compiled by author from various sources

Earlier, when Gen. Stan McChrystal took over command of the war in Afghanistan, he had noted that he was the twelfth commander. Moreover,

---

2   Wesley Morgan, 'Meet the next American Commander in Afghanistan, who has deeper experience there than almost any U.S. general', *The Washington Post*, 28 January 2016, https://www.washingtonpost.com/news/checkpoint/ wp/2016/01/28/meet-the-next-commander-in-afghanistan-who-has-deeper-experience-there-than-almost-any-u-s-general/?utm_term=.660a160b3a10

McChrystal came to the rapid conclusion there was not one but ten different wars being fought in Afghanistan, something that NATO commander and SACEUR Gen. Jim Jones had also noted very early in the conflict, as had Lt. Gen. Doug Lute at the White House. Each allied commander had his own rules of engagement. And he brought his own team and set of experiences to the war zone, confusing allies and giving solace to the enemy that took advantage of the fresh learning curve each time the command changed hands. Each had his 100-Day Plan.

Nicholson had served in Afghanistan earlier, under Gen. James Mattis, during a time of a new form of aggression at the tactical level (the main exhibit of that was the series of attacks on Pakistani posts culminating in the Salala incident that took twenty-four Pakistani soldiers' and officers' lives). Many US officers who had fought in Afghanistan and lost comrades to the Taliban, whom they saw as being abetted by Pakistan, saw the Taliban as 'The Wrong Enemy'[3] and Pakistan as the real enemy. As a result, Nicholson took a harder line on Pakistan than many of his predecessors.

Normally, the commander CENTCOM was the main interlocutor with the Pakistan Army chief. Each one had a different style. Gen. David Petraeus was seen as a political general and his acuity created suspicions in the minds of his counterparts in Pakistan. Some Pakistani generals privately called him 'Mr Petraeus', perhaps out of grudging respect for his political skills. Generals McChrystal, Mattis and Allen developed good relationships and were seen as soldiers primarily. They also maintained a high profile in Washington as well as in the region. By 2018, even the Department of State appeared to cede the diplomatic lead to Gen. Joseph L. Votel, then the head of CENTCOM. Trump's first Secretary of State, Rex Tillerson, was a ghost as far as policy-making

---

[3]   *The Wrong Enemy: America in Afghanistan 2001–2014* (New York: Houghton Mifflin, 2014) was the title of a book by Carlotta Gall of the *New York Times*, who had been reporting extensively from Pakistan and Afghanistan and had even been roughed up by Pakistani intelligence operatives in Quetta, Balochistan, when she went in search of Taliban belonging to the fabled Quetta Shura. Gall had a family connection to the region. Her father, the legendary Sandy Gall of ITN TV News, had covered the 1971 Indo-Pak War. (I recalled meeting him in Rawalpindi at that time, in my early days as a TV newsman for Pakistan Television.) He later authored at least five books on Afghanistan related to the Soviet War and after, including *War against the Taliban: Why It All Went Wrong* (Bloomsbury, 2013).

in the Afghan theatre was concerned. His department lost experienced hands by the dozen. And even into the second year of the new Trump administration, diplomatic posts (including the ambassador to Pakistan, after Ambassador David Hale moved to State as Under Secretary from Islamabad) and policy positions at Foggy Bottom remained filled by temporary staff. He ended up being summarily fired via a tweet from President Trump on 13 March 2018. Before that, the diplomatic lead was often taken by the US ambassadors, who met regularly with both the civilian and military leadership in Pakistan, and served as a strong listening post and sometimes even as a personal 'shrink' to Pakistani leaders. Overall direction came from the seventh floor of the Department of State, where the senior executives sat, either independently or in concert with the NSC staff.

Ambassador Richard Olson recalled that President Zardari 'was keen on having a regular contact with the American ambassador. We had lunch together probably every two weeks during the time that he was in office. We developed a personal rapport, a friendship. Interestingly, one of the things that was important for him . . . [and] that he most wanted to know from me at every session was what his army was up to.' In other words he feared his 'army was going to overthrow him. They weren't, as far as I could tell.' Olson thought Zardari 'saw the role of the US ambassador as being someone who could talk candidly with Pindi [army headquarters] and actually warn him, frankly, if he was going to get in trouble with Pindi'. Later on, Olson had a close relationship with the army chief who succeeded Kayani, Gen. Raheel Sharif, whom he also met 'every two weeks . . . probably fifty or sixty times'. Unlike his much more opaque predecessor, Kayani, Olson thought Raheel Sharif had a remarkable 'perceptiveness and understanding of how other people are thinking about issues and seeing things'. He also had an ability to 'convey to the prime minister that he was just a simple, loyal soldier . . . He spoke in a very straightforward way.'[4] This relationship, Olson felt, played a key role in the conversations during the six months leading up to the army's action in North Waziristan. According to Olson and others, Raheel Sharif was not seen as a profound thinker or reader like Kayani. He was less risk-averse too, and became popular as a man of action, based on what his colleagues told him.

---

[4]   Interview with Amb. Richard Olson, January 2017.

Most of the hard work involved quiet diplomacy, listening to each other's complaints and trying to find solutions. The US coverage of Pakistani military and civilian activities, both overt and covert, yielded valuable information from time to time. Despite the differences between the Obama administration and Pakistan, on Afghanistan, on the use of drones and on India, conversations continued. At the White House, under the Trump administration, the role of the NSC became more that of an enforcer than a problem solver. The Trump team blamed what they saw as the Obama era's softness and decided to change their stance to include greater pressure and tighter deadlines for Pakistan.

Peter Lavoy, who had begun his academic career studying the Soviet Union, learning Russian and focusing on nuclear proliferation issues, had shifted his direction to South Asia after a trip to the region. He enrolled in Hindi classes and then added Urdu over time, starting a long career in South Asian studies and conflict resolution, as well as a key role in the National Intelligence Council, culminating in the NSC. Of the many people who claim to be experts in Washington DC on Pakistan and its surrounding region, Lavoy genuinely understands the people and governments of the region. He spoke with me about the historical sweep of the US–Pakistan relationship that brought Musharraf into the US camp and 'a level of support to Pakistan that the country hadn't seen since certainly the nuclear tests. Musharraf managed to get an agreement for resumption of supplies of F-16s, and normalization and upgrading of the security relationship.' But then things went awry.

That relationship was a victim of its own success, the success in removing Al-Qaeda from the settled areas in Pakistan—they took refuge in the tribal belt. That created friction between Washington and Islamabad, or more importantly Rawalpindi, over the new constrictions on the freedom of operation enjoyed by the Americans. That is when tensions really developed between the two sides, according to Lavoy.

> At the same time also you had the re-emergence of the Taliban and a new series of attacks against not just Afghans but Americans in Afghanistan. You had different bureaucratic agencies promoting different issues. From a military point of view, the growing spate of attacks against American forces, native forces, was a huge disruptive influence or issue. For CIA and for the counter terrorism establishment, the constriction on the ability to operate, conduct counter terrorist operations against suspected

or known al-Qaeda cells in FATA was also very, very challenging. That tension still hasn't been resolved. That has been really a central tension that bilaterally we've been trying to navigate [since 2008].[5]

The Congressional Research Service had also found early on that 'While Obama administration officials and most senior congressional leaders have continued to recognize Pakistan as a crucial partner in US-led counterterrorism and counter-insurgency efforts, long-held doubts about Islamabad's commitment to core US interests have deepened considerably in 2011'.

Lavoy maintained: 'Ultimately Pakistan correctly recognized that it needed to maintain a security relationship with the US, and it recognized that the US has had a vital interest, certainly in the period [since 2001], in defeating terrorism in that region. There was only so far that Pakistan could go without fundamentally disrupting the relationship with the US.'

At the same time, the warming US relationship with India intruded into this relationship with Pakistan to the detriment of Pakistan. Earlier, the US insisted in its conduct of South Asian policy on a balance with India with regard for Pakistan's interests when it looked at Afghanistan as well. 'Over time the US shifted away from a balanced relationship because it was getting less out of the Pakistan relationship; [there were] more challenges, the grievances weren't being addressed, and the relationship with India was born and viewed, I think correctly, as of major significance to the United States', according to Lavoy.[6]

Adding to the difficulty in the US–Pakistan relationship were the differences between the civil and the military in Pakistan. According to the CRS, 'Most independent analysts view the Pakistani military and intelligence services as too willing to distinguish among Islamist extremist groups, maintaining links to some as a means of forwarding Pakistani's perceived security interests.'[7] Secretary of State Clinton had warned Pakistani officials after a quick one-day visit in May 2011 that 'we're going to continue to try to work with them across the entire political spectrum, we're going to demand more from them'. Yet she was realistic in seeing this as 'a long-term,

---

[5]   Interview with Peter Lavoy, Washington DC, February 2017.

[6]   Ibid.

[7]   K. Alan Kronstadt, 'Pakistan–US Relations: A Summary', 21 October 2011, https://www.refworld.org/pdfid/4edc8dc62.pdf

frustrating, frankly, sometimes very outraging kind of experience . . . and yet, I don't see any alternative if you look at vital American national interests.'[8] Therein lay the dilemma of US foreign policy and Pakistan's hold over it, despite Pakistan's preference for and dependence on US military aid and funding under the CSF. The US and Pakistan had become co-dependent, despite the flow of US funds to Pakistan.

Military Assistance since 2001

Since 2001 (US FY2002), Pakistan had received some $8 billion of direct and overt security-related assistance. These flows had hit a peak in FY2011 before declining steadily, with FY2018 producing a total of only some $134 million programmed. In addition, Pakistan received CSF of some $14.6 billion from FY2002 to FY2017, though the FY2017 amount remained subject to certification requirements. It was the largest recipient of CSF money from the US worldwide. CSF monies were supposed to be reimbursement for Pakistani expenditures related to support for the US war against terrorism in Afghanistan.

But that programme had been plagued by bickering and dissent between the two putative allies and was increasingly subjected to scrutiny from the Government Accountability Office in the US.

US officials widely believed that Pakistan was padding the bill. They tended to ignore this in the earlier years in the interest of getting Pakistani support in the border region as well as intelligence cooperation. Ambassador Richard Holbrooke asked me once why Pakistan needed the same large amount of barbed wire each year. A Pakistani officer involved in producing the CSF bill had explained to me that the annual exercise was painful and they had to struggle to fill in the various categories. For example, one question that had come up in preparing the CSF bill one year related to the loss of a jeep at naval headquarters. The vehicle had caught fire and been destroyed. It ended up being included in the CSF bill! A basic issue was that the Pakistan military did not have sophisticated budgeting and financial monitoring systems in place within the armed forces as a line management tool. Also, there was little established, detailed and formal oversight of its expenditures by the civilian authorities and parliament.

---

[8]   'Senate Foreign Relations Committee Holds Hearing on Goals and Progress in Afghanistan and Pakistan', CQ Transcriptions, 23 June 2011. Cited by Kronstadt.

By 2008, in the seventh year of the Afghan war, the US had given some $5.56 billion in CSF reimbursement payments to Pakistan ostensibly for its efforts to fight terrorism along the Afghan border. But alarm signals had been going off in Washington about the extent to which the DoD had issued strict guidelines for reviewing and monitoring the bills from Pakistan and the payments due to it. So, the Government Accountability Office investigated this issue.

It discovered that in 2003 the DoD had issued a new guidance to enhance CSF oversight. The guidance called

for, among other things, CSF reimbursement claims to contain quantifiable information that indicates the incremental nature of support (i.e., above and beyond normal operations), validation that the support or service was provided, and copies of invoices or documentation supporting how the costs were calculated. [*So, for example, for food items, this ought to have covered only extra costs associated with provision of food to troops in the field, not the actual rations themselves that would have been provided anyway in peacetime locations at their base.*] While Defense generally conducted macro-level analytical reviews called for in its guidance, such as determining whether the cost is less than that which would be incurred by the US for the same service, for a large number of reimbursement claims Defense did not obtain detailed documentation to verify that claimed costs were valid, actually incurred, or correctly calculated. GAO found that Defense did not consistently apply its existing CSF oversight guidance. For example, as of May 2008, Defense paid over $2 billion in Pakistani reimbursement claims for military activities covering January 2004 through June 2007 without obtaining sufficient information that would enable a third party to recalculate these costs. Furthermore, Defense may have reimbursed costs that (1) were not incremental, (2) were not based on actual activity, or (3) were potentially duplicative. GAO also found that additional oversight controls were needed. For example, there is no guidance for Defense to verify currency conversion rates used by Pakistan, which if performed would enhance Defense's ability to monitor for potential overbillings.[9]

---

9   'Combating Terrorism: Increased Oversight and Accountability Needed over Pakistan Reimbursement Claims for Coalition Support Funds', US Government Accountability Office, June 2008.

The ODRP staff had not been specifically ordered by the DoD to verify the Pakistani support and expenses, though they were best positioned to do so, being in close touch with their Pakistani counterparts. ODRP began trying to validate the Pakistani claims for reimbursement on its own in September 2006, producing an immediate increase in the amount of claims 'disallowed or deferred'. The percentage of claims disallowed or deferred rose from an average of 2 per cent prior to August 2006 to 6 per cent for the period September 2006–February 2007 and 22 per cent for the period March 2007–June 2007 (actually processed after a necessary built-in delay).[10] Later, these percentages rose as high as 40 per cent, producing enormous problems in the relationship. Further, delays in processing of payments meant that the US ended up in arrears to Pakistan for up to two years, creating a budgeting nightmare for the Pakistani Ministry of Finance that used to plan for these inflows each year and in their absence had to deal with substantial ensuing deficits.[11]

The CSF Process

US personnel involved in monitoring the flow of financial assistance and reimbursements to Pakistan tried to assist their Pakistani colleagues to better prepare their bills and thereby speed up the verification of costs incurred. In July 2006, the Pakistani government was given a cost template and information to assist it in clarifying the types of costs that would support claims for reimbursement. One US officer recalled visiting JCS Headquarters and explaining the processes to junior captains and majors. 'They got it immediately!' he exclaimed. But when the colonels and brigadiers got into the act, things got clogged up. They had little background in budget management and no desire to learn accounting processes!

Depending on whom one spoke to, the CSF accounting and billing process was simple or complicated. It did have many moving parts.

The Pakistan Ministry of Finance and no doubt the Pakistan Army had the following detailed process template available to them:

---

[10] Ibid.

[11] After a GAO Report on Pakistan in 2013, there were no further reports available till 2018.

Scrutiny and Reimbursement Procedure of CSF

The detailed, some would say convoluted, procedure relating to processing of CSF claims, its reimbursement and monitoring expenditure is detailed below:

Step 1: Consolidated claims from Service Headquarters [GHQ, Air Force and Navy] are forwarded to Joint Staff Headquarters (JSHQs) where these are scrutinized and consolidated.

Step 2: JSHQs forward the details of claims to the ODRP, US embassy, in Islamabad, and a summary of claims to Ministries of Finance and Defense.

Step 3: ODRP in the US embassy thoroughly scrutinizes these claims in coordination with JSHQs and processes them after back and forth verification.

Step 4: After scrutiny by the ODRP, these claims are forwarded to US CENTCOM HQ at Tampa where these claims are again scrutinized and reconciled.

Step 5: Once satisfied, US CENTCOM HQ forwards these bills to Comptroller Office in the DoD where these claims are processed.

Step 6: DoD at the same time sends these claims for review to
(i) OMB Coord [Office of Management and Budget Coordination]
(ii) US State Department
(iii) Office of General Counsel in DoD.

Step 7: Once these are cleared, the claims are processed and submitted to the Deputy Secretary DoD through normal hierarchy, for authorization.

Step 8: After authorization by the Deputy Secretary, Defense, and clearance from the US State Department, Comptroller Office notifies the Congress and waits for full two weeks.

Step 9: In case of no objection or observation within two weeks after notifying the Congress, Comptroller Office transfer funds to the State Bank of Pakistan through the Federal Reserve Bank New York.[12]

---

12 Courtesy of S. Wajid Rana, former secretary, Ministry of Finance, Government of Pakistan, and former minister, economic, at the Pakistan embassy in Washington DC. He is one of the most knowledgeable economists on the Pakistani side, with detailed knowledge of the IFIs and the US financial system.

So much for the theory. The practice was much more convoluted and subject to delays, resulting in constant arrears in payment and huge battles within the systems on either side.

The GAO caught many instances of questionable billing, including for radar, considering that the Taliban did not have an air force. ODRP explained that this may be related to assistance in overflights of US aircraft supporting the war effort in Afghanistan.

Two other specific examples were noted by the GAO:

- Approximately $30 million for army road construction and $15 million for bunker construction without evidence that the roads and bunkers had been built; and
- An average of more than $19,000 per vehicle per month for Pakistani navy reimbursement claims that appeared to contain duplicative charges for a fleet of fewer than twenty passenger vehicles.

The Pakistan Navy, for some reason, figured often in the questionable claims. The GAO found that 'Navy claims for food rapidly increased from approximately $445 per sailor in June 2005 to $800 per sailor in December 2005, while Air Force and Army food costs per person remained stable.' The Air Force cost was $800 per person in 2004, then dropped to $400. The Army cost per person was steadily at $200. The GAO also found that 'On average, Defense paid the Pakistani navy more than $5,700 per vehicle per month in damages, in comparison with the army's average claim of less than $100 per vehicle per month'. And the navy continued to charge a high amount for its vehicular costs. 'Defense paid the Pakistani Navy an average of over $19,000 per vehicle per month (more than $3.7 million per year) to operate, maintain, and repair a fleet of fewer than 20 passenger vehicles without sufficient information to determine that these costs were not duplicative'.[13] It was almost as if the three services inside Pakistan were competing to see who would garner more US payments as reimbursements.

The Tierney Report Focus on Military Aid

As discussed earlier, the US Congress also piled on to both the US administration and the Government of Pakistan in the mismanagement of

---

[13]   GAO, 'Combating Terrorism'.

the war against terrorism in the region. It also criticized the CSF system in place to help Pakistan defray its costs of doing battle in its marcher regions abutting Afghanistan: 'The Coalition Support Funds program encapsulates much of what is currently problematic about the US's ad hoc policies when it comes to securing our national security interests in Pakistan . . .' The Committee on Oversight and Reform's Subcommittee on National Security and Foreign Affairs released its report on 25 September 2008 that examined CSF 'from perspectives of efficacy, accountability, and diplomatic complications'. It concluded, 'By the metrics that ought to matter most from the United States perspective—success at defeating al Qaeda and dismantling the Taliban—United States efforts to date have amounted to costly, strategic failure. Coalition Support Funds, as the backbone of United States security activities, deserve strict scrutiny.'

The Tierney Report highlighted the intrinsic problems of the CSF system that had been seen originally as *an ad-hoc, short-term, emergency method* [emphasis added] of paying for services in support of US war efforts, and was explicitly created outside of any existing programme or accountability measures. It would appear that, with respect to accountability, the Defense Department has been playing catch-up ever since.

During the course of this investigation, the subcommittee took testimony, received information and reviewed documents related to the reliability of invoices submitted by the Pakistani military, and the ability of US officials to verify these claims. For example, the US has been repeatedly invoiced for medical evacuation costs for the Pakistan Army and FC, while the FC leadership has suggested its units have not received the medical support on the battlefield. In another instance, the US was invoiced for helicopter maintenance in an amount that, US military officials later learned, vastly outstripped *the entire budget* of the relevant Pakistani air wing component.

In December 2007, the *New York Times* published a significant investigative article quoting unnamed Bush administration and military officials that the CSF programme was rife with waste. The article cites US military officials in their concern that the funds were not reaching the frontline Pakistani soldiers in need, with vast amounts being siphoned off for other purposes.[14]

---

[14] David Rohde, Carlotta Gall, et al., 'U.S. Officials See Waste in Billions Sent to Pakistan', *New York Times*, 24 December 2007.

Another report—this one by the *Guardian*—details allegations that 'as much as 70%' of the then-over $5 billion in CSF claimed by Pakistan had not been for legitimate expenditures. The subcommittee has not found evidence of waste, fraud or abuse rising to the level suggested by the *Guardian*.[15] However, anecdotal evidence, coupled with the GAO reporting on lack of documentation, leaves matters in doubt.

CSF were paid directly into the Pakistan government's treasury and became sovereign funds, for which the US was not able to determine the final destination or application of CSF reimbursements. Internal DoD guidance noted that the 'Department does not track how countries spend the reimbursements'. A senior US military official told a subcommittee-sponsored Congressional delegation that he believed approximately 40–50 per cent of the CSF have not reached the military components that provided the services rendered, and instead have been used for other Pakistani government priorities such as food and energy subsidies.[16]

Noting that the US brand in Pakistan had become 'toxic' over time, the Tierney Report laid the blame at the feet of the US administration cosying up to a military dictator, Gen. Pervez Musharraf, at the expense of the Pakistani people. Military aid to Musharraf rather than economic aid to improve the lives of average Pakistanis fed the animus.

> This dynamic is borne out by the fact that the United States' effective response to the earthquake disaster in Kashmir resulted in the only significant spike in United States popularity during the post-9/11 period. Over the last fiscal year, the United States government has done a better job of programming US aid programs and, when applicable, using a shared objectives process to influence Pakistan's use of US budgetary support for critical societal needs, like education and health care. However, nonmilitary aid to Pakistan is dwarfed by security assistance and Coalition Support Funds reimbursements.
>
> Some of the US image problems in Pakistan are more resistant to near-term programmatic changes. The war in Iraq, nuclear arrangements with India, and the perception that the war on terror

---

[15] 'Up to 70% of US Aid to Pakistan "Misspent",' *The Guardian* (27 February 2008).

[16] Tierney Report, pp. 17–18.

is fundamentally anti-Islam are more structural obstacles to any public relations battle.[17]

The Tierney Report also recognized that the CSF further strengthened the view among ordinary Pakistanis that the US favoured relations with the military over the civilians in Pakistan and also criticized the US for the wrong emphasis. 'The Department of Defense budget justifications for Coalition Support Funds do little to promote any notion of Pakistan's own interests at stake in the fight against terrorist networks, the pacification of destabilizing militant forces within its own borders, and the benefits of regional stability.'[18]

The report then proceeded to produce a comprehensive series of proposals dealing with military, strategic and economic issues that pointed to the need for a new approach to CSF and for overall US assistance to Pakistan as well as US policies in the region. The focus was on engaging with Pakistan to help it reorder its own priorities for its own benefit. The 'Keys to Success' of the road map suggested by the report involved a major shift in priorities:

- Enhance non-military, programmed foreign assistance to Pakistan for the public education, health, energy and economic sectors by orders of magnitude. This type of aid should be visible and will be meaningful to the Pakistani populace.
- Strengthen the democratically elected government. This can be done by assisting it in its efforts to improve the quality of life of its citizens. In addition, skilful diplomacy could help establish an environment in which the new government can credibly claim credit for redefining the Pakistan–US relationship in a manner that is advantageous to Pakistani citizens and consistent with Pakistan's standing as a mutual ally.
- Offer the government of Pakistan an immediate and dramatic infusion of assistance designed to help Pakistan deal with its two current crises of energy production and food prices.[19]

---

[17] Ibid., pp. 24–25.

[18] Ibid., p. 28.

[19] Ibid., p. 35.

All these were desirable changes and made sense for the US to help build Pakistan's polity. But US policymakers seemed to be myopic, and failed to appreciate the nature and role of aid from Pakistan's perspective. The Pakistani establishment, civil and military, also failed to come up with a clear long-term view on aid. For ten years, the Tierney Report proposals lay effectively dormant, as the US policy lurched from one fighting season to the other in Afghanistan, and Pakistani governments lived from day to day, fighting the battle with other political parties and with their own military that sought to operate autonomously as far as possible, except when it came to funding its operations.

The Original Sin

The specific details of the problems in the CSF system were overshadowed by a bigger and more fundamental issue. Under the mistaken mantra of 'Yes, we can!', Pakistan had made a serious error in accepting CSF when it signed up for the Global War on Terror of the Bush administration. Then President Musharraf was keen to rapidly accede to US demands for help in Afghanistan. His finance minister at the time, Shaukat Aziz, told me that he supported the arrangement. In retrospect, it appears the agreement may have been based on faulty Pakistani assumptions: first, that the conflict would be of a short duration; and second, that a marginal cost pricing applied to the expenditures related to moving Pakistani forces into the border region would more than cover the costs to Pakistan, leaving a profit of some kind. In fact, the conflict became prolonged, and the real costs of the movement and placement of troops to the army and the general economy, through damage to equipment, infrastructure and morale, was much higher than calculated.

The Pakistan military may have tried to save by cutting back on maintenance. For example, the helicopters were overused in the operations in the border region. The GAO reported that 'ODRP found that even though the US had paid Pakistan $55 million in CSF reimbursements for maintenance of helicopters in the border area, only a few of these helicopters were fully operational. According to ODRP officials, the Pakistani army was not maintaining the helicopters, causing essential systems to malfunction.'[20]

---

[20] GAO, 'Combating Terrorism'.

Military Supplies

Pakistan generally prefers the latest US military equipment and training over all others, despite its long and growing relationship with China. This is reflected in the fact that it was willing to use its own resources for the purchase of most of the US arms and equipment since 2001, though US grants gradually overtook that total in recent years. The armed forces Capital Fund of Rs 100 billion in 2006–07 helped with military purchases. Some $2.9 billion of military equipment was purchased from the US out of Pakistan's own funds.[21]

Between FY2002 and FY2015, the DoD reported some $6.7 billion of military sales to Pakistan, mainly via the Foreign Military Sales of the FMF (Foreign Military Financing) programme. Congress appropriated some $3.8 billion in FMF since 2001, allowing to Pakistan to modernize its equipment and systems. FMF is a programme that allows eligible partner nations to purchase US defence articles, services and training through either Foreign Military Sales or, for a limited number of countries, through the FMF or direct commercial contracts (FMF/DCC) programme, either as a grant or as a direct loan. In addition, under the Excess Defense Articles heading, Pakistan received defence supplies, including thirteen F-16A/B Fighting Falcon combat aircraft, fifty-nine T-37 Tweet military trainer jets and 500 M113 armoured personnel carriers.

Among the major defence materiel provided to Pakistan by the US after 2001 were the following:

Under FMF:

- eight P-3C Orion maritime patrol aircraft and their refurbishment (valued at $474 million, seven delivered, three of which were destroyed in a 2011 attack by Islamist militants);
- 2007 TOW anti-armour missiles ($186 million);
- at least 5750 military radio sets ($222 million);
- six AN/TPS-77 surveillance radars ($100 million);
- six C-130E Hercules transport aircraft and their refurbishment ($88 million);
- the Perry-class missile frigate USS *McInerney* (now PNS *Alamgir*), via special EDA authorization ($65 million for refurbishment);

---

21 Ishrat Husain. See page 254 for items purchased with Pakistani national funds.

- twenty AH-1F Cobra attack helicopters via EDA ($48 million for refurbishment, twelve delivered); and
- fifteen Scan Eagle unmanned aerial reconnaissance vehicles ($30 million).

Supplies paid for with *a mix of Pakistani national funds and FMF* included:

- forty-five Mid-Life Update kits for F-16A/B combat aircraft valued at $891 million (with $477 million of this in FMF); and
- 115 M-109 self-propelled howitzers ($87 million, with $53 million in FMF).

Notable items paid or to be paid for *entirely with Pakistani national funds* included:

- eighteen new F-16C/D Block 52 Fighting Falcon combat aircraft (valued at $1.32 billion);
- F-16 armaments including 500 AMRAAM air-to-air missiles, 1450 1-ton bombs, 500 JDAM Tail Kits for gravity bombs and 1600 Enhanced Paveway laser-guided kits, also for gravity bombs ($629 million);
- 100 Harpoon anti-ship missiles ($298 million);
- 500 Sidewinder air-to-air missiles ($95 million); and
- seven Phalanx Close-In Weapons System naval guns ($80 million).

According to the intrepid Congressional Research Service specialist, Alan Kronstadt, who has made a lifetime's work in tracking and analysing these flows for Congress and Pakistan watchers, Pakistan also received via CSF (in the DoD budget), twenty-six Bell 412EP utility helicopters, with related parts and maintenance, valued at $235 million. Under Section 1206 and Pakistan COIN fund authorities, the US has provided *four* Mi-17 multirole helicopters (another *six* provided temporarily at no cost), *four* King Air B-350 surveillance aircraft, 450 vehicles for the FC, twenty Buffalo explosives detection and disposal vehicles, helicopter spare parts, night-vision devices, radios, body armour, helmets, first-aid kits, litters and other individual soldier equipment.

Through International Military Education and Training (IMET) and other programmes, the US has funded and provided training for more than 3,800 Pakistani military officers. The ODRP managed to expand opportunities for such training and visits by diving into dozens of pots of money that were available to the DoD so it could go beyond the IMET funding available via the programme operated by the State Department. Col. Robin Fuentes, later a Defense Attaché in India, and rumoured to be heading to the NSC under the Trump administration when the NSA Lt. Gen. Michael Flynn got fired, was particularly adept at finding such funding, according to Vice Admiral Mike LeFever, her boss at ODRP. In 2018, the Trump administration ended IMET for Pakistan, repeating the mistake made by the US in the 1990s.

Three noteworthy defence sales approved by the State Department and notified to Congress were pending in early 2017: an estimated $952 million for fifteen AH-1Z Viper attack helicopters, 1000 Hellfire II missiles, thirty-two T-700 helicopter engines, and advanced avionics; $100 million for 100 Mine Resistant Ambush Protected vehicles; and $62 million for three additional Bell 412EP utility helicopters. The future sale of naval surface vessels was still being studied. In 2014, the DoD notified Congress of a possible $350 million deal for eight GRC43M Global Response Cutters, along with naval guns, navigation and other systems. A proposed sale of eight additional new F-16 Block 52 Fighting Falcons and related avionics for $699 million (notified in February 2016) foundered when Congress declined to allow the partial FMF financing sought by the administration and the government of Pakistan.[22] Pakistan then declined the offer.

Pakistan had been demanding more helicopters to battle the militants inside Pakistan in the rugged terrain of the FATA abutting Afghanistan. The US was parsimonious in providing it the helicopters it needed, citing paucity of spare helicopters. After a meeting with and briefing of Chairman JCS Admiral Mullen in 2010, I was informed by a senior aide to Mullen that helicopters were in short supply.[23] 'We deal in onesies and twosies and call it strategic.' However, the entire Blackhawk fleet of Belgium was up for replacement, according to one of my sources in the US defence industry

---

[22] Data courtesy of K. Alan Kronstadt, CRS.

[23] I recall Steve Coll and C. Christine Fair being in our group that Mullen invited to speak with him on Pakistan. He exhibited an avuncular air with his softly articulated but penetrating questions that contrasted with his starched military look. His love of the navy was evident in the office decor. My striking memory is of a bookshelf to the left of his office door as one entered, which had been cut at a cant to mimic the slanted feeling of being in a ship!

whose firm provided the engines for those aircraft. When I conveyed this to Mullen's aide, I was told those aircraft were due for 'refurbishment'. Well over 200 Blackhawks were available at that time in various National Guard units in the continental US—units that were not involved in any overseas action. It appeared that the US was not approaching Pakistan's needs for helicopters on a war footing.

What if it had provided these resources? The Pakistani forces would not have had any excuse to delay clearing operations in FATA, something that was only done over six years later. The US also feared that Pakistan might shift attack helicopters to its eastern border, an eventuality that could have been prevented by putting them under a lease agreement that the US could have ended at will. Pakistan did test the boundaries of its leasing rules later though, by shifting some of the MI-17s the US had leased to it to a UN peacekeeping operation in Africa, provoking a US protest. In contrast, 150 helicopters were found for Afghan forces in 2017. Uncle Sam did not play with a straight bat either, in Pakistani eyes.

Intelligence Cooperation and Clashes

Some of the more successful examples of US–Pakistan cooperation over the years involved the ISI and the CIA, though both sides tried to maintain a subterranean operating system in each other's country. Personal relationships between the various DGs of the ISI and the local CIA station chiefs in Islamabad as well as the director of the CIA played a huge role in the quality of cooperation, especially when things went awry. For example, during the tenure of then Lt. Gen. Ehsan ul Haq, according to a former CIA station chief, the relationship flourished. There was easy access, and local resolution of issues was swift and relatively cordial. At the start of the Afghan war, Robert Grenier also found easy access to his ISI colleagues. Many of these were initiatives aligned for tactical reasons due to pressures from the Department of State or the CIA.

As one CIA station chief, Kevin Hulbert, put it: paradoxically, Pakistan was 'the best partner in the world on CT, and one of the worst partners on CT!' He cited the cooperation that yielded the capture of Al-Qaeda operatives like Khalid Sheikh Mohammed and Abu Anas al Libi, describing the ISI as 'forward leaning on Al Qaeda. But was it always perfect? No! Did it chase OBL? No!'

Hulbert's frustrations were reflected in the views of other US intelligence experts who dealt with Pakistan. Most of the ISI's successes in the CT field, they maintained, were based on provision of US intelligence. As one expert put it, 'it was amazing how little they knew about AQ. Equally amazing was that the ISI did not know what was going on inside the city of Miram Shah.'[24] This may not be entirely true. Perhaps the ISI knew but did not share that information with their CIA counterparts. After all the army's 7 Division field headquarters lay just outside the city limits of Miram Shah. The Pakistan military chose to ignore the operations of the Haqqani Network in North Waziristan even after US officials provided them videos of Haqqani fighters going past Pakistani check posts without any let or hindrance.

Under Lt. Gen. Ahmed Shuja Pasha, there were a number of road bumps largely due to the confluence of major issues of discord, especially in 2011. Pasha, a straight-shooting super-nationalist general had come into the world of intelligence at the insistence of Gen. Kayani. He became an activist and an aggressive head of the country's largest intelligence agency, expanding its operations and remit virtually at will and demanding greater access to information on US operations and operatives inside Pakistan. CIA Director Leon Panetta, himself new to the world of intelligence, parried him at every step, and used the discovery of Osama bin Laden in Abbottabad as a wedge to expose what he saw as Pakistan's duplicitous behaviour. Pakistan shut down three joint intelligence fusion cells that had been recently established in Quetta and Peshawar and asked for the CIA-led drone programme to be cut back or be more coordinated with Pakistan. Pasha became the bête noire of the Americans he dealt with.

They found all kinds of ways to criticize and neutralize him. He was the subject of heightened US intelligence surveillance. His travels were monitored carefully, especially to Germany, where the Americans even tracked his extracurricular social activities. Such information could potentially be used as leverage against an official. They also noted, with some element of glee, his serious lapse of tradecraft when on one visit to CIA Headquarters in Langley VA he reportedly brought along and had to surrender his personal iPad. And, the US delegation noted with some amusement that Pasha showed up at a meeting along with Jalaluddin Haqqani's brother Ibrahim in Doha, after having professed to have no deep

---

[24] Interview with Kevin Hulbert, Washington DC, July 2017.

connections with the Haqqani leadership.[25] By that time US intelligence had penetrated many Pakistani organizations, according to a now retired US intelligence official. Pakistan may well have suspected this. And only in 2019 it tried and convicted three senior officials for espionage, including two army officers and one doctor working for a 'sensitive agency', most likely a nuclear body.[26]

Pasha also came under pressure from another quarter. Earlier, his name was mentioned in a civil case filed in a Brooklyn court by a US citizen affected by the 26/11 Mumbai attack:

> The 26-page lawsuit accusing the ISI of aiding and abetting the Lashkar-e-Taiba in the slaughter of 166 people was filed before a New York Court on November 19, following which the Brooklyn court issued summons to Major Samir Ali, Azam Cheema, Ahmed Shuja Pasha, Nadeem Taj and Major Iqbal of the Inter-Services Intelligence of the Islamic Republic of Pakistan, Zakiur Rehman Lakhvi of the Lashkar-e-Tayiba and Hafiz Saeed of the Jammat ud Dawaa.
>
> 'The ISI has long nurtured and used international terrorist groups, including the LeT, to accomplish its goals and has provided material support to LeT and other international terrorist groups,' said the lawsuit filed by relatives of the slain Rabbi. 'Pasha, who has been director general of the ISI since September 2008, has been summoned, so is Nadeem Taj, the director general of ISI from September 2007 to September 2008. Major Iqbal and Major Samir Ali are other ISI officers who have been issued summons.[27]

Pasha suspected the CIA was trying to tighten the screws on him. The government of Pakistan protested this action by a US court. Pasha refused to visit the US till the US government gave him immunity in that case, which it did by telling the federal court:

---

[25] Background information from former US officials. Pasha did not respond to requests for an interview after his return from his post-retirement overseas sojourn in the UAE.

[26] https://www.aljazeera.com/news/2019/05/pakistan-military-sentences-officer-death-espionage-190530142947938.html

[27] Rediff News, 'US Court Summons ISI Chief in 26/11 Case', 24 November 2010, http://www.rediff.com/news/report/anniversary-26-11-us-court-issues-summons-to-pak-isi-chief-lashkar-operatives/20101124.htm

'In the view of the United States, the ISI is entitled to immunity because it is part of a foreign state within the meaning of the FSIA (Foreign Sovereign Immunities Act).'

Stuart Delery, principal deputy assistant attorney general, said in a 12-page affidavit submitted to the court on December 17 : 'Furthermore, the department of state has determined that former (ISI) directors-general Pasha and Taj are immune because the plaintiffs' allegations relate to acts that these defendants allegedly took in their official capacities as directors of an entity that is undeniably a fundamental part of the Government of Pakistan.'[28]

Then there was the publication of the CIA Station Chief Jonathan Banks's name in a drone attack–related court case (something that the US believed would have only happened with ISI connivance).[29]

Pasha was an influential voice inside the Pakistani government, especially when it came to the passive Prime Minister Yousaf Raza Gilani, who rarely ever asked for a briefing from his ISI chief. As a rule, Pasha and other ISI chiefs had to essentially force briefings on the prime ministers. A few weeks before the bin Laden raid, Pasha accompanied PM Gilani to Kabul to meet Karzai in order to set up an Afghanistan–Pakistan Joint Commission to speed up the peace process under Afghan aegis. According to the *Wall Street Journal*, Gilani used the meeting with President Karzai to persuade Karzai to align Afghanistan more with Pakistan and China than the US, despite Afghanistan's deep dependence on the United States.

The pitch was made at an April 16 meeting in Kabul by Pakistani Prime Minister Yousaf Raza Gilani, who bluntly told Afghan President Hamid Karzai that the Americans had failed them both, according to Afghans familiar with the meeting. Mr Karzai should forget about allowing a long-term US military presence in his country, Mr Gilani said, according to the Afghans. Pakistan's bid to cut the US out of Afghanistan's future is the clearest sign to date that, as the nearly 10-year war's endgame

---

28   Press Trust of India, 'US Immunity for ISI and Its Ex-Chief in 26/11 Case', *Daily Mail India*, 19 December 2012, http://www.dailymail.co.uk/indiahome/indianews/article-2250718/US-immunity-ISI-ex-chief-26-11-case.html

29   Mark Mazzetti and Salman Masood, 'Pakistan Role Is Suspected in Revealing US Spy's Name', *New York Times*, December 2010, http://www.nytimes.com/2010/12/18/world/asia/18pstan.html

begins, tensions between Washington and Islamabad threaten to scuttle America's prospects of ending the conflict on its own terms.[30]

Needless to say, as was often the case of such 'secret' exchanges with a divided Afghan officialdom, the story was leaked to the US media by some Afghan officials, perhaps even Karzai himself.

One week after bin Laden's death, the name of another CIA station chief in Islamabad appeared in a Pakistani paper, *The Nation*. Though the name as published was incorrect, it was close to the name of the official in the US embassy.[31] The official, Mark Kelton, had been at loggerheads with Ambassador Cameron Munter on approval of drone strikes that Munter felt undermined his efforts to build confidence in the US–Pakistan relationship. After the bin Laden raid, the DG-ISI reportedly was furious with Kelton, with whom he had had a frosty relationship. But the US embassy maintained that Kelton would remain in Islamabad.

Yet, Kelton left Pakistan in a hurry soon after the raid, under mysterious circumstances that were only revealed publicly five years later:

> Two months after Osama bin Laden was killed, the CIA's top operative in Pakistan was pulled out of the country in an abrupt move vaguely attributed to health concerns and his strained relationship with Islamabad.
>
> In reality, the CIA station chief was so violently ill that he was often doubled over in pain, current and former US officials said. Trips out of the country for treatment proved futile. And the cause of his ailment was so mysterious, the officials said, that both he and the agency began to suspect that he had been poisoned.
>
> Mark Kelton retired from the CIA, and his health has recovered after he had abdominal surgery. But agency officials continue to think that it is plausible—if not provable—that Kelton's sudden illness was somehow orchestrated by Pakistan's ISI.

---

[30] Mathew Rosenberg, 'Karzai Told to Dump US', *Wall Street Journal*, 27 April 2011, https://www.wsj.com/articles/SB100014240527487047293045762870 41094035816

[31] Declan Walsh, 'Pakistani Media "Name" CIA Station Chief in Islamabad', *The Guardian*, 9 May 2011, https://www.theguardian.com/world/2011/ may/09/pakistan-media-name-cia-chief. Kelton is now a senior adviser with the Chertoff Group, a firm headed by former head of the Department of Homeland Security, Michael Chertoff, in Washington DC.

The disclosure is a disturbing postscript to the sequence of events surrounding the bin Laden operation five years ago and adds new intrigue to a counterterrorism partnership that has often been consumed by conspiracy theories.[32]

Despite these apparent conflicts, many US intelligence experts valued Pakistan's cooperation in this field. As one put it, 'the Predator program is a joint program', though the Pakistanis may disagree. They wanted targeting control, and at one time Gen. Kayani was prepared to base the control centres in Pakistan, but only if Pakistan was to become involved in targeting decisions. This was not acceptable to the Americans. At the personal level, though, even intelligence operatives from the US had one-year tours, in general, in Pakistan. This did not allow them to develop relationships with their counterparts. When they did, they produced the kind of positive results that Kevin Hulbert recalled. Pakistan went after the militants hiding in the Shaqai Valley in 2004, aided by US intelligence. Hulbert remembered being with his ISI counterparts one evening after the Shaqai operation. 'Good day today?' they asked him. 'Yes!' he replied enthusiastically. It was a 'huge event for them to go into Shaqai', he maintained.

After Pasha, the new ISI head, Lt. Gen. Zahir-ul-Islam, was consumed by domestic issues as the turmoil following the 2013 elections enveloped the political system, producing public sit-ins or dharnas by Imran Khan's PTI and allies against the government. Both Pasha and Islam's names were associated with the street opposition to Prime Minister Nawaz Sharif, though no solid evidence came to the surface. Islam was also a former head of one of the ISI's wings or directorates, and then had been in the hurly burly of Karachi politics as the corps commander there.[33] Islam's earlier experience at the ISI had been in monitoring Pakistani internal politics.

---

[32] Greg Miller, 'After Presiding over Bin Laden Raid, CIA Chief in Pakistan Came Home Suspecting He Was Poisoned by ISI', *Washington Post*, 5 May 2016, https://www.washingtonpost.com/world/national-security/in-bin-laden-raids-shadow-bad-blood-and-the-suspected-poisoning-of-a-cia-officer/2016/05/05/ace85354-0c83-11e6-a6b6-2e6de3695b0e_story, html?utm_term=.ed48aecf9264

[33] He belonged to a well-known Janjua Rajput family from Maira Matore near Kahuta. His elder brother, Azhar ul Islam, had been a Sword of Honour winner at the PMA, but had been removed from service after participating in

Zahir's activism was not lost on the US embassy. Ambassador Olson recalled during the dharna of Imran Khan when the Grand Trunk Road and the Islamabad Motorway were blocked,

> We received information that Zahir [-ul-Islam, the DG-ISI] was mobilizing for a coup in September of 2014. [Army chief] Raheel [Sharif] blocked it by, in effect, removing Zahir, by announcing his successor . . . [Zahir] was talking to the corps commanders and was talking to like-minded army officers . . . He was prepared to do it and had the chief been willing, even tacitly, it would have happened. But the chief was not willing, so it didn't happen.[34]

US surveillance of the ISI and its head was also ongoing. Islam's successor, Rizwan Akhtar, was a US-trained officer and maintained a good relationship with his US counterparts. But he did not impress all his interlocutors, especially when it came to matters of detail in discussions about the Afghan War. Their criticism was brutal. One US official recalled that in a meeting on Afghan reconciliation efforts Akhtar did not even remember the names of the leading Taliban field commanders. He was a hands-on DG-ISI and reportedly showed up in Karachi, where he had earlier served as DG Rangers, and took over an operation without even informing his brigadier who was the ISI's sector commander in that city. This kind of criticism did not serve him well in the ISI or even the army. In the event, Akhtar failed to win the confidence of the new army chief, Gen. Bajwa, and resigned by taking early retirement. He was succeeded by another US-trained officer.[35]

Lt. Gen. Naveed Mukhtar, who took over from Akhtar, had been a successful and active corps commander in Karachi. He was a graduate of the Army War College at Carlisle, PA. Earlier, he had served on the staff of Army Chief Gen. Jehangir Karamat. In his tenure in Karachi, he had

---

an attempted coup against Zulfikar Ali Bhutto in 1973. Another cousin, and coincidentally another Sword of Honour winner, Khalid Nawaz, was a corps commander of X Corps in Rawalpindi. Two uncles of his had been generals, as were two cousins.

[34] Interview with Amb. Richard Olson, January 2017.

[35] After his retirement, I was in contact with DG-ISI Akhtar. He tentatively agreed to an interview but then did not respond.

developed a sophisticated understanding of the broader landscape of the city and the terrorism and militancy that had engulfed that city of close to 25 million. Aided by an able and activist commander of the Rangers, then Maj. Gen. Bilal Akbar, they brought the city under control and put the MQM party on the skids. Both of them also supported the few professional senior police officers who were considered honest and not in the pay of the politicians of Sindh. But the military was unable to fundamentally alter the political landscape of Karachi, given the deep-seated roots of both the MQM and the PPP. Despite lip service to support police operations, the military continued to garnish most of the resources and foreign aid for COIN and CT.

Mukhtar, whose father had been a brigadier, was also an alumnus of the ISI, having been DGCT (director general counter terrorism) as a major general, in which capacity he had interacted often with the CIA at home and in the US. Ambassador Olson called the CT Wing or Directorate of the ISI the 'good ISI'. Mukhtar had a low-profile approach to things and helped keep an even keel during a period of declining US–Pakistan relations.

He was succeeded by the former DG of Military Intelligence at army headquarters, Lt. Gen. Asim Munir. He had also served in the Northern Areas of Pakistan and had the reputation of being a tough officer rooted in Islamic tradition. He was rumoured to have become a *Hafiz ul Quran*, having committed the Quran to memory. More importantly in the context of the civil–military tensions, he was reported to have been behind the sacking of a high court judge who had been critical of the ISI.

> Within Army ranks Asim Munir has the reputation of a 'hardliner'. His subordinates maintain that his strictness has a cult status among the troops he has managed. Observers have expressed concern that Munir will bring a similar hardline approach as the spymaster, increasing the involvement of the intelligence agency in civilian matters even more than it already has.
>
> A recent [example] of this 'over-reach' can be seen in the Supreme Court's sacking of Islamabad High Court judge Justice Shaukat Aziz on Thursday for criticizing the ISI and noting its involvement in the disqualification and imprisonment of former prime minister, Nawaz Sharif.

The decision last week to expel 18 international non-governmental organizations (INGOs) from Pakistan was also taken at the behest of the ISI as well, well-placed sources in the Interior Ministry have confirmed.

Similarly, authorities on Friday arrested rights activist Gulalai Ismail, who is a member of the Pashtun Tahaffuz Movement (PTM)—a Pashtun nationalist movement that is critical of the Pakistan Army.

Military sources say that Munir is a no-nonsense ideologue, who will not tolerate any dissent or spreading of narratives that don't toe the line defined by the Army.[36]

How he would translate his activism on the domestic front to the external relationship with the US was unclear during a period of tension between the two countries. Within eight months of his appointment, he was replaced by another former DG of the ISI. Lt. Gen. Faiz Hameed, who had been recently promoted and assigned as DG I, T & E at GHQ, was sent back to the ISI to take over as DG from Lt. Gen. Munir. He had been active earlier in the exchanges with a radical Islamist group that had blockaded the Rawalpindi–Islamabad main road at Faizabad and authored and signed the deal with the protesters. An unusual step for an army officer during a civilian government's rule. At the same time, another major general, in charge of the Punjab Rangers was seen distributing funds to the protesters, ostensibly to cover their travel expenses. This provoked much commentary and questions about the military's sympathies for such groups. Lt. Gen. Hameed accompanied PM Imran Khan on his maiden visit to the United States in July 2019 to renew a relationship with the Director CIA.

At the heart of the US–Pakistan relationship was a strong military relationship, built on nearly two decades of intensive training and collaboration since 9/11. Though not always perfect, it provided the basis for dialogue and debate, both. Much better than disengagement, the ill-informed path seemingly chosen by the Trump administration in its early days, at a critical juncture in the Afghanistan conflict. It set aside earlier serious efforts at dialogue that had been launched by well-meaning persons in both the US and Pakistan to reset the relationship on a sustainable path. Only in July 2019 was an attempt made to repair the relationship when

---

[36]   Kunwar Khuldune Shahid, 'Pakistan Gets a Hardliner Spymaster to Head the ISI', *Asia Times*, 15 October 2018, https://www.asiatimes.com/2018/10/article/pakistan-gets-a-hardline-spy-master-to-head-the-isi/

President Trump attempted to win over PM Khan with fulsome praise in a hastily organized White House visit, transparently linked to the need for Pakistan to assist the US withdrawal from Afghanistan and Pakistan's help in getting the Taliban to the table. But many efforts were made in this direction in the decade preceding that visit, with the two militaries carrying the weight.

10

Standing in the Right Corner

'Pakistan would like to remain a part of the solution and not the problem. At the end of the day, we would like to be standing in the right corner of the room.'

—Gen. Ashfaq Parvez Kayani[1]

The core of the US–Pakistan relationship over 2008–16 continued to be the direct link between the two militaries. Aiding this was the fact that the Obama administration relied on two military men to handle key relations with Pakistan during its early days. Gen. James Jones, the NSA, took advantage of his earlier experience as SACEUR and head of NATO forces to build on his knowledge of Afghanistan and Pakistan, and his contacts there to reopen the engagement. He was assisted by the Senior Director for the Region at the NSC, Lt. Gen. Doug Lute, a holdover from the Bush administration who had endeared himself to the Obama White House with his diligence and willingness to work even with the most difficult partners at the Department of State. Jones recalled how he requested that the Pakistani team meeting him on his first visit to Pakistan as the NSA should be a combined group of civilians and military men. He felt this would be more effective than meeting them separately. When he got there, the Pakistanis came in a jovial mood, smiling and bantering among themselves, but then some confusion ensued as they tried to sort out who would sit where! They were not used to being in the same room in a large group.[2]

---

[1] Final sentence in the document presented by General Kayani to President Obama in October 2010 in the Roosevelt Room at the White House.

[2] Interview with Gen. James (Jim) L. Jones, Tyson's Corner, VA, September 2016.

As a norm, though, the lead American negotiator with Pakistan was Admiral Mike Mullen, and his principal interlocutor was the Army Chief Gen. Ashfaq Parvez Kayani. Both took great pride in their frequent meetings. Kayani recounted that they had met twenty-six times officially during their tenures, plus one last meeting that took place in Seville, Spain, just before Mullen went public with his criticism of the ISI and its links with the Taliban via the Haqqani Network.[3] An interesting footnote to the Mullen testimony was what seemed to have been an end-run by him of the White House. His testimony on the Hill containing the allegation that the Haqqani Network was a veritable 'arm of the ISI' was not the text that White House had cleared. He was taken to task for taking this public position at the next meeting of Principals of the NSC at the White House, where the feeling was that this parting shot by Mullen would make it hard for his successor, Gen. Martin Dempsey, to build a relationship with Pakistan.[4] According to a senior NSC official at that time, Mullen said he wanted to clear the deck for Dempsey to craft his own relationship. As later events showed, that did not work.

Despite the desire to strengthen the civilian side in Pakistan, the US tended to favour contacts with the military, even on wider diplomatic issues. There was a sixteen-hour meeting with a small group of senior US officials in Abu Dhabi that Kayani recalled. He handled them alone, fuelled famously by nicotine. Secretary of State Kerry sought a private meeting with Kayani prior to his own visit to Kabul as the new Secretary of State. Kayani arranged to see him in Jordan in 2011, 'one on one'. In a set of separate meetings with Kerry and Lute, Kayani recalls Lute asking to 'help us'. They wished Pakistan to persuade the Taliban to issue a statement that they were prepared to join the talks. Kerry said it would be a miracle if the Taliban issued a statement, recalls Kayani. 'We delivered it for them!' Kayani also recalls warning his American counterparts that the Taliban were stronger than before and controlled more territory. In his view, Mullah Omar helped keep control over the Taliban and that splintering them would create more extreme groups. Kayani believed that Mullah Mansour, who took over from Omar 'has to establish his independence from Pakistan to establish his credentials'. As a corollary, he believed that

---

[3] Mullen's testimony before the Armed Services Committee of the Senate became the signature denunciation of Pakistan as a double-dealing ally.

[4] Comments on background by former officials who were at the NSC meeting.

'Talks inside Pakistan [with the Taliban] would create the impression that Pakistan owns the process.' In his calculation, 'the US never had a clear, consistent view of the end game' for Afghanistan.[5]

Yet, the Pakistan military, primarily the army, preferred to deal with its counterparts in the Pentagon, CENTCOM or the ISAF in Afghanistan unencumbered by the protocols and constraints of diplomacy imposed by their Foreign Office colleagues. They preferred the same direct communication with the Afghan leadership. This led to meetings with the Afghan president, and tripartite meetings with the Afghan military leadership and ISAF commanders. The result was a lack of cohesion in the overall Pakistani position and the reduction of the status and capacity of the Pakistani diplomatic corps.

The military agreed to participate in the strategic dialogue that was initiated between Pakistan and the US to discuss mutually agreed topics ranging from economics and trade to security and technical issues. The Pakistani team was nominally led by the PPP Foreign Minister Shah Mehmood Qureshi and, after he left the PPP government in a huff, by Hina Rabbani Khar. Although, all American eyes tended to shift to the army chief whenever he participated in those meetings.

Gen. Kayani had a scholarly inclination that was unusual among Pakistani military commanders, who liked to see and present themselves as men of action. Many of them did not read much, relying on the oral tradition more than diligent study. Kayani was a reader. He also paid particular attention to his public image. He mentioned with some amusement and a sense of hurt, an article that had appeared in America after one of his visits that quoted Gen. Jones as saying words to the effect that Kayani talks of what he will do after leaving university! He explained to me in 2010 in his office at GHQ that he was preparing a statement that would present Pakistan's strategic case to the US in a logical manner.[6] He said he thought Obama was a logical thinker too and this approach

---

[5]   Author interview with Gen. Kayani, February 2016.

[6]   Gen. Kayani normally preferred to meet on Friday afternoons in his office, after other staff at GHQ had gone home for lunch and mid-day prayers. He could then smoke seemingly incessantly and speak in his soft murmur, bouncing ideas and sharing insights about regional and US relations, often conveying messages that he knew would be carried back to Washington. I found him to be a good listener, even though he dominated the exchange. Unlike many of his colleagues, he did not wish to be acknowledged as right on every point he made.

would appeal to the American president. Then he proceeded to outline his approach, point-by-point, in cascading order. Those notes became the basis of a talk at NATO headquarters in Brussels. He later put them down into an essay of sorts.

Various iterations of that paper were handed to the Americans. These are referred to as Kayani 1.0, 2.0 and 3.0. The first two papers were long and seem to have relied on a lot of Foreign Office verbiage, so they may not truly be Kayani 1.0 or 2.0 . . . The first one led to the Strategic Dialogue. The second was handed over to the US team in Islamabad in July 2010. It had a letter to Obama's NSA Gen. Jones signed by Kayani and therefore went to the president, as he intended.[7] The third was the paper he handed to Obama in October 2010 at the White House. The shorter, later versions are more in Kayani's own voice.[8] They reflected not only his pride in learning the US methodology for research and presentation of ideas on paper but also a desire to couch ideas in terms that the audience wanted to hear. He succeeded for long in playing his American interlocutors to his advantage, even while the actions of his army, intelligence and government were at odds with what the US wanted. He also recounted the salient points of the document he had presented to President Obama in October 2010 at the White House, without divulging their provenance at the time, to visitors from the Atlantic Council in December 2010. I saw then that the notes for the Brussels meeting that he had discussed with me earlier had become a cohesive and important Pakistani document.[9] Nothing reflecting Pakistan's point of view cogently has emerged since then. Nor America's understanding of that point of view.

During a meeting at the White House of the US–Pakistan Strategic Dialogue in October 2010 that Lute had arranged, a pithier version of that Kayani essay, dubbed Kayani 3.0 by Steve Coll, was launched with dramatic effect. Lute had a high opinion of Kayani, seeing him as someone with a 'nuanced, calibrated, and intellectual approach. A serious professional.' But he 'did not wish to promote Kayani as a proxy Head of State'. The meeting

---

7   Author interview with Gen. Kayani, February 2016.

8   Coll, *Directorate S.*

9   This particular meeting on 2 December 2010 was during office hours for him to meet Fred Kempe, the CEO and president of the Atlantic Council, whom I was taking around Pakistan after a long hiatus. Kempe had previously been there during the Soviet Afghan war as a correspondent for the *Wall Street Journal*.

that Lute set up at the White House was in the Roosevelt Room, centrally located in the West Wing, a few steps from the Oval Office. The room, named after two American presidents who had led their country during wars, is cosy. No windows, only a little natural light from the roof. It has a table surrounded by comfortable padded brown leather chairs studded with brass tacks, seven across from each other with two at either head of the table. A line of the same stuffed leather chairs extended the length of the room against the wall on either side. Obama would normally prefer to sit in the middle on one side, looking across at a portrait of Franklin Delano Roosevelt to his right on the opposite wall. A painting of Rough Rider Teddy Roosevelt on a rampant horse adorned the wall above the mantle over the fireplace to the president's right.

Jones was chairing the US team that included Lute and US ambassador to Pakistan Cameron Munter, from that central perch that Obama favoured, when the Pakistani team joined them in the Roosevelt Room. Across from him were Kayani and Qureshi, accompanied by Ambassador Husain Haqqani. The American team had prepared a surprise. Fifteen minutes into the meeting, Obama dropped into the room and Jones relinquished his seat for the President, allowing Obama to take centre stage. As the discussion got under way, Kayani spoke briefly and then leaned over and presented Obama a fourteen-page (1.5-line-spaced) document entitled 'Pakistan's Perspective'. This was the 'logical' presentation that he had talked about in his office in Rawalpindi many months earlier. Obama said he would read it with interest. Clearly, the Pakistani side was equally surprised by Kayani's move.

Lute described the document as written in the Fort Leavenworth style, the approach taught at the US Command and Staff College that Kayani had attended some years ago. Others were less generous, calling it 'sophomoric'. Regardless, Kayani achieved his effect. It forced an immediate US response, led by Lute's team and including Holbrooke's experts. Though 'immediate' meant some three-plus months. The response was carried to Islamabad by Secretary Hillary Clinton in February 2011, by which time the US and Pakistan were well on their way to the worst year in recent memory.

Interestingly, when the Pakistani team was preparing for this Washington meeting, Foreign Minister Shah Mehmood Qureshi had gotten into an argument with the PPP leadership. It was widely believed he considered himself as a better candidate for prime minister than his fellow

Multan politician Yousaf Raza Gilani. As a result, he did not participate in a key preparatory meeting just before the team left for Washington, leaving instead for a family weekend in Lahore. Kayani meanwhile had been pressing ahead with the meetings. He called a few meetings at army headquarters, inviting the civilians, both politicians and foreign office staff, to meetings that he chaired. His statement in the Roosevelt Room, however, was a revelation to even his own side. Over time, he had discussed it with his key corps commanders and principal staff officers and the DGMO, Maj. Gen. Javed Iqbal, but not with the civilians. That Kayani paper remains a clear statement of the issues that bedevilled US–Pakistan relations. It was candid and concise.

What Kayani Said[10]

Kayani's five-part assessment began by focusing on Afghanistan, the Pakistan–Afghanistan relationship, the FATA, the Pakistan–India relationship, and concluded with Pakistan's concerns. It made deft use of bullet points and highlighted sections and key points in boldface. Its tone was clinical and sometimes theoretical, relying on the jargon of military schools and presenting Pakistan as a victim of circumstances and the predations of terrorist groups.

Citing the need for 'inclusive and lasting peace', Kayani stipulated that 'Unless people of Afghanistan consider themselves to be part of the process, achievement of this objective will remain elusive.' He then talked about shaping the strategic environment in Afghanistan by taking into account Afghanistan's ethnic mix, and suggested there be no preconditions for talks among Afghans. He suggested sequencing steps: 'reduction in violence, renouncing Al Qaeda and developing consensus on Constitution'. These should be seen as 'end' conditions, not 'pre' conditions. He then cited 'the prerequisite for a strong Central Government' as one where 'the Centre is "giving" to the regions. It has strong Armed Forces and a strong federal structure.' His conclusion: 'If people of Afghanistan and their coming generations view the US and the Coalition as friends, the war would be won.' To some extent. Kayani was cleverly trying to second-guess the US policy towards the

---

[10] Based on the non-paper prepared by Gen. Kayani and shared with President Obama.

Taliban and create resonance on how they wanted to shape the Afghan peace process.

Looking at the Pakistan–Afghanistan relationship, Kayani wrote: 'For Pakistan, the outcome of the war in Afghanistan is a question of life and death.' Earlier, he had told another visitor to his office that if the Taliban were to take Kabul, it would be bad for Afghanistan but much worse for Pakistan. He saw Pakistan being at the receiving end of a serious threat led by Al-Qaeda and its 'conglomerate of terrorist organizations'. He then praised the US as being 'the most important friend and biggest donor of aid to Pakistan' and spoke of their effort to forge a strategic partnership, 'decisively moving away from the transitional nature of the relationship'. (It is not clear if he really meant 'transitional' or 'transactional'.) He then bemoaned the 'vitriolic and biased coverage of Pakistan in the electronic and print media' in the US that made 'support to Pakistan . . . more tentative and future relationship more uncertain'. At the same time, this weakened the cause of 'those in Pakistan who are supportive of the US–Pakistan strategic relationship'. Most military officers in Pakistan, used to the control of media outlets in their own country, held a strong belief that the US government guided and shaped newspapers in their coverage of overseas issues.

Kayani then presented a list of US concerns and complaints about Pakistan that was impressive in its comprehensiveness as well as frankness. Most interestingly, this list remains unchanged to this day and could have been taken from even the US–Pakistan dialogues in 2018 or been drafted by his American counterparts! He highlighted the major points in bold type.

- **Pakistan provides safe havens** to Quetta Shura, Taliban, Haqqanis and other anti-Coalition forces.
- ISI is harbouring and supporting Haqqani Network.
- **Pakistan is selective and duplicitous** in its efforts against radical forces attacking Coalition in Afghanistan.
- **Pakistan is supporting Taliban and keeping them alive as AN OPTION** if Coalition fails in Afghanistan.
- **Pakistan Army is either unwilling or incapable** of tackling those who attack US interests in Afghanistan. It operates against only those who pose a direct threat to Pakistan.
- **Pakistan Army is India centric.** Its focus on terrorist threats in Pakistan is blurred.

- Al Qaeda lives and grows in Pakistan. All threats to the World security thus emanate from Pakistan.
- Pakistan is a **reluctant and unreliable partner.**

He blamed this list for creating 'a low degree of trust' and having 'far reaching effects on the morale and motivation of [Pakistani] troops in the field'. And he countered with Pakistan's own concerns and complaints. He criticized the US for keeping Pakistan in the dark regarding peace efforts and for blaming Pakistan for 'each and every act of violence in Afghanistan'. In his view, Pakistan was being made a scapegoat for the 'inadequacies of the Coalition and overall situation in Afghanistan. All this does not portend well for the future.'

Kayani saw a direct linkage between the stability and future of Afghanistan and Pakistan. '**It cannot, therefore, wish for Afghanistan anything other than what it wishes for itself.**' He stated firmly: '**Pakistan has no right or desire to dictate Afghanistan's relations with other countries.** This includes relations with India.' This must have been music to the Americans' ears, but the reality on the ground was at a tangent from this statement of Pakistani policy; Pakistan wanted Afghanistan, at every step, to expunge India's presence and influence. He extolled the need for development and stability in Afghanistan since it would benefit Pakistan directly. But he also presented the need for Afghan Pashtuns to be 'accommodated in the political dispensation of Afghanistan', not realizing that this broke the rule he had established in his own list about Afghanistan being a sovereign state. He went on to add that 'Pakistan neither desires nor has the capacity to control Afghanistan let alone undertake the imprudence of setting up a government of its choice'.

He chose not to break the Pashtun prism through which Pakistan views the mosaic of Afghan polity and society. He ended this section by stating: 'A peaceful, stable and friendly Afghanistan provides us the strategic depth—a concept that is totally misunderstood.' Kayani repeated this thought in different fora and in private conversations with visitors from the United States. I was at the NDU in Washington DC in February 2010, when he startled his audience by stating point blank: 'We want Strategic Depth in Afghanistan,'[11] but then promptly redefined the

---

[11] Zahid Hussain, 'Pakistan Spells Out Terms for Regional Stability', *Dawn*, 2 February 2010.

idea of Strategic Depth as not being physical depth but the presence of a neighbour to the west that was stable and not hostile to Pakistani interests in the region. The defunct and unworkable concept of Strategic Depth continued to enthral and consume Pakistani military thinking. It detracted from Pakistan's ability to craft an effective security environment built on an educated and empowered population and a vibrant economy.

The ISI Nexus

He then segued into a hot issue—the relationship between the ISI and Taliban groups like the Haqqanis—saying that Pakistan was 'maligned' by this accusation based on the assumption that Pakistan wanted to retain the Taliban option if the situation merited it after the Coalition draw down. In fact, he posited that the ISI had broken off 'all contacts' with the 'Mujahideen', as he called the Taliban groups after 9/11, and this was seen by them as dishonourable conduct. 'Pakistan identifies Taliban and Haqqani Network to be one of the **biggest irritants in its relations with US.**' This led to a series of rhetorical questions about the role of extremist militants and radicals and whether Pakistan wished to see them as an alternative to US friendship and as shapers of Pakistan's polity. His answer was 'Negative'.

But was all this verifiable? No. Nor did Pakistan work to make it so. At various times, Pakistan cited the need to maintain contact with such groups though it maintained this did not translate to support for them. Much later, in 2016, Sartaj Aziz, then adviser in charge of the foreign ministry, acknowledged that Taliban leaders and their families were living in Pakistan. 'We have some influence on them because their leadership is in Pakistan, and they get some medical facilities, their families are here,' Aziz said, responding to a question about Pakistan's role in peace talks between the Taliban and Afghanistan government. 'So we can use those levers to pressurize them to say "come to the table",' he said, 'but we can't negotiate on behalf of the Afghan government because we can't offer them what the Afghan government can.'[12]

US intelligence routinely captured transmissions of communications between what they termed officials from Pakistan with the Taliban as well

---

[12]   Rishi Iyengar, 'Pakistan Has Finally Admitted That Afghan Taliban Leaders Are Living There', *TIME*, 4 March 2016.

as relatively unhindered movement of the Haqqani group inside North Waziristan.

Next, Kayani spoke about a perennial issue: when would Pakistan move to clear all the FATA of militants, especially in North Waziristan, which remained a hideout for the Haqqanis and a pathway for Punjabi Taliban sympathizers to enter the fray inside Afghanistan. 'The question is not "if" but "when" and "how" to tackle it militarily.' This was a sentence he used frequently in discussions of this topic, with Admiral Mullen, and other official and think tank visitors (including me).

The army had already moved into South Waziristan in force, but many militants escaped into Afghanistan or into North Waziristan and other agencies of FATA. Kayani spoke about the fact that the Pakistan Army was 'stretched' in FATA and also by relief efforts for the floods that had ravaged Pakistan. He cited logistical issues in moving into North Waziristan via South Waziristan, where displaced persons had yet to be resettled and roads were under construction. He also cited the conflicting demands of closing the border with Afghanistan and controlling the population centres inside the agencies of FATA. All this required help on the economic front as well as filling 'deficiencies in critical capability i.e. transport/attack helicopters and Intelligence Surveillance and Reconnaissance (ISR) etc.' The US never really delivered what Pakistan needed on this front. Its military aid was slow and stingy. And Pakistani leadership, especially in the military, continued to delay and dissemble in the search or Al-Qaeda and other terrorists inside Pakistani territory . . .

The India Factor

A surging economic and military India and fears of its hegemonic designs in the Greater South Asian region, that encompassed also Iran, Afghanistan and Central Asia, guided Pakistani political and military doctrine and strategy. In an earlier conversation with me, Kayani had taken umbrage at what he called a partial quotation of his views leaked to Bob Woodward by NSC officials in the Obama White House. 'I am India-centric' is how he had been portrayed in the book *Obama's Wars*.[13] In one of his closed-door sessions with me in his GHQ office, Kayani had told me that he had gone

---

[13]   Bob Woodward, *Obama's Wars* (Simon and Schuster, New York, September 2010).

beyond that stark statement to explain to his White House interlocutors that no Pakistani Army chief could ignore India and its huge army and air force deployments on Pakistan's eastern border (three strike corps and three dozen airfields, according to Pakistani calculations). Ignoring the huge Indian military presence on the eastern border would be dereliction of duty. So, he *had* to be India-centric in preparing to defend Pakistan against a country that had been continuously hostile towards Pakistan since Independence in 1947. When India could leverage its numerical strength against Pakistan, it did, as was the case with East Pakistan to create the independent state of Bangladesh in 1971. Kayani had seen action in that war as a freshly commissioned second lieutenant, his course at the PMA having been released earlier than scheduled in 1971 to allow the young cadets to join their regiments and prepare for the impending battle with India of December that year. That experience left a deep imprint on his mind and generation.

But Kayani took a different tack in this note for Obama in order to create some cognitive dissonance and then some eventual resonance in his American readers' minds. '**India is an important neighbor**,' he wrote, using boldface type to highlight his argument, but slipped in the Pakistani expectation that the US would '**facilitate a rapprochement,** despite the limits of its leverage over India'. He extolled the need for '**peaceful coexistence**' with India and wrote that Pakistan could '**not afford to be in a perpetual state of confrontation and competition with India**'. Yet he recognized the need to '**strike a balance between defence and development**' while stating that 'we cannot, however, remain oblivious to our basic defence needs'. He felt that India needed to play a 'more positive and accommodating role in understanding and responding to Pakistan's legitimate security concerns, without defining them'. And he spelled out Pakistan's desire that India should exhibit 'strategic altruism'[14] and keep in mind Pakistan's self-respect, sovereignty and the aspirations of its people. He recognized that Pakistan should not expect to compare the India–US relationship with the Pakistan–US relationship, but warned that the people of Pakistan

---

[14] Kayani could well have, but did not use this apt term that had been coined by Peter Jones of the University of Ottawa, a leading proponent of Track 2 diplomacy in South Asia and the Middle East, with whom the Atlantic Council launched an India–Pakistan Military Track 2 dialogue. Under the rubric of Waging Peace, the South Asia Center of the Atlantic Council also launched its own Indo-Pakistan Trade and Business Track 2 as well as one on Water Issues.

would continue to see the US relations with India as yardstick. He threw in Pakistan's expectation of a **'mutually beneficial relationship with India'**, but skipped over details of the various opportunities that had been lost on trade with India, transit trade for both Afghanistan and India and resolving the low-hanging fruits of past conflicts involving water in the north and disputed territory around Sir Creek in the south of the country.

The Bottom Line

All of Kayani's self-described 'logical' argument led to a recitation of Pakistan's concerns, nay complaints (the bold face is from the original document):

- **US is disregardful** (*sic*) **of Pakistan's efforts and its support.** It takes Pakistan for granted.
- The US 'is reluctant to help Pakistan resolve its disputes with India'. It discusses rather than delivers.
- 'Pakistan is not important for US' and hence it gets a 'raw deal' whenever it cooperates with the United States.
- **'US is hesitant to crystallize the end state** and decisively move towards that end.' (He did not define the meaning of the 'end state' and whether it referred solely to Afghanistan or to Pakistan too. But he also mentioned that the notion of 'victory' was affecting US strategy.)
- **Pakistan is being made a scapegoat.**
- He then blamed the US for maintaining a **'transitional relationship with Pakistan'** though it was unclear if this was seen as a synonym for 'temporary' or 'transactional'.
- Finally he accused the US of being 'intrusive' and 'overbearing' and **'causing and maintaining a controlled chaos in Pakistan'** with the **'real aim'** being to **'de-nuclearize Pakistan'.**

Kayani tried to end on a more positive note, having shared his innermost thoughts in the final concerns about the US relationship. He praised the **'Strategic Relationship' with the US as 'a very important initiative of President Obama'.** But emphasized the need for it to be a relationship based on a better understanding of each other's 'frames of references' between the people of the two countries and to develop favourable public opinion on both sides. He decried constant US pressure on Pakistan **'to do** more', especially since 'Pakistan feels that it is being pushed in a different direction than the one US itself is likely to ultimately take.'

He ended with Pakistan's bottom line: 'Pakistan would like to remain a part of the solution and not the problem. At the end of the day, we would like to be standing in the right corner of the room.'

The Delayed US Response

It took the US almost three months before it finalized a response to Kayani's short and pithy missive. There was no established centre of gravity for decision making in Washington DC. Especially on the Af–Pak theatre. The CIA, DOD, State and the NSC at the White House, each had its own preferences and methods of operating. There were long discussions about who should reply. 'There was a conversation about Mullen staff preparing to respond because they were the Pakistani military's counterparts in a sense and had a relationship, but eventually, the responsibility fell to NSC because it [the Kayani document] was literally given to the president,' recalled Shamila Chaudhary, the Pakistani–American director responsible for Pakistan at the NSC. Chaudhary had started at the NSC in April 2010. She left the NSC in June 2011. The first set of replies from other agencies that came to the NSC were found wanting so Doug Lute put his own team, led by Chaudhary, to come up with a comprehensive answer to Kayani. Lute recalls working on the final draft at home in Arlington, VA, while trying to keep track of a Washington Redskins football game one weekend.

While Kayani and his team remained in charge of decision making on India and Afghanistan and the relationship with the US on the Pakistani side, and despite their clear differences with their own civilian government on many issues related to India and Afghanistan, they had a clear notion of what they wanted. And they had continuity. The US bureaucracy, on the other hand, suffered from a routine transfer of staff across the board. Because of security concerns, Pakistan was a short-term posting for many staff. State also had a parallel set of changes, though some changes did allow old Pakistan or regional hands to occupy key slots at State and thus continue dealing with Pakistan. The same transfer syndrome afflicted the NSC and DOD. And often, all these changes in the different agencies would occur roughly at the same time, creating issues of continuity in building relationships and of faulty or missing institutional memory. Finding new staff who had the experience and knowledge needed to hit the ground running was a major problem.[15] Lute at NSC was the constant. So he took on the central role for the Americans to respond to Kayani.

Chaudhary's approach to her task at crafting a reply was clear-cut. 'My strategy was to write something in the same voice as the Pakistani letter was written. The Kayani voice was very straightforward and direct, and he didn't mince words, nor did he try to be very showy. He wasn't trying to write a fancy letter with a lot of flowery language. He was just trying to tell us what their perspective was . . . This message from Kayani was the first time someone in the Pakistani government had actually admitted to us that the Haqqani Network was part of Pakistan's strategic national security interest, that the way they looked at these groups was part of their strategic approach to national security. We had never gotten that before.' She thought the Kayani message was a milestone and was 'something to work with actually because he wants to have a real conversation about it'.[16]

The end result was a US document that was long and therefore may not have been totally effective in responding to Kayani or getting the attention of his titular civilian bosses with their famously short attention spans. Some 5000-plus words long, the US perspective that was issued as a White Paper in February 2011 ran on to eighteen pages of a single-spaced document and attempted to capture all the different points from other US agencies. However, it failed to highlight two underlying and explicit fears reflected prominently in Kayani's paper, treating them inside the paper as ancillary functions. First, it tried to downplay the India factor and any US role, either public or behind the scenes, to broker better relations between India and Pakistan. There were good reasons from the American side to do this, since this would have involved a long inter-agency debate. Second, it did not address prominently the Pakistani plea to be treated with respect and trust and not to have the persistent fear that the US had ulterior motives for being in the region, including the defanging of Pakistan's nuclear arsenal. While reiterating the US's views on nuclear safety and safeguards and stating that the US had no desire to denuclearize Pakistan, the reply did not create a clearer path forward other than continuing the Strategic

---

[15]   Shuja Nawaz, 'Exeunt Pakistan Experts, Pursued by Bear', *Foreign Policy*, 14 June 2011.

[16]   Op. cit. Interview with NSC Director Shamila Chaudhary.

Dialogue that was destined to meet its demise in the wake of the tumult of 2011.

Kayani seemed pleased with the fact that he had received the answer from Secretary Clinton during her February 2011 visit to Pakistan, even as the US and Pakistan were dealing with the effects of the Raymond Davis affair. He recalled that the US quoted his own ideas back at him and tried to respond to some of them. A real dialogue seemed to be brewing.

In restating Pakistan's key perspectives, the US reply focused largely on Pakistan's relations with Afghanistan and the prosecution of the war in that country and how that affected relations with the US. And it appeared to agree with the points made by Kayani in that regard, while continuing the dialogue on all these issues, as well as other issues of mutual concern. Of course, most of the drafters were not part of the Inner Circle at the White House and the CIA which was already zeroing in on the lair of Osama bin Laden in Abbottabad during that period. It suggested sustaining during 2011 the momentum built in the Strategic Dialogue in 2010, exhibiting, in hindsight, the ignorance of the drafters about the events that were *en train* in the US and that would derail the relationship irrevocably.

The US recognized Pakistan's fight, not only for itself but also for the world. But it also acknowledged that Pakistan's fears about India's hostile intentions prevented it from moving more forces to the Afghan border or to deal with internal militancy. Yet, the US appeared ready to expand support against domestic extremist networks and those that threatened Afghanistan and the US. On the nuclear issue, the US statement assured Pakistan that it did not aim to control Pakistan's nuclear weapons directly or via the proposed Fissile Materials Cutoff Treaty, but it continued to express US concerns about Pakistani nuclear materials getting into the hands of terrorists who might use them against the US and its allies.

It then turned to what Kayani had termed in his paper for Obama as the 'transitional' US relationship with Pakistan. It read 'transitional' as meaning transactional and said that Pakistan appeared to the US as only interested in doing the minimum necessary on CT cooperation to continue to receive US aid. It then cited reports of Pakistan's clandestine support to militants who targeted Afghanistan or the US.

Citing the need to change the relationship between the US and Pakistan, the US document raised the issue of America's broad interests in the region, including with India and Afghanistan. The US wished to create a similar long-term relationship with Pakistan based on a shared vision via the ongoing Strategic Dialogue scheduled for a meeting in April 2011. Clearly, the authors were not aware of the Abbottabad Raid plan that was then reaching its final stage.

Turning to Afghanistan, the document agreed with Kayani that Afghan forces would not be self-sufficient by the time of the proposed drawdown of US forces in 2014, and that is why the US and NATO had committed to a long-term partnership. This was in accord with what the National Training Mission Afghanistan (NTMA), headed at one time by Kayani's Fort Leavenworth coursemate, Lt. Gen. William B. Caldwell, believed to be the case. Caldwell had taken over the NTMA in 2009 and also spent time at Kayani's invitation visiting Pakistani training establishments. Kayani made sure he spent time looking at the COIN training being imparted to Pakistani troops prior to their injection into the fight in the western borderlands. In a meeting of an NTMA team with us at the South Asia Center of the Atlantic Council, when I asked at the end of our discussions about the size of the Afghan security forces that could go into battle autonomously, the reply I got was '5,000'. They were aiming to create a total force of 350,000, but were constantly stymied by high attrition rates and an imbalance in the ethnic mix, especially in the ANA officer corps.

The American document was in line with Kayani on one major issue. There was no purely military solution for Afghanistan. (Something that successive Pakistani prime ministers, especially Imran Khan, also stipulated over the years.) It was critical to get the reconcilable Afghan insurgents into a durable political process to ensure the stability of both Afghanistan and Pakistan. It also recognized the supremacy of the people of Afghanistan in deciding the final outcome, and noted that Pakistan had strategic interests in Afghanistan. Therefore, it suggested that the end result needed to take into account Pakistan's legitimate interests. Interestingly, a similar sentiment was expressed by Pakistan's bête noire Amrullah Saleh, the former Afghan intelligence chief, at a CENTCOM conference on the region that I attended in Tampa, Florida. But his comment was lost in his obligatory broader diatribe against Pakistani intelligence meddling in Afghanistan.

The Americans warned of a real threat to Pakistan if the Taliban won the war in Afghanistan, and noted that no major change had been visible in the ability of groups like the Haqqanis to operate from Pakistani territory. Saving the most blunt rebuttal for the last, the US disputed Kayani's statement that Pakistan's ISI 'broke all contacts with "mujahideen" after September 11, 2001'. In the US view, senior Afghan leaders continued to find refuge not only in the borderlands but also in major cities, including Quetta and Karachi. The Americans also warned of the shared interests and goals of the various local and foreign terrorist networks operating inside Pakistan. They recognized the danger of blowback from actions in North Waziristan, but offered to help the broader economic and political development and improved governance of FATA.

On India, the US understood Pakistan's concerns and Kayani's hope that India and Pakistan needed to understand and respond to each other's legitimate security concerns. But, it challenged the notion that the Pakistani people measured the US relationship in light of its relationship with Pakistan's arch-rival, India. The Americans tried to allay Pakistani concerns by not portraying the relationship as zero-sum. But America demurred on its ability to broker confidence-building between the two arch-rivals unless they themselves accepted the US role. And it suggested India and Pakistan needed to define a road map to reduce tensions before the US would consider a role in the process. It pointed out the need to act against the accused in the Mumbai attacks and to recognize that both India and Pakistan had legitimate strategic interests in Afghanistan. Concluding by citing Kayani's own final statement that had expressed a desire on Pakistan's part to stand in the right corner, the US response to Kayani said that they ought to stand together in the same corner of the room that Kayani had described.

That togetherness did not materialize, as the earth-shaking events of 2011 inside Pakistan took the erstwhile and aspiring 'allies' into a deep well of hurt and disappointment for both. US aid to Pakistan declined steadily. The Strategic Dialogue collapsed. Both sides continued to talk past each other or to resort to half-truths or outright lies, for tactical advantage. Ambassador Olson captured the nature of this dialogue in his exit interview with DG-ISI Rizwan Akhtar in the latter's camp office in the Chaklala section of Rawalpindi. During an unusually frank conversation, Akhtar told a long story, according to Olson. 'It was about how in South Asian culture, his essential message . . . done through parable and anecdote, [was] that when a South Asian lies to you, he defends that lie to the death. He will never admit that he was lying. He will just keep piling lie on top of lie.'[17]

---

[17]   Interview with Amb. Richard Olson, January 2017.

This frank admission captured the difficulty of a dialogue where both sides were talking but had difficulty hearing each other.

Kayani 4.0

Kayani though was not giving up on his effort to educate his NATO colleagues and especially the Americans and their 'logic-driven' president. He made another attempt to recast his earlier paper and produced another concise document of just over eleven pages, double-spaced text,[18] encompassing his view of the lessons that America and Pakistan had learned in the process and presenting it as 'our collective experience'. This comprehensive and data-backed document was presented at a NATO meeting in Seville, Spain in September 2011 and later given to Commander CENTCOM Gen. James Mattis on Saturday, 24 September 2011, during the latter's visit to GHQ,[19] where they discussed a series of militant attacks in Afghanistan including one on the US embassy that the US felt had ISI involvement. It had been produced inside GHQ with key input from the Military Operations Directorate. The meeting with Mattis also took place in the shadow of the testimony of Admiral Mullen citing the ISI links to the Haqqani Network.

> Sources said the issue of Haqqani Network was discussed in detail during the meeting. General Kayani highlighted the fact that statements from US officials alleging Inter-Services Intelligence (ISI) support for the group was disturbing cooperation between the US and Pakistan.

---

[18] 'Ten Years since 9/11: Our Collective Experience'. (Pakistan's Perspective.) This document was presented by Gen. Kayani to mark the tenth anniversary of the terrorist attacks on the US mainland, just before the NATO Chiefs of Defense Staff meeting in Seville, Spain, 16–18 September 2011 (including Adm. Mullen, who bid farewell to the group on the 18th) and later shared by Pakistan Army Chief Gen. Kayani, with Gen. James Mattis of CENTCOM, United States, in Rawalpindi, on 24 September 2011. Gen. Kayani confirmed some of these details in a telephone call to me, 1 November 2018. In his recollection, the paper was delivered 11 September, when NATO commemorated the tenth anniversary of 9/11.

[19] Senior Pakistani official.

The issue of cross-border raids was also discussed during the meeting.[20]

Mattis had come to Pakistan for a short visit during a whirlwind tour of the region, accompanied by journalists. His primary message was about the need to curb the Haqqanis and to convey the anger in the US about the attacks on the US embassy in Kabul the previous week as well as the truck bombing of 10 September on a NATO outpost south of Kabul in which five persons were killed and seventy-seven Coalition soldiers were wounded. Mullen had reacted to those attacks in his own testimony on Capitol Hill on 22 September.

'With ISI support, Haqqani operatives planned and conducted that truck bomb attack, as well as the assault on our embassy,' Admiral Mullen said in a hearing of the Senate Armed Services Committee. 'We also have credible evidence that they were behind the June 28th attack against the Intercontinental Hotel in Kabul and a host of other smaller but effective operations.' In short, he said, 'the Haqqani Network acts as a veritable arm of Pakistan's Inter-Services Intelligence agency.'

His remarks were part of a deliberate effort by American officials to ratchet up pressure on Pakistan and perhaps pave the way for more American drone strikes or even cross-border raids into Pakistan to root out insurgents from their havens. American military officials refused to discuss what steps they were prepared to take, although Admiral Mullen's statement made clear that taking on the Haqqanis had become an urgent priority.[21]

Kayani immediately countered Mullen's attack, terming it 'unfortunate', and 'not based on facts'.

'In the first official reaction to the slew of public statements made by various levels of the US administration against the ISI and suspected links between the Haqqani Network and the Pakistan establishment, Kayani said that he had held a constructive meeting with Admiral Mullen in Spain last week.'[22] In a later conversation with me, Kayani recounted the friendly

---

[20] 'US CENTCOM Chief in Pakistan: Meets Kayani', *Express Tribune*, 24 September 2011.

[21] Elisabeth Bumiller and Jane Perlez, 'Pakistan's Spy Agency Is Tied to Attack on U.S. Embassy', *New York Times*, 22 September 2011.

[22] 'Kayani Terms Mullen's Haqqani Accusations as "Baseless"', *Express Tribune*, Pakistan, 23 September 2011.

exchange with Mullen in Spain—something that led to his surprise and anger at the Mullen statement.

Against the backdrop of a deteriorating situation between the US and Pakistan, Kayani apparently wanted to be seen as broadly aligned with the Americans. In his view, both sides had learned the difficulty of waging war and the greater difficulty of achieving peace, as well as the need for subordinating the military to political strategy. Here, he was using the time-tested Pakistani approach of telling the Americans what he thought they wanted to hear, using the language of the seminars at Fort Leavenworth. 'Now we can better appreciate the need for [a] comprehensive approach i.e., clear, hold, build and transfer.' Kayani wanted his American audience to join him in using 'our collective experience and wisdom' to 'forget about past differences and opinions and be wiser on achieving a better peace'.

He emphasized the need to build on the success of the joint CT effort against Al-Qaeda, and the shift from the surge to transition and reconciliation, reflecting a change of emphasis from the military to political strategy. For him, the way forward in Afghanistan was for 'enduring peace based on [a] stable environment' attained by 'an all inclusive approach which is open to all Afghans'. He then presented the basic parameters of an approach that, in his view, would resolve the Afghanistan issue beyond 2014 and create a conducive strategic environment that would allow a hand over 'to a "capable" Afghan Government and the ANA'. In the process of trying to attain peace, 'achieving less which is sustainable is more important than attempting more that is not sustainable,' he added.

'Given the above guidelines, it has to be determined whether to reconcile or not? And if yes, then with whom, a select group or all? Once that has been determined by Afghanistan and ISAF, Pakistan is prepared to help. However, the extent of this help should be correctly appreciated. We can facilitate but not guarantee. Ultimately it will remain Afghan responsibility,' said Kayani.[23]

How to translate these goals into an operating strategy? Kayani thought geography and history were two major constraints. (1) 2611 kilometres of the Afghanistan–Pakistan border over rough terrain was a major hurdle. (2) The division of Pashtun tribes by the border based on

---

[23] Op. cit. 'Ten Years since 9/11: Our Collective Experience'. (Pakistan's Perspective.) Also dubbed Kayani 4.0, this is the source document for most of his views in this section.

the Durand Line and Easement Rights of tribes people across the border without visas (under locally issued *rahdari* or travel permissions, or often without such permission by local authorities) created obstacles, rooted in historical custom, to managing the porous border. A further constraint was the dire economic situation of Pakistan, with low growth and massive floods affecting some 21 million persons, which meant diversion of 70,000 troops from fighting terrorism and militancy to providing flood relief and rehabilitation.

He then went into the challenges for the Pakistan military. An army of some 500,000 had over 150,000 deployed on the western border abutting Afghanistan, and another 80,000 facing India. (The total number of Pakistan's deployed forces roughly equalled the total ISAF deployment of forty-eight countries per Kayani's calculations.) Another 10,000 were committed to UN Peacekeeping duties. Citing the Pakistan's army's 'Tail to Tooth ratio', that is the quantum of fighting forces relative to those who provided support and logistics, only 30 per cent of the force ought to be deployable. In fact, Pakistan had over 40 per cent of its force deployed, stretching its resources. The forward deployments in Pakistan were averaging thirty months, compared with six months for ISAF soldiers, according to Kayani. The army's budget was also stretched. Even at a relatively low $6,000 per soldier per annum, it had a hard time meeting its operational needs with a total budget of $2.5 billion, Kayani stated, making the point that over the previous decade the military budget had declined from 4.5 per cent to 3 per cent of the GDP, and from 37 per cent of the budget to 14 per cent. 'Our argument is not to seek military aid but to improve our economy so that we can sustain the war against terrorism,' he added, as a coda that became the mantra of succeeding Pakistani military leaders, especially Gen. Qamar Javed Bajwa, even as they continued to seek or accept US funding and military aid.

All this was a preamble to a series of tables and charts indicating the size and number of military operations over time versus the rising tide of suicide bombings inside Pakistan. The Pakistan military had lost by that time some 11,000 dead or wounded due to the blowback from its operations, while the overall casualties in the country resulting from terrorist attacks was 40,000. Kayani then cited the ratio of 1 officer to 10 soldiers killed in action. This was a fact noted by a number of American military leaders, such as Gen. Petraeus and Gen. McChrystal, especially the loss of nine Pakistani generals, including one three-star. The ISI also came in for attacks by terrorists, losing 250 dead or wounded in attacks on three of its five regional headquarters inside Pakistan. Against this background, Kayani pointed to the success of the operations in Swat that cleared the region of terrorists within four months and helped evacuate and then rehabilitate some 2 million inhabitants, challenging his American readers: 'Do we have a comparable example?'

From the particular, he zoomed out to the general again, placing Pakistan's security calculations in 'a broader regional context' that involved 'a stable and peaceful Afghanistan on our west' and also 'peace and stability on our eastern border with India'. He recognized India again, as he had done in Kayani 3.0, as an 'important neighbour' and an 'emerging power with potential to influence global politics'. Noting Pakistan's 'limited military potential, essentially defensive in nature', he stated that the Indian military capability was 'Pakistan specific'. But Pakistan was 'committed to resolving outstanding issues with India and line in peace with dignity'. Ending with a Yoda-like statement with chosen capital letters: 'BIG POWER is about SIZE but GREAT POWER is about CONDUCT. We wish India to be a GREAT POWER.'

He concluded by reiterating the need for a stable and peaceful Afghanistan as a necessary end condition. Quoting the *Economist* of 3 September 2011, 'there can be no return to the innocence of September 10th 2001—and sadly no end to the vigilance', Kayani added. 'In our fight against terrorism we shall remain mindful that at the end of the day our children should live in a better world.'

Kayani badly wanted to stand in the same corner as the US. But the US kept redrawing the boundaries of that room, changing commanders and strategies in Afghanistan. The relationship with Pakistan was on the downswing again. It is not clear how widely Kayani 4.0 was shared by Mattis in the US system. Nor did Kayani share it widely with civilian counterparts in Pakistan. Army commanders did employ the document in PowerPoint presentations with counterparts in NATO. A senior army officer in Pakistan acknowledged that they tried to engage a number of times after the Mattis meeting with their US counterparts but did not get much traction. A number of senior diplomatic and administration officials in Washington did not recall seeing the document, including senior Trump administration officials who were dealing with the new president's critique of Pakistan as a bad partner. Other events in the region overshadowed this attempt by Kayani to right the floundering US–Pakistan relationship.

US military commanders did not view Pakistan very favourably in the wake of repeated attacks on their forces by militants they believed were getting support from Pakistani-based Taliban commanders. The roller coaster that had reached its apogee in 2010 was hurtling downward, and would reach a seemingly irretrievable condition by the time the disruptive force of President Trump arrived on the scene in 2017. And like Ground-Hog Day, the earlier arguments of 2010 and 2011 would be repeated by both American and Pakistani leaders, without much success in convincing each other that they meant well and were indeed committed for the long haul to protecting Afghanistan.

Internally, Pakistan was undergoing a massive shift in the nature and capacity of its army, from a conventional force to one that was fighting an existential battle against internal militancy and terrorism, generated by domestic forces but in some cases abetted by external or foreign-based actors. Its politics was also changing from alternating rule by the two leading dynastic parties to a new, unproven populist leader with strong Islamist leanings and a huge energized youth following in the shape of Imran Khan. The Battle for Pakistan was not over. Critical in its success was to be the speed and nature of the change in the Pakistan military, paradoxically a potential partner as well as powerful foe of the over-weaning US influence in the region. It was significant therefore that PM Khan took both the army chief and the DG-ISI with him on his first visit to Washington DC in July 2019, to indicate that they spoke as one and to help lay the foundation for a new and improved US–Pakistan relationship and to rejuvenate the Pakistani military.

11

Transforming the Pakistan Army

'Successful, resource-efficient counterinsurgency campaigns have by their nature tended to be low-profile precisely because they dealt with the issue discretely and with political sensitivity.'

—Emile Simpson[1]

Pakistan has fought numerous external wars with its bigger neighbour, India. The biggest lesson from those encounters appears to be that Pakistan must have a proactive defence that will allow it to protect its territory while making India pay a heavy price in case it ever invades Pakistan. Hence, its forward nuclear posture and support of irregular warfare to keep India busy in Kashmir. And its ambivalence in the war inside Afghanistan that remains a bone of contention with the US.

Its military has learned much from its internal wars since 9/11. It has much more to learn if it is to reorient its role inside the country as well as change its relationships with neighbours, near and far. In that context, the words of a young captain from the Royal Gurkha Rifles, a thinking warrior in the mould of another Gurkha Rifles officer, Bill Slim, whose campaign and memoir of his battles in Burma during the Second World War are still providing lessons to aspiring soldiers across the world, ring true for the seemingly endless wars raging in Afghanistan and Pakistan. The challenge for Pakistan has been to transform not only its fighting forces but also the foundational thinking that has informed its military

---

[1] Emile Simpson, *War from the Ground Up: Twenty-First Century Combat as Politics* (Oxford University Press, New York, 2015).

operations and organizations for decades. Only then will it be able to win the Battle for Pakistan.

Emile Simpson served three tours in Afghanistan and took to heart the lessons of war from his perspective as a junior officer, captured in a slim volume that was described by no less an authority than Sir Michael Howard as a befitting 'coda to Clausewitz'. His comment about COIN exposes the inherent weakness of conventional military thinking that does not recognize that all military action is, in fact, political at heart and you cannot separate the military from the political domain. Indeed, the non-kinetic aspect must take precedence over the kinetic approach rather than the other way around.

Observing the Pakistan Army in action in the field and in its training institutions brings me in accord with Simpson. There is less likelihood of victory in the traditional sense on the battlefield. Rather, victory encompasses success in a broader 'battlespace' that extends beyond the physical field of military conflict into the heart of societies, economies, and political systems. Until you can alter the landscape in which the insurgent or militant operates, and be prepared to understand, accept and accommodate differences of opinions and purpose, there is no clear-cut victory. Neither is there a linear relationship between the use of force and the achievement of political outcomes, a lesson that both the Soviet Union and the US learned over time.

Since the 2001 US and Coalition invasion of Afghanistan and the move of Pakistani forces into the borderlands with Afghanistan, Pakistan has been learning these lessons the hard way. It has been forced to adjust to new realities and learn by doing. The transition has been less than smooth. The Pakistani military, and especially the Pakistan Army, still is in many ways a traditional organization, bound by the broad structures and experiences of its predecessor, the British Indian Army. It has attempted to reorganize piecemeal, but there has been little impetus internally for a wholesale rethinking of the nature of the military force that Pakistan needs going into the middle of the twenty-first century.

It is large, around 500,000 strong, and fairly immobile. Rather than seeking a radical transformation, it has added layers of modernity over crusted layers of outmoded structures and thinking.

Over the seventy-plus years of independence, it has changed, as needed, largely in reaction to the types of conflicts it became involved with. Hence, it adopted a makeshift COIN approach in 1971 against what it termed 'miscreants' in East Pakistan that badly missed the political dimension of the conflict and allowed a larger conventional Indian army to throttle it with the aid of the local Mukti Bahini of ex-Pakistan Army Bengalis and trained guerrillas operating from bases in India. In Balochistan, in the 1970s, it adopted more conventional tactics, using air power, with assistance from the Shah of Iran who lent it helicopters, and cordon-and-clear operations against local tribesmen, some of whom sought refuge and training in Afghanistan and other sites. Baloch nationalism still simmers.

Via the ISI, it also became a party to the struggle inside Kashmir, helping train and equip Islamist fighters and militants who infiltrated and injected themselves into the battle between Kashmiris and the huge Indian military and paramilitary force that was sent to quell the insurgency in Kashmir. This approach was predicated on the idea that India could be made to pay for its hostility towards Pakistan with a War of a Thousand Cuts, by forcing India to deploy large numbers of troops against a small and elusive enemy in Kashmir. The actual numbers of Kashmiri militants fighting on the Indian side of the LoC in Jammu and Kashmir is much debated. According to Ajai Shukla, a former commanding officer of the famous Hodson's Horse cavalry regiment, and now a leading Indian defence analyst:

> The most accurate militancy figures are from the J&K Police CID [Criminal Investigation Department of Jammu and Kashmir] in Srinagar, which—at 300 militants currently—is slightly higher than the army figure. I would go by the CID figure. It is twice what it was since Burhan Wani's killing. And that is even though some 400 local militants have been killed in this period.

Shukla adds:

> The figure for total Indian military presence in J&K is pretty straightforward. As is well known, there are eight infantry divisions—8, 28, 19, 25, 10, 26, 29 and 39—deployed on the LoC and 'working boundary' in Ladakh, Kashmir and Jammu regions. At 18,000 troops per division, that is 1,44,000 soldiers. In addition, there are 5 Rashtriya Rifles formations—Kilo Force, Victor Force, Romeo Force, Uniform Force and Delta Force—deployed in the CI grid, at about 10,000 soldiers

per 'Force', that is another 50,000 soldiers. The total adds up to a little bit short of 2,00,000 soldiers.

Naturally, there are nuances to this. At any given time, at least 30 % are out on leave, courses, temporary duty, etc. That means there are about 1,40,000 soldiers physically deployed in managing the LoC and the CI grid in J&K.

Shukla does not take into account Indian forces in Ladakh facing China. These figures, which sometimes are inflated by Pakistani sources, give strength to the Pakistani strategic aim of forcing India to expend massive amounts in support of its efforts to control the militancy in Kashmir. Any forces that are thus employed are not available for deployment against Pakistan proper according to the traditional Pakistani calculus.

The Pakistan Army also was involved in conventional conflicts with India, largely on the eastern border of its western wing that it claimed were victories, since it managed to avoid being overwhelmed by a much larger Indian Army and Air Force and traded territory with India along the border of West Pakistan. The Pakistani Air Force played a key role in 1965, and a limited one in 1971. Their navies played a tertiary role in these conflicts.

The regular Pakistan Army played only a tangential role in the battle of the Afghan Mujahideen against the Soviet occupation of their country. The vanguard here was the ISI Directorate, with logistical support provided as needed by frontline army formations facing Afghanistan. The army created a new corps headquarters (12 Corps) in Quetta, as a potential conventional barrier to any Soviet incursion into Pakistan, if the Soviet army was to head to the warm waters of the Gulf. Indeed, there was some resentment against the ISI by regular army officers at the vast resources being made available to the ISI without adequate controls or oversight. Many saw this as a key element in changing the traditional discipline and thinking of the army officers seconded to the ISI.

What complicated the situation was the continuation of a military dictatorship legitimized by the US and other foreign support for Gen. Zia-ul-Haq's regime and the infiltration of senior military brass and even some lower-level officers into the administration of martial law as well as civilian departments. Not all of these seconded officers enjoyed these roles. But it certainly created a greater sense among the officer corps that they could do the job of the civilians and maybe better! After a brief interregnum of civilian rule with the untimely departure of Zia-ul-Haq another military coup d'état took place that upended Prime Minister Nawaz Sharif's government in October 1999, bringing in the regime of Gen. Pervez Musharraf, a former commando with enormous confidence about his ability to transform the country. He took the country into a new type of war, pitching the army and the FC against local insurgents as well as a congeries of disaffected militants from Central Asia and elsewhere in the Muslim world on the border with Afghanistan. But, the public record indicates he fought this war from afar—having been ostracized by the liberal Western order, after his coup in 1999.

Musharraf was readmitted to the comity of nations by the US and others after the terrorist attacks on the US mainland of 11 September 2001, leading to the invasion of Afghanistan. He signed up with the Coalition. The war between the Taliban insurgents and the Coalition Forces ensued and continued for nearly two decades without resolution. It led to the rapid movement of some 35,000 Pakistani regular forces, initially by Musharraf, into the borderlands of Pakistan with Afghanistan that had been left by the Pakistani forces soon after Independence in 1947.

This spawned an immediate backlash and insurgency among the tribal youth that Pakistan refused at first to recognize as such. The term 'miscreant' was dusted off and reissued by the ISPR Directorate, partially because it wished to minimize the nature of the conflict and partially because it failed to understand the nature of the conflict, as did its bosses at army headquarters. Many of the generals described this internal war as a 'low-intensity conflict' (LIC) even after their Coalition allies began to use the acronym COIN. In other words, the Pakistani military view was that all you needed was conventional force employed at a smaller scale than in a regular war against say India. They saw the fight taking place largely on the physical battlefield. And they were woefully unprepared in terms of training and equipment for this war. It would take years and many casualties for them to adjust their thinking and actions.

Moreover, in the rush to do the bidding of his newly rediscovered allies in the US and NATO, Musharraf and his generals immediately moved regular army units that were posted in peacetime locations near the western border into the FATA. Proximity seemed to be key to these deployments. Most of these units and formations had little operational knowledge of the frontier terrain or language and customs. For instance, 7 Division that was based in Peshawar moved its forward headquarters to Miram Shah in North Waziristan. Its training and battle assignment in all Pakistani conflicts with India had been in the southern half of Kashmir. It had no direct knowledge of the terrain or the people of FATA. As late as 2010, when I visited North Waziristan, the 7 Division officer accompanying me during my visit, who had been there for two years by then, admitted to knowing no Pashto. The army had numerous regiments that had 50 per cent Pakhtun complement and whose officers were expected to learn Pashto and were given allowances for the extra language skill. Rather than preparing and deploying those Pashto-speaking formations, the contiguous forces from Peshawar, Bannu, Kohat, etc., were pushed into FATA with an unclear mission. They found themselves, as had their predecessors in East Pakistan in 1971, as strangers in their own homeland.

It also appears that the calculations made by Musharraf and his then Finance Minister Shaukat Aziz did not foresee a long conflict and deployment. So they accepted US assistance via the CSF largely on the basis of a formula that used the marginal cost of moving troops to the border region. The related agreement signed with the US regarding the 'Transit of US Cargo to and from the Islamic Republic of Afghanistan through the Territory of the Islamic Republic of Pakistan' was only produced as an MoU in 2012.[2] This covered the transport of non-lethal materials, and no taxes or charges were to be collected by Pakistan. The agreement was to serve as the basis of later agreements for NATO and would only last for three years, subject to renewal. It is not clear if this was formally renewed. There is no role assigned to the Pakistani Ministry of Foreign Affairs in this MOU or its implementation, nor in an earlier agreement titled US-PK01 on the 'Acquisition and Cross Servicing' between the DoD of the US and the MoD of Pakistan on 9 February 2002. This agreement was 'for the purpose of establishing basic terms, conditions, and procedures to facilitate the reciprocal provision of logistic support, [non-lethal] supplies, and services' related to the US and allied war in Afghanistan, establishing the general principles for pricing and reimbursement, tying Pakistan to charge no more than what it paid for such services for its own operations and acquisitions. The agreement was to last ten years unless terminated by either party with 180 days' notice. As was the case of the later 2012 MOU,

---

[2]   The MOU was signed by Amb. Richard Hoagland, Charge d'Affaires, a.i. of the US embassy in Islamabad and Rear Admiral Farrokh Ahmad, Additional Secretary of the Ministry of Defence.

this agreement was between the Pakistani MoD and the US DoD, without any defined role for the Ministry of Foreign Affairs of Pakistan.[3]

Musharraf, who had shown a willingness to face risks as a young officer, for some reason did not appear to have visited FATA as army chief and president of Pakistan, when the insurgency was being fought there by his troops, other than visits to Peshawar to meet tribal elders. Musharraf challenges that by saying that he 'went many times' and even crossed the Indian LoC in Kargil.[4] Inexplicably, there is no record of his visits to FATA on the Web, or publicly available at the ISPR Directorate. A number of his subordinates said that he essentially farmed out the operational management of the army to his vice chiefs and was not a frequent visitor to GHQ.

When one of them, Gen. Kayani, became the army chief, he undertook to engage publicly with his troops in the field and to clarify their mission in a manner that helped stem the desertions and faltering initial performance of the regular military against an irregular force. Not unsurprisingly, his immediate task was to focus on the troops by declaring his first year as chief to be the Year of the Soldier and the second year the Year of Training.

Most of the army's training had been following the grand and long campaigns of the Second World War and even as far back as the American Civil War. The lessons learned by the British in Frontier Warfare at the outset of the twentieth century had gradually been discarded in the 1970s and replaced with a different kind of mountain warfare: fighting in high snow-covered mountains in the frozen wastelands of northern Kashmir where most of the casualties were not from Indian action but from frost bite and oedema caused by the heights of the battle stations—over 15,000 feet or thereabouts. Over time, Pakistan produced a generation of army leaders who were trained in high-level strategic thinking for extended campaigns despite the fact that even the conventional wars with India had been of short duration and had their roots in political conflicts and that were ended by political agreements. All, except the case of 1971, when Pakistan lost the war to India on the battlefield and surrendered some 93,000 persons,

---

[3]   This agreement was signed by Maj. Gen. Dennis K. Jackson, US Army, Director of Logistics for the US DoD, on 4 February 2002, and Rear Admiral Irfan Ahmed, Additional Secretary of the Ministry of Defence of Pakistan, on 9 February 2002, and became effective on 9 February.

[4]   Telephone conversation, 17 March 2018, from Dubai.

including its entire military force in East Pakistan, the territory that became the new state of Bangladesh. The mental straitjacket of what was known as the Staff Solution to military problems came to be the Rule of the Day. Officers who came up with unusual solutions and ideas found themselves discarded in the promotion process.[5] Extended martial law also meant that there was little turnover in the uppermost ranks, leading to the promotion of favourites and creation of clones or those who had served with the senior officers in earlier postings.

Musharraf himself had been very critical of martial law:

> First, whenever the army gets involved with martial law, it gets distracted from its vital military duties. Military training and operational readiness suffer. Second, when we superimpose martial law and place the military over the civilian government, the latter ceases functioning. When martial law is later lifted, the civilian functionaries remain ineffective. Their growth is stunted. Last, I learned that whatever the law, civil or military, the poor are always victims of oppression. The rich and the powerful generally remain above the law.[6]

His actions as COAS and president over time ran counter to these liberal instincts as he inducted more and more army officers into the civil services and spent more time playing the politician on the basis of the military's latent coercive power rather than a broad base of political support. His successor, Kayani, had to recall most of the army officers from civilian posts after taking over and forbade meetings of serving officers with politicians, including President Musharraf.

Extended military rule fostered the formation of closed kinship networks of officers who had served with each other or belonged to the same arm or service groups. Group-think took root and prevented the kind of massive transformation of military thought and operation that was needed to cope with the new warfare, inside Pakistani territory, against its own people, against fellow Muslims who said they were fighting in the name of Islam.

---

[5]   This is based on a review of papers produced at the National Defence College by the author and relating the later trajectory of promotions of officers who produced creative papers.

[6]   Op. cit. Musharraf, *In the Line of Fire*, p. 65.

Potentially adding to the difficulty was the infusion into the military of deeply conservative Islamic thinking and the formation of *Pir Bhai* networks of spiritual bands that included civilians and military men and threatened the discipline and rank order of the military. This began in the Zia-ul-Haq period, but appears to be extant to some extent even today, according to those who follow these networks. (I received examples from serving and retired military officers citing instances of behaviour that was unacceptable in military circles, e.g., senior officers opening the door for a junior officer who outranked them in the *Pir Bhai* network. Or, an officer refusing to take part in a water-crossing exercise because it was 'unIslamic' for him to wear shorts that exposed his knees, according to the regimental maulvi! The commanding officer who had to deal with this intransigence had to read the riot act to both the maulvi and the officer concerned and reassembled the entire regiment to watch the officer try to swim across the canal water obstacle the next day in his shorts!)

The Tablighi Jamaat, a proselytizing group, had already penetrated the upper echelons of the military. Two DGs of the ISI and some corps commanders had been members of this group and, like their colleagues, they favoured others from their own group. Members of the group were duty-bound to take leave of absence to do missionary work each year at home or abroad. These issues bedevilled the military's operations and processes. The army did take steps to reduce the visible aspects of some of these trends, but at the same time, the use of Islamic symbolism in signage inside cantonments remains a visible reminder of the difficulty of removing the powerful role of religion in the army. It also tried to identify some radicalized officers and purged them from the ranks. But as recruitment became urbanized and broad-based, it was difficult to totally remove this potential threat.

'Learning by Doing'

In the absence of formal training methodologies and doctrines for fighting the insurgency epitomized by the TTP and the Baloch nationalist groups, the military improvised on the run. Field commanders learned on the job, often at a high cost in terms of men lost or wounded. Some of them shared their experiences with others. More often than not, the experience was lost during rotations. These rotations started initially for one year at a time and then were extended to one and a half years and eventually to two years at

a time in FATA, according to Kayani's DGMO Maj. Gen. Javed Iqbal.[7]
The army had calculated by 2010 that some 80 per cent of all operations
since 2001 had taken place in the previous two years. All this had occurred
at a time when Pakistan faced massive flooding that temporarily took away
military resources in aid of civil power to help with the flood relief work.
While infantry regiments undertook the brunt of the COIN work, they
received support from armour, engineering and other services in holding
cleared areas and participating in rebuilding work.

Meanwhile, US and Coalition assistance had begun arriving, in
the shape of military supplies, as well as forensic facilities in Islamabad,
equipped by the US, UK and Australia, according to DGMO Iqbal. The
ISI was given the lead role in this area. These facilities helped counter a
rising tide of Improvised Explosive Device (IED) attacks that emerged as
a response to the increased military operations in FATA. A key element
that Iqbal noted was that the officer-to-soldier casualty ratio was high,
10:1, indicating that officers led from the front. Kayani also echoed this
sentiment and shared it with his ISAF counterparts frequently. Iqbal and
his director, Brig. Waseem Ashraf, also from the FF Regiment, gave me a
breakdown of Pakistan Army deployments in the field and in different parts
of the country that were largely reflected in the September 2011 document
handed by Kayani to Gen. James Mattis of CENTCOM. Some 147,000
Pakistani troops were on the western border, out of a total of 480,000. Some
37,000 were deployed in North Waziristan but had not been launched into
a clearing operation. These included 10,000 members of the FC, locally
recruited but commanded by regular Pakistan Army officers.

By 2010, the Pakistan Army had had 11,037 casualties, including
7,684 killed in action, much larger than the combined total of Coalition
and especially American casualties inside Afghanistan (though civil and
military Afghan casualties were much higher). The running joke was that
ISAF stood for 'I See Americans Fight', since many of the members of
the Coalition were operating under severe constraints imposed by their
respective governments and chose not to engage in battle with the enemy!

---

[7]   Interview at GHQ 2010, following my meeting with Gen. Kayani. Iqbal was
       an officer from the 9 Frontier Force regiment, commissioned into the army
       in 1979. He had commanded the 34 FF Regiment. As mentioned earlier in
       this book, he was convicted and sentenced to life imprisonment, effectively
       fourteen years, in 2019 in a secret military trial, allegedly for espionage during
       the period when he was at GHQ.

Yet, Pakistan operated with limited weapon systems. Gunship helicopters were the most effective for providing mobility and firepower in the rugged terrain of FATA, in an area that was missing roads. A total of twenty-nine Cobra helicopters had been provided to Pakistan by the US after 9/11, much less than Pakistan had demanded and needed. Brig. Ashraf confirmed that the Cobras, despite their limitations, had been extensively used, flying some 6,010 sorties in 2009 and 4,190 in 2010. The Pakistan Army struggled to keep maintenance at a high level, some 75 per cent, compared with the 50–60 per cent that is considered normal. Compounding the difficulties was the fact that ISAF had pulled troops back from the Pakistan–Afghanistan border to guard the cities. At the lower level in the Pakistan Army, the call was to prepare for clearing operations in North Waziristan, using a cordon-and-search method. But the green light was not given during Kayani's tenure.

In an effort to come up with a makeshift COIN strategy, the army was trying to introduce the concept of Quick Impact Projects in the FATA region. Since the civil administration had been decimated and local Tribal Maliks targeted by the Taliban, the army was trying to initiate the building of roads and water projects, funded by the US and the UAE. The latter especially assisted with works in Swat, South Waziristan and Bajaur. The US aid extended also to intelligence, surveillance and reconnaissance, albeit very slowly, and in the use of night-vision devices. Although, the first batch of night-vision goggles were vintage models that did not operate effectively on full-moon nights, and the American ODRP sought to take an inventory of the devices regularly so they had to be withdrawn from service too frequently. This was eventually changed, but the policy of checking on the location of the devices (the US feared they might be moved to the Indian border!) reflected the short leash on which the US commanders wanted Pakistan to operate.

The FC provided a necessary but much neglected component of the battle against militancy in FATA. Its advantage was that it was comprised of locals and most of the time the 59 Wings (roughly equivalent to a regiment each), supported by a limited three squadrons of armour. According to a retired armour officer, old T-59 tanks were manned by crews from the FC and trained by the Pakistan Armoured Corps. It was the first time that tanks were deployed in COIN operations (Shangla, Dir, Bajaur) and proved to be very effective not only in leading the advance but also in Casualty Evacuation (CASEVAC) and resupply of infantry since they could run the gauntlet of fire. Some were repeatedly hit by Rocket-Propelled Grenades (RPGs) and survived to fight on. Taking a cue from this, when the Pakistan Army went into Waziristan, tanks were an essential component of the combat teams and much feared by the militants. They have traversed terrain that was previously considered untankable, and operated at heights of 6,000–7,000 feet. Some seventeen artillery batteries also had a permanent presence in some 616 posts. FC presence was continuous and often within their tribal boundaries. Some thirty-four tribes from FATA were represented in the FC. Although, unlike the regular Pakistan Army, their battlefield rotations were not to peacetime locations inside Pakistan but to other parts of FATA. In effect, the FC was fighting nonstop since 2001! As the Deputy IG Brig. Usman explained to me, since 2008 they had become the spearhead of the anti-terror operations.

A key element in this was the change in leadership that brought Maj. Gen. Tariq Khan to become the IG of the FC. He helped transform the FC from a backwater to an active and very proud element of the Pakistan military, so that it began attracting good army officers rather than the discarded lot that had earlier been sent to serve in the perceived backwater of FATA.[8] The elder Bhutto had created a special Tribal Service that attracted top civilian talent.

Gen. Tariq Khan, himself a Pakhtun from a military family of Tank, instilled a new activism among the FC, regularly visiting his troops in the field and exhorting them to take the fight to the enemy.[9] Sitting in on one of his command meetings, I heard him advising his commanders to 'own the night' by active patrolling and setting up ambushes so that the Taliban would be forced to operate in daytime when they were more vulnerable. 'When you operate at night, you've won!' he said. He also took advantage of American cash assistance from SOCOM that allowed him to bypass administrative systems and build outposts and reward soldiers. Occasionally, he lapsed into Americanisms, picked up during his assignment at CENTCOM headquarters, as a liaison officer. His final

---

[8]   In the more distant past, especially up to the 1970s, the FC attracted eager officers who took pride in the adventure of serving in the rough borderlands. Their civilian counterparts were also the best and the brightest civil servants. All this changed in the martial law days of Zia-ul-Haq.

[9]   Tariq Khan was a Sword of Honour winner from the PMA at Kakul, and joined his father's 4 Cavalry regiment, in which my cousin Asmat Nawaz Janjua fought in 1965. He later commanded I Corps in Mangla.

message at the end of one commander's meeting was: 'Kick some ass out there!' Landing at an FOB in Jhansi fort by helicopter, he was mobbed by the soldiers and sought out an NCO who had been cited for bravery, embraced the man and immediately gave him a handgun as a reward. The fact that he had come under fire during one of his aggressive forays in northern FATA and participated in the fight added to his stature with his troops. Under him, his deputy over 2008–2010, Brig. Nadir Zeb, was promoted to Maj. Gen. in command of an armoured division in the regular Pakistan Army. This was the first high-level promotion from within the FC, and a sign that the Corps had been elevated in stature.

A key difference that Tariq Khan explained between the army and the FC was that the FC was 'not an army. We are scouts. Army is mission-based. We stay. We anticipate and take pre-emptive action. The army has fixed drills. We have tribal bonds.' He took issue with the use of the term COIN for the fighting in FATA. 'People [of FATA] are not with the bad guys. This is a militancy, sparked by economic things. We do not need outsiders to teach us. Their signatures are huge. We are light.' But he acknowledged American help from Adm. Eric Olson of SOCOM, and trainers as well as American presence at medical camps run by FC troops. The Americans asked him why FC casualties from IEDs were the lowest in FATA. His response was that 'we cannot rely on technology. We walk the road. Patrols go 4–5 kilometres, eyeballing the ground. Establish perimeters of security with confidence and then march perimeters' before allowing traffic. Brig. Nadir Zeb added that, 'People are with you, if you show courage.'

But the cost of this new kind of warfare was high. In 2010, the FC budget was around $88 million, and the overall cost of continuous operations was $230 million, according to the IGFC, with the difference being made up by the army. The US offered $111 million spread over five years. Tariq Khan believed and told US NSA Gen. James Jones that the 'Pashtuns will throw out Al Qaeda'. According to Khan, militants from South Waziristan had escaped into North Waziristan. 'We need to go to NWA to sort them out. The chief [Kayani] may be ready.' He believed that the Haqqanis were the wrong group to be aligned with. 'They have never ruled Afghanistan. Durranis ruled. You will never find a Durrani [seeking refuge] in Pakistan. Haqqani comes here because he has no base. Why are we tolerating this?' His voice was the lone one in the corridors of power as the ISI and other senior commanders continued to toe the line on support for or condoning of the Haqqanis' presence in Pakistani territory.

The new type of warfare provided an opportunity for a new generation of commanders to show their mettle and to knit the Pakistan Army into a fighting machine that not only understood why it was fighting but also knit the officer corps and the soldiers into a more cohesive unit rather than the postcolonial class-based Pakistan Army. At GHQ, an energetic DGMO Maj. Gen. Ahmed Shuja Pasha took to crafting a new strategy for the unconventional war. In the field, in Swat, for example, division commanders like Maj. Gen. Nasser Khan Janjua (17 Division) and Maj. Gen. Ishfaq Nadeem Ahmed (37 Division) quickly learned to adapt their conventional training to wrest the initiative from the militants, involve the locals to either deny space or push the terrorists out of the villages and small towns, and occupied and travelled along the heights so they could contain and then interdict the movement of the militants. Swat also saw the introduction of the air assault and the Special Services Group commandos for interdicting and clearing up pockets of insurgents, particularly when they holed up in the Peochar Valley.

Although the overall strategy in Swat of emptying the battlespace of civilian presence created huge logistical issues involving some 2 million internally displaced persons, it gave the military room to adapt its conventional training and forces to roust the militants from the territory they had occupied. Initially, there was massive use of artillery that damaged a lot of property—the military did adapt its approach to fight IEDs and roving bands of militants with its own roving patrols and radio-based counter-propaganda. Both the division commanders in the initial battle for Swat took back their experience to GHQ and shared it widely inside the Pakistan Army, a change from earlier operational commanders who did not capture their experiences in writing. Janjua became the Vice CGS. Nadeem Ahmad became the DGMO and later CGS. The military had started on a learning curve.

Change in Training

By 2010, training of the army had become the top priority. Central facilities had been set up, notably in the Pabbi Hills south-west of Islamabad, and at corps and divisional headquarters, so designated troop formations were sent for battle inoculation under realistic conditions simulating the FATA experience. Battalions earmarked for FATA were re-equipped with NVGs, Motorola communication gear, bulletproof vests, etc., and put through a training regime of four months, at the end of which they were tested and declared certified.

Officer training was critical in this endeavour. The PMA was the basic foundation stone of the change in army thinking and training for the new kind of warfare that demanded rapid movement and reaction. Added to the regular training syllabus in the third term at the PMA in Kakul, near Abbottabad, was a Quick Reaction Course that employed both electronic and real fire drills. A training circuit was set up by the PMA under its new commander, then Maj. Gen. Raheel Sharif.[10] It included seven fundamentals of room-clearing, a maze and live-fire exercises in the final term. Everywhere, one could see posted signs with the principles of COIN and LIC, and all cadets took part in the training, including 'lady cadets', many of them medical professionals. Gen. Sharif invited guest speakers to help cadets understand the softer side of LIC and COIN. How to negotiate and to operate in the field under a 'buddy system' were part of the new training regimen.

The live ammunition firing range was supplemented by an indoor electronic range with moving targets, simulating militant activity. Gen. Sharif used his first-hand knowledge of and contacts with the German defence industry to get German equipment for this purpose. The lessons of LIC were summarized into a handbook for cadets to add to their hands-on training. Sharif took me proudly around PMA to show the new and improved training facilities and explain the changes in the syllabus.[11] Major changes included de-emphasizing India as the enemy and focusing on

---

[10] He was a graduate of the military academy in the class of 1976 (54th Long Course), and joined his famous brother Shabbir Sharif's 6 Frontier Force regiment (Piffers). His brother had won a posthumous *Nishan-e-Haider*, the highest valour award of the Pakistan Army, in the 1971 war against India. Raheel Sharif attended a company commanders' course in Germany and served a one-year attachment with the German Army after that, becoming fluent in German in the process. A graduate of the Staff College of Canada and the Royal College of Defence Studies of the United Kingdom, he had also been an instructor at the PMA and the School of Infantry and Tactics. His earlier stint at PMA Kakul began when Maj. Sharif returned from his course in Germany and joined as an adjutant to my late brother, then Maj. Gen. Asif Nawaz, commandant at that time. He later was a Chief of Staff at a Corps headquarters and then commanded 11 Division.

[11] Maj. Gen. Raheel Sharif, Commandant, PMA Kakul, showed me around the academy on 10 April 2010 and explained the changes in training.

internal militancy. Even in the military exercises, the stereotypes of the past were removed and replaced. In war games, he explained, a mullah-type was the antagonist. A bearded profile would be placed on an easel sometimes to underscore that point. The IED Room in the Quick Response Course exercises included lectures by engineering bomb experts from the GHQ, who used cut-outs of different types of IEDs to familiarize cadets with the structure of IEDs.

Thus equipped for the new warfare, many cadets from the PMA ended up heading straight to FATA upon getting their commission as officers in the Pakistan Army. Raheel Sharif said they had 'done very well, because they are well prepared'. One newly commissioned officer won the *Sitara-e-Jurat*, the second highest award for valour for the Pakistan Army, according to Raheel Sharif.

Infantry School, Quetta

The Pakistan Army's leading weapons training establishment for young officers was set up in 1947, immediately after Independence, in Kakul as the Infantry School, relocating to Quetta a year later. It underwent change over time, absorbing the Tactical Wing of the Command and Staff College of Quetta in 1956, when it was renamed the School of Infantry and Tactics. Over time, it acquired additional responsibilities, including the training of army personnel for UN peacekeeping duties, a lucrative venture (under which Pakistan reportedly received roughly $1,000 per month for each 'peacekeeper') and a good way to reward officers and soldiers for their services by earning international pay scales and experience. Its stated aim is 'to produce combat worthy Junior Leaders, equipped with requisite professional knowledge and competence to effectively respond to changing/fluid combat situations, through a directive (*sic*) control, by focusing on development of leadership traits and basic skills for conventional and unconventional operations'.[12]

As the internal war against militancy became protracted and costly in terms of expenditure and casualties, the school focused more and more on a different kind of training. It also expanded its intake to cover JCOs and NCOs. In addition to basic command and tactical training, and

---

[12]   https://www.pakistanarmy.gov.pk/AWPReview/TextContentb1b1.html

peacekeeping duties, it began to focus on specialized and unconventional conflicts, including nuclear and biological warfare, and countering IEDs.[13]

The seminar rooms were populated by young officers who had served in FATA as had their instructors. This allowed them to operate on a common intellectual base and to further hone their skills to fight unconventional battles inside Pakistan. The class instruction was supplemented by TEWTs in the rugged terrain surrounding Quetta, where they could simulate movement and attacks and defences against insurgents and militants. The training is based on modules and scenarios that have been developed with knowledge and help garnered from at least five countries around the world. Trainees undergo field demonstrations of LIC (the Pakistani appellation for COIN warfare) and CT, a course in firing against moving targets as well as hand-to-hand combat. Counter-IED training and warfare on a nuclear battlefield are also an integral part of the programme. Annually, some 3,000 officers and soldiers are processed by the school each year, including allied officers. Over 800 Sri Lankan officers have undergone training at the school.

The instructors were increasingly officers who had themselves received specialized training and served in battle in FATA. When I visited the school, one of them told me that he had been to a COIN course in Australia and was employing some of the same training techniques in Quetta. These included the use of tutorial methods. An Australian team was invited to share its experience during a three-week stay at the school during the LIC package. The training also encompasses brigade-level exercises and scenarios dealing with the linkage between urban and general LIC, using a disguised Karachi landscape and Taliban bases in an urban environment, and the employment of civil armed forces, such as the Rangers, against urban militancy. They also run scenarios at the division level within the framework of a corps. The training is at a granular level,

---

13 When I spent time at the school in Quetta, it was led by Maj. Gen. Agha Umer Farooq, who later became president of the National Defence University and had coined the concept of 'No Peace, No War' to reflect the hybridization of the threat environment facing Pakistan. Commissioned in April 1977 into 12 Baloch regiment, Farooq was a graduate of the war course in 1988 in Pakistan and then the US Army War College at Carlisle, PA, in 2003 as a brigadier. His deputy, Brig. Tariq Javed, had been approved for promotion to major general. Javed was a graduate of the German Company Commanders' course that later Army Chief Raheel Sharif had also attended.

often employing the use of Unmanned Aerial Vehicles, and bringing in civil administration officials for role-playing.

As Maj. Gen. Farooq explained to me, the aim is to train people to 'react rather than be guided' in their actions. Hand-to-hand combat skills were also honed. A big change was that training extended to all arms of the Pakistan Army and was not restricted to the Infantry. Young officers were encouraged to come up with ideas to battle external and internal enemies, and their suggestions (some of them wild and woolly!) were captured in a publication without much regimentation of thought. As in other leading training institutions, the army sent its smartest officers to lead this school and to occupy its training slots.

Staff College

Not far from the Infantry School in Quetta lies one of the most venerable institutions in Indian and Pakistani military history. It was set up in 1905. The Command and Staff College prepares some 365 junior officers for senior management roles in the army. Some thirty-five to forty allied officers are included in each course. It has produced famous alumni who have later commanded forces in Britain, India, Pakistan and allied forces, including the US. Competition to get into the Staff College is always intense. Once there, the officers are subjected to a rigorous routine. However, the dreaded Staff Solution does intrude, and savvy officers learn to negotiate its perils but hold their tongues and, only in rare cases, share their creative ideas with others![14]

The Staff College has changed considerably from its past leisurely and genteel approach to learning, laced with a heavy dose of social activities, including fancy-dress parties. Only those who have passed the captain to major examination and been cleared by Military Intelligence can apply for entrance in the Staff College. Once applicants have made it through the hurdle of the entrance exam with its heavy reading, they are subjected to an eighteen-week pre-course preparatory regimen to help them achieve a common base of military knowledge for the forty-five-week course in Quetta. In earlier years,

---

[14] Some US students were horrified to learn that NCOs on the training staff were helping some officers with materials from previous courses. The culture was such that it allowed such behaviour and relied on subsequent sifting by promotion boards to separate the truly bright from the less capable officers.

the reading concentrated heavily on World War II campaigns and even the US Civil War. Currently, the emphasis has shifted to more contemporary topics, including a compilation of articles on terrorism and CT. After the preparatory course, the students undergo a Technical Orientation Term run by instructors from the College of Electrical and Mechanical Engineering to help them master the role of technology in military operations in the context of Pakistan. The actual forty-five-week course is divided into four terms and also includes a couple of breaks, including one that allows groups of students to travel overseas to learn how other countries train and operate their armies and to better understand strategic issues.

During my visit, the then commandant Maj. Gen. Khalid Nawaz[15] spoke about the renewed emphasis on frontier warfare, LIC and COIN, and how the Staff College had brought in Australians and others to observe his training programme and to advise them. The LIC instructional package of some eighty-seven instructional hours is supplemented with a detailed course on dealing with IEDs and the experience with countering them. Jammers often do not work, pointing to the need for better frequency coverage. The Pakistan Army has also learned that militants had learned to avoid road-level scanners by planting IEDs in overhanging branches of trees in Swat. Militants also have resorted to booby-trapping the bodies of Pakistani soldiers killed in combat.

Interestingly, the Frontier Warfare course and reading materials did not exist in the Staff College till 2006. It had dropped off the radar in the 1970s. The first LIC exercise was started in 2006 and an LIC course was added in 2009. In the scenario-based training, allied officers, especially those who had served in Afghanistan, were useful in playing the role of the 'Chief Miscreant' (to present his strategy) as well as Coalition force commanders across the Pakistan–Afghanistan border. British, Canadian and American officers served in such roles.

The nature and intellectual make-up of the student body at the Staff College reflects the general shift in the demographics and thinking of the new officer class in the Pakistan Army. In some ways, the twenty-first century ushered in a more urban petit bourgeoisie into the armed forces, many officers being first-generation military and reflecting the general trend to ritualistic

---

[15] He was a Sword of Honour winner at the PMA in Kakul and belonged to a well-known Janjua Rajput family of Maira Matore, not far from Kahuta and Rawalpindi, which produced many generals.

religion and conservative value systems of many in contemporary Pakistan. No more the raucous partying and alcohol-lubricated exchanges of the past. An interesting aspect of my own visit to the Staff College was the very first question by an instructor following my lecture on US–Pakistan relations. He cited an injunction from the Prophet Muhammad that warned against trusting Christians and Jews. He then questioned the idea of friendly relations with a 'Christian' power like the US. It was not the question per se (it is one that visitors to Pakistan often face) but the fact that it was not considered unusual by his seniors that took me by surprise. Such out-of-context references to Islamic texts (this particular quotation had been taken from a battle situation where the Prophet felt that the Jews and Christians had betrayed the Muslims with whom they had made a pact prior to a battle) tend to provide ammunition to those who wish Pakistan to remain distant from its traditional Western allies and strengthen the growth of an inward-looking officer corps that may move increasingly along the path of conservatism towards a more rigid and perhaps even radical view of the conflict between Pakistan and the West.

This trend was underscored by a conversation with the DG Analysis of the ISI over a dinner he hosted for Fred Kempe, president of the Atlantic Council, and me in Islamabad. When asked about the danger of the spread of radical religious thought in Pakistani society, he did not challenge the assumption of the question but replied, 'It is a slow process and will take many years.' This sanguine response reminded me of the image of a frog in boiling water. Interestingly, a number of senior army officers were candid enough to take note of these trends, though none offered any firm measures to deal with the potential shape-shifting of the Pakistan officer corps. A former army chief had pushed back against my assertion that the Islamists were gaining a foothold in the army by stating that promotion review boards were a good filter against such developments, only to come back to me a year or so later to acknowledge that indeed the Islamization trend seemed to have taken hold. How Pakistan copes with this trend will determine the nature of its fighting force as well as its relationship with partners in other countries.

Other Challenges for Pakistan's Army

Over seventy years after the birth of Pakistan and the reduction of the size of the country to what used to be West Pakistan, Pakistan today has an army that is roughly the same size as the regular US Army, if not marginally larger. And its structure has undergone some changes. It is still a heavily centralized command system that does not allow devolution of command to forces close to the action. Nor does it allow optimal and well-coordinated use of air, land and (in the south) sea power against external enemies at the sector level. Since there has not been much public discussion of this situation in Pakistan, particularly in parliament, it is difficult to offer specific commentary on what needs to be changed and how. But some issues can be identified.

Under President Musharraf, some new command structures were announced. Main among these was a Southern Command encompassing XII Corps and V Corps, the former facing west to Afghanistan and the latter facing east to India. But all the commanders of these new regional commands were the same rank (three-star lieutenant generals) as the corps commanders. In the hierarchical model of the military, this is a recipe for confusion during war, when instant decisions need to be taken. Pakistan missed an opportunity to reassess its higher defence organizational structure that had been originally envisaged in the unfinished plan presented during the elder Bhutto's tenure, when the JCS Committee was first set up under a four-star. Lack of follow-up on that plan effectively left the JCS set-up without real power, and the centre of gravity remained with the army chief. Moreover, by not elevating regional commanders to four-star rank, the civilian authorities (both government and parliament) missed a real opportunity to participate fully in selection of the four-star officers, even if they were based on the army chief's recommendations. Ideally, the creation of a more powerful JCS or Chief of Defence Staff position would allow better coordination of all services during peace and war. But, given current dynamics and in the presence of a fledgling civilian government and an all-powerful army chief, there is likely to be little movement towards this goal.

In the waning period of Gen. Kayani's tenure, a Central and Northern Command was mooted, one facing east and the other primarily facing west. This was seen as a response to India's Cold Start strategy that was premised on a rapid Indian thrust into Pakistan to capture and hold key territory and make Pakistan sue for peace. Strategically, the creation of the Central Command comprising of I and XXX Corps, accompanied by the provision of an armour division from Kharian to XXX Corps in Gujranwala, effectively blocked any Indian move into the Sialkot and adjacent sectors. Meanwhile, the Northern Command (a name shared by the British formations headquartered in Rawalpindi in pre-Partition India) would comprise of X and XI Corps with their headquarters in Rawalpindi and Peshawar respectively.

Despite some criticisms for Gen. Kayani near the end of his term as army chief, those who served with him continue to laud him, even well after he had left the scene, for transforming the army. In the judgement of Lt. Gen. Asif Yasin Malik, who served as a corps commander under Kayani and later as Secretary of Defence:

> Transformation of Pakistani Armed Forces cannot be discussed without a reference to Gen. Ashfaq Pervez Kayani. In my opinion all the alleged controversies aside, the General will be remembered the best chief this Army has ever had. First of all his personal competence is just beyond comprehension of a common man. His clarity of Operational Thought and Strategic Concepts is very unique and sharp. His print on the military is very dark and very long lasting. I have used the term military intentionally instead of Army as he gelled the three services in operations as well as on the Strategic Plane . . .
>
> Apart from that he touched every big or small domain starting from uniform to accommodation to rations to physical fitness to firing standards to LIC training to pension to post retirement benefits to welfare of dependents of shaheeds [martyrs] to rehab of injured . . .
>
> Overall probably this was the most meaningful transformation of the Army after the setbacks of 1971, Siachen and Kargil. Also the poor public image during the last year of Musharraf era was not only restored but a national pride re-emerged within the military. The Officer to Jawan causality ratio reflects the sky rocketing morale and highest standard of leadership along with dedication and devotion. Most of all the complete depoliticizing of rank and file was a major step too. The support for democracy was critical during his tenure and he withstood tremendous pressures to intervene in the political arena.[16]

While one may debate some issues related to increasing political influence of the army, it is rare in the culture of Pakistan and the army for a former chief to receive such praise from his contemporaries. In many ways, Kayani's ability to reshape thinking inside the army helped prepare the

---

[16] Written communication from Lt. Gen. (retd) Asif Yasin Malik.

foundation for action by his successor Gen. Raheel Sharif to move against the militants in FATA under Operation 'Zarb-e-Azb', and for Gen. Qamer Javed Bajwa to build on that clean-up operation with his own Operation 'Radd-ul-Fasaad', the well-intentioned but still unfinished effort to eradicate militancy and terrorism from the hinterland via deweaponization and deradicalization

Other issues still remain. More needs to be done to turn back the forces of religious obscurantism and ritualism that have crept into Pakistani society and even the military. And, despite protestation by both sides to the contrary, the communication gap between the civil and the military remains. A battle of tweets or statements from media spokesmen for either side does not reflect well on either. The performance gap both reflects this chasm and affects it. Also, the enhanced ability of the army to shape public opinion directly through liberal use of funding for contractual services by media firms and indirectly by exercising censorship directly or by using the Pakistan Electronic Media Regulatory Authority to exert pressure on recalcitrant media has led to charges of self-censorship by media from the Musharraf period onwards.[17]

The ISPR has also been accused of drawing a sharp line between journalists and scholars who are seen as cheerleaders and those who are prone to being critical at times. It needs to win the confidence of international media. It could do this partially by improving its outmoded website with its twentieth-century bulletin-board approach to pushing information, by allowing media and scholars to pull well-presented, verifiable and updated data, information and analyses on current operations and issues, and better search functions. The use of Twitter as a substitute for fuller, well-thought-through and well-crafted briefings, commentaries and press releases has also been detrimental to its objectives. ISPR effectively functions as the media office of the Pakistan Army. Its equivalent in the Pentagon is headed by a chief spokesperson of the rank of colonel.

Since ISPR is a joint service, its operations could be better placed under the chairman of the JCS, as could the work of the ISI, another joint service. The public face of the military would then be better located within the MoD rather than as an enormous and autonomous enterprise that can and does produce conflict between the civilian government and the military.

---

[17]   Background information on specific cases, provided by serving military officers.

Finally, the ability of military institutions, such as the ISI and Military Intelligence, to transgress their remit by undertaking functions of arrest has been enhanced by political cover provided by changes in the laws of the land, often ex post. A glaring example of this was the retroactive application of laws passed by the Zardari government to cover the actions of the Pakistan Army in Swat and Malakand against suspected militants and the expansion of the remit of military courts, ostensibly to expedite the processing of terrorism cases. The military continues to be under pressure by the courts to answer for hundreds of persons who have disappeared and who are suspected of being held by the army. ISI and MI have also been accused of harassing and manhandling journalists who do not toe the official line.

According to the US Library of Congress research report:

On February 7, 2014, the National Assembly of Pakistan, the lower house of the country's legislature, passed a resolution to extend three anti-terrorism ordinances for a 120-day period, including the controversial anti-terrorism law, The Protection of Pakistan Ordinance (PPO). Among other measures, the PPO grants extensive arrest and detention powers to security agencies in the context of military- and terrorism-related operations. (Ordinance No. 9 of 2013, GAZETTE OF PAKISTAN [Oct. 21, 2013].) The PPO has come under heavy criticism from human rights groups and opposition political parties. (Nasir Iqbal, *Indefinite Detention Gets Legal Cover*, DAWN.COM [Jan. 23, 2014].) . . .

Some of the controversial clauses in the newly amended PPO include:

- granting security agencies extensive powers of arrest, search, and seizure without a court-ordered warrant (PPO . . . 3(2)(b)—(c));
- allowing the government to authorize preventative detention of a person for up to 90 days 'if there are grounds to infer that such person is acting in a manner prejudicial to the integrity, security, [or] defense of Pakistan . . .' (*id*. . . . 6(1));
- permitting indefinite detention for a person who is designated as an 'enemy alien' or 'combatant enemy' (*id*.);
- giving power to military and civil law enforcement forces to establish internment camps to 'detain any enemy alien, combatant enemy, or any person connected or reasonably believed to be connected with the commission of a Scheduled Offence . . .' (*id*. . . . 6(2));

- providing legal cover for past arrests and detentions by security
  agencies, stating 'any person arrested or detained by the Armed
  Forces or Civil Armed Forces and kept under arrest or detention
  before the coming into force of this Ordinance shall be deemed to
  have been arrested or detained pursuant to the provisions of this
  Ordinance' (*id.* . . . 6(5)). This provision is particularly controversial
  because it attempts to provide legal protection for alleged enforced
  disappearances of terrorism suspects during past military and anti-
  terrorism operations, disappearances that are currently subject to
  being handled as missing persons cases;[18] and
- establishing separate special anti-terrorism courts and a separate
  prosecuting agency (PPO . . . 8).[19]

In the period leading to the end of the PML-N government's tenure, the
broad assumption in Pakistan was that the army silently influenced the
political balance against the sitting government with a view to affecting
the election results. In the face of groups like the Pakhtun Tahafuz
Movement launched by Pakhtun youth and other civic groups, the
abduction and manhandling of journalists and civic activists by 'unknown
persons' (*Na maloom afraad* according to the vernacular description)
places the military in an adversarial position to civil society in Pakistan.
This does not help to create the conditions of public support that it needs
to operate in crises. Why is the ISI feared? According to a former DG-
ISI, as reported in the deliberations of the Abbottabad Commission
report, words to the effect that the only people who are afraid of the ISI
are those that need to fear it.

The power and expanding role of the ISI could well be turned to its
professional pursuits and away from concentrating on domestic spying
and enforcement activities, by reverting its command and control to the
chairman of the JCS Committee, since it is an Inter-Services body, truly
removing it from political engineering. This would allow it to concentrate
more effectively on CT as well as external-facing counter-intelligence

[18] Nasir Iqbal, 'Legal Experts Reject PPO', *Dawn*, 25 January 2014.

[19] *Global Legal Monitor*, US Library of Congress, 'Pakistan: National Assembly
      Extends Ordinance on Protection of Pakistan', 11 February 2014, http://
      www.loc.gov/law/foreign-news/article/pakistan-national-assembly-extends-
      ordinance-on-protection-of-pakistan/

activities. A trend that needs to be monitored carefully is the movement of purged or superseded intelligence officers towards militant Islamist organizations, whom they previously had been tracking or managing. Placing these joint services bodies under civilian scrutiny via parliament and adding transparency in handling of their affairs would make their work more credible. The military needs public support to be effective. It also needs public scrutiny to become more efficient, especially as it fights the Long War against militancy and terrorism at home and faces expanding threats on its international borders.

12

Pakistan's Military Dilemma

Understanding the dynamic behind Pakistan's security fears and its defence strategy is critical for US policy-making in South Asia, since Pakistan remains a powerful regional player and sees itself often as a counterpoint to the US interest in developing stronger ties with India. In dealing with the region and Pakistan specifically, the US sometime appears to push to the background the doctrinal and existential issues that Pakistan faces, and which continue to shape its thinking and actions. It needs to better understand Pakistan's fears and capabilities.

The emergence of Pakistan's military doctrine in this current precarious stage of its political and economic development needs careful consideration in order to delineate its approach to a conventional war with India and how India's emerging and as yet publicly unstated nuclear doctrine affects its stance. It will emerge in light of the historical context of the India–Pakistan rivalry and Pakistan's current economic and political condition.

Broad guidance comes from its own constitution. 'The Armed Forces shall under the direction of the Federal Government defend Pakistan against external aggression or threat of war, and, subject to law, act in aid of civil power when called upon to do so,' states the constitution of Pakistan. So much for the theory. In practice, 'Pakistan's defence budget is made in India,' said former Pakistan ambassador to the US, Jamsheed Marker, an astute observer of the domestic and foreign scene for his country to the author. His comment to me a couple of decades ago encapsulates Pakistan's perennial conundrum. Must it forever remain imprisoned by the prospect of hostility or active war with India and can it afford to match India's rapid economic growth and military strength?

Answers to these questions will help clarify Pakistan's relationships in the region and beyond, particularly with the US. As the US National Intelligence Council Global Trends 2030 report and other analyses have clearly pointed out, the current trajectory has the Indian economy rising from seven to nine times Pakistan's size to sixteen times by 2030. Both the absolute and the relative costs of defence spending by Pakistan will become a heavier burden over time, requiring a smarter strategy going forward. Added to the difficulty of this calculation vis-à-vis India is the increasing danger of internal militancy and an insurgency in its western marcher regions, a spillover from the seemingly forever war in Afghanistan and Pakistan's own tardiness in fully assimilating the FATA since its birth in 1947.

Not only is the opportunity cost of conflict with India high, but also the opportunity cost of those expenditures on the Battle for Pakistan raging inside the country remains a huge challenge. Pakistan's military doctrine, such as it is, is caught between the rock of India and the hard place of its growing internal threats and economic difficulties. It is not clear if there is as yet a coherent and consensual national view on how it must proceed, although the Pakistan Army has produced a doctrine that may be used as a proxy for a national definition of threats and likely responses.

Pakistan Today

Pakistan remains a fragile and dysfunctional polity, still not recovered from the lingering effects of extended military rule under Gen. Pervez Musharraf and the detritus of previous military regimes that have left civilian administrations and the political system stunted, unable to exercise the control that the constitution devolves upon them. The military, and especially the all-powerful army, pays ritualistic obeisance to the concept of civilian supremacy, as evident in numerous statements from its headquarters over the years, but actual decision making on defence matters tends still to be largely in the hands of the men in uniform rather than a truly civilianized MoD or the national government.

The national economy is in dire shape. Annual growth has plummeted from the heady 6–8 per cent of the early Musharraf days to around 3-4 per cent today. Foreign reserves and foreign direct investment are shrinking. (A rise of one per cent in growth would enormously increase the GDP of the country each year.) Repayments to foreign debtors will present the prospect of a fiscal cliff in the short run, as large outflows deplete the state's coffers. The prospects of governmental instability emerging from the 2018 elections makes the role of the army even more powerful, given the general perception that the military collaborated with the judiciary in eliminating the major political parties on the national scene to allow Imran Khan's party to become ascendant. If the new government falters or fails, there is the perennial spectre of the much-discussed Soft Coup of the military being followed by a Hard Coup to establish an 'Egypt on the Indus'; especially if the army calculates that the US is distracted by crises elsewhere in the world and discounts its ability to react to the emergence of a Sisi-like dictator in Pakistan.

State Bank reserves are on a downward path. Of these reserves, a substantial amount is due for paying the IMF and other foreign debts. By 2018, the situation had become much worse, with a potential $25 billion financing gap looming, prompting recourse to Saudi Arabia for short-term relief, as a precursor to a fresh IMF programme. That robust IMF programme was agreed in July 2019, designed to stop the rot of the economy, improve tax administration and revenues, and restore growth over time. It brought in $6 billion, provided Pakistan met its terms over time.

However, the inflows from the CSF of the US for operations of the 140,000-strong Pakistan military on the Afghan border had begun to dwindle as US military operations in Afghanistan began winding down. These were eventually halted by the Trump administration. Only two options remain in Pakistani hands: either draw down those Pakistan military operations, allowing the domestic insurgency to gain the upper hand, or finance them with inflationary deficit financing and dig a deeper economic hole for the country. Or, President Trump restores US funding and pays arrears on the CSF, withheld since 2018.

Though the constitution of Pakistan established civilian supremacy over the military, the armed forces, and in particular the army, continue to dominate decision making in Pakistan. This has emerged largely because of its experience in running the country through successive military regimes and, to some extent, by the inability of civilian regimes to exhibit the political vision and will necessary to exert their constitutional control over the military. Current trends indicate that this situation is not likely to change in the near term. Swimming against the tide of history will be tough for a new government that is facing continuous sniping from the ancien régime.

A dynastic political system and politics as family business continue to infect Pakistan. All this despite the clear defeat of some of the dynastic leaders in the 2018 elections and the reduction of others from the national to the provincial stage. Peaceful and successful elections help validate civil power, while gradual changes in the military high command structure, by an informed and engaged civilian leadership, offer a chance for the government to shape the future of the civil–military relationship. The force of personalities on both sides will determine the future path.

The Shadow of India

Yet the dominating issue facing Pakistan's defence strategy is its continuing 'no peace, no war' relationship with its dominant neighbour to the east, India.[1] This historical rivalry continues to inform Pakistani military thinking to a great extent. And Pakistan's military doctrine, which has long been based on defending Pakistan's territory against an Indian attack in an effort to undo the Partition of British India in 1947, is now shifting to what is being called a 'comprehensive doctrine' to combat both the potential Indian capability to attack and weaken Pakistan and the growing threat of internal militancy and insurgency.

As Pakistan's former Army Chief Gen. Ashfaq Pervez Kayani asserted in his introduction to the restricted circulation army doctrine:

> The prevalent regional and internal environment is ominous of very complex, multidimensional, multifaceted *direct and indirect* [emphasis added] security challenges for the Army . . . The emerging asymmetry in conventional forces vis-à-vis the threat [India, a name that is never once mentioned in the document—author] (and avoidance of arms race) calls for harmonisation of all elements of national power, extraordinary commitment, ingenious planning, non-traditional thinking and decisive superiority in quality of leadership to ensure fulfillment of the army's obligations.[2]

---

[1] The 'no peace, no war' formulation has been used by Lt. Gen. Agha Umer Farooq, among others.

[2] *Pakistan Army Doctrine 2011—Comprehensive Response*, Pakistan Army General Headquarters, Rawalpindi, 2012. Distributed widely inside military and retired military circles in Pakistan from where it made its way to the West.

While India is not named in the doctrine, clearly the doctrine is aimed primarily at India while a new facet is added: internal militancy. The expression of continuing fear of India's growing ability to use what the doctrine calls 'coercive diplomacy' retains the key elements of Pakistan's conventional response and the development of its nuclear capacity to deter any Indian military threat.

Its origins lie in the development of Pakistan's successive War Directives that represent the expression of its government's orders to the military for the defence of the country since its inception. Though secret, these directives have occasionally been mentioned and indeed in the post mortem on the lost 1971 war, when Pakistan ceded East Pakistan to India, leading to the birth of the independent state of Bangladesh, the Hamoodur Rehman Commission Report refers to War Directive Number 2 that essentially enjoined the military to defend every inch of its borders with India.[3] This near-impossible task led to an approach under which the Pakistani leadership chose to defend itself in the west, and thought that strategy would keep India occupied and prevent it from encircling and taking over East Pakistan. It was a serious miscalculation that cost them dearly and led to the imprisonment of over 90,000 Pakistanis in Indian PoW camps in December 1971.

In an elliptical and obtuse way, the new army doctrine also refers to sub-conventional warfare and points to the internal threats that have occupied the Pakistan Army in the past decade or so. But there is no evidence that there has been much debate of this aspect of its stance within the middle and lower ranks in the run-up to the issuance of the new doctrine. This document apparently was crafted entirely in army headquarters and reviewed only by the senior brass. It borrows heavily from language used in other military doctrines, ranging from the US and Britain to New Zealand. And its excessive verbiage adds to its opacity. No Urdu version is as yet available, so most of the lower ranks will not have easy access to it.

The new doctrine does not explicitly discuss the imbalance in the size of conventional forces in the subcontinent. The numbers for both rivals are hard to pin down but provide a reasonable relative size. In 2011, India's armed forces, with an army of 1.2 million, heavily outweighed Pakistan's armed forces of some 610,000, and an army of over 500,000.[4] But on the

---

[3]   The Report of the Hamoodur Rehman Commission of Inquiry into the 1971 war (as declassified by the Government of Pakistan), Vanguard, Lahore, 2001.

[4]   Author's estimates derived from International Institute of Strategic Studies, *The Military Balance 2011* (London: IISS, 2011) and by Anthony H.

ground, Pakistan's armour at 2,656 was more than half the size of India's 4,117 tanks, and armoured infantry vehicles or personnel carriers at 1,266 were close to India's 1,786. India's navy far outnumbers Pakistan's, and in the air India's 365 modern combat aircraft far outnumbered Pakistan's fifty-eight.[5] Pakistan is estimated to have over 190 surface-to-surface missiles, while India has not released any data on its missile strength. What shifts the balance somewhat in Pakistan's favour is the lack of readiness of the huge Indian military, and increasingly a hodge-podge of new equipment from different sources being inducted into the Indian armed forces that will exacerbate the logistical and communications and training problems bedevilling India's military operations. Added to this mess is the dominant Indian bureaucracy that slows down the acquisition and induction of new weapon systems. But this advantage may not last for Pakistan, if mutual hostility remains the hallmark of its relationship with India.

Despite the recent slowdown of the Indian economic growth, India has the reserves to invest in large defence purchases according to a 2013 calculation by SIPRI:

> Over the next decade . . . India plans to spend $150 bn modernizing, upgrading, and maintaining its military equipment. IHS Jane's, the defence analysts, predicted this month [February 2013] that India would surpass France, Japan and the UK to become the fourth-biggest defence spender in the world by 2020 after the US, China and Russia. Over the next five years, the Indian defence budget would rise to more than $55 bn.[6]

This would make it some ten times Pakistan's military budget. The Indian defence budget shows an average annual increase of 5 per cent. Pakistan's budget follows India's by a few months and it is likely that yet again, as Ambassador Marker predicted, Pakistan will get its cue from India and raise its defence spending to try to maintain some sort of equilibrium. Yet, it cannot be expected to maintain that equilibrium over the long term given

---

Cordesman, *The Military Balance in Asia: 1990-2011—A Quantitative* Analysis (Washington DC: CSIS, 16 May 2011).

[5]   Ibid. These numbers are hard to pin down given the inclusion of aging aircraft on both sides of the Indo-Pakistan border.

[6]   Victor Mallet, 'India's Slow March', *Financial Times*, 16–17 February 2013.

the rising trajectory of India's economic growth compared to Pakistan's in the foreseeable future. Over time, India's larger economy will allow it to use a smaller proportion of its GDP for its defence. Pakistan's smaller economic pie will not afford it that luxury, unless it begins growing close to 7 per cent or more a year and cuts unproductive expenditures, including within the military.

Pakistan's military doctrine and planning also suffers from ad hocism rather than a predictable, repetitive and inclusive system for updating it, involving both civilian and military actors.

The Process

The reality is that the War Directive in Pakistan emerges sporadically rather than regularly from the military and is merely rubber-stamped by the civilian leadership. It is not built from the ground up as a routine. Meanwhile in India, the Ministry of Defence issues a new War Directive every five years, and service headquarters update their war operations instructions every two years or with a change in command. The legwork is done by the joint headquarters with input from the services and is presented to the Defence Advisory Board, a body of elders that is not duplicated in Pakistan.

The last known War Directive in Pakistan emerged in 2000. When Gen. Mirza Aslam Beg inherited command of the army following the death of Gen. Zia-ul-Haq in a plane crash in August 1988, he sought a new War Directive to update the Pakistanis' thinking, but with no success. Beg lauds a recent effort by the Senate to look at this issue:

The Senate Standing Committee on Defence (SSCD) is presently [sic] engaged in devising a robust defence policy that is aimed at making policy guidelines for the parliamentarians' with three objectives in mind:

* To review current issues pertaining to defence;
* To determine mandatory changes to the defence policy; and
* To provide new policy guidelines for better national defence.

Its intentions are noble, but it has started the exercise from the wrong end. The first step that it must take is to assist Pakistani government to issue the war directive, which lays down policy guidelines for the armed forces.

War Directive (WD): A new WD is long overdue. Some of the main objectives it sets are:

* The structure of Higher Defence Organization (HDO);
* Level and size of the armed forces;
* War stamina to be developed;
* War objectives to be achieved;
* Capability to be achieved within a given timeframe.

After issue of the WD, the armed forces carry out in-depth studies to evolve the defence policy based on the available resources. Once the government approves it, they evolve a joint defence strategy and the strategies of army, navy and air force.[7]

Gen. Beg is right. I first heard Beg's views on the War Directive while interviewing him in his office in 1990 when he bemoaned the strictures of the antiquated directive under which he was operating. There is no evidence to date of the results of the Pakistani Senate effort to update the War Directive. Nor should one hold one's breath, given the lack of visible initiative of the Senate Defence Committee on such critical matters, which needs to be more of a guiding and overseeing entity. Despite some efforts by a few members of this committee to bring their oversight and investigation of the defence services and policies into the public eye, there has been resistance from the military, especially the army. The military wishes to keep the briefings in camera, according to Senator Mushahid Hussain, former chairman of the committee. And some topics are taboo, only on the basis of the preferences of the COAS. This makes the committee appear to be more of a cheerleader rather than a public watchdog. Among the many topics that the public was unaware of was the matter of the purchase by both the military and civil security agencies of so-called bomb detection wands that had been declared fake by the British authorities investigating their sale to Iraq and that were sold by a retired Pakistan Army officer to the government at enormous cost. They did not work. In fact, they were then sold under a local name to keep them separate from the name they were sold under internationally, even to neighbouring India! The committee needs

---

7   Mirza Aslam Beg, 'Devising a Robust Defence Policy', *Nation*, Lahore, 7 October 2012.

qualified research and support staff to keep it informed and equipped to deal with complex and sometimes technical issues so it can perform its functions for the national good. As a result of these constraints on its operations, there has been no public discussion of the War Directive in parliament.

During the Musharraf period, despite efforts by some of his commanders and the joint headquarters, he refused to open discussion of a new directive, dismissing such requests with the retort that 'we know what to do'.[8] The unity of command for civil and military decision making in a single person (Musharraf) made this possible. In 2012, the MoD, run by a retired army general, began seeking inputs from the services for a new War Directive. The civilian Minister of Defence 'has no interest' in such matters, according to the then secretary.[9] He went on to state that the Joint Chiefs Headquarters helps provide coordination for this effort and supports the work of the Defence Committee of the Cabinet. The civilian authorities have not established any mechanism for studying or supporting decisions on military matters or broader defence policy. 'The War Directive should be updated before doctrine is defined. Pakistan went in reverse order, with the army taking the lead on its new doctrine,' stated a former defence secretary. It is possible that the new doctrine could lead to updating of the War Directive. But there are few signs of movement on this front.

According to another former defence secretary, the new version is 'already outdated, since it did not take into account 9/11 and its subsequent fallout for Pakistan'. An earlier effort in 2005–06 fizzled out after the Joint Headquarters tried to enlist support from the NDU in lieu of think tanks inside Pakistan. They then came up with a Joint Strategic Directive for the individual armed services to come up with their operational plans. That effort was completed in 2007 but never got formal governmental approval.

Much of the focus was on high-level conventional defence. Nuclear policy began intervening in conventional defence policy by 2004. Musharraf had combined all his civilian and military functions by then. By 2007–08, the NDU had also begun including discussion of the nuclear threshold

---

[8] Interview with a former Musharraf Corps Commander and a former defence secretary.

[9] Ibid.

vis-à-vis India in its war games. The concept of combined deterrence emerged, informed by the experience of the 2001–02 escalation of tensions with India. Pakistan realized the value of dovetailing conventional and nuclear posture and plans. In its thinking, this led the US to lean on India to draw down its forward deployment during that crisis. The subsequent emergence of the new defence policy against India was seen as a response to the so-called Cold Start doctrine of India, now better known as the Proactive Strategy.

Cold Start or False Start?

India continues to publicly disavow the premise of Cold Start, that its forward-deployed Integrated Battle Groups could move rapidly into Pakistani territory, capture key cities and territory and make Pakistan sue for terms. Pakistan continues to see this as an emerging threat and considers the 1980s thinking that led to the Brasstacks exercise as a testing of the idea of such rapid combined manoeuvres designed to hit Pakistan at multiple points of vulnerability in a modern version of the German blitzkrieg. It countered with an offensive–defensive approach that was based on hitting India in response with a counter-strike and capturing key territory for itself. Its conventional riposte, based on a net-centric doctrine of well-planned counterattacks, was bolstered over time by the testing and development of a tactical nuclear capability by Pakistan (countered by India). This took the form of short-range so-called tactical weapons mounted on ballistic and cruise missiles, adding to the potential for a nuclear holocaust in the region with global consequences.

The Pakistani army chief, Gen. Kayani, spelt out his view of the new strategy in January 2010 according to an official military press release: 'COAS stated proponents of conventional application of military forces, in a "nuclear overhang" are chartering an adventurous and dangerous path; the consequences of which could be both unintended and uncontrollable.'[10]

The army tested its new doctrine through a series of exercises or war games called Azm-e-Nau (Fresh Resolve). The third one in the series was conducted in the Cholistan Desert from 10 April to 13 May 2010, involving up to 50,000 troops, and even included a final segment that showed anti-aircraft gunners shooting down a drone.

---

[10]   ISPR Directorate, 1 January 2010.

As mentioned earlier, Gen. Kayani also introduced what he considers a suitable riposte or deterrent to Indian conventional plans by shifting control of his key armour division from its base in Kharian, facing Kashmir, to the Gujranwala corps. In his view, this would blunt any Indian armour thrust into the Ravi–Chenab corridor of the Punjab plains, the traditional tank battleground of Sialkot and its environs.[11]

At the conventional level, despite the current disparity in size and growing disparity in the nature of conventional weaponry available to India that promises to give it overwhelming superiority over time, Pakistan operates on the assumption of 'strategic equivalence'. Loosely translated, this means that Pakistani forces can blunt any conventional Indian attack and respond effectively by undertaking its own offensive actions into Indian territory. All under a nuclear overhang.

Pakistan's new army doctrine recognizes a wider spectrum of conflict that includes sub-conventional warfare in addition to conventional warfare that, in turn, includes low-intensity operations, conventional war and nuclear warfare. The latter is aimed at complementing comprehensive deterrence and adding to the combat potential of the regular forces, leading to a potentially heavy cost for any aggressor. Nuclear war is seen 'only as a last resort'.[12] Moreover, while conventional warfare is to be conducted under the devolved authority given by the National Command Authority to the military high command, the decision to go to nuclear war can only be initiated by the civilian authority under 'the exclusive right of the NCA headed by the prime minister'. But no one has any doubts that should India launch a serious and deep conventional strike into Pakistan, the army would take the lead in deciding how to respond rapidly, with or without formal approval by the NCA.

Increasingly, Pakistan sees itself subject to potentially hostile activity from India, under the assumption that a sort of nuclear parity has led to maintenance of the status quo. So, it expects India (the unnamed South Asian foe in its new Army doctrine) to synchronize activities at various levels to: 'subtly erode [Pakistan's] . . . national resilience and force compliance'. India's willingness to bear the cost of war will help define the intensity, scale and nature of any future conflict, according to this view.

---

[11]   Conversation with me, June 2012.

[12]   Op. cit. Pakistan Army Doctrine, p. 11.

At the same time, Pakistan's own calculations rest on the intensity of a nuclear exchange that would be Counter Value in nature rather than Counter Force. Potentially, ten major Indian urban centres and all seven of Pakistan's major cities might be the targets in a nuclear exchange. The end result would be the destruction of large tracts of India and most of Pakistani territory, and the release of dust and debris into the atmosphere that would travel eastwards, eventually covering the entire Northern Hemisphere. In effect, Nuclear Winter could descend on the northern half of the globe for as much as six months. India's own calculations may well mirror those of Pakistan.

Hence, a backward glance at previous crises shows a remarkable degree of restraint in the deployment of nuclear assets in times of tension between India and Pakistan. Yet, Pakistan, the smaller adversary, chose to flex its nuclear muscles via testing of delivery vehicles such as the Ghauri and Hatf missiles. In the 2002 crisis, following the attack by non-state actors on the Indian parliament, Pakistan chose to reduce the talk of nuclear weapons and continued to deny that it readied its nuclear arsenal when India moved conventional forces to its eastern border. It maintains that it would only use nuclear weapons if India attacks and occupies large tracts of Pakistani territory and attempts to stifle Pakistan's economy or weaken its polity by internal subversion.[13] In essence, as Feroz Hassan Khan maintains: 'The Pakistanis see no role for nuclear weapons than to deter India from waging a conventional war.'[14]

The issue still remains that when the polity and economy become weak over time, nuclear deterrence may lose its viability, as in the implosion of the former Soviet Union. At the same time, Pakistani experts continue to see the modest attempts to develop conventional confidence-building measures, with India being overshadowed by developments that may be inherently antithetical to Pakistani interests vis-à-vis India. They see the Indo-US nuclear agreement tilting the balance in India's favour, posing a continuous challenge for Pakistan. By keeping India's strategic nuclear weapons systems out of safeguards, India retains the right to improve and deploy its nuclear weapons without let or hindrance, according to this view. In their calculation, the only way the balance could be maintained would be to offer a package approach that allowed Pakistan the same access to

---

[13] Feroz Hassan Khan, *Eating Grass: The Making of the Pakistan Bomb* (Stanford, CA: Stanford Security Studies, 2012), pp. 350–53.

[14] Ibid., p. 380.

nuclear material that India gained from this agreement.[15] The US and its allies have not been inclined to head in this direction.

Meanwhile, Pakistan, perhaps under the influence of its artillery-dominated leadership of the SPD, continues to develop longer-range delivery vehicles that might belie its claim of deterrence against neighbouring India. One reason for this may be, according to one leading US observer, the control of the SPD by artillery officers who are fixated on missile ranges and payloads! Even as the overall costs continue to mount. This fixation may well be one of the stumbling blocks in the path to Pakistan's membership in the Nuclear Suppliers Group, in addition to opposition from the US.

Costs of Defence

By all accounts, Pakistan continues to operate under the Armed Forces Development Plan instituted by Musharraf for 2004–19 with a total outlay of $18 billion, for essential requirements of all services, with fund allocations locked in place. But this plan suffered mightily during the financial crisis of 2005 and with the front-loading of expenditures by the services. After Musharraf's departure, the period covered by this plan, under the same total outlays of $18 billion, was extended to 2025 and tied to a national GDP growth rate of 4 per cent per annum. An annual outlay of $5 billion means that the ceiling for this plan will be breached sooner than 2025. Meanwhile, the asymmetry with India has begun increasing. At some point, it is possible that the growing disparity may increase the propensity to use so-called tactical nuclear weapons. But India would then respond with full force. With unimaginable results.

As Pakistan's internal militancy and insurgency occupies greater space and use of its forces, and as CSF dry up, it will need to weigh carefully the costs of war, conventional or nuclear or both.

Two major principles will inform the Pakistani decision:

1. Any conventional conflict could trigger a nuclear war with results that neither India nor Pakistan could survive easily.

---

[15] Tariq Osman Hyder, 'Concerns over Pakistan's Nuclear Program: Perceptions and Reality', *Policy Perspectives* 9, no. 2 (Islamabad: Institute of Policy Studies, 2012).

2. It does not benefit either side in this heightened nuclear environment to launch a surprise move or attack. Hair-trigger responses are built into both systems in the subcontinent, given the lack of warning time. India's much publicized 'surgical strikes' might be the fuse for a rapid escalation of conflict.

The answer rests on a Strategic Restraint Regime, rooted in continuing and deepening contacts between India and Pakistan at all levels of government and society to reduce the risk of accidental conflict. And by increased focus within Pakistan on rebalancing its economic and political systems to make them inclusive and equitable. The US can play a more active role between India and Pakistan in this regard while helping Pakistan economically so it does not feel threatened by India as a regional hegemon. A sustainable doctrine in these conditions can only emerge with the combined efforts of the civil and the military, while involving civil society in their decision making. Muddling through is not a viable option.

13

Choices

In the aftermath of the third elections to produce a civilian government in July 2018 headed by Imran Khan, a non-traditional politician, Pakistan has an opportunity to lay the foundation for a vibrant economy and polity and reduce the overarching shadow of the military on its political system over time. The relatively strong electoral position of Prime Minister Imran Khan and a powerful position in the major provinces of the Punjab and Khyber Pakhtunkhwa promises some stability, despite his many domestic and regional challenges and a seemingly unending election campaign by the other parties with a view to toppling his government via street action. Ironically, these were the tactics he employed with eventual success to galvanize support.

Pakistan can play an important security and development role in the region and as a partner of the US, even as it maintains its separate relationships with its immediate neighbours, China, Afghanistan, India and Iran. Imran Khan's apparent efforts to work with the military on national economic and strategic issues will stand him in good stead but they may also delay the establishment of civilian supremacy in a democratic Pakistan. The country and its surrounds have changed dramatically in the past two decades. If current trends bear out, populations in the greater South Asia region will continue to become more politically and economically active. If its leaders can provide responsive governance and a clear and consistent economic direction, South Asia may be able to surmount over time its persistent security challenges, both within countries and from hostile neighbours. And they may be able to lay the basis for connectivity of their economies.

The challenge for Pakistan will be to balance its internal battles with the need to create a more congenial regional atmosphere that fosters stability and economic growth. Imprisoned by its geography, Pakistan must learn to live and thrive in its neighbourhood without becoming a vassal of surging India. Otherwise, it risks becoming a backwater and asterisk in future atlases. Especially if its centrifugal forces triumph over the centripetal forces holding it together. In fighting this hostile future, it needs to learn from its history and those of other countries that have struggled to establish a clear and sustainable national identity. And it will need to balance carefully its quest for security against its need to develop economically and to ask itself if its investment in defence has effectively purchased it adequate security.

Regarding its external relations, Pakistan does not have to choose between its traditional ally, the US, and its relatively newer friend, China. On its part, the US can take advantage of the presence in the same region of two relatively sophisticated military and political systems in India and Pakistan that together could provide stability and growth to the wider region.

The US cannot afford to create or encourage divisions in South Asia. Over the next ten to fifteen years, South Asia could be poised to play a pivotal role on the global economic and political scene. Given its size, India is in a position to take the regional lead, and Pakistan could end up playing either a major supporting role or the role of a critical spoiler, if its polity deteriorates instead of stabilizing and improving. Afghanistan also may well offer a springboard for a new regionalism, reverting to its historical role as the gateway to South and Central Asia. And Iran, if it can fully rejoin the global community, may successfully hook into South Asia's economy, while playing a key role in the stabilization of Afghanistan and the neighbourhood. But only if the US reopens its discussions with Iran rather than taking the path of confrontation. An economically and militarily stronger India may well work out a balanced relationship with arch-rival China, building on trade dependency to either dampen territorial disputes or to resolve them through quiet negotiations.

Pakistan's developing relationship with China under the China–Pakistan Economic Cooperation Corridor or CPEC, linked to China's broader Belt and Road Initiative may give it a chance to connect with its neighbours too and become the 'game changer' that Pakistani leaders talk about. But that will demand much more preparedness and transparency in Pakistan. Much more than has been evident to date. China will also need to give Pakistan breathing room to undertake and participate in the

Belt and Road Initiative so that it brings investments into Pakistan rather than burdensome debt or commitments on the rates of return promised to Chinese investing firms that Pakistan may have difficulty in servicing. Deeds, not words, matter.

Pakistan looks to reap some benefits from the emergence of the CPEC that will start bearing fruit in the next five years by creating jobs in the infrastructure sector and by alleviating the energy shortages that have held back the economy in the past decade or so. It remains to be seen if China reduces its reliance on its own labour to speedily complete the jobs or relies on Pakistani labour to build and maintain the projects.

Another possible impediment might be the speed with which Pakistan can muster counterpart funding and institution building for these projects. Initial reports indicate that the development budget will be cannibalized to give priority to the CPEC effort, including funding the security forces to protect construction work. Much of the $46 billion investment promised by China over the next fifteen years is in the energy and infrastructure sectors, with energy taking the lion's share at nearly $38 billion. If the government can deftly manage the initial investment in the pathway from China to Gwadar on the Arabian Sea by not tilting the investment first towards the easternmost Punjab-centric highway, Pakistan could help knit the provinces together. It would behoove the government to begin work on the Baloch segment first, mandating the use of local labour and bringing the tribal populations into ownership, given the strategic location of Balochistan across three countries of the region. The US could lay the foundation for a long-term investment in Pakistan's future by helping Pakistan undertake speedily the Western Corridor traversing Khyber Pakhtunkhwa and Balochistan, and including a tributary linked to Afghanistan. Such a signature project would be a lasting symbol of US relations with Pakistan, much like the Mangla and Tarbela dams were in the 1960s and '70s. The undisbursed KLB funds amounting to an estimated $2 billion and withheld CSF and other funding by the Trump administration might provide the seed money for this project.

To date, Pakistan has chosen to avoid making decisions on the $46 billion in Chinese investments that would speedily integrate its marcher regions into the economy and body politic of the country. Of these, some $36 billion are energy related and the remaining $10 billion are for infrastructure. It has favoured the Punjab for the main route connecting China to the Arabian Sea, given the presence of the current motorways.

The Western Corridor is supposed to be built with local financing. China did not provide loans for three infrastructure projects of the western route. Pakistan had to scramble to find funding for one of the three projects related to that segment of the CPEC corridor. But, lack of preparation has dogged it and many other projects.

China has provided a number of heavy loans to Pakistan and some balance of payment financing. But nothing of the quantum that would meet Pakistan's immediate financing needs to service its obligations and imports.

Both Pakistan and China need to better publicize China's investment flows into Pakistan as a counter to the impression that most of its funding is in the form of loans. At the same time, both China and Pakistan need to make a special effort to share openly and widely their plans and processing of contracts. This would help counter the surging conspiracy theories of those who oppose this relationship, both inside Pakistan and in other countries, near and far.

But in all this it would be critical for Pakistan not to present China as an alternative to the US and the West. Rather, Pakistan needs to reshape its regional and global alliances in light of the blueprint that Gen. Ashfaq Kayani had presented to the US and NATO in September 2011 (Kayani 4.0). Ending the no-war-no-peace condition in South Asia and working with friends, near and far, to help stabilize its own economy and polity will be key to Pakistan's economic growth.

Regional security issues also dog Pakistan. The growing arsenal of nuclear weapons in the hands of India and Pakistan and the potential ability to deliver them from sea, land and air platforms as well the emergence of 'MIRVing' (i.e., the ability to produce missiles carrying Multiple Independently Targeted Re-entry Vehicles) and tactical weapon capabilities could create a nuclear standoff that paradoxically might forestall regional conflict. Pakistan's search for developing MIRV capacity might be its best counter to India's planned acquisition of advanced Anti-Ballistic Missile Defence systems from Russia or elsewhere. Growing economies and the presence of more involved and affluent urban populations could act as an additional break on conflict. But, both countries would have too much to lose if they stray from the path of socioeconomic development. And unfettered expenditures in developing advanced weapons systems at the expense of needed socioeconomic development for the poorest segments of their populations would be a big price to pay in terms of forgone benefits for the broader population.

The scary part of looking at the crystal ball for the region is the possibility that the conflict scenario is probable. If individual countries fall into the trap of religious, sectarian, or economic selfishness and intolerance, and if external actors, especially the US, fail to exercise their important roles in forging regional economic integration rather than setting up India to be the regional hegemon and local power broker, the prospects look dim indeed. Indo-Pakistan conflict definitely retards economic growth in both countries and is now involving Afghanistan as an ancillary to India's regional political moves to isolate Pakistan.

Economic actions and developments in the region and the world will lie at the heart of change in the region over the next two decades. They will be the accelerant for reversing several negative trends that have emerged in the past three decades, especially in Pakistan and India, and mitigate the corrosive effects of religious ideology on political thinking. The solidification of a Culture of Entitlement, based on preferred access to state resources, and lack of transparency and accountability, has undermined the effectiveness of civil and military institutions, especially in Pakistan. In the long run, Pakistan's security will stem from economic development and concomitant social and political progress. Overlaying everything will be the state of governance, that is, the orderly provision of services and the regulation of economic and political activity that is transparent, efficient and effectively managed, with accountability and transparency in expenditures by both the civil and the military.

But a potentially major disruptive trend is the rapid urbanization of South Asia. Coupled with a rising population and the rapid introduction of labour-saving technologies, this promises to create a massive challenge to business and government both. A look at the night-time map of the region indicates how massive the urban agglomeration has become.[1] In northern India and along its coastline and in the Punjab in Pakistan is evidence of a growing phenomenon of linked urban centres called conurbation, which extends cities in a shiny necklace of light across the night-time map of South Asia. Essentially, the world's largest city now extends from Delhi to Islamabad! Of the world's thirty leading megacities, with populations of over 7 million, five are in South Asia (Karachi, Mumbai, Delhi, Lahore

---

[1] NASA issued a photograph of lights during the night of Diwali in 2012 that illustrates this point. https://earthobservatory.nasa.gov/images/79682/south-asian-night-lights

and Dhaka).[2] Three of these: Karachi, Delhi and Mumbai, each has a population exceeding 20 million. This massive urbanization also creates an accompanying problem of pollution, in effect creating micro-climatic zones in and around these major cities and adding to the health and other economic costs of living in their environs. While these megacities often contribute to overall economic growth in each country, they also spawn sharp contrasts between the rich and the poor. They are home to the largest slums in the world, and create economic inequality that can lead to social unrest based on both ideology and pure economic deprivation.

Cities of 5 million or more inhabitants will continue to grow in number and size, changing the social and political maps of the countries in the region, raising the level of (largely unmet) expectations, especially of the still massive youth bulge. This trend is not likely to change in the near term or even up to 2035. The penetration of new communication technologies, such as the cell phone and the Internet, into the cities and countryside, and the interconnectedness of youth across the globe, has led to a network of discontent with the status quo. It also facilitates ideological recruitment and sustainment of subversive ideas, as recent events in Syria and Iraq have shown with the self-styled Islamic State or Daesh enticing youth from South Asia and the South Asian diaspora in the West, in particular, to join its ranks. This disruption will likely continue in the near term, but the future of IS remains uncertain given its own inability to govern the space that it occupies. Yet, it has metastasized into Afghanistan, Pakistan and India, adding to the uncertainty about political stability.

Dark Scenarios

Black Swan events, by their very nature, are unpredictable. However, certain looming worries will play a key role in shaping future events. In the near term, Iran's rivalry with Saudi Arabia and the Gulf states could suck South Asian states into the Shia–Sunni squabble, further exacerbating Shia–Sunni tensions within the countries of the region. Countries like Pakistan and Bangladesh may take political positions that may not accord with those of labour-hosting countries in the Arabian Peninsula; displacement of South Asian labour from the Gulf and Saudi Arabia may well accelerate, with

---

[2]   Nations Online, 'Megacities of the World', http://www.nationsonline.org/oneworld/bigcities.htm

South East Asian workers potentially filing the gap. Returning labour would inject a heavy dose of disgruntlement into the domestic labour markets of the exporting countries that have been unprepared for a reverse flow of these workers. (Expelled Bangladeshi workers have already felt the short-term wrath of Saudi unhappiness. The Gulf states may well turn on Pakistan in the wake of Pakistan's hesitancy to enter the Saudi campaign against the Houthi in Yemen.) Pakistan could face severe difficulties adjusting to the loss of approximately $6–8 billion annual remittances from its workers in this region if its workers are ejected from the Gulf and Saudi Arabia. These remittances are crucial in meeting about half of Pakistan's import bill and in covering deficits in the trade of goods account.

The potential for nuclear proliferation or extension of the Pakistani nuclear umbrella to the Arabian Peninsula will add to regional tensions and imbalances. China's announced plans to use South Asia as an economic gateway to the Bay of Bengal and the Arabian Sea, if they reach satisfactory fruition, will pose new challenges to its relationship with India. Access to ports in Sri Lanka and Pakistan potentially give it a foothold in the Indian Ocean without subjecting itself to the danger of a long line of communication for its maritime Silk Road through the chokepoint of the Malacca Straits and a potentially hostile South China Sea.

Exogenous environmental factors, including massive earthquakes, a secular shift in the monsoon patterns from the Gangetic Plains northwards to the Himalayas and ending in the mountainous northern Pakistan rather than on the Potohar Plateau, could multiply the dangers that have been witnessed in recent years with the all-too-frequent appearance of '100-year floods'. Rain falling on deforested mountains and ravines in northern Pakistan creates speeding trains of floodwaters that cannot be contained by the dams and barrages on Pakistan's rivers. Extreme fluctuation of monsoon patterns is another issue that will lead to uncertainty for South Asian farmers.[3] Delayed arrival of the monsoon and higher temperatures would create challenging conditions of large swathes of South Asia, according to research done at Purdue University. Noah Diffenbaugh, whose research group led the study, said the summer

---

[3]   Devjyot Ghoshal, 'India's Vital Monsoon Rains Are Changing—and Not for the Better', *Quartz India*, 10 August 2014, http://qz.com/246563/indias-vital-monsoon-rains-are-changing-and-not-for-the-better/

monsoon affects water resources, agriculture, economics, ecosystems and
human health throughout South Asia.

> Almost half of the world's population lives in areas affected by these
> monsoons, and even slight deviations from the normal monsoon pattern
> can have great impact . . . Agricultural production, water availability and
> hydroelectric power generation could be substantially affected by delayed
> monsoon onset and reduced surface runoff. Alternatively, the model
> projects increases in precipitation over some areas, including Bangladesh,
> which could exacerbate seasonal flood risks.[4]

Climate change, fuelled in part by local pollution, could accelerate,
leading to a faster melting of the glaciers in the Pamir Knot that seed
the northern rivers of Pakistan and India. Notwithstanding the powerful
influence of natural and manmade disasters, overall and in the longer
term, domestic issues and actions will likely play the greatest role in
determining the future of South Asia as a region and in shaping the path
of Pakistan.

The Near-Term Continuum

South Asia's tradition-bound societies are not designed for rapid change.
Complicated and overlapping caste, religious divisions, language and ethnic
barriers, and geography that both divides neighbours within countries and
from other states, all help shape the nature and retard the speed of change.
Despite these and the huge demographic challenges facing the region,
individual countries have shown a remarkable resilience and produced an
enviable economic growth record.

As former Governor of the State Bank of Pakistan Ishrat Husain
put it:

> In the 1960s Pakistan was considered as a model developing country and
> its manufactured exports were higher than those of Thailand, Malaysia,

---

[4]   Purdue University, 'Purdue Study Projects Weakened Monsoon
      Season in South Asia', 26 February 2009, http://www.purdue.edu/uns/
      x/2009a/090226DiffenbaughMonsoon.html

Philippines and Indonesia.[5] While our larger next-door neighbor [India] was stuck with 3 percent growth rate Pakistan was averaging six percent annual growth rate. The Eastern wing of the country felt left behind in this rapid progress and decided to become independent in 1971. At that time Bangladesh's economic prospects were dubbed by the international community in most uncharitable terms.[6]

World Bank economist Shahid Yusuf also discovered in a review for the World Bank that Pakistan maintained a long-term growth rate that only came in second to China's growth from the late 1970s to the early years of the 2000s, while India maintained a much lower 'Hindu rate of growth' hovering around 3 per cent. India, however, caught up and accelerated past Pakistan in the 1990s and is now poised to overtake China's growth rate in the next decade, if it can maintain its momentum of change and reform. But the relative size of India's economy will likely remain much smaller than China in the next two decades. Arvind Subramanian, then chief economic adviser to the Government of India, opined that India's natural growth rate was around 7 per cent, ascribing the drag to rampant rent-seeking in India.[7] He later lowered the real growth rate, blaming official miscounting.

None of these shares or trends is likely to change in the short run (till around 2024). Government regulations and controls need to become more transparent and less onerous, and bureaucratic inefficiencies removed. At the same time, political rent-seeking needs to be replaced by less obtrusive governmental regulation of the economy. Only then will Pakistan change the underlying conditions that are holding it back. Evidence of sclerotic governmental behaviour of the past does not lend much optimism on this front.

Pakistan, like other countries of the region, suffers from vast inequalities in its component provinces, states or regions. Both democratic and autocratic governments have favoured a centralized command structure,

---

5   World Bank, Development Policy Review (Washington DC: World Bank, 2002).

6   Ishrat Husain, 'Economic Reforms in Pakistan: One Step Forward, Two Steps Backwards', Quaid-i-Azam Lecture at the Annual Conference of Pakistan Society for Development Economics, 15 November 2012.

7   Arvind Subramanian, 'Arvind Subramanian: What Is India's Real Growth Potential?' Business Standard, 20 January 2013, http://www.business-standard.com/article/opinion/arvind-subramanian-what-is-india-s-real-growth-potential-112052300014_1.html

despite attempts at freeing market forces to open up their economies. Local government is treated more as an afterthought than a critical foundation for a burgeoning democratic system that could foster an open economy.

Meanwhile, in Pakistan's western border region, the potential for economic interaction with Afghanistan still remains more a hope than a reality. Decades of distrust and the underlying Indo-Pakistani rivalry inside Afghanistan will stand in the way of better integration, despite the aspirations of the new Afghan leadership to make Afghanistan a regional trade hub and a revived terminus of the Grand Trunk Road that links Kabul to Dhaka. A Grand Trunk Road Initiative, backed, among others, by the US and other Western countries, would be a good counter as well as complement to the Belt and Road Initiative of China and help better integrate the South Asia region. It may well outdo the Silk Road initiatives that are on everyone's lips these days.

The best that can be hoped in keeping the centre meaningfully tied to its periphery would be to work with regional political parties in crafting links with potential economic partners across international borders. For Pakistan, this means Afghanistan and Iran in the west, China in the north, and India to the east. For India, this would mean opening up trade routes and travel points into Pakistani Punjab and Sindh, and facilitating the formation of regional markets in the south to include Sri Lanka, and in the east to include Bangladesh and Myanmar. Pakistan is trying in concert with India to open up religious tourism for Sikh pilgrims from India, with either visas upon arrival or a no-visa policy, and thereby garner immense economic and political benefits. Why not extend this to opening of more border crossings in southern Punjab and Sindh?

The lesson from the Nepalese experience with India on the removal of visas for travel between the two countries could well be applied to other regions on the periphery in South Asia. Despite the presence of such an open visa regime on paper under the aegis of the SAARC (the eight-nation South Asian Association for Regional Cooperation that includes Afghanistan as well as other South Asian countries and the Maldives) grouping, there does not appear to be a strong movement towards a change in the visa regime in practice over the next five years. In the past, India and Pakistan have raised security-related concerns about visa-free travel. When I posed the question to some former DGs of the ISI in Pakistan, all of them, whom I asked whether open visas would endanger security, responded with a resounding 'No'. The explanation one gave me was that 'people with bad intentions don't apply for visas. They can just come across the border.' A new push by the Asian Development Bank to expand visa-free travel appears to be gaining some traction. But Indian and Pakistani bureaucracies and security services will likely continue to drag their feet unless bold political leaders show them the lead.

The counterfactual may support the strengthening of regional groupings at the periphery of the region that could splinter the major states of South Asia. Pakistan appears the most vulnerable, with Balochistan becoming even more restive, unhappy with what some of its native population sees as an invasion of people from other provinces and an export of its natural resources to the Centre without commensurate benefits to the province. The continued availability of sanctuary in Afghanistan for Baloch nationalists and reported Indian assistance as a response to Pakistan's fomenting of trouble in Kashmir raises the spectre of the separation of that province with links to both Afghanistan and Iran. But this is avoidable via more informed and inclusive policies.

The creation of new provinces in Pakistan could forestall some of these moves, especially the treatment of the 25-million-strong population of Karachi demanding greater autonomy and the splitting of the dominant Punjab into a Seraiki province in the south and potentially a Potohar province in the north. Khyber Pakhtunkhwa has seen the rise of a youth-led Pakhtun movement demanding greater citizen rights and access to the erstwhile FATA. Khyber Pakhtunkhwa might eventually see and accept the emergence of a Hindko-speaking Hazara province abutting the Punjab with which it shares a similar language. Finally, there is the issue of the future of FATA, changing it from a buffer territory ruled from Islamabad to a full participating region of Pakistan proper. The legal process has begun. It needs to be completed quickly and effectively, taking into account the needs and views of its largely youthful population and not by alienating them with threats or coercion. Successful elections in July 2019 augur well for the transition to the merger of FATA with Khyber Pakhtunkhwa. The best scenario is the emergence of a true Pakistani confederation as envisaged in the original call for Pakistan during the waning days of British India.

Kashmiris also demand more autonomy on both sides of the Line of Control. Pakistan has failed to allow its part of Kashmir to operate autonomously and has already sliced off the northern areas of Gilgit-Baltistan, in the face of strong Indian protests. Every time a government changes in Islamabad, the government in Muzaffarabad changes as well. Meanwhile, Pakistan continues to seek greater autonomy for the Kashmiri people on the Indian side of the LOC. India wants them folded into the Union.

The greatest change in the region with regard to Centre–Periphery relations has occurred in Pakistan. The 18th Amendment laid the basis for reorganizing the fiscal and financial ties between the Centre and the provinces. Concurrently, the National Finance Commission Award recast the revenue-sharing formulae, giving the relatively poorer states a larger share of federal revenues. It took eighteen years for the National Finance Commission to reach agreement on its award. While politically this is a beneficial move that will tie the provinces together, it also created a financial nightmare and raises the spectre of unfettered provincial spending and revenue generation from unpaid loans that could well become liabilities for the Centre. The Bank of the Punjab model is eagerly being emulated by the other provinces, and if not monitored closely could well become an ATM machine for deficit spending by inept or corrupt provincial governments.

Devolution in Pakistan stopped at the provincial capitals. For it to take root and succeed, it needs to move further downward to local governments and must include the provision of services at the local community level. External threats, to Pakistan from India (and to India from China), will help hold the unions together. And as growth resumes in the region, the larger economic pie will generate a larger share for the constituent units. But much effort will be needed to make the stars align. Mere rhetoric will not suffice.

Security concerns and long-lasting territorial and natural resource issues (for example, sharing and managing of above-ground water and aquifers across borders) add to the difficulties of intra-regional trade. Opening borders would enhance the natural complementarities that exist among countries in South Asia. Enhanced trade would benefit consumers but is constrained largely due to manmade barriers that will require far-sighted political leadership to surmount. And sharing of water resources and cooperation across borders to deal with climatic changes and to stem environmental degradation that has no respect for manmade boundaries is also held hostage by politics. There does not appear to be much movement towards reaching practicable regional agreements. High tariffs and non-tariff barriers persist. The opportunity cost of conflict in the region remains high. Both India and Pakistan lose the equivalent of some 1.5 per cent of GDP because of their continuing hostilities.[8] They lose even greater proportions in wasteful expenditures and forgone tax revenues.

The near-term prospects could be bleak, if leaders remain caught up in domestic squabbles and internal security challenges. Added to these problems are sectarian and ethnic conflicts, and lack of protection of minorities and of human rights in general in all South Asian countries. If their growing urban and middle-class populations become politically aware and active over the next decade or so, they may precipitate a change in political behaviour, by wresting control from dynastic political systems. But external pressures from major neighbours like China, Saudi Arabia and distant trading and political allies like Europe and the US would be needed to alter behaviour. Saudi Arabia in particular would need to stop allowing the export of extremist jihadi ideology and cease its proxy wars against Iran in this region. Iran would also need to reduce its external footprint in the Middle East and on the Arabian Peninsula.

The rising share of the middle class in Pakistan may become another game changer for domestic and external politics and hence economics. According to the Asian Development Bank, some 32.94 per cent of Pakistan's population falls into the middle-class category. The share of the middle class increased over the period 1990–2008 by 12.8 per cent. This trend likely will continue.[9] Though the majority of the middle class belong to the relatively lower-income brackets within that grouping, collectively they represent a growing and potentially important economic and political entity. As this growing class becomes more educated and politically active, it may produce checks and balances on traditionally heavy-handed governments and challenge also the hegemony of the security establishment.

Leading Edge of Change: Governance

The continued presence of a youth bulge in Pakistan in particular promises to be a double-edged sword. If conditions are created to provide a secure environment for growing numbers of young people and better equip them

---

[8]   Shuja Nawaz and Mohan Guruswamy, *India and Pakistan: The Opportunity Cost of Conflict* (Atlantic Council, Washington DC, 2014).

[9]   'The Rise of Asia's Middle Class', Special Chapter in *Key Indicators for Asia and the Pacific 2010*, http://www.adb.org/sites/default/files/publication/27726/ki2010-special-chapter.pdf

with education and the opportunities for economic activity, Pakistan will flourish. The counterfactual points to chaotic conditions and violent conflicts at the local, provincial and regional levels. The use of state force will not be sufficient to change this situation permanently, as both India and Pakistan have discovered in Kashmir and FATA respectively.

In the 2018 elections in Pakistan, some 22 million new voters entered the rolls, mainly the youth cohort that helped give Imran Khan his victory. But the census that preceded the election did not fully recognize the dominant urban landscape of Pakistan, continuing instead to cede space to rural constituencies. Yet Pakistan's major challenges and promises lie in its burgeoning cities.

Strong and consistent governance will be the key to altering this landscape. Ceding fiscal and management authorities to local communities, creating a more balanced regional and sub-regional set of administrative structures (read new provinces in Pakistan) and greater transparency in the use of domestic and foreign resources will be critical if Pakistan is to prosper and grow in the next two decades. Domestic investment will be key to moving its economy to a higher plane. Pakistan needs to double its foreign exchange reserves, domestic investment and foreign direct investment in the next five years to transform its economic system.

All this is doable, if the government does not take a breather after successfully surmounting the immediate hurdles it faces and as it implements an IMF programme. If the government is prepared to take many of these measures on its own, before turning to external financing, Pakistan's annual growth rate could return to the 7–8 per cent range.

As discussed earlier, the dynastic and spoils-based system of political parties that suffered a setback in the 2018 elections still remains a major hindrance to change, forcing some of the best and brightest Pakistanis to exit their own countries and head to developed countries to create new opportunities for themselves. Many of Pakistan's leading political parties are non-democratic in their internal structure and management. Power resides in the hands of families or individuals. The rise of the PTI under Imran Khan is a break with this trend but faces huge odds in governing a fractured polity, especially since he had to rely on imported politicians from other parties, many of whom are feudals, or politicians and technocrats associated with previous military regimes. And though the Islamists did not fare well at the polls again, they remain a threat to the progressive political order, especially if they continue to be available and are used as clients of political parties or military agencies for domestic or external purposes.

The national system of decision making has been whimsical and prompted more by personal gain than public good. It shuns institutions in favour of individual actions. Kitchen cabinets have undermined the process of elections and systems of government. The persistence of antique bureaucratic systems adds to the ballast holding back change. Pakistani leaders need to understand that good government is the best antidote to the creeping menace of religious extremism, signs of which have begun appearing in all South Asian countries.

Security remains a looming concern. But the current sequencing of security and then economic development needs to be reversed. Expanding economic opportunities can help trigger and sustain changes in social systems. If these developments are accompanied by better governance and the devolution of fiscal authority to local levels, security would become the business of the populace and not just the state alone. The command economy approach has not worked well in South Asia. Its leaders need to trust the inherent capacity of their people to work hard and to innovate, as they do when they resettle in the developed world. If this happens, South Asia could create the world's largest contiguous market and a source of jobs not just for itself but also for the developed world with which the region now has burgeoning economic, trade and investment ties.

Internal security will continue to be a drag on political and economic decision making, despite heavy military presence and operations. The contagion of jihadi ideology, assisted by speedy web-based transmission mechanisms, will add an extra layer of uncertainty. Protected economies operating at sub-optimal levels may lead South Asia and particularly Pakistan to miss the opportunity to make the region the fulcrum of the global economy by 2035.

Pakistan has the ability to stay ahead of the curve and help transform itself as well as the region around it. If it makes the right choices, and receives the right kind of advice and assistance from its friends.

Improving the US–Pakistan Relationship

Among those friends, the US is the oldest major power to have had a relationship with Pakistan. But, the US has failed to develop a steady relationship with Pakistan despite its potential leverage of direct economic and military assistance, including a large quantum of training for the best and brightest military officers from Pakistan, and assistance from US-dominated international financial institutions such as the World Bank, the IMF and the Asian Development Bank. Pakistan continues to view its regional interests and strategies at a tangent from the views of the US and its Coalition partners, while ostensibly working with the Coalition Forces in return for Coalition Support Funding (or any successor arrangement).

This will be a major challenge for the Imran Khan government, as it balances sovereignty against the need to have relationships with the West and China. Pakistan needs to free itself of economic dependence on US aid by undertaking reforms internally and reducing tensions with India and Afghanistan. It can do this. Rather, it *must* do this.

There are a number of critical factors that will affect Pakistan's view of India and the US in the next few years:

The below par state of the economy in Pakistan is a serious cause for concern. Increased pressures from the return of migrant workers from the Middle East, and demographic pressures internally, leading to a sharp increase in the Youth Bulge and a rapid urbanization, will add to Pakistan's difficulties at achieving stability at home. Compounding these will be a lack of institution-building, and weak decision-making systems in managing the economy. For example, the PML-N government was unprepared for the roughly $7.4 billion 'budgetary savings' windfall per annum that resulted from the drop in the price of imported energy in 2015 and beyond and frittered it away on inconsequential projects and pork barrel politics. A senior minister, who was a member of the prime minister's inner circle, told me the 'savings' from the energy import bill had 'gone down the hole'. The reality is that both Pakistan and the US will have to do more with less in the next decade or so.

A persistent dynastic and corrupt political system under which the major Old Guard political parties are led by autocrats or run as family businesses is increasingly coming under fire from Pakistani society. The 2018 elections reflected this changing trend. Opposing them, increasingly through extra-legal and subterranean operations, are a growing number of extremist militant groups that use Islam as a rallying cry against the state and neighbours, including India and Afghanistan.

At the same time, a powerful military establishment continues to foster a 'culture of entitlement' for its senior ranks. (This is mimicked by civilian entities.) It actively protects its turf even against the constitutionally superior civilian government. Yet, despite being the best organized group in Pakistan today, the Pakistan military remains organizationally stuck with administrative systems that rely on outmoded budgetary and management systems. There is very little active or open oversight and accountability of military finances and management systems by the civilian rulers of Pakistan. The military can and should achieve much-needed economies and efficiencies in its operations autonomously as well as with greater oversight and inquiry from the peoples' elected representatives in parliament. A leaner, more mobile and more effective military may offer a more powerful defence of the country against internal and external threats.

On the positive side, the Pakistani military, particularly the army and air force, have been transformed in recent years into a force that is focused on fighting internal militancy and insurgency. Younger officers are routinely sent from the PMA to the border region. They are all battle-inoculated and tend to view unfavourably the corruption of their civilian masters as well as the visible wealth acquired by senior military officers through the acquisition of real estate via the proliferation of the defence housing schemes that provide windfall profits with relatively small investments. Continued urban recruitment will strengthen such views among the younger recruits.

The multiple ethnic and sectarian wars within Pakistan will persist for some time to come and drain the ability of the state and the military to de-weaponize and de-radicalize Pakistani society. Some political parties are seen as beholden to jihadi groups with whom they have electoral alliances. Others use militant wings of their parties to amass wealth through kidnappings, extortion and coercion. But the state and the military should not strengthen the hands of militant sectarian groups by so-called 'mainstreaming' initiatives. As in the past, the fostering of such groups may boomerang on the patrons over time.

What Can the US Do?

There are persistent Pakistani suspicions, particularly in the senior leadership of the army, that the US aims to defang Pakistan's nuclear capacity and will countenance or even support Indian moves against Pakistan as a regional surrogate for the US in that regard. Lack of a centre of gravity in decision making inside Pakistan, with the civil and the military often at loggerheads, and the heavy reliance by the US on its mil-to-mil contacts to affect decisions inside Pakistan, has exacerbated the problems of communication and cooperation between these so-called allies.

The US can work on multiple fronts to build Pakistani confidence in this relationship, while shifting the onus on to the Pakistanis to craft mechanisms for implementing, benchmarking and reviewing projects and cooperative operations in both the civil and military sectors. Creating Pakistani ownership of these operations is critical to instilling confidence and fostering trust. This approach also makes it easier for the US to turn off the aid spigot if Pakistan fails to meet its own self-imposed targets without the US being seen as arbitrary or antagonistic.

Some in the early Trump administration's military leadership often cited Thucydides' dictum of 'Fear, Respect and Honour' as guiding principles in approaching relationships with other countries or institutions.[10] This needs to be applied to relations with Pakistan, putting the US decision makers in Pakistani shoes and seeing how Pakistanis measure US actions in light of Pakistani fears, their need for respect, and an honourable method of interaction. Both sides would do well to dust off and review the Kayani 3.0 and Kayani 4.0 documents so they can mutually agree on updating and revalidating the issues Gen. Kayani outlined in those seminal documents in 2010 and 2011. Prime Minister Khan also echoed these sentiments when he said that his maiden visit to Washington DC in July 2019 was not to ask for anything other than 'understanding'.

Pakistan also needs to understand and verify that the US does not wish to take away its nuclear capabilities but wishes to help safeguard its sovereignty and assets. Moreover, the US must work to help Pakistan understand that it will not assist any foreign attempt to undermine Pakistan's integrity and independence. Finally, the US must make it clear that it can bolster Pakistan's defence but will not support offensive capabilities. Candour and honesty from the Pakistani side would help demolish some of the fears of the American counterparts.

A number of approaches could be explored by the US:

- Employ the US influence directly and through international financial institutions to transform Pakistan's management of the economy, especially its longer-term strategies to deal with growing

---

10   Notable among these were Secretary James Mattis and NSA H.R. McMaster, both departed from the administration.

demographic pressures and changing economic situations in the
Middle East. A more efficient system of employing economic aid,
monitoring and reviewing its use at the provincial level and setting
of attainable targets by the Pakistanis themselves would engender
great confidence among donors and potential donors. This will
require transforming the Economic Affairs Division into a more
professional and active body inside the Government of Pakistan.
Pakistan tends to over-promise and under-deliver on economic
aid. It needs to become more realistic in its planning, and the US
could help it draft achievable plans and projects. The US could
follow the Chinese model of insisting on a strong US presence
at the federal and provincial level to help monitor progress of
implementation. But this needs to be done in a quieter and low-
key manner so the US is not seen as hegemonic.

- Help Pakistan achieve a bigger bang for its military dollars.
  This could be done by providing Pakistan advice and assistance
  in adopting a practicable taxonomy for defence planning and
  management, revamping the budget system so it is driven by results
  rather than wishlists of the military. Helping Pakistan understand
  the need for longer-term defence planning and budgeting along the
  lines of the quadrennial review in the US may be a start. The US
  could provide expertise in the theoretical construct of such reviews
  and budgetary mechanisms without requiring Pakistan to share
  sensitive details of its plans and expenditures with the US. Use of
  NATO partners, especially the British, in this process would make
  it less US-dominated and more palatable to the Pakistani military.
  If the US can help the Pakistan military remove the fat inside its
  own system, it might help it understand that US intentions are
  not mala fide and they can do much more with what they have
  rather than constantly demanding more resources from their own
  government and the US.

- The US could help improve Pakistan's defences while
  exercising greater influence over its offensive capabilities in the
  neighbourhood. Pakistan has a relatively immobile land army that
  forces it to rely on tactical nuclear weapons for defence. Provision
  of three helicopter fleets (fifty helicopters each) with troop-lifting
  capacity for the long eastern border and another fleet of fifty
  helicopters for use in monitoring the western border and attacking

insurgents in the difficult terrain of the western marcher regions
would enhance Pakistan's defences. Prohibitions on the movement
of the western fleet to the eastern border could be imposed if the
supply of helicopters were under a lease agreement rather than
outright purchase.

- Reducing Pakistan's paranoia of India's growing military might
  is a more difficult task. If India could be persuaded to shift one
  or more of its three strike corps facing Pakistan to the Chinese
  border or deeper into the heartland, the signalling effect on
  Pakistan would be enormous. So long as a third of the Indian
  military budget continues to be spent on troops arrayed against
  Pakistan, it is hard to convince the Pakistanis that India does not
  wish to coerce Pakistan into submission.[11] The US could quietly
  help India make this strategic shift to reduce regional tensions.

- The White House and Department of State also need to work
  in tandem with the Pakistani government and the US Congress
  with the Pakistani parliament to help make government more
  open, inclusive, and pluralistic in running the country. In other
  words, make Pakistan truly the federation that its constitution
  has defined. A greater review and public scrutiny by parliament
  of economic and military matters would assist the growing media
  inside Pakistan to play a more useful role in informing the public
  about key issues and answers. Engaging with and educating civil
  society and media in this direction would act as a multiplier for the
  US efforts to assist Pakistan. Much has already been done by the
  US to build these relationships with Pakistani civil society. But it
  could be better branded and publicized and owned by Pakistani
  counterparts.

The US needs to craft a clearer and longer-term Pakistan strategy and not
see it as a spin-off or subset of its Afghanistan or India strategies. Once
Pakistanis understand this to be the case, they will feel more respected
and comfortable in taking the US at its word. While it may be tempting

---

[11] Bharat Karnad, 'Rethinking Indian Policies towards Pakistan', *Security Wise*, a
blog by Bharat Karnad, 2 May 2012, https://bharatkarnad.com/2012/05/02/
rethinking-indian-policies-towards-pakistan-2/ and Bharat Karnad,
'Rethinking Pakistan', *Asian Age*, 31 March 2011, http://archive.asianage.
com/columnists/rethinking-pakistan-898

to follow a 'feel good' policy of isolating or containing Pakistan, those approaches confuse America's friends within the country and weaken their position while achieving little by way of influence in what still remains a critically important country in a tough neighbourhood.

History has taught us that crises will continue to erupt in the Arc of Instability that extends from Turkey to Indonesia. Who knows when the US may need to have Pakistan on its side again? Therefore, it should eschew the short-term fix and over-reliance on the military channel to solve problems as they arise.

The Americans should ask the Pakistanis to help identify ways its allies can work with them to improve nuclear safety and the prevention of leakage of nuclear materials and weapons into the hands of unsavoury groups, and work with them to further strengthen safeguards. This approach is better than offering unsolicited public advice. The US has provided more aid without strings and more grant aid to Pakistan than China, yet the Chinese are perceived by the Pakistan government and the public as a better friend of Pakistan than the US. One reason is that they lower the boom quietly and privately, while the different branches of the US government and political system resort to public criticism that provokes perverse behaviour from counterparts inside Pakistan. Here the constraints of the US system with its different centres of power in Washington DC come into play. But the Executive Branch needs to take the lead as a champion of a new policy.

The US need not always be the lead Western agency for change in Pakistan. Use of key NATO allies, especially the British, the Germans and the Turks, could help it achieve its goals. This bank-shot approach might sometimes be preferred, since on some issues Pakistanis listen more to the British and the Germans and Turks. The NATO office in Islamabad, populated by the Turks, has been one of the best-kept secrets in Pakistan! A growing number of senior military officers in today's Pakistan Army have been trained in Germany and Britain. The Australians also could help Pakistan think through the institutional changes needed to assess the structure to support the work of the newly minted National Security Committee. Their own experience in reshaping their security structure would help.[12]

---

[12] Aaron Phillip Waddell, 'Cooperation and Integration among Australia's National Security Community', *Studies in Intelligence*, 59, no. 3, extracts (September 2015), https://www.cia.gov/library/center-for-the-study-of-intelligence/csi-publications/csi-studies/studies/vol-59-no-3/pdfs/Cooperation-and-Integration-Among-Australias-NSC.pdf

In the end, Pakistan itself is key to its change and development. It has the people, the ideas, the strategic location and untapped resources to make it a peaceful hub for economic activity in South and Central Asia. If it chooses that objective, the US, China and others could help it reach its goals. But it needs to define its goals and stick to them. It should avoid the popular American Sage Yogi Berra's advice: 'When you get to the fork in the road, take it!'

Epilogue

'A Series of Unfortunate Events'

As Pakistan lurched toward the end of the second decade of the twenty-first century, its bubbling political and economic cauldron produced a series of unfortunate domestic events with all the drama of a Bollywood film. Added to this internal tumult were external challenges: Indian Prime Minister Narendra Modi's attempted final annexation of Kashmir and apparent disenfranchisement of Muslim minorities in the borderlands and the protracted attempt by the Trump administration to end the American adventure in Afghanistan with a whimper before the presidential election of 2020. Meanwhile, the mirage of a fresh and close relationship between Pakistani Prime Minister Imran Khan and mercurial US President Donald J. Trump continued to hold the Pakistani leadership in thrall, with little to show for the false bonhomie that had greeted the Pakistani leader in the White House in the summer of 2019. Trump had offered to mediate in the Kashmir dispute between India and Pakistan, stating that Prime Minister Modi had asked him to do so, but then retreated in the face of Indian opposition.

Trump had much more to worry about by December 2019, including his impeachment by the House of Representatives and a potentially messy trial in the Senate as he entered the final year of his first term, complicating his re-election hopes. America once more turned inward, leaving Pakistan confused and perhaps abandoned. Would it be a case of déjà vu all over again? But Pakistan had much to be responsible for with its own travails at home and in the neighborhood. Much that could not be passed off on its narrative of victimhood and constant attack came under the military's favorite menace, 'Fifth-Generation Warfare (5GW)', an old wine in new bottles of jargon.

Domestic Turmoil

Many of the problems facing Prime Minister Khan in his second year in office were the result of what had happened during his election and his first year. The persistence of allegations by the opposition parties that the persuasive Inter-Services Intelligence had facilitated his electoral victory dogged him at every move and was used by the opposition to mount street protests in its unending campaign to oust him. His government reacted by unleashing the National Accountability Bureau to pursue cases of corruption against the leadership of both the Pakistan Peoples Party and the Pakistan Muslim League, Nawaz Group (PML-N), seemingly with a view to expunging them from the body politic of Pakistan.[1] The United States did not make much of these claims and a State Department spokesperson refused to deem the elections 'free and fair'.[2]

Looking back on the 2018 elections, the Pakistan Institute of Legislative Development and Transparency (PILDAT) assessed that while actual polling day performance had been better than in the previous 2013 elections, the pre-poll phase was 'unfair' in 'the period between April to July 2018 and in particular is low on the parameters of neutrality of the Federal and Provincial Caretaker Governments, impartiality of the intelligence agencies and independence of the Judiciary'.[3] Sporadically documented efforts by the ISI, for instance, to suggest to candidates that they either run as Independents or join the Pakistan Tehreek-e-Insaaf lineup helped create the impression of a new wave of support for Imran Khan's party. Defections from the PML-N and the PPP ensued, including groups of candidates who chose to declare themselves Independents, while waiting to see if a PTI victory occurred so they could then join that party. This happened in Southern Punjab for instance, with a group of candidates who had canvassed for a language-based Seraiki province in southern Punjab. In the event, PTI's victory produced a party of turncoats of many

---

[1] https://warontherocks.com/2018/08/a-tilted-playing-field-what-pakistans-electoral-shifts-could-mean-for-imran-khans-government/

[2] https://www.express.co.uk/news/world/994419/Pakistan-election-2018-Trump-imran-khan-election-commission-live-results-rigging-won

[3] 'Assessment of the quality of general elections 2018' by PILDAT. Page 8. https://pildat.org/wp-content/uploads/woocommerce_uploads/2018/09/AssessmentoftheQualityofGeneralElection2018b.pdf?

colors, with many of them swamping the old revolutionary guard of the PTI in the corridors of power in Islamabad. The fractures began to emerge between the party loyalists and the carpetbaggers, often evident in public spats on Twitter on major and minor issues alike, leading to difficulty in creating momentum for legislative change.

Adding to this was the unorthodox management style of the inexperienced new prime minister, who relied heavily on his close and dependent relationship with the military high command to shape his agenda and less on the bureaucratic institutions of the state. He reportedly spurned written briefs and chose to speak extemporaneously, without care for the time allotted to his speeches, even at the rules-bound United Nations General Assembly or the Organization of the Islamic Conference. The PTI also struggled against the reality of Pakistan's political calendar. Senate elections were not due until 2021, when half the senate would be up for grabs.

The National Assembly elections gave the PTI and its coalition partners a majority of sorts with some 182 members out of a total of 342 in the National assembly, of which only 156 were PTI members. The rest belonged to a hastily assembled coalition of disparate parties.[4] But it faced a senate that was commanded by the opposition groups. As a result, it failed to legislate change, relying instead on the frequent suspension of rules in parliament to approve presidential ordinances, which did not require senate approval, for short periods (120 days at a time) to govern. In effect, the election squabbling continued in the chambers of parliament, creating uncertainty. The cabinet grew to over fifty persons with ministerial rank, many of whom were unelected advisors who had held similar offices in previous governments, including those of the military autocrat General Pervez Musharraf, adding to the unhappiness within the party faithful. Decision making became opaque and seemingly whimsical at a time when Pakistan urgently needed certainty and constancy.

The cases of corruption against former Prime Minister Sharif dragged on. Sharif's ill health became an issue, forcing the government to accede to his demand to be allowed under court order to leave for treatment abroad with a promise to return as soon as doctors permitted. A ham-handed and unprepared attempt to exact some kind of financial retribution from the former prime minister as a surety that he would return to face trial failed.

---

[4]   https://www.dawn.com/news/1528265

A combination of court orders and medical reports sprung Sharif from detention and took him back to his base in London. This escape technique had been used earlier in other cases, including that of General Musharraf, who had been aided by his protectors in the army. Most such defendants chose not to return while their cases remained stuck in legal limbo at home.

Adding to the mix was the impending changing of the guard at the helm of both the Pakistan Army and the Joint Chiefs of Staff Committee. Both incumbents, General Qamer Javed Bajwa and General Zubair Mahmood Hayat, were completing their customary three-year terms in November 2019. Khan took the apparently wise and unexpected step of ending conspiracy theories by announcing the reappointment of the army chief General Bajwa for another full term on 19 August 2019. His co-dependence with the army chief seemed complete, though many saw this as an effective state capture by the more powerful military without mounting a coup.

But the emergence of a seemingly independent judiciary stymied this move, accepting a public interest plea by the Jurists Foundation against the federal government's legal basis for the extension of the army chief's tenure and the peremptory manner in which the prime minister handled the notification of the extension order. Under Supreme Court Chief Justice Asif Saeed Khosa, and a bench including Justice Mian Mazhar Alam Khan Miankhel and Justice Syed Mansoor Ali Shah, the Supreme Court challenged the legality of the extension order as well as the lack of written rules and procedures for according an extension to a service chief in both the Constitution and the Army Rules and Regulations. Past custom, in the opinion of the court, was not enough. This threw the fledgling government into turmoil with bluster and legal arguments employed to dominate the public discussion of this unexpected turn of events.

The government scrambled retroactively to get its bureaucratic ducks in a row, but it was too late for the Supreme Court. Subsequently, the court issued its short order giving the government a six-month period to sort out its affairs 'to clearly specify the terms and condition of the COAS through an Act of Parliament and to clarify the scope of Article 243 of the Constitution in this regard'.[5] It allowed General Bajwa to remain in his post for this six-month period. Suddenly the power balance seemed to shift temporarily from the civil-military alliance toward the court

---

[5]   https://www.supremecourt.gov.pk/constitution-petition-no-39-of-2019/

and parliament, giving the opposition a hold on determining whether a simple parliamentary act with a simple majority might suffice or a basic change in the Constitution was needed. The Constitution was the only document where the appointment of the service chiefs was stipulated. A constitutional change would necessarily increase the difficulty of passing a law through both houses with a two-thirds majority.

The government appealed the court order and sought a review. Surprisingly, the respondents in the appeal included the army chief, perhaps the first time that an army chief had been placed in such an awkward legal position. Political posturing ensued from the opposition benches, with an opening gambit being offered that they might support the extension if the army helped remove Imran Khan from government, even if the PTI remained in power. This 'Minus One' formula rattled around the corridors of Islamabad for a short period, even as other issues arose to capture the attention of the flustered government.

But the extension issue combined with other matters, related to the relationship between the army and the government on the one hand and the army and the constitution on the other, and sowed confusion and chaos, especially within the government, as it prepared to resolve the extension issue. Then, suddenly, both the PPP and the PML-N for their own reasons folded on the extension issue and agreed to support another three years for the army chief. There was no real debate in parliament. Clearly, no party wanted to take on the military, instead hoping for political payback in due course. The usually reliable but sometimes wishful rumor mill churned out detailed accounts of a meeting of the director general of the ISI with opposition leaders in a safe house near Islamabad to talk about future adjustments in provincial power with the assistance of the military. None of this helped strengthen the government's position at home.

Musharraf's Ghost

Other issues remained to provide ammunition for their attacks on the PTI government. In mid-December 2019, a special Court in Islamabad declared former president General Pervez Musharraf guilty of high treason for subverting the Constitution by removing the chief justice and declaring a state of emergency. The case went back to his action of 3 November 2007, when Musharraf put Supreme Court judges under house arrest. The ensuing public protest and crisis led to pressure on Musharraf to resign and leave the country for exile in Dubai and London. Pressing him to leave was the senior leadership of his own army. He eventually returned to Pakistan on 24 March 2013, against the wishes of the army high command, though to a very tepid welcome. But he was barred against running in the elections or from leaving the country. Prime Minister Nawaz Sharif then ordered a probe in June 2015 by the Federal Investigation Agency to see if Musharraf had violated Article 6 of the constitution and thus committed treason by dismissing the judges. Five months later the FIA inquiry found him 'solely responsible' for suspending the constitution. Interestingly, the list of those who left him hanging high and dry on this issue were his favorites of yore, including his prime minister, Shaukat Aziz, and his governor of the Punjab, retired lieutenant general Khalid Maqbool. On 24 December he was ordered to appear before a special court.

Initially the army appeared to distance itself from him. A senior military source told me that they had warned him against returning. 'Now let him enjoy the courts for a while', one senior general wrote to me. But the institutional imperative took over, as did Musharraf's close relationship with the army chief Raheel Sharif's late brother, and the army eventually gave him cover by admitting him to a military hospital and then helping spirit him out of the country to Dubai for medical treatment in March 2016. Long-distance bargaining continued between the court and Musharraf until the new Imran Khan government appeared to resile from its adversarial position in the case and de-notified (that is, dismissed) the prosecution team in the case of high treason on 23 October 2019. By that time, the court had decided to proceed against him anyway and stated it would announce its verdict on 28 November. More jousting with a new state prosecution team did not produce results. The special court then declared Musharraf a traitor and sentenced him to death on 17 December 2019.

A gory section in the verdict written by the chief justice of the Khyber Pakhtunkhwa High Court went a step further, declaring that if Musharraf died before the verdict was carried, his body should be hung in D Chowk in the heart of Islamabad. This non-binding suggestion created a sideshow of no substance. But the lines were drawn, with the army issuing a challenge to the verdict via the spokesperson of the Inter Service Public Relations Directorate and expressing the 'pain and anguish' of its troops. 'However, for us, the country comes first', he said. 'We'll not step back. We'll frustrate the designs of internal and external enemies. . . . At the same time, we'll defend the honour of the country and our institution by thwarting the designs of the enemy, its operatives and facilitators', he added.[6]

Musharraf tried to reopen the case. Even as he prepared to appeal the verdict, by declaring that he had consulted his prime minister, Shaukat Aziz, the army chief, General Kayani, and others before declaring the emergency. He had raised this argument earlier in 2015 to no avail.[7] But the ISPR's veiled threat was not lost on the public and evoked full-throated responses from pro-army and ex-servicemen on the one hand and anti-army interference calls from civil society groups and opinion leaders. Among others, the Pakistan Bar Council condemned the military spokesperson's statement. But the virtual toothpaste could not be put back into its tube, even as the legal drama continued via appeals.

Economic and Regional Challenges

At the heart of the government's travails were its lack of institutional capacity for decision making, which was exacerbated by its unfinished battles against the opposition parties, with assistance from the military, and the openly hostile policies of its powerful eastern neighbor, India. Despite the efforts of Prime Minister Khan to create some thaw in the India relationship by opening a corridor to the Sikh holy shrine at Kartarpur inside Pakistan and allowing visa-free travel by Indian Sikh pilgrims, India took a hard line. India's effort to remove Kashmir from its special status as a disputed territory and make it part of the Union sowed further discord with Pakistan and inside India's Muslim community, leading to the closure by Prime Minister Khan of the Indo-Pak border for trade.

Meanwhile the economy sputtered along, even while the International Monetary Fund's program for Pakistan moved into the second tranche of an extended credit line for Pakistan. Despite falling growth rates and Foreign Direct Investment, as well as poor performance on the foreign exchange reserves, Pakistan's exchange rate seemed to stabilize and reserves steadied somewhat. But its underlying fiscal system and revenues remained suspect and weak. Inflation became a challenge. And doubts remained about its

---

[6]   https://tribune.com.pk/story/2121253/1-dg-ispr-major-general-asif-ghafoor-addresses-news-conference/

[7]   'Musharraf says he invoked emergency after consulting Gen Kayani' by Malik Asad, Dawn, 23 December 2015. https://www.dawn/news/1228255

ability to continue to meet the rising conditionality of IMF lending as it went for the higher tranches.

The US influence in the IMF and other international financial institutions was also a factor, as the United States pushed for Pakistan to deliver the Afghan Taliban to the peace talks that might allow the US to exit Afghanistan relatively quickly and without further loss of face. As a sop to Pakistan, the United States restored International Military Education and Training (IMET) program grants worth about $2 million a year to Pakistan under a program run by the Department of State for the Department of Defense. But, Pakistan still had to wait for the release of arrears of the Coalition Support Funds owed to it to the tune of $800 million and even the undisbursed funds from the lapsed Kerry-Lugar-Berman aid package of $7.5 billion that still had $2 billion unallocated for Pakistan. The transactional relationship remained intact. There was little sign of a strategic vision or reset, though both sides kept a smiley face and lobbed softball words of praise to each other. President Trump was now deep into his impeachment battle and a re-election campaign at home, leaving Pakistan the same two options it had had before: act as a spoiler and thus draw US attention or bend to American will in the region either directly or through its surrogates, such as Saudi Arabia.

Pakistan thus sailed into choppy waters with an untrained hand on its tiller, as the third decade of the twenty-first century dawned. Would it be able to master its course or would it be buffeted by forces beyond its control?

Scenarios

The most favorable scenario for the 2020s for Pakistan includes a settlement in Afghanistan that would gradually draw down the fighting in that benighted land, allow the US military to exit gracefully, and reduce the threat to Pakistan of Afghanistan-based insurgents. This might help re-open trade with Afghanistan and Central Asia, and even link up the Afghan tributary with the China-Pakistan Economic Corridor (CPEC). But the lack of an opening to the East with an increasingly hostile right-wing Indian government that had enflamed Muslim minority sentiments inside the Union and the rebellious state of Kashmir would stymie Pakistan's efforts to expand trade with India and extend it to Afghanistan and Central Asia.

Pakistan would continue to be dependent on the promise of new jobs migrating from China along the CPEC route, though much of Chinese manufacturing is seeking overseas production bases in India and South East Asia, even as it makes the shift to robotic manufacturing instead of human labor at home. According to one estimate, in 2018 China installed some 154,000 units of manufacturing robots compared with 55,000 units in Japan and only 40,300 in the United States.[8] Moreover, China spread its foreign direct investment net far and wide across the globe, ranging from Latin America and Africa to India and South East Asia. 'China has strengthened its bilateral relations across the region [that contains Pakistan] through development aid. In addition to policy banks such as Chexim, China has set up development funds for projects such as the China-Pakistan Economic Corridor. This project is *backed* by Chexim and the Silk Road Fund, and its overall value is expected to *eclipse* the development assistance given by the US to Pakistan between 2005 and 2015'.[9] Yet Pakistan remained a relatively small part of this vast network of Chinese investments exceeding $350 billion in Asia. According to one Pakistani estimate that gained traction within the government and even the military, some 85 million jobs could potentially come into Pakistan. This is an unbelievable dream, since Pakistan does not have the education system to support a trained and disciplined labor source for the manufacturing sector, nor the power sector to support the growth of manufacturing at a scale to accommodate such a massive increase of its manufacturing base.

Moreover, the potential for the return of its vast labor force from the Arabian Peninsula remains a real threat. Despite warnings about this eventual flood of workers from overseas, including by me while at the Atlantic Council since 2009, Pakistan has made no preparations to absorb these workers into its labor market. Pakistan may also be overestimating its relationship with China, whose global strategy relies on a diversified set of economic and political partnerships in its neighborhood as well as across the globe, ranging from the Arctic Circle to Latin America.

Pakistan's anachronistic political ecosystem will resist change vigorously, creating turmoil when it needs a steady course to economic recovery. It is possible that the creeping expansion of the military's

---

[8]   https://ifr.org/downloads/press2018/2019-09-18_Press_Release_IFR_World_Robotics_2019_Industrial_Robots_English.pdf P. 3

[9]   https://chinapower.csis.org/china-foreign-direct-investment/

influence in the running of the government could be replaced with more direct intervention if the system of governance collapses or street protests create serious disruption in the economy and polity. An 'Egypt on the Indus' scenario, though tempting as a source of temporary stability, would be disastrous for Pakistan, taking it back into the mid-twentieth century.

Prime Minister Khan faces two broad kinds of issues—those that he has some control over, and those that are beyond his control. In the first group are political issues at home and allocation of domestic resources to growth-oriented projects for the longer term that would lay the basis for equitable growth and development. Good governance trumps everything else that he can do. In the second category are global economic slowdown, pandemics (such as the novel coronavirus, COVID-19), natural disasters, weather-related events, global resource shifts, especially increase of energy prices due to security flare-ups in the Middle East, and the possibility of new conflicts between Shia and Sunni groups in the Middle East or between the United States and Iran.

The United States remains a wild card in Central Asian and Middle Eastern politics. The US election fever in 2020 and a fresh Trump presidency may create further turmoil and muscularity in foreign policy making. A Democratic president in 2021 and beyond may find it difficult to garner support from those in the United States who paradoxically yearn to pull back from the global stage on the one hand while demanding swift use of American power against perceived enemies abroad. Increasing US tensions with Iran and the growing Saudi influence on Pakistan will put Pakistan in a difficult situation regarding whom it aligns with. If it continues to make diplomatic mistakes like choosing between the Saudis and Iran, or aligning with the new Muslim coalition of relatively progressive states like Malaysia and Turkey, it might find itself being punished economically and politically.

Ideally, the United States could continue to de-hyphenate India and Pakistan, crafting its separate relationships with each country based on its own vision of an Indo-Pacific partnership with India while using Pakistan as a steady bulwark of its Central Asian and Middle Eastern policy. But this would demand a clearly enunciated Pakistan policy, not one that was an afterthought or linked to short-term moves on Afghanistan or Iran. Pakistan would need to play its part too, aiming for the longer-term benefits of using US aid to build a more stable set of relationships with its neighbors, and serving as a conduit for US relations with even potentially hostile countries like Iran. Reducing tensions in the Gulf and opening trade routes to the south and west from Central Asia might also assist the United States in countering China's penetration of Central Asia as part of its One Belt, One Road strategy. This would imply a change in the stance of President Trump during his first term. Without such a shift, the United States risks becoming embroiled in regional rivalries and reverting to its role as a global policeman.

Against this background, the battle for Pakistan's soul and its future will be an abiding feature of the new decade of the twenty-first century. Barring unforeseen natural or economic challenges, Pakistan could make the right choices to hold things together and prosper. Otherwise, it risks the fallout of centrifugal forces that will threaten its existence. Muddling through is not an option.

Note: I borrowed the title of this Epilogue from the work of Daniel Handler, an American writer and musician who publishes under the nom de plume Lemony Snicket. His best-known series of children's books is *A Series of Unfortunate Events*, also a popular film.

Select Bibliography

Abbas, Hassan. *The Taliban Revival: Violence and Extremism on the Pakistan–Afghanistan Frontier*. New Haven: Yale University Press, 2015.

Afzal, Madiha. *Pakistan under Siege*. Washington DC: Brookings Institution Press, 2018.

Ahmed, Akbar S. *The Thistle and the Drone*. Washington DC: Brookings Institution Press, 2013; Bozorg Press, 2015.

Ahmed, Khaled. *Sectarian War: Pakistan's Sunni-Shia Violence and its Links to the Middle East*. Karachi: Oxford University Press, 2012.

—. *Sleepwalking to Surrender*. Gurgaon: Penguin Random House, Viking, 2016.

Amjad, Rashid, ed. *The Pakistani Diaspora*. Lahore: The Lahore School of Economics, 2018.

Anonymous [Michael Scheuer]. *Imperial Hubris: Why the West Is Losing the War on Terror*. Nebraska: Potomac Books, 2007.

Ayub, Mahmood Ali, and Syed Turab Hussain. *Candles in the Dark: Successful Organizations in Pakistan's Weak Constitutional Environment*. Karachi: Oxford University Press, 2016.

Bergen, Peter. *The Longest War: The Enduring Conflict between America and Al Qaeda*. London and New York: Free Press, 2011

—. *Manhunt: The Ten-Year Search for Bin Laden from 9/11 to Abbottabad*. New York: Crown Publishers, 2013;

Bergen, Peter, and Katherine Tiedeman (eds), *Talibanistan: Negotiating the Borders between Terror, Politics, and Religion*. New York: Oxford University Press, 2013.

Berntsen, Gary, and Ralph Pezzulla. *Jawbreaker: The Attack on Bin Laden and Al-Qaeda: A Personal Account by the CIA's Key Field Commander*. New York: Three River Press, 2006.

Broadwell, Paula, and Vernon Loeb. *All In: The Education of General David Petraeus*. New York: Penguin Press, 2012.

Burton, Fred. *Ghost: Confessions of a Counterterrorism Agent*. New York: Penguin Random House, 2008.

Chivers, C.J. *The Fighters*. New York: Simon and Schuster, 2018.

Clinton, Hillary Rodham. *Hard Choices: A Memoir*. New York: Simon and Schuster, 2014.

Cohen, Stephen, ed. *The Future of Pakistan*. Karachi: Oxford University Press, 2012.

Coll, Steve. *Directorate S*. New York: Penguin Press, 2018.

Connable, Ben, and Martin C. Libicki. *How Insurgencies End*. Santa Monica CA: RAND Corporation, 2010.

Cowper-Coles, Sherard. *Cables from Kabul: The Inside Story of the West's Afghanistan Campaign*. London and New York: Harper Collins, 2011.

Dalrymple, William. *Return of a King: The Battle for Afghanistan 1839–42*. New York: Vintage, 2014.

Davidsson, Elias. *The Betrayal of India: Revisiting the 26/11 Evidence*. New Delhi: Pharos, 2018.

Dulat, A.S., Asad Durrani and Aditya Sinha. *The Spy Chronicles*. Noida: Harper Collins India, 2018.

Durrani, Asad. *Pakistan Adrift*. London: Hurst; Karachi: Oxford University Press, 2018.

Evans, Duane. *Foxtrot in Kandahar: A Memoir of a CIA Officer in Afghanistan at the Inception of America's Longest War*. El Dorado Hills CA: Savas Beatie, 2017.

Fair, Christine. *Fighting to the End*. New York: Oxford University Press, 2014.

Fuller, Graham. *Breaking Faith*. Online, Bozorg Press, 2015.

Gannon, Kathy. *I Is for Infidel: From Holy War to Holy Terror in Afghanistan*. New York: Public Affairs, 2005.

Garntenstein-Ross, Daveed, and Clifford May (eds), *The Afghanistan–Pakistan Theater: Militant Islam, Security, and Stability*. Washington DC: Foundation for the Defense of Democracies, 2010.

Gates, Robert. *Duty: Memoirs of a Secretary of War*. New York: Knopf, 2014.

Ghani, Ashraf, and Claire Lockhart. *Fixing Failed States: A Framework for Fixing a Fractured World*. New York: Oxford University Press, 2008.

Grenier, Robert L. *88 Days to Kandahar: A CIA Diary*. New York: Simon and Schuster, 2016.

Haqqani, Husain. *Magnificent Delusions: Pakistan, the United States, and an Epic Misunderstanding*. New York: Public Affairs, 2013.

Hashwani, Sadruddin. *Truth Always Prevails: A Memoir*. Gurgaon: Penguin Portfolio, 2014.

Hayden, Michael. *Playing to the Edge: American Intelligence in the Age of Terror.* New York: Penguin Press, 2016.

Hersh, Seymour. *The Killing of Osama Bin Laden.* London: Verso Books, 2016.

Husain, Ishrat. *Governing the Ungovernable.* Karachi: Oxford University Press, 2017.

Ignatius, David. *Blood Money.* New York: W.W. Norton, 2012.

Jaffrelot, Christophe. *The Pakistan Paradox: Instability and Resilience.* New York and Karachi: Oxford University Press; Hurst: London, 2015.

Jalal, Ayesha. *The Struggle for Pakistan.* Cambridge MA: Harvard University Press, 2017.

Jones, Seth, and C. Christine Fair. *Counterinsurgency in Pakistan.* Santa Monica, CA: RAND Corporation, 2010.

Karnad, Bharat. *Staggering Forward: Narendra Modi and India's Global Ambition.* Gurgaon: Penguin Rand House India, Viking, 2018.

Kasuri, Khurshid Mahmud. *Neither a Hawk Nor a Dove.* Karachi: Oxford University Press, 2015.

Khalilzad, Zalmay. *The Envoy: From Kabul to the White House: My Journey through a Turbulent World.* New York: St. Martin's Press, 2016.

Khan, Feroz Hasan. *Eating Grass: The Making of the Pakistani Bomb.* Palo Alto CA: Stanford University Press, 2012.

Khan, Riaz Mohammad. *Afghanistan and Pakistan: Conflict, Extremism, and Resistance to Modernity.* Baltimore MD: Johns Hopkins University Press, 2011.

Kiessling, Hein. *Faith, Unity, Discipline: The ISI of Pakistan.* Noida: HarperCollins India, 2016.

Lamb, Christina. *Farewell Kabul: From Afghanistan to a More Dangerous World.* London: William Collins, 2016.

Lodhi, Maleeha (ed.), *Pakistan: Beyond the Crisis Stage.* London; Hurst; Karachi: Oxford University Press, 2011.

Maqsood, Ammara. *The New Pakistan Middle Class,* Cambridge, MA: Harvard University Press, 2017.

Markey, Daniel S. *No Exit from Pakistan: America's Troubled Relationship with Pakistan.* New York: Cambridge University Press, 2013.

Mazzetti, Mark. *The Way of the Knife: The CIA, a Secret Army, and a War at the Ends of the Earth.* New York: Penguin Press, 2013.

Mir, Amir. *Talibanisation of Pakistan: From 9/11 to 26/11 and Beyond.* New York: Pentagon Press, 2010.

Morell, Michael, with contributor Bill Harlow. *The Great War of Our Time: The CIA's Fight Against Terrorism—From al Qa'ida to ISIS.* New York: Twelve, 2015.

Muñoz, Heraldo, *Getting Away with Murder: Benazir Bhutto's Assassination and the Politics of Pakistan*. New York: W.W. Norton, 2013.

Nasr, Vali. *The Dispensable Nation: American Foreign Policy in Retreat*. New York: Doubleday. 2013.

Nawaz, Shuja. 'Why Can't the Afghans Fight Their Own War?' *Foreign Policy*, 25 August 2009.

—. 'Ungovernable'. *American Interest*, 1 September 2011.

—. 'Can Zardari Deliver the Aid?' *New York Times*, 12 April 2011.

—. 'Why the US Still Needs Pakistan'. *New York Times*, 10 May 2011.

—. 'Feeding Pakistan's Paranoia'. *New York Times*, 9 May 2011.

—. 'The Pakistan Dilemma'. *Foreign Affairs*, 2 May 2011

—. 'Trump's Flawed Pakistan Policy', *Foreign Affairs*, 10 January 2018.

—. 'The bin Laden Aftermath: The Future of the US–Pakistan Relationship'. *Foreign Policy*, 2 May 2011.

—. 'Raging at Rawalpindi'. *Foreign Policy*, 13 May 2011.

—. 'The US–Pakistan Roller Coaster Relationship'. *Huffington Post*, 25 May 2011

—. 'General Petraeus's Reality', *Foreign Policy*, 24 June 2010

—. 'Pakistan on the Brink, Again'. *Foreign Policy*, 27 August 2014

Nawaz, Shuja, with Michele Dunne. 'Can Egypt Avoid Pakistan's Fate?' *New York Times*, 3 February 2012.

Nawaz, Shuja. *Crossed Swords: Pakistan, Its Army, and the Wars Within*. Karachi: Oxford University Press, 2008, 2017.

—. *FATA: A Most Dangerous Place*. Washington DC: CSIS, 2009.

—. *Pakistan in the Danger Zone: A Tenuous US–Pakistan Relationship*. Washington DC: Atlantic Council, 2010.

—. *Learning by Doing: The Pakistan Army's Experience with Counterinsurgency*. Washington DC: Altantic Council, 2011.

Nawaz, Shuja, with Mohan Guruswamy. *India–Pakistan: The Opportunity Cost of Conflict*. Washington DC: Atlantic Council, 2014.

O'Neill, Robert. *The Operator: Firing the Shots That Killed Osama bin Laden and My Years as a SEAL Team Warrior*. New York: Scribner, 2017.

Panetta, Leon, with Jim Newton. *Worthy Fights: A Memoir of Leadership in War and Peace*. New York: Penguin Books, 2014.

Puri, Luv. *Across the LOC: Inside Pakistan-Administered Jammu and Kashmir*. Gurgaon: Penguin India, 2010.

Rhodes, Ben. *The World As It Is: A Memoir of the Obama White House*. New York: Random House, 2018.

Riedel, Bruce. *The Search for al Qaeda: Its Leadership, Ideology, and Future.* Washington DC: Brookings Institution Press, 2008.

—. *Deadly Embrace: Pakistan, America, and the Future of the Global Jihad.* Washington DC: Brookings Institution Press, 2011.

—. *Avoiding Armageddon: America, India, and Pakistan to the Brink and Back.* Washington DC: Brookings Institution Press, 2013.

Robinson, Linda. *One Hundred Victories: Special Ops and the Future of American Warfare.* New York: Public Affairs, 2013.

Rubin, Barnett. *Afghanistan: From the Cold War through the War on Terror.* New York: Oxford University Press, 2013.

Sanger, David E. *Confront and Conceal: Obama's Secret Wars and Surprising Use of American Power.* New York: Crown, 2012.

Sanger, David E., with Dean, Robertson. *The Inheritance: The World Obama Confronts and the Challenges to American Power.* New York: Bantam Press, 2009.

Schaeffer, Teresita C., and Howard B. Schaeffer. *How Pakistan Negotiates with the United States: Riding the Roller Coaster.* Washington DC: United States Institute of Peace, 2011.

Schmidt, John. *The Unraveling: Pakistan in the Age of Jihad.* New York: Farrar, Straus and Giroux, 2011.

Schmitt, Eric, and Thom Shanker. *Counterstrike: The Untold Story of America's Secret Campaign Against Al Qaeda.* New York: Times Books, 2011.

Schroen, Gary C., *First In: An Insider's Account of How the CIA Spearheaded the War on Terror in Afghanistan.* New York: Presidio Press, 2006.

Scott-Clark, Catherine, and Adrian Levy. *The Exile: The Stunning Inside Story of Osama bin Laden and Al Qaeda.* London and New York: Bloomsbury, 2017.

Siddique, Abubakkar. *The Pashtun Question: The Unresolved Key to the Future of Afghanistan and Pakistan.* London: Hurst, 2001.

Simpson, Emile. *War from the Ground Up: Twenty-First Century Combat as Politics.* New York: Oxford University Press, 2012.

Small, Andrew. *The China–Pakistan Axis: Asia's New Geopolitics.* New York: Oxford University Press, 2015.

van Linschoten, Alex Strick, and Felix Kuehn, eds. *The Taliban Reader: War, Islam and Politics in Their Own Words.* New York: Oxford University Press, 2018.

Wilkinson, Steven. *Army and Nation: The Military and Indian Democracy since Independence.* Cambridge MA: Harvard University Press, 2015.

Woodward, Bob. *Obama's Wars.* New York: Simon and Schuster, 2011.

Yusuf, Moeed (ed.), *Pakistan's Counterinsurgency Challenge*. Washington DC: Georgetown University Press, 2014.

Yusuf, Moeed. *Brokering Peace in Nuclear Environments*. Palo Alto CA: Stanford University Press, 2018.

Zaeef, Abdul Salam. *My Life with the Taliban*. New York: Columbia University Press, 2010.

Acknowledgements

While this book is my personal effort and responsibility, it would not have been possible without the wisdom and information from many in Europe, Pakistan, Afghanistan and the United States over the past decade. Some cannot be identified, because of the nature of their assistance and our personal relationships, especially the many military, civil and police officers, of all ranks, and politicians who helped me understand from the ground up the complex reality of Pakistan today and its relations with the US over 2008–19.

Among those that I want to mention are the many who agreed to being interviewed, mostly on the record, or provided key documentation and shared their notes and thoughts over the past decade. My special thanks go to them and others who helped me better understand Washington, London, Islamabad, Rawalpindi and the turbulent region where Pakistan resides.

I am grateful to Fred Kempe, president and CEO of the Atlantic Council, for inviting me to participate in the Pakistan Task Force of 2008 and then entrusting me with the launch of the South Asia Center in January 2009. I must acknowledge my many talented colleagues at the South Asia Center, the wider Atlantic Council, and fellow think-tankers in Washington DC and Islamabad for their input and advice. Fred supported our small but energetic team's efforts towards Waging Peace in the Greater South Asia region and fostered our search for solutions to the region's problems and improvements in the shaping of US and Pakistani policies.

In Pakistan, I wish to thank in particular former President Pervez Musharraf, four other army chiefs—Generals Jehangir Karamat, Ashfaq Pervez Kayani, Raheel Sharif and Qamar Javed Bajwa—Ishrat Husain, Hina Rabbani Khar, Sartaj Aziz, Shah Mehmood Qureshi, Aitzaz Ahsan,

Rehman Malik, Chaudhry Nisar Ali Khan, Shehbaz Sharif, Imran Khan, Asad Umar, Aftab Sultan, Ihsan Ghani, Tariq Parvez, Lt. Gen. Masood Aslam, Lt. Gen. Naveed Mukhtar, Lt. Gen. Ahmed Shuja Pasha, Lt. Gen. Zahir-ul-Islam, Lt. Gen. Nasser Khan Janjua, Lt. Gen. Ishfaq Nadeem, Lt. Gen. Tariq Khan, Lt. Gen. Hidayat ur Rahman, Lt. Gen. Naweed Zaman, Brig. Moghisuddin, Maj. Gen. Sahibzada Isfandiyar Ali Khan Pataudi, Maj. Gen. Ahmed Mahmood Hayat, Maj. Gen. Niaz Khokhar, Maj. Gen. Farooq Ahmad Khan, Ahsan Iqbal, Tariq Fatemi, Governor Owais Ghani, Wajahat S. Khan, Saba Imtiaz, Raashid Wali Janjua, Babar Sattar, Cyril Almeida, Lt. Gen. Agha Umer Farooq, Omar Shahid Hamid, the Lahore Study Group, Lt. Gen. Tariq Waseem Ghazi, Lt. Gen. Asif Yasin Malik, Lt. Gen. Naeem Khalid Lodhi, Nargis Sethi, A. Wajid Rana, Nadeem ul Haque, Khaled Ahmed, Amb. Mahmud Ali Durrani, Lt. Gen. Javed Iqbal, Owais Tohid, Maj. Gen. Syed Ali Hamid, Brig. (now Maj. Gen.) Ch. Sarfraz Ali, Maj. Gen. Khawar Hanif, Brig. (later Lt. Gen.) Nazir Butt, Senator Mushahid Hussain, Amb. Riaz Mohammed Khan, Amb. Salman Bashir, Amb. Tehmina Janjua, Amb. Jalil Abbas Jilani, Amb. Aizaz Ahmed Chaudhry and President Asif Ali Zardari. All have helped me understand Pakistan today and the challenges it faces.

In the United States and Europe, I benefited from the advice and knowledge of Secretaries George Shultz and William Perry, Andrew Wilder, Moeed Yusuf, Dan Markey, Alex Thier, Greg Gottlieb, Amb. Doug Lute, Gen. James Jones, Gen. David Petraeus, Gen. Stan McChrystal, Gen. James Mattis, Gen. John Allen, Amb. Robin Raphel, Lt. Col. Eliot Evans, Lt. Col. Tom Lynch, Amb. Rick Olson, Amb. Cameron Munter, Amb. Dan Feldman, Jasmeet Ahuja, Jonah Blank, Alan Kronstadt, Nancy Birdsall, Masood Ahmed, David Ignatius, Peter Lavoy, Bruce Riedel, Khalid Ikram, Ali Jafri, Amb. Anne Patterson, Amb. Gerald Feierstein, Vice Admiral Mike LeFever, Amb. Husain Haqqani, Mansoor Ijaz, Amb. Marc Grossman, Kevin Hulbert, Eric Schmitt, Marc Ambinder, Shamila Chaudhary, Tamanna Salikuddin, Eric Lebson, Phillip Reiner, Robert Grenier, Duane Evans, Damian Murphy, Peter Bergen, Larry Sampler, Vali Nasr, Alexander Evans, Amb. Sir Adam Thomson, the analysts at the Foreign and Commonwealth Office of the United Kingdom and the German BND, Jeff Lightfoot, Joseph Syder, Tom Sanderson, David Sedney and Ashraf Ghani (later president of Afghanistan). My childhood friend Shahid Yusuf read the first rambling draft and guided me into trimming it from 'three books' into one cohesive volume.

I especially want to thank my friend and mentor, the late Arnaud de Borchgrave, whom I had admired for decades from afar as a dashing foreign correspondent, but who entered my professional life late by taking a chance and bringing me into the world of think tanks in 2008. He entrusted me with the lead role in producing our CSIS report on FATA for the incoming CENTCOM commander Gen. Petraeus in 2009. Arnaud was always ready to inject a dose of reality, notably by accusing me of being a perennial optimist and reminding me that 'a pessimist is an optimist with experience'!

Thank you to Paul Werdel, our talented son-in-law for the superb photographs of the author and for his astute editorial suggestions. And a big thanks to my super agent, Priya Doraiswamy of Lotus Lane Literary Agency, and Milee Ashwarya, who heads Penguin Random House India, her colleagues Shantanu Ray Chaudhuri, Mriga Maithel and Peter Modoli, who helped transmute my manuscript into an accessible book. Thank you to Susan McEachern of Rowman & Littlefield, who suggested the change of title way back from *Misalliance* to *The Battle for Pakistan* and for making the book available to a US and global audience.

Finally, I must thank my wife, Seema, and our daughters, Zaynab, Amna and Zahra, who have been my anchors in this turbulent world, with their love, understanding and advice. All of them are the best sounding board for my ideas and simultaneously the most trenchant critics and cheerleaders of my work, both poetry and prose.

All the errors of omission and commission are mine alone.

Index

About the Author

Shuja Nawaz, a globally recognized political and strategic analyst, is a distinguished fellow at the South Asia Center at the Atlantic Council. He has been a journalist in Pakistan and the United States and worked at the World Health Organization, on the senior staff of the International Atomic Energy Agency, and the International Monetary Fund, as well as been a consultant with leading think tanks in Washington, DC.

He is the author of *Crossed Swords: Pakistan, Its Army, and the Wars Within*. He is also the principal author of *FATA: A Most Dangerous Place, Pakistan in the Danger Zone: A Tenuous US–Pakistan Relationship, Learning by Doing: The Pakistan Army's Experience with Counterinsurgency, Who Controls Pakistan's Security Forces?, Countering Militancy and Terrorism in Pakistan: The Civil-Military Nexus*, and with Mohan Guruswamy, with a foreword by former Secretary of State George Shultz, *India–Pakistan: The Opportunity Cost of Conflict*.

www.shujanawaz.com

Lightning Source UK Ltd.
Milton Keynes UK
UKHW010628310520
364102UK00001B/30